THE CHURCH:
Its Nature, Ordinances and Offices

ALSO BY JOHN W KEDDIE

The Five Points of Calvinism (Finding out about... series)

Sing the Lord's Song: Biblical Psalms in Worship

George Smeaton: Learned Theologian and Biblical Scholar

Running the Race: Eric Liddell, Olympic Champion and Missionary

Finish the Race (Eric Liddell) (Trail Blazers)

James MacGregor: Preacher, Theologian and Defender of the Faith

Preserving a Reformed Heritage: The Free Church of Scotland in the 20th Century

A Divided Church: An Account of the Division in the Free Church of Scotland in 2000

THE CHURCH:

Its Nature, Ordinances and Offices

John W Keddie

Foreword by Maurice J Roberts

**Scottish Reformed
Heritage Publications**

Copyright © John W. Keddie 2018

The moral right of John W Keddie to be identified
as the author of this work has been asserted by
him in accordance with the
Copyright, Designs and Patents Act, 1988.
All rights reserved.

No part of this book may be reproduced
in any form or by any means without the
prior written permission from the publisher.

Unless otherwise stated, Scripture quotations
are taken from the King James Version (KJV).

Scripture verses marked NKJV are from
the New King James Version.
Copyright© 1982. Thomas Nelson, Inc.
Used by permission.

First Published – December 2018

ISBN: 978-1-326-83069-4

Front Cover: Free North, Free Church of Scotland building in Inverness, from across the River Ness. The building was opened on 7th June 1893. (Photo by John W Keddie).

Publisher:
Scottish Reformed Heritage Publications
19 Newton Park
Kirkhill
Inverness-shire
IV5 7QB

Printed and bound by Lulu (www.lulu.com)

CONTENTS

Foreword by Maurice J Roberts — 5

Introduction — 7

Section A: The Church: Its Nature & Government
1. What the Church is — 11
2. Head of the Church — 19
3. Marks of the Church — 31
4. Purpose of the Church — 39
5. Membership of the Church — 49
6. Discipline of the Church — 61
7. Forms of Church Government — 81
8. Church and State (1) — 91
9. Church and State (2) — 101
10. The Church and Antichrist — 113

Section B: The Church: Its Creeds & Confessions
1. General Considerations — 127
2. Place and Usefulness of Confessions — 135
3. The Westminster Confession of Faith — 147

Section C: The Church: Its Worship
1. Regulative Principle for Worship — 163
2. Singing of Psalms: (1) Principles — 173
3. Singing of Psalms: (2) Scriptural basis — 187
4. Singing of Psalms: (3) Imprecatory Psalms — 201
5. Instrumental music — 209
6. Posture in Public Prayer — 219
7. Women's head-coverings in Public Worship — 227
8. Collections and Offerings — 239
9. Public Prayer, Reading the Word, Benediction — 253
10. Christian Sabbath — 259

Section D: The Church: Its Sacraments

1. Sacraments — 271
2. Baptism: (1) Mode and Meaning — 279
3. Baptism: (2) Subjects — 289
4. Baptism: (3) Responsibilities — 301
5. Lord's Supper: (1) Institution and Benefits — 307
6. Lord's Supper: (2) Partaking — 319

Section E: The Church: Its Officers

1. Minister of the Word — 331
2. Ruling Elder: (1) Calling — 345
3. Ruling Elder: (2) Qualifications — 349
4. Ruling Elder: (3) Responsibilities — 355
5. Ruling Elder: (4) Respect — 361
6. Deacon — 367

Questions for Study and Group Discussion — 379

Selected Reading List — 383

Scripture Index — 385

FOREWORD

The spiritual health of any nation is closely related to the health of the church within that nation. Christ is the only true Head of the church and the health and well-being of a church therefore must be gauged by the measure of its conformity to the teaching of the Bible, which is the written and unchangeable revelation of God. The measure of good which a church can do is inevitably bound up with the degree to which that church is obedient to and patterned after the doctrine, worship, discipline and practice laid down by Christ in holy scripture. Tragically, the Western world has, for over a century now, imbibed an anti-scriptural philosophy which treats the Bible more as the word of man than as the Word of God. The consequences of this Bible-denying philosophy can be seen in the fearful degree to which the church's influence has declined in Europe and in other nations once blessed with excellent churches. It is a mistake to think that the weakness of the modern church can be healed by modernising church worship and church government so as to make them more conformed to the spirit of our age. The proper attitude is to see that the present-day church's weakness can only be healed by our return to the doctrines and principles laid down by God in the Bible.

If the question be asked, 'In what areas has the church received authority from Christ to act?', the answer is made clear in this book. The church has authority from the Lord Jesus Christ to do the following: (1) to teach doctrine on all points on which the Bible itself speaks; (2) to insist on the proper biblical worship of God; (3) to maintain the spiritual independence of the church over against possible intrusion by civil government; (4) to preserve good biblical discipline among the lives of all who profess to be church members.

One area of modern church life which has suffered greatly over recent years is that of worship. Too often the view has been taken in churches that people are free to worship in any way they choose. But the Bible has God-given principles which are to be carefully observed.

Mr Keddie looks at this vital subject at length in Section C of this book, where the subject of the Regulative Principle of Worship and its application are explained. It is, sad to say, a neglected subject in most churches today. But God only accepts as worship what He himself has taught us to adopt in worship. Man is not free to invent his own style of worship. True worship must be "in spirit and in truth" (John 4:23).

Similarly, it is typical of the spirit of our day to ask, 'Why do we need any Confession of Faith?' But our godly forefathers at the time of the Reformation and in Puritan times where absolutely right to teach that we must, in our churches, teach and believe only such truths as God has taught in His word, which is the Bible. The theology of the Bible, as this book makes clear, is revealed to us as a system of truth. The Bible alone is the supreme authority in all matters of doctrine. The *Confession of Faith* is the Presbyterian church's subordinate standard. This term makes it clear that whatsoever is taught in the Confession is subordinate to what is taught in the Bible. However, when the Confession teaches what is clearly and demonstrably the same as what the Bible teaches, it is our duty to God to accept its teaching and to pass the teaching on to our church members. It must always be remembered in church life that the principal means of grace is the Bible. All that we believe, teach and practice, must, if we are to be obedient to God, always conform to the Bible's teaching.

One of the excellent features of this carefully written book by John Keddie is that it always aims at being theologically sound and morally responsible. Its treatment of the subjects which it covers is comprehensive and thorough. Careful readers will learn much from a study of these valuable chapters. Whether they be office bearers, church members, or only enquirers into church practice, they will find here a wealth of sound, solid and satisfying information. The chapters of the book are written so as to build up the reader in genuine Christian faith, life and practice.

MAURICE J ROBERTS

INTRODUCTION

The renowned 19th century Scottish theologian, John ('Rabbi') Duncan (1796-1870) in one of his quaint but perceptive sayings stated: "I'm first a Christian, next a Catholic, then a Calvinist, fourth a Paedobaptist, and fifth a Presbyterian. I cannot reverse this order." Someone asked if this could be likened to circles within each other, the first the widest and best. To this, Duncan replied: "I like better to think of them as towers rising one above the other, though narrowing as they rise. The first is the broadest, and is the foundation laid by Christ; but we are to build on that foundation, and, as we ascend, our outlook widens."[1] In a distinct way the book reflects such an outlook!

The chapters in this book are intended to cover most aspects of the Church as an institution, in its nature, government, worship, sacraments and offices. The subject of ecclesiology (doctrine relating to the church) is not easy to address today.[2] This is because there is such diversity among, and even within, churches on Church government, worship, sacraments and offices. In the light of such diversity it is considered by many to be unrealistic to claim a divine right (*jus divinum*) for any particular Church government or practices. So far as a 'regulative principle' may be applied, the ready acceptance of diversity in Church order and ordinances make it so mutable that the very idea of maintaining a *jus divinum* in ecclesiology is considered by many to be passé. The present volume, however, seeks to base Church principles squarely upon what is warranted by the teaching of Scripture.

The doctrine of the Church and its practices are of importance because it is not just a man-made institution simply ruled and governed by men and changed at their whim. It is an institution ordained by

---

[1] 'The Creed within the Creed,' in, William Knight, *Colloquia Peripatetica*, Edinburgh and London, 61907, 8.
[2] See, for example, Derek W H Thomas's contribution, 'The Doctrine of the Church in the Twenty-First Century,' in, A T B McGowan (Editor), *Always Reforming: Explorations in systematic theology*, Leicester: Apollos, 2006, 328-352.

Christ of which He is Head. His rule and authority are not to be usurped. He determines how the Church is to function and how He is to be worshipped. It is not a matter either of indifference (*adiaphora*) or mere pragmatism. Rather it is a matter of seeking to maintain a *jus divinum* (divine right) for Church government and practice. This inevitably relates to the supreme authority and application of Scripture in all matters of faith, worship and Church governance and practices. Such concerns are behind the publication of the present volume.

It is the hope and prayer of the writer that this study in Church principles will prove to be a helpful overview of the subject and will reflect accurately the teaching of God's Word in that connection. It is designed to be informative and of practical help to divinity students, ministers and other office-bearers and, indeed, to any who may enquire as to the nature and functions of a Christian Church. It is written from a perspective which is both Reformed and Presbyterian.

To assist in personal study or group discussions some questions have been included and in addition an index has been provided of Scripture verses and passages referred to in the text. These are found at the end of the book. Other resources are indicated by suggestions for further reading at the end of some of the chapters, in addition to references in footnotes and a selected reading list of useful works on the various topics covered. Thanks are due to the Rev. Maurice Roberts for his kind Foreword.

May the Lord Jesus Christ, the Head of the Church, be pleased to bless this study to the challenge and strengthening of His Church in these days. May He be pleased to send the Spirit in reviving and reforming power to the recovery of the Church as an institution for the advance of the gospel in these days of declension and confusion about what the Church should be and how it should function so that He as its Head might be glorified.

JOHN W KEDDIE
Kirkhill
Inverness-shire
December 2018

SECTION A

THE CHURCH
ITS NATURE & GOVERNMENT

THE CHURCH

1. What it is and where it is to be found

A. What is the Church?

The Greek word ἐκκλησία (ekklesia) is translated 'Church' in the New Testament.[1] It means 'meeting,' 'assembly' or 'congregation.' In Acts 19 ἐκκλησία is used in verse 39 to indicate an official gathering and in verses 32 and 41 as a sort of crowd gathered together 'unofficially' as it were. In Acts 7:38 ἐκκλησία is used of the congregation of the children of Israel in the wilderness. Elsewhere in Acts the word describes a Christian assembly or congregation. This is the more general sense of the term. There are, however, some varieties of meaning, e.g.:

1. *The company of people gathered/associated together for Christian worship/service in a particular locality.* This is commonly used in Paul's letters, as, for example: "the church of God which is at Corinth" (1 Corinthians 1:2); "the church of the Thessalonians" (1 Thessalonians 1:1); and in all the letters to the 'churches' (ἐκκλησίας) in Asia Minor in Revelation chapters 2 and 3.

2. *The company of professing Christians actually gathered for worship.* This is the meaning, for example, in 1 Corinthians 14, verse 19 "…in the church I had rather speak five words with my understanding, that I might teach others also, than ten thousand words in an unknown tongue" (see also verse 35).

3. *The whole body of professing Christians throughout a particular region or world-wide.* We have, for example, reference to "the churches (ἐκκλησίαις) of Galatia" (Galatians 1:2). In places Paul uses the suggestive expression "the church of God" (1 Corinthians 15:9;

---

[1] 'Ekklesia' is the transliteration of the Greek word. It is the word from which 'ecclesiastical' is derived, meaning 'pertaining to the Church' in English.

Galatians 1:13). Jesus in one place speaks about the apostolic testimony as the rock upon which he would build his church (Matthew 16:18).
4. *The sum total of those given to Christ by the Father, whom He will present faultless in the last day.* This is the sense in which Paul uses the word in Ephesians 5, when he speaks of Christ being "head of the church" (v23); and Christ loving the Church (v25); and of a "glorious church" (v27, and v32).

The word 'Church' has no linguistic connection with ἐκκλησία. It actually comes from another Greek work κυριακη (kuriake) meaning that which pertains to the Lord (as in *Lord's* Supper and *Lord's* Day). The early church fathers used the term to describe the Christian meeting places as 'the Lord's house.' Thus, we have the connotation in the German *Kirche*, the Dutch *Kerke*, and the Scottish *Kirk*. Naturally, we must be careful to distinguish this idea of the Church as a particular meeting place, from the basic idea of ἐκκλησία in which the emphasis is upon the *people who worship together* and not the *place* in which they worship. William Binnie summarises the position well: "...the Church, or company of the faithful, is in Scripture presented to our faith in three phases, or at three distinct stages. It comes in view as the Local Church; as the entire Community of Christians dispersed through the world; and as the Bride of Christ, the total company of the redeemed."[2]

B. Where is the Church to be found?
(1) *The Local Church*
It is important to state that it is the duty of men and women who have come to take the word and worship of Christ seriously, to associate themselves together for His worship, service, and mutual edification (see Matthew 18:17; 28:19-20; 1 Corinthians 11:23-34; Hebrews 10:23-25). The Old and New Testaments cannot be properly understood without this corporate aspect of like-minded souls gathering together for the praise of the Lord in worship and service. It is a sin if anyone

---

[2] William Binnie, *The Church*, Edinburgh, 1882, 4.

forsakes the society and fellowship of the Christian Church in their locality, or at least as near them as their conscience and convictions dictate. It is an anomaly and a serious inconsistency at best for any professing believer not thus to be associated with the gathered and worshipping Church in any given locality. And furthermore, they ought willingly to submit to the oversight and discipline of such a properly constituted, biblically based and sound Christian congregation. Christ promises His presence where there are men, women and children gathered in His name (Matthew 18:20) and therefore at the very least they should be found gathering together for worship in such a congregation. This is complicated by two factors:

(a) One is the fact of diversity among visible churches, i.e. denominations often significantly differing from one another. Whilst retaining a love for all Christian brethren (see 1 John *passim*) the individual/family will be guided by the principle, "Let every man be fully persuaded in his own mind" (Romans 14:5), whilst deploring the fact of so many outward divisions among those truly professing the gospel;

(b) The other is the fact of Churches claiming to be Christian which are sadly shot through by doctrinal error, forms of worship and practices not warranted by the Word of God, and with a 'nominal' outlook. This is a particular phenomenon in what might be termed 'broad' churches that have embraced liberal theology effectively undermining the authority of the Word of God as the supreme standard for faith and life. The Bible itself warns of Churches that may even become Synagogues of Satan (see Revelation 2:9; 3:9). The letters to the Churches in Revelation 2 and 3 constitute serious warnings of the danger of the decline and fall of churches, whether as local churches or denominations. They may become enemies of the truth.

(2) The Worldwide visible Church

The Church is not just to be considered as a local phenomenon. It also has a worldwide aspect. This is often described as the 'Church Catholic,' meaning universal or worldwide. It is a pity that the word 'catholic' has been so bound up with one Church, the *Roman* Catholic Church. It has a worldwide aspect of course, though it is deeply in error over a range of dogmas from a strictly Biblical standpoint. The true evangelical, Bible-believing Church has a 'catholic' or universal aspect. It is not just a matter of local Churches. The Church as a visible body of believers on this earth is wider than that and due recognition of this is necessary. As Binnie put it: "Christians owe allegiance not only to the Church of their own city or province, but to the general Church of Christ, the great community of those who throughout the world profess and call themselves Christians."[3] The question does arise about the nature of the 'allegiance' and the relationship or extent of fellowship between Churches of Christ throughout the world. This takes us into the whole 'ecumenical' debate. William Binnie helpfully makes three points which we summarise here:

    (a) Church members should not stay apart from congregations or fellowships of gospel churches if they move into areas beyond the limits of their own church (denomination). And such churches should welcome professing Christians from other areas notwithstanding differences in particulars (such as baptism or church government). Obviously, there may be convictions which will preclude taking office, but the principles stated in the *Westminster Confession of Faith* would apply: "Saints by profession are bound to maintain a holy fellowship and communion in the worship of God, and in performing such other spiritual services as tend to their mutual edification; as also in relieving each other on outward things according to their several abilities and necessities. Which communion, as God offereth opportunity, is to be extended unto all those who

---

[3] Binnie, op. cit., 11.

in every place call upon the name of the Lord Jesus" (26:2). This all assumes the soundness and faithfulness to Scripture in the Churches in question. Discernment would require to be exercised in not being exposed to liberal or heretical teachings.

(b) Churches which are for the greater part agreed in doctrine and practice ought to cultivate friendly relations as far as possible. There is good reason for this. It makes stronger the witness to the gospel truth and encourages a spirit of mutual love which is such a strong element in the character of a truly Christian disposition, for Churches as for individuals. We may cite here 1 Corinthians 13, where love (αγαπη) is stated as the 'greatest gift,' as well as the first letter of John throughout. Such co-operation and friendly relations will not be at the expense of convictions about the truth and its application, in which the two communions may not exactly be at one, though in time there may be a coming together, which is no bad thing to desire. Though there were no such things, strictly speaking, as denominations in the New Testament era, nevertheless there were clearly differences between Churches (see e.g. Revelation 2 and 3), and stresses and strains within them (see e.g. 1 Corinthians 1:11-17; 3:1-4; etc). The tenor of the apostle's argument, however, is that these were not good. Everyone must be persuaded in their own mind before the Lord, but at the very least there ought to be strong friendly and co-operative ties between churches of basically the same faith and order.

(c) In a sinful, fallen world of imperfection Christian denominations may in many ways be thought inevitable. At heart there may be significant differences over the principles that regulate the doctrine and practice of the Church, i.e. what may be called the 'regulative principle.' That will make it very hard to avoid differences and consequently the polarisation into what are called 'denominations.' The question will arise, however, about the desirability and feasibility for denominations to unite. This has become a contentious and perplexing issue, not least since the 19th century with the rise of the Ecumenical Movement and organisation of various Councils of Churches, either at national or international levels. In the Scottish Church situation, it should not be assumed that Church unions since the 19th century have benefitted the Church in the longer term. This is because such unions usually involve compromise on previously established positions. This was classically the case in the union of the Free Church and United Presbyterian Church in Scotland in 1900 and the later union of the resulting United Free Church with the Church of Scotland in 1929. These were crafted on the basis of the broadening of the creedal position and loosening of the relation of the ministers and other office bearers to the whole-orbed Biblical doctrine and practice and government hitherto established. Nevertheless, there is truth in what William Binnie has written that, "the union of sister Churches occupying the same territory is obligatory, unless stringent reasons are forthcoming that it cannot take place without the sacrifice of truth or duty."[4]

(3) The Church 'invisible'
No local Church or denomination is exclusively the one 'true church' on earth at any given time. As the *Westminster Confession of Faith* recognises: "The purest Churches under heaven are subject both to mixture and error;…" (25:5). This said, it is true to say that "there shall always be a Church on earth to worship God according to His will." Christ will build His Church (Matthew 16:18) and the end will come only when the gospel has been preached to all the nations (Mark 13:10). So, there will always be visibility of the Church on earth, however limited that may be in some eras. At the same time the Church on earth will always be mixed, containing some who make no profession – and give no indication – of being saved; and others who will be found to be

---

[4] Binnie, op. cit., 15.

false converts. This is a state reflected, e.g., in the parable of the wheat and tares (Matthew 13:24-43).

The visible Church on earth is divided into numerous denominations. However, the truth is that there is *one true Church*. It comprises all the saved at any given time, of whatever denomination, on earth and in heaven. It is sometimes called, the 'Church Invisible.' That is not a felicitous expression, because there is a sense in which the Church always inevitably has visibility, here and hereafter. But it is a truth that the Church of Christ which He has purchased with His own blood is not tied down to this world but encompasses all the saved in every generation on earth and in heaven (Ephesians 5:25). The fortunes of the visible church may wax and wane from one generation to the next. This is not the case with the one true Church comprising all the saved. There is only addition to this Church; there is only growth. Local Churches and even denominations may disappear from the earth, but the Church which Christ has purchased with His own blood can never fail or disappear. It is as permanent and sure as all those known to the Father and given to the Son in the Covenant of Redemption (John 10:22-30). We cannot infallibly tell who the members are of the one true Church of redeemed souls on earth. That, however, does not justify looseness in the application of discipline or admission to sacraments on the part of the Churches on earth, nor any dimming of zeal for the free offer of the gospel to all and sundry. As far as possible Churches on earth under the headship of Christ must attend with care to all the spiritual interests of the flock (Acts 20:27-31) on behalf of the One who is "the head over all things to the church" (Ephesians 1:22), as well as calling upon all people everywhere to repent and turn to the Lord (Acts 17:30).

(4) The Church Triumphant
It is common to describe the professing Church on earth as the 'Church Militant.' It is engaged in the spiritual warfare referred to by the Apostle Paul in Ephesians 6:10-20. There Paul encourages Christians to put on "the whole armour of God" so that they may be

able "to stand against the wiles of the devil" (v11). In the same Epistle Paul uses the analogy of the marriage state to speak of the headship of Christ in His Church: "Christ is the head of the church: and he is the saviour of the body" (5:23). Furthermore, Christ "loved the church and gave himself for it" (v25). The Church as the true people of God is His "bride." In that context the reference is to all the elect of God. The divine purpose is, "That he might present it to himself a glorious church, not having spot, or wrinkle, or any such thing; but that it should be holy and without blemish" (v27). When will that be? It will be hereafter, in the "new heavens and new earth, wherein dwelleth righteousness" (2 Peter 3:13; Revelation 21:1). That is the "glorious church," the heavenly country (Hebrews 11:16), the "church of the firstborn, which are written in heaven" (Hebrews 12:23). True believers are part of a 'Church triumphant' awaiting the final consummation of the last day when Christ comes again. Little wonder they are exhorted to set their "affection on things above, not on things on the earth," for "when Christ, who is our life, shall appear, then shall ye also appear with him in glory" (Colossians 3:2, 4). For this reason, Christians are to be concerned to be holy now and Churches are to be concerned with doctrinal and practical purity (Ephesians 5:26; 2 Peter 3:14).

This is the final prospect for the "true church" comprising all the elect in every age. The visible churches on earth – even the best of them – are flawed on account of sin. True believers in the Lord Jesus Christ are part of His "body" and will finally share in His triumph in the place prepared for them, where He is (John 14:3). In Christ's Kingdom of Glory there will be no flaw, no sin to mar the life of the redeemed saints. The believer in the Church militant on earth will always live in anticipation of this prospect of glory. In the verse of Anne Ross Cousin on the last words of Samuel Rutherford (1600-1661) we see this reflected:

> The sands of time are sinking, the dawn of Heaven breaks,
> The summer morn I've sighed for, the fair sweet morn awakes:
> Dark, dark hath been the midnight, but dayspring is at hand,
> And glory – glory dwelleth in Immanuel's land.

THE CHURCH

2. The Head of the Church

1. Is the Church just a human organisation?
The proper nature of the Church as an institution in the world is often missed. It is often thought of simply in human organisational terms. Superficially people in the world may speak of the Christian community as adherents of Christian Churches, as the Muslim community is represented by followers of the prophet Mohammad, and so on, as a merely human religious institution like any other. This, however, is only part of the story. From one aspect the visible Church is represented by professing *followers of Christ* in various congregations and worshipping in various buildings or meeting places. The Church, though, ought to be viewed from a very much higher perspective as *the body of Christ*. It ought, therefore, to be seen first and foremost as a body of which Christ is head. That is true principally in relation to the 'invisible Church,' that is to say, the sum total of truly converted people the world over, also embracing the redeemed in glory. But it is also important for the visible Church, numbering among it at any given time unconverted or nominal members or adherents, to recognise Christ as its head and law-maker.

There ought to be recognition in the Church on earth of answerability not to any mere human organisation or authority, but to the Lord Jesus Christ Himself and His authority as revealed in the Scriptures. As we read in Paul's letter to the Colossians: "he is the head of the body, the church: who is the beginning, the firstborn from the dead; that in all things he might have the pre-eminence" (1:18). His Headship is unlimited, as Paul makes clear in his letter to the Ephesians: "[the Father] hath put all things under his [Christ's] feet, and gave him to be head over all things to the church, which is his body, the fulness of him that filleth all in all" (1:22-23). This relates to the proper nature of the Church. And the truth of the Headship of Christ is clearly a central one for any professing Christian Church. We consider, firstly:

2. The truth of the Headship of Christ

Scripture clearly teaches concerning Christ that He is the Head of the Church. The verses already cited indicate that (Colossians 1:18; Ephesians 1:22-23). We may distinguish two distinct aspects of the exercise of His Headship over the Church.

1. *He has authority over it*

In terms of Ephesians 1:22 the Headship of the Lord has been bestowed on Him as the God-man as a reward for His atoning work. As the eternal divine Son He possesses an inherent sovereign Lordship. But this Headship is a specific bestowal of the Father upon the Son *as the God-man*. The authority that He therefore or thereby possesses comes to focus in several ways:

(1) *He instituted the Church*. Speaking of the apostolic testimony of Peter at Caesarea Philippi, Jesus said that it was on that rock that He would build His church (Matthew 16:18). His institution of the Christian Church is clear from the Great Commission of Matthew 28 (18-20). There are certain institutions that are divinely ordained. We find this, for example, with the family and the state. Parents have a divine right to rule their children and magistrates have a divine right to rule in a nation. This does not justify any oppressive unrighteous abuse of authority in such areas of life. But the Church, too, is of divine appointment. In a sense it comprises voluntary associations of people acting according to their own will. However, the Church does not derive its *warrant* or *functions* from its members. It derives its warrant and functions from Christ Himself – not from members, or office-bearers, or Presbyteries or Church Councils, but from Christ. In the case of the family and state, these are institutions only for this world, though they, too, are obliged to be subject to Christ, and, as we have said, should not abuse

their authority. The Church is, however, His special institution, His 'body' in a special way.

(2) *He prescribes the ordinances within it.* This is clearly seen in the two sacraments He instituted. They have their authority from Him. However, the same principle holds good in relation to all the ordinances of worship. The Church is bound to seek warrant *in His Word*, the Scriptures, for all the ordinances, lest it be accused of mere human will-worship. The Church on earth must recognise that what it does is not to be according to the wit or wisdom of man, but according to Christ speaking through His Word. That is the sphere of its responsibility. In one place the Scottish Reformer, John Knox, writing in terms common to the Reformed Churches in those days, had this to say: "If He [Christ] be King, then must He do the office of a king, which is not only to guide, rule, and defend His subjects, but also to make the statute laws; which laws only His subjects are bound to obey."[1]

(3) *He provides its constitution and office-bearers.* What is the Church's constitution? It is the belief and confession of the truth regarding Christ and His saving purposes. It can perhaps be summed up in Christ's own exclusive assertion: "I am the way, the truth, and the life: no man cometh unto the Father, but by me" (John 14:6). Or as Peter confessed at Caesarea Philippi: "Thou art the Christ, the Son of the living God" (Matthew 16:16). After all, Jesus Himself stated that "on this rock I will build my church" (v18). It therefore comprises those and only those who are 'of the truth.' This comes in to His conversation with Pilate at His trial, in which He also states an important feature of His Church, namely, that it is not like the Kingdoms of this world but acts according to persuasion and admonition with the weapon of truth (John 18:36-38). The 'weapons' of the Christian's and Church's warfare are outlined clearly in Ephesians 6:13-18. He establishes the Church's constitution. He also appoints its office-bearers to administer the constitution. In his

---

[1] John Knox, *Works*, III, [Laing], Edinburgh, 1854, 41.

farewell exhortations to the elders of Ephesus at Miletus Paul includes this telling point: "Therefore take heed to yourselves and to all the flock, among which the Holy Spirit has made you overseers, to shepherd the church of God which He purchased with His own blood" (Acts 20:28, NKJV). To the same Ephesians Paul later teaches that "he [the Lord Jesus Christ] gave some, apostles; and some, prophets; and some, evangelists; and some, pastors and teachers, for the perfecting of the saints, for the work of ministry, for the edifying of the body of Christ, till we all come in the unity of the faith, and of the knowledge of the Son of God, unto a perfect man, unto the stature of the fulness of Christ" (4:11-13).

(4) *He continues to exercise authority and rule in administration of the Church's life.* It is not that He gives a constitution and officers and simply lets them get on with it in the best or most pragmatic way they can. That has often happened and continues to happen in the visible Church, to its detriment and decline. He still lives and reigns and all such officers are answerable to Him, as they are to have a felt dependence upon Him. William Binnie uses an analogy of a business corporation that may have had a very clear 'mission statement' at the outset and specific company policy. In the course of time the original founders of the corporation will leave it to others who may not have the same vision at all and take it in an entirely different direction and 'change the rules.' This may do despite to the original founders though their unfaithful successors will not fear their displeasure, because after all they have passed away. It's not like that with the Church. The founder still lives and reigns and any who act unfaithfully to His constitution and rule have to answer to Him and will incur His displeasure. This is something very clear in the addresses of the Lord Jesus to the various churches in Asia Minor of Revelation 2 and 3. After all, the risen Lord already intimated that: "I am the first and the last: I am he that liveth, and was dead; and, behold, I am alive for evermore, Amen" (Revelation 1:17-18). This puts an altogether different complexion on what the Church is to be and is to do: *it is not warranted to act in the administration of the affairs of*

Christ's Church beyond what He has taught and appointed, with a full recognition of its answerability to Him as its Head.

2. He has a vital influence in it

Christ's authority as a king is one thing. His relationship to His people goes further than kingly rule. Writing to the Colossians Paul speaks of believers being united to Christ as their Head: "from which all the body by joints and bands having nourishment ministered, and knit together, increaseth with the increase of God" (2:19). Christ Himself speaks of the relationship of His people to Him in terms of a vine and its branches. Christ encouraged them: "abide in me" (John 15:4). There is a clear experiential aspect to the teaching of Paul when he writes: "if any man have not the Spirit of Christ, he is none of his" (Romans 8:9). Here is a vital aspect of the Headship of Christ in relation to the Church: His influence in it experientially.

(1) *This explains how Christian ordinances are made effective in people's experience.* We call the ordinances – the worship of God, preaching of the word, the sacraments, the reading of the word, and prayer – the 'means of grace,' and so they are. How? It is because by the work of the Holy Spirit Christ blesses sinners through them. It must be remembered that Christ rose from the dead and ascended to heaven. Consequently, it is He who dispenses spiritual life. This is how He revealed Himself to John at Patmos: "I am he that liveth, and was dead; and behold, I am alive for evermore, Amen; and have the keys of hell and of death" (Revelation 1:18). He has been "exalted…to be Prince and a Saviour, for to give repentance to Israel and forgiveness of sins" (Acts 5:31). He does this according to His will through His executive, the Holy Spirit: "and we are His witnesses to these things, and so also is the Holy Spirit whom God has given to those who obey Him" (v32, NKJV). But it is Christ as Head who dispenses the grace by which sinners are saved, and the grace by which they benefit from all the ordinances. William Binnie put it well: "Whenever Christ's word is truly preached, He is Himself there, and His power is able and ready to make the word victorious in

men's hearts. Wherever the sacraments are [ad]ministered according to Christ's appointment, He is Himself there, able and willing to bestow the benefits of which they are the pledges."[2] He is – to use the figure of the Book or Revelation – in the midst of the seven golden lampstands, that is to say, the visible Churches on earth (Revelation 1:13, 20).

(2) Christ provides the Church with faithful ministers. This is clear in what Paul writes to the Ephesians: "he [the Lord Jesus Christ] gave some, apostles; and some, prophets; and some, evangelists; and some, pastors and teachers, for the perfecting of the saints, for the work of ministry, for the edifying of the body of Christ, till we all come in the unity of the faith, and of the knowledge of the Son of God, unto a perfect man, unto the stature of the fulness of Christ" (4:11-13). In accomplishing the Church's mission, it is Christ Himself who raises up and equips His instruments for the accomplishment of His predestined ends. This is obviously a very important factor when it comes to determining who should be ordained into the ministry in the Church of Christ, or even for that matter the other offices: elders and deacons. The Church on earth will look for men patently equipped spiritually by Christ Himself for such Christian service. Where care is not taken in this adequately, the seeds of declension and spiritual decay will soon become all too evident.

(3) The Church's life is His. This is to say that where it can be said that there is true spiritual life in any Church, to that extent it can be detected that Christ is there in the midst. Where it is clear that in a Church there is a concern to work out the will of Christ in the life of the Church, to that extent it can be said that Christ is there, giving such spiritual life to that Church. When a faithful Church is persecuted it can be said in that case that Christ is persecuted. A Church is sustained by the reality of the Headship of One who is touched by their afflictions and triumphs (Hebrews 4:14-16).

---

[2] Binnie, op. cit., 26.

3. The Practical Application of Christ's Headship

1. *The Headship of Christ helps delineate the power belonging to the Church.*
Lawful Church authority flows from the Headship of Christ. It is therefore an antidote to tyrannical authority of Church courts and rulers. Christ has not delegated His power to Church bodies or individuals – Roman Catholic or Protestant – to do with as they will. The power He vests in His officers in the visible Church is strictly *ministerial*. And such power itself flows from the sole Lordship of Jesus Christ. This principle applies to doctrine, worship and discipline.

(1) *The Church has authority to teach.* Christ promised His Spirit to lead His Church into truth (John 14:15-18; 16:12-15). This means, that in exercising power as vested by Christ in His officers they are warranted only to act *in accordance with His written word*. In other words, they must have warrant in Scripture for their doctrine/teaching. To go beyond that is to impose what is not in line with His will and therefore a denial of His prerogatives.

(2) *The Church has authority to ensure that the proper worship of God is carried out.* Again, this is limited to their giving effect to His express command and warrant. This is an extremely important principle that we shall return to in discussing the regulative principle of worship and the express warrant for the elements of worship. A Church should not presume to lay down elements in the worship of God that go beyond what is warranted in His word. That is a prerogative of the Headship of Christ in relation to the Worship of His Church. If a Church presumes to do such a thing, Christ's people are not bound to obey, but may refuse obedience out of regard for the honour of Christ. Again, William Binnie made a strong point: "The reason annexed to the second commandment warns us that the practice of introducing into the house of God new ordinances of worship, however plausibly it may shelter itself under the plea that it is a devout attempt to honour Christ by adding new allurements of beauty and grandeur to His worship,

involves a presumptuous disparagement of the simplicity of His appointments, and is regarded with jealous displeasure."[3]

(3) The Church has authority to exercise discipline. The keys of the kingdom of heaven have been given to Church officers/rulers (Matthew 16:19). These are bound to be exercised in the oversight of Christ's Church on earth. This covers the exercise of discipline involving infringements of Biblical standards of life and doctrine, as well as the admission or exclusion from sealing ordinances, sacraments, Church membership and the like. There are limits determined by the Head. The civil powers that be have a right to do justice, but no right to do wrong. The power of the sword is limited. So, too, in Church matters, is the power of the keys. This is a ministerial function and the Church has no divine right to judge unjustly. In all such cases, in which recourse to correcting any such bad decisions is followed through, there is a right of appeal from the judgement of men to the judgement of God. In that connection there may never be complete satisfaction on this earth.

2. The Headship of Christ is a protection for true liberty of conscience.
Oppression of enlightened conscience may arise from more than one source:
(1) *From the powers that be, state authorities.* This occurs when a state or civil magistrate imposes upon its subjects legislation which would require them to act contrary to conscience in relation to biblical faith or morality. We have this sort of imposition illustrated in the Scriptures, for example in the book of Daniel. On the one hand we have the case of Nebuchadnezzar's image of gold that the young faithful Israelites refused to bow down to, being contrary to the commandment of God (Exodus 20:4-6). It seemed that they would pay the price for this disobedience to the ruler as they were committed to the fiery furnace, from which, however, they were spared (Daniel 3). On the other hand, Daniel is prohibited by the law of the land to bow down to any other than the King. Yet this was contrary to his enlightened conscience and

---

[3] Binnie, op. cit., 29-30.

Daniel refused and was cast into a den of lions. From that situation he was spared (Daniel 6). This has become an increasing concern for evangelical believers/Churches in recent times in the West, what with, for example, the decriminalisation of homosexual activities and subsequent moves to redefine marriage itself by legislating for 'same-sex' marriage. No civil government is beyond such imposition on the conscience. But they do not have authority over Christ and the law of Christ, and therefore they do not have absolute authority over the consciences of men under Christ. Paul makes this clear writing to the Corinthians: "he that is called in the Lord, being a servant, is the Lord's freeman: likewise also he that is called, being free, is Christ's servant. Ye are bought at a price; be not ye the servants of men" (1 Corinthians 7:22-23). Binnie asks: "How was the dominion over conscience to be met?" People instinctively fall back on right of private judgement. But is that sufficient in facing imposition on conscience in religion? No person is bound to die for *their own* rights. Yet a Christian will be prepared to suffer or die *out of duty to Christ*. The Headship of Christ is the bulwark of such liberty in the face of contrary impositions. It is to be understood that this liberty is not inconsistent with the *properly exercised power* of civil or ecclesiastical authorities. As the *Westminster Confession of Faith* expresses it: "… because the powers which God hath ordained, and the liberty which Christ hath purchased, are not intended by God to destroy, but mutually to uphold and preserve one another, they who, upon pretence of Christian liberty, shall oppose the lawful power, or the lawful exercise of it, whether it be civil or ecclesiastical, resist the ordinance of God" (20:4).

(2) *From Church authorities.* This is a subtler form of imposition on the consciences of Christians and Churches. This may come in the form of revised statements of doctrine or practice by a Church subsequently imposed on those who did not see such changes as being agreeable to God's Word. There have been many cases of this in the history of the Church. It may be illustrated with reference to the whole Reformation movement which was in effect a protest movement against the

imposition on men's consciences of Church doctrines, dogmas and practices which had no warrant from the Word of God. The principle is well stated in the *Westminster Confession of Faith*: "God alone is Lord of the conscience, and hath left it free from the doctrines and commandments of men, which are, in any thing, contrary to His word; or beside it, if matters of faith and worship. So that, to believe such doctrines, or to obey such commands, out of conscience, is to betray true liberty of conscience: and the requiring of an implicit faith, and an absolute and blind obedience, is to destroy liberty of conscience, and reason also" (20:2). Christ is the head of the Church and the bounds on what may be appointed in the Church are set by Him speaking through His word.

3. *The Headship of Christ preserves the spiritual independence of the Church.*
The State has no right to rule the Church in its particular affairs and sphere of authority. The carrying out of the Great Commission (Matthew 28:18-20) is vested in the visible Church and is not to be suppressed by the State, nor is it to be assumed by the State, albeit they ought to provide support and encouragement to Christianity in the nation; that is a moral responsibility of a State, however little it may be carried out. Professed followers of Christ are to gather themselves in Churches, taking their order from the Word of Christ, ensuring that the Word is faithfully preached, the worship properly carried out and the exercise of discipline within its membership rightly applied. It is not for the State or any other body to take upon themselves that responsibility. In other words, the visible Church is to maintain its spiritual independence. After all, Christ's Kingdom is "not of this world." Therefore, it will be maintained that under the Headship of Christ the affairs of Christ's Church belong to the body of the faithful and the officers appointed by them. These have the right to discharge that function without any interference by the State authorities.

In asserting this spiritual independence there is no denial of the propriety of the State giving support and encouragement to the Christian religion, which indeed would be seen to be its responsibility also under the Headship of Christ over the nations. That support and encouragement, however, would not extend to the functions of the Church itself in maintaining its doctrine, worship, government and discipline. Wrote William Binnie: "We condemn the antichristian domination of the Church over the State, as strongly as the domination of the State over the Church. We plead for the co-ordinate jurisdiction of the two powers. We desire to give to Caesar the things that are Caesar's, and to Christ the things that are Christ's."[4]

---

[4] Binnie, op. cit., 34-35.

THE CHURCH

3. The Marks of the Church

1. Introduction

The Reformation of the 16th Century was a radical movement for Biblical standards in Church life in the face of a Roman Catholic Church in which there had been a myriad of accretions for which there was scant if any Biblical warrant. The Reformation Churches, driven by the concern for Biblical principles in Church life, were concerned to establish proper standards in the Church that reflected these principles. They wished to make clear what the marks of a true Church were. This is perfectly understandable given the state of corruption in terms of doctrine, worship and practice in the pre-Reformation Church. The Reformed Churches, therefore, were concerned to establish proper marks by which a true Christian Church may be identified. We look at some of the representative confessions on this matter of the 'marks' of the Christian Church, before discussing their significance.

1.1 The Scots Confession (1560) and Belgic Confession (1561)

One of the first of the Reformation Confessions to outline marks or 'notes' of the true Church was *The Scots Confession* of 1560. "It is essential," says that *Confession*, "that the true Kirk be distinguished from the filthy synagogues by clear perfect notes lest we, being deceived, receive and embrace, to our own condemnation, the one for the other." So, what 'notes' did the *Scots Confession* recognise as agreeable to the Word of God? "The notes of the true Kirk, therefore, we believe, confess, and avow to be: first, the true preaching of the Word of God, in which God has revealed Himself to us, as the writings of the prophets and apostles declare; secondly, the right administration of the sacraments of Christ Jesus, with which must be associated the Word and promise of God to seal and confirm them in our hearts; and lastly, ecclesiastical discipline rightly administered, as God's Word prescribes, whereby vice is repressed and virtue nourished" (Chapter XVIII). Within a year the *Belgic Confession* was drawn up in what is now Belgium (but was then Southern Netherlands, 1561). It stated the marks of the Church to be: "[1] if the pure preaching of the gospel is preached therein; [2] if it maintains the pure administration of the sacraments as instituted by Christ; [3] if church discipline is exercised in punishing of sin; in short, if all things are managed according to the pure Word of God, all things contrary thereto rejected, and Jesus Christ acknowledged as the only Head of the Church" (Article 29).

1.2 The Westminster Confession of Faith (1647)

It is interesting that in its statement about the Church the *Westminster Confession of Faith* is somewhat less explicit than these 16th Century Confessions. In Chapter 25 the *Confession* simply states that "The visible Church, which is also catholic or universal under the Gospel (not confined to one nation as before under the law), consists of all those throughout the world that profess the true religion; and of their children: and is the kingdom of the Lord Jesus Christ, the house and family of God, out of which there is no ordinary possibility of salvation." This is a definition in line with how Paul addresses the Corinthians in his first letter: "To the church of God which is at Corinth, to those that are sanctified in Christ Jesus, called to be saints, with all that in every place call on the name of Jesus Christ our Lord, both theirs and ours" (1:2). Yet the Westminster definition still begs the question as to how the 'true religion' was to be understood, something which the *Confession* is at pains throughout to establish, including the nature of the true gospel, the right understanding and administration of the sacraments, and the necessity for biblical Church discipline.

1.3 *The Church of Christ* (James Bannerman)

In a chapter on 'The Notes of the Church' in his lectures on *The Church of Christ* (1869), James Bannerman distinguishes what the *essential characteristics* of a Church of Christ are from the *notes* by which it may be known, or by which its *spiritual health* may be discerned. In other words, he distinguishes what is necessary for the *being* of a Church and what is necessary to its *well-being*. He puts the notes or marks of a Church of Christ in the category of *properties* belonging to it, though not strictly entering in to the *essence* of a Church.[1] Bannerman put it this way: "The one note or mark, then, which is common to every true Church, and peculiar to every true Church, is the profession of faith in Christ. Whatever be the differences in other respects, – whatever be the distinction in outward form or administration, in ordinances, in government, in worship, – these things are subordinate to the one criterion of the profession of the true faith, which marks by its presence a true Church, and declares by its absence an apostate one."[2] Its *existence* is proven by this mark, though its *well-being* will be demonstrated by other marks, such as those identified in the Scots and Belgic Confessions. However, with good grounds Bannerman identifies the one mark of a profession of the true religion as *primary*, whereas those involving outward ordinances are *secondary*, though not insignificant or unimportant for all that. Bannerman made the valid point that defining the essence of the Church by 'secondary' marks in relation to ordinances, etc., "begins that error which is developed in the intolerant principles of many in the present day who would unchurch all denominations but their own; and which manifests itself also in that outward formalism – Popish or Tractarian – which ascribes to external ordinances a value and sacredness which belong only to the truth as it is in Jesus."[3]

1.4 The well-being of a Church indicated by its marks

Notwithstanding Bannerman's advocacy of the one essential mark of a Church, consistently with the *Westminster Confession of Faith*, it is clear that such 'secondary' marks in relation to ordinances, etc., will enter in to the *well-being* of a Church. A Church will be marked by doctrine,

---

[1] James Bannerman, *The Church of Christ*, Vol. 1, Edinburgh 1960 [1869], 54ff.
[2] ibid., 60.
[3] ibid., 61.

worship and government one way or another. The question will be, is that worship, doctrine and government sound and biblical? In that sense there are certainly good marks you would expect to find in a Church professing the true religion. How do you know it is professing the true religion if it does not have a clear view of what the true religion is, who Christ Himself is and how He is regarded, and what He has done and is doing to build His Church on earth? From Christ's observations on the Seven Churches of Asia Minor in the second and third chapters of the Book of Revelation it is clear that such matters as orthodoxy, purity of worship and proper discipline are to be serious concerns for any Church concerned to reflect what a Christian Church should be in making a true profession of Christian faith.

2. Marks of a True Church

2.1 The faithful preaching of the Word

In encouraging Timothy in his ministry Paul emphasises the place and importance of the Scriptures in his work (2 Timothy 3:16-17). He immediately goes on to write of the implications of that in terms of preaching: "I charge thee therefore before God, and the Lord Jesus Christ, who shall judge the quick [living] and the dead at his appearing and his kingdom; Preach the word; be instant [ready] in season and out of season; reprove, rebuke, exhort with all longsuffering and doctrine. For the time will come when they will not endure sound doctrine; but after their own lusts shall they heap up to themselves teachers, having itching ears; and they shall turn away their ears from the truth, and shall be turned unto fables" (2 Timothy 4:1-4). We can understand the stress given on the preaching of the Word when we take account of how Paul deals with it in writing to the Corinthians: "the preaching of the cross is to them that perish foolishness; but unto us which are saved it is the power of God." After all, "it pleased God by the foolishness of preaching to save them that believe" (1 Corinthians 1:18, 21). The preaching of the Word is one of these 'ordinary means' by which the Holy Spirit awakens souls. It is one of the principal means God uses for the salvation of sinners and their subsequent instruction in the truth. It stands to reason, therefore, that a Church weak on the function of preaching the message of the Scriptures; the message concerning sin and salvation, heaven and hell, will be sadly lacking. For these are things the Lord has positively appointed to be instrumental in the conviction, conversion, instruction and edification of sinners. As Martin Luther put it, pithily: "Where thou findest the word [i.e. preached word], doubtless a Church is there." When we consider that John the Baptist came preaching (Matthew 3:1), and Jesus came preaching (Matthew 4:23), and the apostles went about preaching (Acts 5:42; 8:4, etc.), little wonder that this should be considered a 'property' or 'mark' of a true Christian Church. As Paul wrote to the Romans: "whosoever shall call upon the name of the Lord shall be saved. How then shall they call on him of whom they have not believed? and how shall they believe in Him of whom they have not heard? and how shall they hear without a preacher?" (Romans 10:13-14). And later to Titus the Apostle writes: "God, that cannot lie,…manifested his word through preaching, which is committed unto me according to the commandment of God our Saviour" (Titus 1:2-3).

2.2 The proper administration of the sacraments

The sacraments of the New Testament according to the Protestant interpretation of Scripture are Baptism and the Lord's Supper. These are seen to be instituted by the Lord Jesus Christ Himself and replace the Old Testament rites of Circumcision and the Passover. The warrant for Baptism is found in the Great Commission: "Go ye therefore, and teach all nations, baptizing them in the name of the Father, and of the Son, and of the Holy Ghost: teaching them to observe all things whatsoever I have commanded you: and, lo, I am with you alway, even unto the end of the age" (Matthew 28:19-20). The warrant for the Lord's Supper is found in Paul's letter to the Corinthians: "I have received of the Lord that which I also delivered unto you, that the Lord Jesus the same night in which he was betrayed took bread; and when he had given thanks, he brake it, and said, Take, eat: this is my body, which is broken for you: this do in remembrance of me. After the same manner also he took the cup, when he had supped, saying, This cup is the new testament in my blood: this do ye, as oft as ye drink it, in remembrance of me" (1 Corinthians 11:23-25). Wrote William Binnie: "the Sacraments are notes of the Church in this respect, that when we find them annexed to the word, they strengthen very materially the proof afforded by the presence of the word, that the society which enjoys it and them, enjoys also the gracious presence of Christ Himself and the continual ministration of the Spirit, and forms part of the true Church of Christ."[4] Perhaps it is proof enough of the importance of Baptism for the Church, that it speaks so eloquently of covenant relations and is therefore a sign (in its symbolism) of spiritual life within the Church. And it is perhaps proof enough of the importance of the Lord's Supper for the Church that Christ says, "This do in remembrance of me." Besides, His concern for the proper administration of the ordinance is clear from the fact that He encourages self-examination. It seems clear that the Church ought not to allow the improper administration of either sacrament, the one being the sign and seal of the Covenant; and the other speaking so strongly on what is so central to sinners' acceptance with God through the death of Christ. Binnie again: "when I find the word faithfully taught and the other ordinances purely administered, I may well presume that the true Church – the congregation of the saints – has more or less an existence there."[5]

2.3 The preservation of vital Christian faith

It is one thing for a Church/congregation to have the faithful preaching of the word in its midst, and to administer the sacraments carefully to members. However, it is another thing to say that that means there will be the presence of vital religion. It is not just a mark of the Church that the outward ordinances are in place, but also that there is real spiritual life in the body. That is the implication of the 'mark' of the right

---

[4] Binnie, op. cit., 6-7.
[5] ibid., 7.

application of discipline in the church. The whole tenor of the Lord Jesus' remarks to the Churches of Asia Minor in Revelation 2 and 3 is that there must be the exercise of right discipline in the body or else its integrity will be undermined and the lampstand finally removed. One of the clear lessons in Church history is that Churches will decline where discipline becomes lax; it imperils the well-being of a Church. In any case the 'keys of the kingdom' are given to the Church, to be used judiciously according to the word of Christ: "And I will give unto thee the keys of the kingdom of heaven: and whatsoever you bind on earth will be bound in heaven, and whatsoever thou shalt loose on earth shall be loosed in heaven" (Matthew 16:19). The question of discipline was clearly crucial in the early Church (see Matthew 18:15-20; Acts 5:1-11; 15:6-29; 20:28). However, the health of the Church is not determined just by the right application of discipline when necessary, but more positively, the evident spiritual evangelical life of the professing members of the Church.

3. Conclusion

The aim of every Church which claims allegiance to Christ and faithfulness to His Word ought to be that it is as pure as a visible Church in earth can be. The *Westminster Confession of Faith* acknowledges what has patently been the case down the millennia, that "This catholic [=universal] Church hath been sometimes more, sometimes less visible. And particular Churches, which are members thereof, are more or less pure, according as the doctrine of the Gospel is taught and embraced, ordinances administered, and public worship performed more or less purely in them" (25:4). As far as the 'marks' of the Church are concerned, we might say that the three principal things normally stated as 'marks' or 'notes' in the Churches of the Reformed tradition – the faithful preaching of the word, proper administration of the sacraments, and right application of Church discipline – will indicate in one degree or another the spiritual health of any visible Church. It would be strange Churches claiming to be Christian that did not have such elements in their Church life.

There are some denominations that claim to be Christian which lack one or other – or more than one – of these elements or properties in their Church life, such as the Salvation Army and the Quakers who have no sacraments. They might be considered Christian Churches by virtue of professing faith in Christ. However, when preaching, ordinances of worship, the sacraments and Church discipline are found to be warranted and instituted in the Word of God for the Church, any professing Church in which such things are held in low esteem, or loosely applied, or perhaps not found at all, must be seriously deficient and at odds with the Lord in their Church life and practices, and will require to learn the way of God more perfectly (Acts 18:24-28). At the same time, mere nominal possession of such 'marks,' outwardly, is insufficient. It appeared that the Church at Ephesus had all the proper marks of a true Church (Revelation 2:1-3), and yet it lacked something serious which could be fatal for its life. They had left their first love (v4), and they required to repent and do the first works (v5). Whatever else a professing Church may be marked by, the most important feature for its well-being is the presence and power of God among the people; the people walking in the Spirit (Galatians 5:16, 25), and Christ in the midst (Revelation 1:12-13).

THE CHURCH

4. The Purpose of the Church

1. Introduction
This is closely connected to the question of the 'marks' of the Church. But the question may be asked: What is the *purpose* of the Church in the world? This is an important issue because sometimes the practice of evangelism is thought to take priority over everything else and is often used as an excuse for admitting elements into such evangelism at odds with what may be thought appropriate in formal worship, because, after all, it is 'evangelism' and therefore it can justify any approach, on the principle that the end justifies the means. This, however, it may be argued, falls seriously foul of Jesus' stricture about the scribes and Pharisees of His day, when He said, "in vain they do worship me, teaching for doctrines the commandments of men" (Matthew 15:9), not to speak of the Great Commission in which He explicitly states to His disciples: "make disciples of all the nations, baptizing them in the name of the Father and of the Son and of the Holy Spirit, teaching them to observe all things that I have commanded you" (Matthew 28:19-20, NKJV). There are several things that go into the purpose of the Church in the world. There is a logical order to these but they must be seen not as mutually exclusive, but rather mutually inclusive.

2. The Church is to bear witness to God and His truth
In the broadest sense this is the overall purpose of the Church in the world. In the Sermon on the Mount Jesus describes His disciples in this way: "Ye are the light of the world. A city that is set on an hill cannot be hid. Neither do men light a candle, and put it under a bushel [basket], but on a candlestick [lampstand]; and it giveth light unto all who are in the house. Let your light so shine before men, that they may

see your good works and glorify your Father which is in heaven" (Matthew 5:14-16). Exactly the same could be said of the Church, for the Church essentially comprises His disciples. Further, in writing to Timothy Paul provides a concise definition of the Church in the world when he calls it, "the house of God, which is the church of the living God, the pillar and ground of the truth" (1 Timothy 3:15). It is on the 'rock' of the clear apostolic testimony to the Saviour given by Peter that the Church would be built (Matthew 16:18).

A primary concern for the church, then, is bearing witness to the truth, especially in relation to God as He is revealed in creation and in the word, and in relation to Christ as Saviour and all He taught. The source of this is not human philosophy, but the God-breathed Scriptures, inerrantly preserved by the Holy Spirit (2 Timothy 3:16; 2 Peter 1:19-21). After all, Jesus is to be confessed as the way and the truth and the life (John 14:6). The relevance and importance of this lies in the fact that, though mankind is fallen and stands under the wrath and curse of God, salvation has been accomplished by Christ and is offered to the sinner. It is a mercy, then, that there is truth revealed and it stands to reason that, in the light of the perilous state of mankind fallen in sin, making the truth of a gracious salvation known should be a primary purpose of the Church in the world. It is necessary, therefore, for the Church to be very clear on what the truth is lest people be deceived or sold short. It is important for all people everywhere to be confronted by the truth offering them free salvation in Christ. There is a need, therefore, for having a clear confessional and doctrinal position (thus the place for Creeds and Confessions) so as accurately to point sinners in the right direction in this life, and accurately reflect the truth of God, sin and salvation, and eternal realities.

3. The Church is to advance the worship of God
In a real sense this is the 'chief end of man.' The commitment of people to glorify God and enjoy Him forever implies engagement in the true worship of the living and true God and His Son Jesus Christ. This indeed is an obligation upon all men everywhere. There is a sense in

which the call of the gospel is precisely a call to worship God. It is the highest exercise in which any one can engage. That is why the manner in which we draw near to Him is so important. It is also the reason why, logically, this is before evangelism and why care should be taken in all evangelistic work to ensure that what is done is positively appointed by the Lord and not just according to man's devices and whims or expediencies, or entertainments.

Worship, then, is a grand purpose of the individual. This seems clear, for example, in Romans 12 where Paul urges this: "I beseech you therefore, brethren, by the mercies of God, that ye present your bodies a living sacrifice, holy, acceptable unto God, which is your reasonable service" (Romans 12:1). That is man's highest responsibility, privilege and purpose: the worship of Almighty God. It stands to reason that the greatest care should be taken as to how we are to approach Him. This is the concern of the first four of the 10 commandments. Worship, then, is not something people should be casual about, whether it be thought of in connection with private or public worship, nor indeed even the duty and responsibility of a nation/state. It is very clear from Scripture that,

(1) all people everywhere individually ought to praise and worship the true God in the Trinity of His persons. Indeed, it is sin for them not to do so;

(2) people ought to gather collectively to worship Him as congregations and hear His word; and,

(3) nations, too, ought to acknowledge the God revealed in Scripture and encourage His worship in the nation. Principally it is the Church that is God's institution on earth for the furtherance of such worship.

In relation to the Church, William Binnie expressed this purpose of worship well: "One principal end for which the Church has been instituted is that, by means of it, God's people may be regularly associated in divine service, and may, by their union, fan each other's devotion into a warmer, brighter glow. This is the highest and most honourable of the Church's functions; and it is that in which the

Church on earth makes the nearest approach to the service of the upper sanctuary, where angels and redeemed men worship God continually."[1] It is impossible to understand the Biblical religion, whether of the Old or New Testament, without the clear obligation of people collectively gathering to praise and worship. 'Church' as the visible gathering for worship of those who profess the true religion is writ large over the whole of the Bible.

4. The Church is to encourage the fellowship of its people
It is clearly a purpose of the Church to encourage submission to Christ and His will among its members and adherents. It therefore is duty bound to encourage fellowship and 'mutual edification' so that those who profess and confess Christ may grow in faith and love and obedience, and in the hope of the gospel. This is very clear in what emerged after Pentecost. After Peter's sermon recorded in Acts 2 this is what happened: "they continued steadfastly in the apostles' doctrine and fellowship, in the breaking of bread, and in prayers…all that believed were together, and had all things in common; and sold their possessions and goods, and parted them to all men, as every man had need. And they, continuing daily with one accord in the temple, and breaking bread from house to house, did eat their food with gladness and singleness of heart, praising God, and having favour with all the people" (Acts 2:42-47). Little wonder that we find that, "the Lord added to the church such as should be saved." This question of fellowship and mutual edification and encouragement in spiritual life through the Church is clear, for example, in the New Testament letters. These obviously vary in their nature and purpose, but they all in one way or another have this context of the Church as a body which is for the mutual help and encouragement of men, women and children in growing in professing faith in Christ and growing in His grace. A cursory glance at all the opening greetings in the New Testament letters will bring this point home. Certainly, the purpose of the letters is to

---

[1] Binnie, op. cit., 45-46.

advance the fellowship of the saints, providing inducements to deal with sins which are destructive of the life of the whole body (the letters to the Corinthians), encouragements to pursue godliness for the good of the whole body (the letters to the Thessalonians), provide the oversight to ensure the cohesion of the body of the Church (the letters to Timothy). In a way this is summed up in the letter to the Hebrews, where we have this exhortation to the Church: "Let us hold fast the confession of our faith without wavering; (for he is faithful that promised;) and let us consider one another to provoke unto love and good works: not forsaking the assembling of ourselves together, as the manner of some is, but exhorting one another: and so much the more as ye see the day approaching" (10:23-5).

In this connection Binnie provides an appropriate word of caution. There is a necessity for the gospel to be preserved in any Church fellowship. It may be lost so that Churches become merely 'nominal' and spiritually lifeless. Binnie points out that there can scarcely be Christian fellowship where "members of a congregation are severally strangers to the grace of God." They may have "neighbourly fellowship with each other, but brotherly and Christian fellowship they cannot have. They cannot love the brethren; they cannot consider one another, or edify one another, as brethren." He utters a timely warning: "Churches which are so lax in their admission of members, and in their oversight of members after admission, that they become flooded with people in no material respect differing from the world around, are thereby disabled from fulfilling the chief end of the Christian Church."[2] Sadly, humanly speaking the failure in this purpose of the Church is usually at the heart of declension in the Church. This may be illustrated in the history of the Church in Scotland. Through the Church unions of 1900 (Free Church and United Presbyterian Church) and 1929 (United Free Church and Church of Scotland), there was both a liberalising of the theological position of the resultant united bodies and, one could argue consequently, the nominalising of the membership. Without true

---

[2] Binnie, op. cit., 43.

spirituality and regard for the mutual edification and fellowship of confessing people; and without a careful regard for sound doctrine, a Church will not fulfil its purpose in this world effectively, and may outwardly decline and die as a spiritual force.

5. The Church is charged with the evangelisation of the world

This is what is charged by the Lord upon the Church in the Great Commission: "Go therefore and make disciples of all the nations, baptizing them in the name of the Father and of the Son and of the Holy Spirit, teaching them to observe all things that I have commanded you; and lo, I am with you always, even to the end of the age" (Matthew 28:19-20, NKJV). Alexander Duff (1806-1878), pioneer missionary to India in the early 19th Century entitled one of his books *Missions the chief end of the Christian Church* (1839). In a real sense, consistently with the other 'purposes' already mentioned above, this is true: a great purpose of the Church is, basically, mission, it is making Christ known throughout the world as the only Saviour for sinners. As mentioned above, this is not somehow detached from the necessity for the Christian Church to be clear on its doctrine and the principles of its operations. Given a true evangelical and biblical basis, however, this is an absolute obligation upon the Christian Church. It is explicit in Christ's Commission, but is also implicit in the giving of the Holy Spirit, as recorded in the Acts of the Apostles. Before His Ascension the Lord made clear the evangelical purpose of the Church's mission: "you shall receive power when the Holy Spirit has come upon you; and you shall be witnesses to me both in Jerusalem, and in all Judæa and in Samaria, and to the end of the earth" (Acts 1:8, NKJV). We have this worked out practically in the missionary ventures of the Apostle Paul, as recorded in Acts and implicit in his epistles. It was something to which the Old Testament pointed forward by way of anticipation, as, for example, in the book of Jonah, and in many of the Psalms. We see this, for example, in such passages as these:

- "All nations whom thou hast made shall come and worship before thee, O Lord, and shall glorify thy name" – Psalm 85:9.

- "God be merciful to us and bless us, and cause His face to shine upon us. Selah. That thy way may be known on earth, thy salvation among all nations. Let the peoples praise thee, O God; Let all the peoples praise thee" – Psalm 67:1-3.

The obligation upon the Church for global evangelisation is related in the Scriptures to the expectation of the Second Coming of Christ. In His discourse recorded in Matthew 24, Jesus speaks of the persecutions His faithful followers will experience in the world. They are, however, to endure to the end, and "he that shall endure to the end, the same shall be saved" (Matthew 24:13). However, the gospel which they will be preaching is to go far and wide. He says, "this gospel of the kingdom shall be preached in all the world for a witness unto all nations; and then shall the end come" (Matthew 24:14). No Church, then, can neglect this calling. But in order properly to fulfil this great purpose of the visible Church in the world, the *content* of the gospel must be clear, whatever inconvenience or troubles may arise on account of maintaining it inviolate. William Binnie emphasised the importance of this well: "There is good reason to believe that the internal prosperity of the Church, at any given time, will largely depend on the measure of her faithful obedience to this part of the Lord's charge. If the Church would enjoy prosperity – if she would have the Lord to bless her, and make her face to shine upon her, she must labour to make His way known on the earth, and His salvation among all the nations."[3]

It is obviously important for the Church to have a clear view of what its purpose is in the world. That purpose is entirely derived from the will of Jesus Christ for it. It is not a question of what men can best think up to advance the cause of the Lord. His revealed will is paramount. The basic purpose is not social change or social action – though there may be social change and social action which flow from Christians being salt in the earth and light in the world; yet the basic purpose is not social change but spiritual transformation and the preparation of men and women and all people everywhere to recognise

---

[3] Binnie, op. cit., 50-51.

the truth of God in His word and submit to it, to see their responsibility to worship and serve Him in this world, and to advance His cause among themselves and others, as well as to prepare for death and eternity. It is summed up in what Paul taught: "For so the Lord hath commanded us, saying, I have set thee to be a light of the Gentiles, that thou shouldest be for salvation unto the ends of the earth" (Acts 13:47).

6. The Church and Social Responsibility

The diaconal function in the offices of the Church implies and even involves the disbursement of a social responsibility aspect of the work of the Church. It involves among other things satisfying the social or financial needs of its own adherents (in the broadest sense) as far as may be practicable within the resources available to the Church. The claims of compassion would imply that this practical concern may extend beyond the immediate congregation. Some of this care might involve the support of Christian-based agencies specialising in particular areas of social need. Many prominent Christians (e.g., Thomas Guthrie, the Earl of Shaftesbury and Dr Barnardo[4]) were at the forefront of such initiatives in the past. In the 20th century the Church of Scotland, Free Church and Free Presbyterian Churches all organised their own Care Homes, something that is perfectly consistent with the diaconal function of the Church.

In a real sense social responsibility arises from the injunction to the Christian to "love thy neighbour as thyself", something that spans Old and New Testaments (Leviticus 19:18, 34; Matthew 19:19; 22:39; Mark 12:31). This is the royal law (James 2:8). The Sermon on the Mount is often highlighted as having practical implications for social responsibility, which it surely has (see especially Matthew 5:21-48). The whole question of Good Works (see *Westminster Confession of Faith*, Chapter 16) is at the heart of the responsibility of the Christian in the

---

[4] See Kathleen Heasman's *Evangelicals in Action: An Appraisal of their Social Work* (London, 1962) for what has been described as "the first survey of the social work of a prominent religious outlook."

world and will inevitably relate to the encouragements and exhortations of the Church in the world. The whole matter of compassion and concern for people's practical social needs as well as for their soul's salvation must be a responsibility for the Christian and Christ's Church on earth in this fallen dysfunctional world. There is the example of the Lord Jesus, who went about doing good, who fed the 5000 and the 4000, and healed the sick. There were also clear 'social responsibility' elements in, for example, the appointment by the Apostles in Acts 6 (1-7) of seven to "serve tables" and to exercise responsibilities towards the "widows" (Acts 6:1; James 1:27).

It is a question to what extent the Church *as an institution* should be engaged in particular works of, broadly speaking, social responsibility or activism. The principal task of the Church is gospel: the calling of men, women and children to come to faith in Christ and the consequent concern to build up believers in the holy faith. Nothing should deflect a Church from that calling and mission for the Lord, as answerable to Him. The Church must therefore be careful not to become simply an agency for a 'social gospel'.[5] The Church, however, will be an indirect force in social life in maintaining truth and justice, as well as Christian love. Obvious areas of influence lie in the fields of education and medicine as well as the media, areas often pursued actively in mission situations.

It is of note that in the 19th century the Free Church maintained its own Schools, motivated by a desire to maintain Christian values and principles among the youth of the Church (and beyond). Whether that was strictly speaking a task for the *Church* is a pertinent question. Unfortunately, the Schools largely passed into a state system after 1872 and there was no subsequent development of distinctly Christian schooling in Scotland (unlike the situation in the Netherlands, the United States of America and some other colonial territories). The drift in the state school system progressively throughout the 20th century

---

[5] See Lit-sen Chang's *The True Gospel vs. Social Activism* (Presbyterian and Reformed Publishing Co., 1976)

unquestionably, humanly speaking, has had a negative impact on Christian faith in Scotland (and, indeed, in the West in general) as education became more and more secular, and humanistic at every level, not least in a commitment to the evolutionary theory of origins in the science class. The responsibility of Christians to organise such things is an imperative in every age and this is something that the Church will encourage through a ministry which emphasises not just personal salvation but also a Christian world-view with covenantal responsibility and righteous action (good works), focussing on concerns for truth, justice, and compassion for the practical as well as spiritual needs of individuals everywhere.

THE CHURCH

5. The Membership of the Church

1. Introduction

The question of Church membership is interwoven with the nature of the Church itself. You cannot ask the question 'What is the Church?' without also asking the supplementary question, 'Who comprises the Church?' and, 'How should they be marked out?' The existence of a Church presupposes individuals who are part of it. The outward marks of a Church body defined in terms of the preaching of the word, the administration of sacraments and the exercise of discipline is one thing. It seems clear, however, that the liveliness, health and strength of a Church under God relates to *the nature of its membership*. What of those who comprise the Church? What is their profession of faith? What is their experience of the grace of God? What spiritual life is there among them? *You cannot ask questions about the health of a Church without examining its membership*. That, as we know, is not necessarily as straightforward a matter as it seems. Not when distinctions are made between members and non-members, or adherents; and when 'adherents' may comprise a significant proportion, or even a majority of those who are associated with a Church congregation and may even receive admission to one of the sacraments but not the other. The question of Christian profession can thereby become blurred and the question of 'membership' muddied. Communicant membership in Churches can become a nominal thing, especially when a Church's position becomes doctrinally compromised and enfeebled, as, sadly, has been the case in mainline Churches in recent history. This has been a harbinger – and indicator – of a Church that has a name that it is alive but is dead – or dying (Revelation 3:1-6).

Clearly the health of a Church will relate to the spiritual health of its membership, the standards of profession of faith and godliness and the presence and power of the Holy Spirit within it, that is to say among those who are part of it. This is a clear lesson from the letters of the Lord Jesus Christ to the seven Churches in Asia Minor, as recorded in Revelation chapters 2 and 3. As we consider this question of membership of, or in, the Church we have to focus on what the members of the Church *should* be, and also what those who are simply attendees should *become*. For our purposes it is presupposed that there is a clear understanding of the faith in the Church, as summarised, for example, in the *Westminster Shorter Catechism*; a clear understanding of an evangelical profession of faith; and a desire for wholehearted obedience to the Lord as He speaks through His Word. Without such things our discussion would be lacking in substance. When we consider this subject, we will look at the *reasons* for Church membership, the *requirements* of Church membership, the *privileges* of Church membership and the *duties* of Church membership.

2. Reasons for Church membership

In speaking of Church membership, we have to define our terms. On the one hand there is the broadest understanding in terms of all who regularly, or more or less regularly, attend Church services and otherwise associate with a particular Church denomination or congregation. However, we have to be more specific and think of membership more strictly in terms of those who personally and voluntarily make profession of faith in the Lord Jesus Christ as their Saviour and Lord. They are professing to be born again and to accept the Scriptures as the rule for faith and life. On examination such souls are admitted to the rights and privileges – and duties – of Church membership which, among other things, gives them rights to receive the Church's sacraments. All others are non-communicant adherents of congregations, albeit they may have been admitted to the visible church by baptism in infancy. There is clearly a call, and indeed a responsibility, of all such to make profession of faith for themselves in due time and be admitted to the communicant membership of their Church/congregation. We are therefore thinking here of what we might call 'communicant membership' to which all 'adherents' or non-communicant members *should* aspire. It is true that adherents may personally or privately give indication of being people of lively faith and piety, but if that is so then they should desire to be members in the fullest sense as those who among other things are obedient to Christ in remembering His death till He come. There are therefore good reasons for Church membership in these respects:

(1) *A clear open confession is made in this world of faith in the Lord Jesus Christ and obedience to Him (so far as fallible human beings can tell)*. This is Scriptural: "if thou shalt confess with thy mouth the Lord Jesus, and shalt believe in thine heart that God hath raised him from the dead, thou shalt be saved. For with the heart man believeth unto righteousness; and with the mouth confession is made unto salvation. For the scripture saith, Whosoever believeth on him shall not be ashamed" (Romans 10:9-11). The importance of an open public profession cannot be minimised: "Whosoever therefore shall confess me before men, him will I confess also before my Father which is in heaven. But whosoever shall deny me before men, him will I also deny before my Father which is in heaven" (Matthew 10:32-33).

(2) *Those who make such profession of faith receive privileges and bring themselves positively under the guidance and discipline of the Church and its offices*. The Church is seen to be an organism and not just an organisation. Members receive the privileges of the sacraments as well as the fellowship of those who make like profession of faith. They affirm that they belong to a body which believes in Christ, seeks to follow Christ and, if you will, they clearly give *visibility* to these things in the world. As believers they are commanded to remember Christ's death till He comes again (1 Corinthians 11:26) it is obviously important for the Church to be clear on who may and who may not receive the sacraments. Inevitably, in obedience to Christ, a Church will be therefore concerned to establish the criteria for such things, which will

be done in terms of 'membership' of a local church. There are therefore good reasons for Church membership. But what of its requirements?

3. Requirements of Church membership

As we have suggested, Church membership relates to the visibility of the Church in the world. Here are people who associate with the Church in the world. What will demonstrate clearly that this body is truly Christian? What would you expect of the individuals who comprise it?

(1) *There will be a credible profession of faith in the Lord Jesus Christ made unashamedly in the face of the local Church.* Whatever else is involved in a *credible* profession of faith, it will involve a clear understanding of sin and righteousness and judgement to come (John 16:8-11). It will involve a satisfactory testimony concerning repentance for sin (2 Corinthians 7:9-11). It will involve a clear understanding of the truth concerning the Person and Work of the Saviour. It will involve sufficient grasp of the teaching of the Bible as God's Word. We do not say a perfect or *thorough* understanding of the basic Bible teaching. It is not a case of having an advanced degree of sanctification. Nevertheless, there must be a clear enough knowledge of the gospel way of salvation and of Christ as the God-man and only Saviour, in whom alone there is forgiveness.

(2) *There will be expected a life of obedience to Christ and the moral and spiritual demands of Scripture teaching.* This, clearly, is an aspect of the *credibility* of a profession of faith in Christ as personal Saviour and Lord. Is there a desire to hide His Word in our hearts that we will not sin against Him (Psalm 119:11)? A wonderful and searching illustration of this is found in Psalm 119, verses 33 to 40. In his general letter, James speaks of 'justification by works.' That does *not* mean we are saved by our works, for the Bible tells as clearly that that is not the case. It *does* mean that believers will give evidence by their works that they have truly received the grace that justifies the sinner. As James wrote: "Even so faith, if it hath not works, is dead, being alone. Yea a man may say, Thou hast faith, and I have works: shew me thy faith without thy works, and I will

shew thee my faith by my works" (2:17-18). He has already exhorted: "be ye doers of the word, and not hearers only, deceiving your own selves" (1:22). The *life* of the professing person, in other words, must be in line with any profession of faith they may make.

(3) *There should be a clear understanding of the privileges and commitments of Church membership and of the meaning of the sacraments.* After all, the desire of the Christian Church must be that the Lord Jesus will be glorified and that its members be fruitful for Him. "For ye are bought with a price: therefore glorify God in your body, and in your spirit, which are God's" (1 Corinthians 6:20). But if that is to be the case then they must be captives to the Word and see themselves as ambassadors for Christ (2 Corinthians 5:20). In addition, they are to be instruments for the gospel as those who heed the Great Commission (Matthew 28:19-20).

4. Privileges of Church membership

So, what are the privileges of Church membership? It is a privilege to be a professing member of a local congregation bearing testimony to the Person of Christ, the claims of the gospel and the demands of godly living. Consider:

(1) *They enjoy the advantages of the true worship of God in the services of the Church.* This is a 'general' point. We sometimes call these the means of grace. They are not to be taken lightly. They are not to be *formalised*. We are never to go through the motions of worship acts. It is a privilege to have a faithful Bible-believing and gospel-holding Church. It is a privilege to have the regular Lord's day ministry to feed your souls. The worship of God is a primary end of our existence. The Church must be faithful to Christ and the doctrine of the word. It is a privilege to worship the Lord with a good conscience together with other like-minded souls. Whatever benefits non-professing people may receive in the worship services, these are to be treasured as privileges by Church members and seen to be such! It is a privilege to be taught what we are to know concerning God and what duties He requires of us, and that is a task of the Church in the world.

(2) *They enjoy the privilege of partaking of the sacraments.* The *Shorter Catechism* is clear on the nature of a sacrament: "a sacrament is a holy ordinance instituted by Christ; wherein by sensible signs, Christ and the benefits of the new covenant are represented, sealed, and applied to believers" (Answer 92). The sacraments are baptism and the Lord's Supper. By means of the sacraments God teaches certain truths and bestows certain blessings. Baptism is applied to adults professing faith in Christ having not been baptised as infants (Acts 2:41), and to the children of those who profess faith in Christ and obedience to Him (*Larger Catechism* 166 & *Shorter Catechism* 95). Likewise, the Lord's Supper is a blessed means of grace for those professing souls exercised in receiving it (1 Corinthians 11:23-34).[1]

(3) *They enjoy the privilege of practical support of the work and ministry of the Church.* It is a privilege to give to the Church of our substance, and to do so 'heartily,' for the Lord loves a cheerful giver. This is the 'tithing' principle. No doubt there is a duty here, which we will consider below.[2] It is sufficient, however, at this point to recognise this as a *privilege* (Luke 8:3; 1 Corinthians 16:2).

(4) *They enjoy the privilege of spiritual guidance and support, and where necessary correction within the fellowship of the Church.* As part of a body of people (Church) who make like profession of faith in Christ and love for the ordinances, and concern for holy living, it is a privilege to be among those who will help (practically as well as spiritually) and guide in the things of the Lord. In our day of 'gathered' congregations and relative isolation we tend to see 'Church' narrowly in terms of *services*. It has to be more than that, with meaningful interaction. As Peter taught: "be ye all of one mind, having compassion one of another, love as brethren, be pitiful [tender-hearted], be courteous" (1 Peter 3:8). He went on to write: "above all things have fervent love for one another…Be hospitable to one another without grumbling. As each one has received

---

[1] For a discussion of Baptism and the Lord's Supper see Section D below.

[2] See Section C, Chapter 8, below.

The Church – Its Membership 55

a gift, minister it to one another, as good stewards of the manifold grace of God" (1 Peter 4:8-10, NKJV).

(5) *They enjoy the privilege of having a voice in the oversight of the Church.* That is to say, the communicant membership has the privilege of voting on pastors, elders and deacons in the local congregation (see Acts 6:1-7). In addition, it is the privilege of male members, when in the view of the Church they have suitable qualifications for office, to be open to election as office-bearers themselves in their local congregation.

5. Commitments of Church membership

So much has been said already to suggest many of the duties or responsibilities of Church membership. One suspects, however, that when people think of Church membership – 'communicant' Church membership – they think in terms of a few privileges rather than *responsibilities* or *commitments*. In relation to 'adherents' – non-communicants – *their* duty is to come to profess faith in Christ and enter in to the *privilege* of testifying to Christ and His claims in the world. Some may indeed do that after a fashion as men or women in Christ. However, in the context of the Church they have no formal standing; they do not remember Christ's death in the sacrament of the Lord's Supper; they do not engage, the men, in public prayer; and they have no direct vote in elections of office bearers. They are called to confess Christ openly and nail their colours to the mast! As for those who *do* openly profess faith in the Lord and a living hope through grace, there are clear commitments to be expected:

(1) *There is a duty to be attentive at the means of grace.* This includes the Sabbath services and weekly prayer meetings. A lack of diligence in such things on the part of members is a bad witness and a discouragement to other members, and ministers. There should not be among members absence from public worship, other than for legitimate reasons, works of genuine necessity or mercy, infirmities or ill health. In relation to public worship members ought to have their minds/hearts set simply on the joy of going to the house of the Lord (Psalm 122:1),

where their Saviour is worshipped, and not on whether or not they 'enjoy' the worship.

In connection with the means of grace there is also responsibility in connection with the sacraments. In relation to baptism this involves commitment to bring up children in the fear and instruction of the Lord; to pray for them and plead with them and encourage them in believing in Christ for themselves and following Him. In relation to the Lord's Supper there is a duty to remember His death till He come by sitting at His table.

(2) *There is a duty of loyalty to the Church.* This relates to the faithfulness of the Church and convictions about the doctrine and practice of the Church/congregation. We seem to be in a fluid situation these days in which people carry around alternative options in Church connections. The member in the faithful gospel Church having a care for the purity of worship and proper exercise of Church practice *ought to be loyal through blessed times and in adversity.* There appears to be a tendency for people to leave Churches for 'personal' reasons rather than out of convictions on principles. Church members ought to be loyal to their local congregation and denomination. This does not mean that they will never attend any other Church. There will be humility in recognising, where that is the case, other Churches and Christian believers who are truly Bible-believing, evangelical and reformed and therefore hold a like precious faith, albeit with some lesser differences.

(3) *There is a duty to observe the Christian Sabbath carefully.* The professing man, woman and family are under scrutiny, both from the Lord and from the world! Keeping the Lord's day is a test of seriousness in Christian faith. How do you observe the Lord's day? What excuse by slackness do you give to people of the world for their indifference or neglect of the day of rest and worship? Members need to be exercised about this so that full benefit spiritually may be enjoyed in that day. I would just suggest here, for example: keep the TV off, and avoid any superfluous travel on the Lord's day, as, for example, travelling for holidays. These are a bad witness.

(4) *There is a duty to give for the cause of the Lord.* This has been mentioned as a privilege and little more need be said, other than the duty to support not only local ministry, but gospel work farther afield, mission work, and the Church fabric needs. When Paul commends the churches of Macedonia for their giving, as an example for the Corinthian Church (2 Corinthians 8:1-7) he does so not just in terms of their giving according to their ability, but beyond it (v3). It pleased the apostle to say that it was not just such giving that marked them: "…and this they did, not as we hoped, but first *gave their own selves to the Lord*, and [then] unto us by the will of God" (v5). Giving is not just from the pocket, but of *ourselves* in prayer and witness to advance His cause.

(5) *There is a duty of pursuing personal devotion and holiness.* This is arguably the most powerful witness in any Church: *the prayer life and holy living of the members.* These are people who take Christ and His Word seriously. These are people who have a desire for likeness to Him. They are lights in the world and salt in the earth. And this will be fuelled by diligent daily Bible reading and prayer. This is the principle set out in Deuteronomy: "these words, which I command thee this day, shall be in thine heart: and thou shalt teach them diligently unto thy children, and shalt talk of them when thou sittest in thine house, and when thou walkest by the way, when thou liest down, and when thou risest up. And thou shall bind them for a sign upon thine hand, and they shall be as frontlets between thine eyes. And shalt write them upon the posts of thy house and on thy gates" (6:6-7). It is the repeated call: "as he which hath called you is holy, so be ye holy in all manner of conversation [conduct]; because it is written, Be holy; for I am holy" (1 Peter 1:15-16).

(6) *There is a duty of comfort and help to others, all people but especially those of the household of faith (Galatians 6:10).* When fellow believers are in need, according to their ability the Church member is to comfort and help. "Bear ye one another's burdens, and so fulfil the law of Christ" (Galatians 6:2). We are to "rejoice with them that do rejoice, and weep with them that weep" (Romans 12:15). This is an aspect of that most important of marks: Christian love. As Paul testifies of the Thessalonian

'members': "We are bound to thank God always for you, brethren, as it is meet [fitting], because that your faith groweth exceedingly, and the charity [love] of every one of you all toward each other aboundeth; so that we ourselves glory in you in the churches of God for your patience and faith in all your persecutions and tribulations that ye endure" (2 Thessalonians 1:3-4). Finally,

(7) *There is a responsibility to give all due deference to those who have the rule over them, the minister and the elders (Hebrews 13:7).* Christ is King and he has set office-bearers in His Church. They may not always act righteously, but so far as they have the rule in the Church, always under charge to act for Christ strictly according to Scripture teaching, it is the duty of members to be submissive and responsive. Among other things this will involve the application of any necessary Church discipline when members stray from the standards of the Word of God.

6. Conclusions

This is an important subject. Because the whole matter of Church membership has to do with the spiritual health and practical work and testimony of local congregations or denominations. What membership standards please the Lord? What are consistent with His character? What brings glory to His name? These are things to think upon deeply. How well does a person's membership reflect on the Saviour? There is a sense in which everyone under the sound of the gospel is called to Church membership. They are called to be *disciples*. They are called to service and worship. The truth? The Church is as lively and healthy as its members (including the leadership in the local Church).

People who believe themselves to be saved by Christ ought readily and happily to profess this openly. They will go to the minister and the Kirk Session. This may be daunting for some. It is usual for the emphasis to be placed on the *spiritual experience* of the person coming for membership. Their life-style may already be a matter of satisfaction to the Session. However, it may be a weakness that nowadays there is little teaching of potential communicants or emphasis on their responsibilities. We perhaps scorn 'communicants' classes.' But would it not be a good thing for Church members to be received as such in the face of the congregation, taking vows as to what is expected of them (as, for example, is the case in the marriage covenant)? That may sound daunting. However, it has the virtue of due emphasis on the *duties* as well as the *privileges* of Church membership.

We are sinful men and women in fallible Churches. Yet we should set our aims high in the life of the Church that the membership be lively and exercised and knowledgeable and holy and *committed*. This way at least the Church will tend to be less marginalised in a society which sadly tends to see little difference between those in Church and those not in Church.

THE CHURCH

6. The Discipline of the Church

1. Historical Introduction

From the outset the Reformed Church in Scotland recognised the necessity of ecclesiastical discipline within the Church. In its 'The Notes by which the True Kirk shall be determined from the false, and who shall judge of Doctrine,' the *Scots Confession* of 1560 stated that one of these 'notes' consisted in "ecclesiastical discipline uprightly ministered, as God's Word prescribes, whereby vice is repressed and virtue nourished."[1] In addition to this, in the Scottish Reformed Church its *First Book of Discipline* (1560) contained a seventh head on 'Ecclesiastical Discipline.'[2] Under this head it is stated that "no commonwealth can flourish or long endure without good laws, and sharp execution of the same, so neither can the church of God be brought to purity, neither yet be retained in the same, without the order of ecclesiastical discipline, which stands in reproving and correcting of those faults which the civil sword does either neglect, either may not punish." In the *First Book* various offences are considered and stipulations for their censure outlined. Where the offence is secret or known to few, private admonishment is deemed sufficient, provided there is due sorrow for the offence, promised circumspection. Where there is no obvious repudiation of such an attitude, due process will be necessary. In cases where the offence is public and 'heinous' formal process is to be followed and (controversially?) public repentance expressed. Even this aspect has a pastoral side as the congregation is encouraged to "pray to God with him for mercy, and to accept him in their society, notwithstanding his former offence, then the church may, and ought

---

[1] *The Scots Confession of 1560*, Edinburgh: The Saint Andrew Press, 1960, 72.
[2] See Appendix 1 below, pages 75 to 79.

[to] receive him as a penitent." The church is not to be more severe than God declares himself to be. "And therefore the church ought diligently to advert that it excommunicate not those whom God absolves." Statements are made concerning stubbornness, impenitence and their seriousness. Even here there is a pastoral aspect: "Request also would be made to the most discreet and to the nearest friends of the offender to travail with him to bring him to a knowledge of himself, and of his dangerous estate…" The idea of some heartless and overly stringent and intrusive discipline applied in the Reformed Churches is a myth, albeit in a liberal age any sort of 'restriction,' moral censorship or *punitive* discipline is alien. However, the question is not whether in any era discipline is discountenanced by the spirit of the age, but whether discipline within the Church is carried out faithfully and biblically.

The *Westminster Confession of Faith (1647)* in a Chapter of 'Church Censures' is actually very brief and generalised in dealing with discipline.[3] It speaks of office-bearers under Christ who are appointed by Him to exercise governance in the Church (30:1). They have the 'power of the keys' to exercise discipline (30:2). The necessity for discipline is stated to be (a) the reclaiming of offending brethren; (b) deterrence to others from such offences; (c) purging out evil influences in the Church; (d) vindicating the honour of Christ; (e) preventing the wrath of God if the Church should suffer any to profane His word (30:3). Mention is then made of the types of discipline: admonition, suspension from the sacrament of the Lord's Supper, and excommunication "according to the nature of the crime, and demerit of the person" (30:4).

Perhaps the most significant advance in the codification of discipline in the Scottish Reformed Church was what became known as the *Form of Process* adopted by the Church of Scotland in 1707. The full title of the Act was: 'Act Approving a Form of Process in the Judicatories of the Church with Relation to Scandals and Censures' (Session 11, April 18, 1707). "Church discipline and censures," says the

---

[3] See Appendix 2 below, page 80.

Act, "for judging and removing offences, are of great use and necessity in the Church, that the name of God, by reason of ungodly and wicked persons living in the Church, be not blasphemed, nor his wrath provoked against his people; that the godly be not leavened with but preserved from the contagion, and stricken with fear; and that sinners who are censured may be ashamed, to the destruction of the flesh and saving of the spirit in the day of the Lord Jesus." But "nothing ought to be admitted to any Church judicature as the ground of a process for censure, but what has been declared censurable by the word of God…" This constitutes a good summary of the correct approach to discipline. The Act in nine chapters goes quite thoroughly into procedures for the application of discipline as it should be in the Christian and Reformed Churches. It covers the responses to a variety of sins, the procedures and evidence necessary and the penalties involved. It is the basis of fair and Bible centred Church discipline still adopted by the smaller conservative Presbyterian denominations as part of their constitutions.

2. Biblical Perspective

"Among the first principles of Church order set forth by our Lord in His personal ministry, this is one, That persons living in open sin are not to be suffered to remain in Church fellowship (Matt. xviii. 15-20)."[4] This is how William Binnie begins his chapter on 'Church Discipline' in his fine Handbook on *The Church*. Secret sin should not be overlooked in an individual Christian. Open sin is not to be overlooked in a Church fellowship. Action must be taken. Because errors and immorality are scars on a Church, and can readily lead to the dissolution of a Church. This is a clear lesson in the letters of the Lord Jesus Christ to the Churches in Asia Minor in Revelation chapters 2 and 3. If a Church does not wish its lampstand to be removed through tolerated sin and error, then it must take action to ensure discipline in the case of erring members. This is clear from Matthew 18 and from cognate passages in the New Testament.

---

[4] Binnie, op. cit., 98.

The general principle of ecclesiastical discipline is older than the New Testament. Provision is found in the law of Moses which obliges the application of discipline among the professed people of God in cases of denial or defiance of God's revealed word and will. This much is clear from the teaching of the Pentateuch. The principle stated in Leviticus 19 is in reality a timeless one: "Thou shalt not hate thy brother in thine heart: thou shalt in any wise rebuke thy neighbour, and not suffer sin upon him" (verse 17). In other words, every effort should be made to recover errant brothers and sisters, so that no shame will fall on the Church of Christ and deliver our own souls. In the case of members of the Church we must go farther. Private admonition is to be given, but if that meets with no positive response and repentance, then witnesses must be brought in to add weight to the admonition. If in turn this is not productive, then the matter must be taken to church courts, with two or more witnesses. This is the thrust of Matthew 18:15-20. It is consistent with Titus 3:9-11. Discipline is also implicit in the statement of the Jerusalem Assembly as recorded in Acts 15:22-29 and in the tone of the letters to the Corinthians (for example 1 Corinthians 5:1-8 regarding sexual immorality in the Church). It is also implicit in admonitions to the Church in Ephesus (see for example chapter 5, verses 1 to 7). Clearly discipline among members is writ large over the New Testament letters. And little wonder, for the honour of Christ and the normative teaching of His word are at stake.

3. Warrant for Church Discipline

It is not uncommon for people to resent Church discipline. It is seen by some to interfere with their rights. It is seen also to be selective because after all there are so many others who do – or think – things that are just as bad, if not worse. In an age of denominations, it is relatively easy for people to avoid or evade discipline by moving from one Church to another, especially a Church less particular about the application of discipline among its members. Some people think it is judgemental, something worse, they may think, than their own fault or sin. However, the Bible makes it clear what righteousness is, what sin is – violation in greater or lesser measure of the word/law/commandments if God – and what a delight righteous actions are, and what an offence all sin is, to a holy God who is "of purer eyes than to behold evil, and canst not look on iniquity" (Habakkuk 1:13). The point is that on the basis of Matthew 18:15-20 and His letters to the Churches in Revelation 2 and 3, Christ does not leave His Church with an option. The Church is bound to take action against an erring brother or sister who are members in the local church. In the context of normal family life a loving father will discipline erring children in their own interests and to preserve the good name of the family. So, it must be with Christ's Church. By all means it must not be degraded by low moral or doctrinal standards.

However, the warrant for Church discipline in a real sense arises from Christ's words to His disciples:

- "I will give unto thee the keys of the kingdom of heaven: and whatsoever thou shalt bind on earth shall be bound in heaven: and whatsoever thou shalt loose on earth shall be loosed in heaven" (Matthew 16:19).
- "Verily, I say unto you, Whatsoever ye shall bind on earth shall be bound in heaven: and whatsoever ye shall loose on earth shall be loosed in heaven" (Matthew 18:18).

In other words, earthly church discipline rightly administered will be ratified in heaven. In this, "one thing… is plain; namely, that the power of authoritative discipline is to be distinguished both from the private influence which Christians may and ought to exercise with each other, and from the power which a private religious society has over its members by their mutual agreement."[5] It seems clear that the Church should not censure a person for that which God's law approves, nor should the church impute to such persons that of which they are not guilty. Churches, wrote Binnie, "in their judicial actings…have need to

---

[5] Binnie, op. cit., 103.

be humble, prayerful, circumspect."⁶ Nevertheless, fear of liability to error, or even a sense of unworthiness, are not reasons for not following through discipline in church affairs when faults are clearly provable. The passage, "where two or three are gathered together I my name, there am I in the midst of them" (Matthew 18:20) is given within the context of Christ's teaching on discipline rather than an encouragement in small gatherings for worship or fellowship!

4. The Intent of Church Discipline

Binnie fairly states that an overall design of Church discipline has a three-fold reference: to the one who is the subject of the discipline; to the other members and adherents of the Church or congregation; and to the on-looking world.⁷

(1) *With reference to the offender himself or herself.* The overall intention must be to bring such an erring person to repentance by awakening them to the seriousness of their offence before God, give them a concern for righteousness and ultimately restore them to the blessing of the Lord.

(2) *With reference to the local congregation or denomination.* The overall intention must be to "strike in their minds a wholesome dread of sin, in order that the contagion of evil may be arrested and the plague stayed."⁸ Such discipline alerts others in the congregation or Church to be watchful in their own lives about the presence and progress of sin in the life and its potential to bring discouragement or carelessness upon a congregation or Church.

(3) *With reference to the watching world.* The intention of such discipline properly exercised is to ensure that the watching world understands the moral and doctrinal standards which the Church seeks to maintain in the world. It is to obviate the Church or local congregation being evil spoken of in the world on account of evident slackness in the behaviour and life-styles and beliefs of its members. It is, in short, to obviate shame being brought upon the Church.

---

⁶ ibid.
⁷ ibid, 99.
⁸ ibid.

All this is very relevant for the Church in the 21st Century, especially in the West. Social standards pay little regard to the moral teaching of the Scriptures. A fruit of the Church's relaxation of the place and authority of the Bible as the Word of God in its life throughout the 20th Century has been the lowering of standards especially within the professing Christian Church in Scotland, Europe and North America. As the mainline Churches have declined in doctrinal standards and weakened on the normative authority of Scripture, the exercise of discipline has been rendered all the harder. In his contribution on 'Heresy, Heresy Trials' in *The Dictionary of Scottish Church History & Theology*, David Wright commented that:

> The impact of the Declaratory Acts, and the doctrinal confusion and indifference of a post-liberal era have conspired to make prosecutions for heresy almost unthinkable in the contemporary CofS [Church of Scotland]. Theological uncertainty has led, by compensation, to a more rigorous attitude towards pastoral and sacramental irregularities. In grotesque disproportion, a minister or elder is much more likely to be disciplined for re-baptizing than for denying the divinity of Christ.[9]

The multiplicity of churches with varying standards has meant that the subjects of discipline in a strictly conservative church may move to a less conservative church and avoid the application of just discipline. The matter of discipline thus tends to lose its restraining power and stigma, and consequently the standing and standards of the Church in the world become undermined.

5. The Types of Censurable Offences

In society at large infringements of its laws may be of a civil or criminal nature. Either way such acts will conflict with good order in society and in relation to their severity they will be punished. We can fully understand that. It happens that we are passing through a period in which good is being called evil and evil good. It can happen in

---

[9] D F Wright, 'Heresy, Heresy Trials,' in, *The Dictionary of Scottish Church History & Theology*, Edinburgh, 1993, 400.

Churches too, as in recent times, when things are passed into legislation clearly at odds with the teaching of Scripture, or discipline misapplied (as in the Free Church of Scotland in 1999/2000[10]). In relation to the Church the issue of infringements of law has reference to the absolute standards of God as expressed through the Holy Scriptures. In answer to the question, 'What is sin?' the *Shorter Catechism* states that, "Sin is any want of conformity unto, or transgression of, the law of God" (Q/A 14). The discipline of the Church relates to censurable sin as thus understood among its members. However, we need to be clear about when censurable action is appropriate.

(1) *Secret sins*. It is true to say that *not all sins will be subject to a formal disciplinary process*. No-one is free from sin in word, thought or deed. Some sins may be in their nature secret. Such sins ought to be repented before God. Such a spirit of repentance may arise in the individual through the ordinary course of the preaching of the word or pastoral visitation. Such repentance and mortification is needed for sanctification and usefulness.

(2) *Sins affecting others, or between members*. Such sins ought to be resolved between themselves according to the principle laid down in Matthew 18. Such disputes *may* lead to more formal action where there is an escalation of conflict, but that would not, initially at any rate, be necessary.

(3) *Scandalous sins*. There are sins which in their nature are 'aggravated' and scandalous. These normally will *require* formal disciplinary action in the Church. The important thing is sin as 'scandal.' A sin will be scandalous when in the public eye, or the eye of the church, it causes others to stumble, or brings shame or disrepute morally or doctrinally upon the individual and, consequently, the Lord and His Church. The high moral and spiritual standards of the Church are always to be upheld for the sake of the reputation of the Lord Jesus Christ. "Judicial action of the Church," wrote Binnie, "has respect to this view of the

---

[10] See the author's *A Divided Church. An Account of the Division in the Free Church of Scotland in 2000*, Scottish Reformed Heritage Publications, 2018, for a detailed examination of the division in the Free Church of Scotland and what was behind it.

matter, and is designed…to 'remove the scandal' – in other words, to prevent the sin from being any more a stumbling-block in men's path."[11]

Distinctions, therefore need to be made in how offences may be subject to discipline. What, then, are the principles relating to the *application* of judicial disciplinary action in the Church in connection with such sins?

6. The Principles relevant for the *Application* of Church Discipline

(1) Not every kind of sin requires to go before the Church
There are secret sins of the individual, that is to say, sins not directly involving or affecting others. These are known only to the sinner and to God. Sins like covetousness and lust, for example, will generally come into this category of 'secret' sins. In such a case confession should be made to Him and such sin repented and mortified, as exhorted in 1 John 1:9: "If we confess our sins, he is faithful and just to forgive us our sins, and to cleanse us from all unrighteousness." Were the individual to *report* the sin before the Church, however, it would cause a scandal. Such sins in themselves are not (so far) *publicly* scandalous. It is sins by their public impact as offence to others and their tendency to tempt others to such sins, which bring reproach upon the cause and are an offence to Christ. This will be true of members and office-bearers, though the discipline will not be carried out in quite the same way. If a sin is private to the extent that only one or two others know of it, such a sin should be dealt with privately and not published abroad. No doubt this is the meaning of the statement quoted in Peter's first letter: "love will cover a multitude of sins" (1 Peter 4:8; Proverbs 10:12, NKJV). There must be care in other words not to bring *unnecessary reproach* on the cause of Christ by imprudently broadcasting the sins and faults of others. This is not to detract from the necessity of self-discipline, repentance and confession before the Lord of *all* secret sins and faults.

---

[11] Binnie, op. cit., 100.

This is necessary for all Christian believers because they daily sin in word, thought and deed. If there is a failure in such personal confession and repentance and forsaking of sin this will diminish the effectiveness and power of a man or woman's spiritual life and consequently the Church's witness in the world. If the 'secret sins' do come out and are scandalous in nature they will then become a subject for more formal censure.

(2) *Church discipline must take account of false unsound doctrine as well as unrighteous immoral behaviour*

The Christian is bound to maintain the sound and wholesome doctrine of God's holy word. This is basic in the Christian Church in its position and the beliefs of its members (1 Timothy 1:10; 2 Timothy 1:13, 4:3; Titus 1:9, 2:1, 8). Especially is this significant in relation to the teaching ministry. Any teaching at odds with the stated and committed position of the Church, expressed for example as the "whole doctrine" contained in the *Westminster Confession of Faith*, would require to be dealt with decisively, every bit as much as a moral lapse on the part of a minister or elder or deacon, or member. In the case of ministers, disciplinary process can only be undertaken by a Presbytery or higher court. The Lord Jesus severely condemned the Churches in Pergamum and Thyatira for suffering false teachers to remain within their fellowships (Revelation 2). Evident deviations from Biblical doctrine and life must in one way or another be the subjects of censure in the Church and may lead to the highest censure where they are not repented or repudiated.

(3) *The infliction of a Church censure does not necessarily pronounce upon the state of the offender's soul before God.*

As Binnie put it: "The Church judges not the man, but his deeds."[12] As Paul wrote to the Thessalonians: "if man obey not our word by this epistle, note that man, and have no company with him, that he may be ashamed. Yet count him not as an enemy, but admonish him as a brother" (2 Thessalonians 3:14-15). At the same time, however, if a

---

[12] ibid., 101.

man or women who professes to be a Christian and is in membership or office in the Church commits a scandalous sin duly established by witnesses and are defiant about it, then they will be duly disciplined and treated as "a heathen and a tax collector" (Matthew 18:17). As Paul taught the troubled Corinthians: "I wrote to you in my epistle not to keep company with sexually immoral people. Yet I certainly did not mean with the sexually immoral people of this world, or with the covetous, or extortioners, or idolaters, since then you would need to go out of the world. But now I have written to you not to keep company with anyone *named a brother*, who is sexually immoral, or covetous, or an idolater, or a reviler, or a drunkard, or an extortioner – not even to eat with such a person. For what have I to do with judging those also who are outside? Do you not judge those who are inside? But those who are outside God judges. Therefore 'put away from yourselves the evil person'" (1 Corinthians 5:9-13, NKJV). Open sin in the world can be denounced by the Church, but it is those within the Church who can – and must – be censured for flagrant and open sin. In such cases the right attitude will involve compassion and desire for recovery. Until there is any such recovery, however, the offender will be outside the fellowship of the Church and not treated as a genuine Christian believer. There will be tares among the wheat and the Church is to be discerning, albeit with love for those who show themselves to be false converts (Matthew 13:24-30; 36-43). The Church in other words, in its discipline will be faithful and just, but not without desire or hope for the *recovery* of the offending soul.

7. The Types of Disciplinary censure

It is clear that censures applied will be as varied as the guilt and aggravation of offences and will ideally be proportional to the offences committed. As already stated, the purpose is the recovery of the offender as well as the purity and harmony of the Church. There are several types of censure consistent with offences committed:

(1) In some cases, *simple admonition* will suffice (Titus 3:10). If someone

has been ignorant or careless, or if they have spoken, say, ill-advisedly or intemperately to others within the Church, or been lax in Church attendance, they may be dealt with pastorally, either by the minister in the course of his pastoral work, or the Session if it is a case that has come before it. Admonition may be sufficient. If the evident fault is not corrected then there may require to be a stronger censure administered. As with all discipline, it is to be given in love, which does not mean that it will not be given in a direct and earnest manner.

(2) A greater degree of guilt will call for *a rebuke*, solemnly administered in the name of Jesus Christ (Titus 1:13; 1 Timothy 5:20). This will be necessary where there is continued behaviour considered to be at odds with Biblical standards or doctrine. The failure to mortify intemperate behaviour or speech, or laxity in attendances at the means of grace or prayer meetings, can itself cause no little discouragement among the other members – and adherents – in the congregation, or beyond. The purpose of rebuke is to correct such faults persisting. Such censures should be effective when there is appropriate positive response on the part of the offender.

(3) More serious scandals will require *suspension* of the offender from the sacraments, or office in the Church, for a period (2 Thessalonians 3:14). This is called the *lesser excommunication*. In this case the offence is such as to cause for a specified time suspension from privileges, *where there has been what appears to be real contrition for the offence*. Common in this area are instances of sins of drunkenness, immorality and revellings. It will also apply to false accusations made against others in the congregation, or such one-off civil 'offences' as proven defalcations, or drink-driving offences.

(4) For more serious offences, doctrinal (heresy) or moral (adultery, fornication, homosexual acts, murder, manslaughter, theft and fraud etc), where there is persistence in maintaining a sinful life-style or indulging in gross sin at variance with the standards of the Church there may be a censure *sine die* (without any fixed time) from office and/or membership. This is called the *greater excommunication*. This latter, however, should never be done other than under the authority of a

Presbytery or a higher Court.[13] This is usually most often applied in connection with office-bearers, who have a more direct responsibility in maintaining the teaching of God's Word, and the Church's standards. Where they are in violation of these standards the discipline will be correspondingly rigorous, albeit always in love and with a desire for restoration. At the same time, it may be applied to any member in a local congregation. And, therefore, its application must be undertaken with extreme care and seriousness.

8. A Mark of a Reformed Church

Discipline is a mark of a healthy Christian Church. The *Scots Confession* got that right, as did other Reformed Confessions, such as the *Belgic Confession (1561)*. Among other things this area raises questions of the Church's Authorised Standards and conformity to them. It raises issues of ordination vows and the doctrine and practice to which office-bearers are formally committed. However, it also involves the application of clear Biblical standards on doctrine and morality, so that, for example unorthodox views on the person of Christ, denial of salvation by grace or justification by faith, denials of the bodily resurrection of Christ and His coming again, unless recanted will receive the highest censure. But so will all scandalous sin when un-repented. It is an irony that where there has been a weakening in ordination vows, and an undermining of the supreme authority of the Bible, the result is that heresy or immorality can pass un-censured. In recent times openly homosexual and lesbian ministers have been tolerated in the mainline Churches. Because of the modification of the standards and loose views of Scripture and its normative authority the Church has come to replace the Scripture as the final arbiter for what is tolerable in the Church. This has led inevitably to man-centred standards and an inability to discipline unbiblical doctrine or practice. In the process the meaning of sin, in a real sense, has been lost, and

---

[13] See, Robert Forbes, *Digest of Rules and Procedure in the Inferior Courts of the Free Church of Scotland*, Edinburgh, 4th 1886, 46-47.

therefore the effective exercise of discipline. In other words, in general there has been a radical breach with the Reformed Church of the past.

Whilst we may bemoan the *want* of sound discipline in the Church, in general, we will also have to recognise disproportion in the exercise of Church discipline. There ought to be care that an 'eye for an eye' and a 'tooth for a tooth' principle is applied. In other words, the censure should be related to the seriousness of the offence. With this there ought to be a spirit of forgiveness, though not without regard for repentance, but with a willingness to forgive sins confessed. This is a Biblical requirement.

Finally, it is wisdom to approach the whole matter of discipline with a pastoral spirit. This is not to say it should be half-hearted or nominal. It is no kindness to be light on discipline for censurable sins. However, there can be too ready a recourse to the 'Practice' or 'Blue Book' without first making all necessary enquiries, pleas, or private admonitions in order to pacify disputes and avoid unnecessary divisiveness in the body. Discipline can often be premature and always ought to be approached with care. At the same time a clear concern for righteousness in word and deed ought to be clearly established in any Christian congregation and denomination.

Further Reading:

For details of the Procedures in connection with the exercise of discipline practically speaking see the relevant portions of The Practice of the Free Church of Scotland in Her Several Courts *(Edinburgh, ⁸1995).*

Though long out of print and hard to acquire, reference might be made to Ivo MacNaughton Clark's A History of Church Discipline in Scotland *(Aberdeen: W. & W. Lindsay, 28 Market Street, 1929). This volume seems to stand alone in addressing the subject historically.*

APPENDIX 1

The First Book of Discipline (1560) on Ecclesiastical Discipline

As that no commonwealth can flourish or long endure without good laws, and sharp execution of the same, so neither can the church of God be brought to purity, neither yet be retained in the same, without the order of ecclesiastical discipline, which stands in reproving and correcting of those faults which the civil sword does either neglect, either may not punish. Blasphemy, adultery, murder, perjury, and other crimes capital, worthy of death, ought not properly to fall under censure of the church; because all such open transgressors of God's laws ought to be taken away by the civil sword. But drunkenness, excess (be it in apparel, or be it in eating and drinking), fornication, oppression of the poor by exactions, deceiving of them in buying or selling by wrong mete or measure, wanton words and licentious living tending to slander, do properly appertain to the church of God, to punish the same as God's word commands.

But because this accursed Papistry has brought in such confusion in the world, that neither was virtue rightly praised, neither vice severely punished; the church of God is compelled to draw the sword, which of God she has received, against such open and manifest offenders, cursing and excommunicating all such, as well those whom the civil sword ought to punish as the others, from all participation with her in prayers and sacraments, till open repentance manifestly appears in them. As the order of excommunication and proceeding to the same ought to be grave and slow, so, being once pronounced against any person, of what estate and condition that ever they be, it must be kept with all severity. For laws made and not kept engenders contempt of virtue and brings in confusion and liberty to sin. And, therefore, this order we think expedient to be observed before and after excommunication.

First, if the offence is secret and known to few, and rather stands in suspicion than in manifest probation, the offender ought to be privately admonished to abstain from all appearance of evil; which, if he promises to do, and to declare himself sober, honest, and one that fears God, and fears to offend his brethren, then may the secret admonition suffice for his correction. But if he either contemns the admonition, or, after promise made, does show himself no more circumspect than he was before, then must the minister admonish him; to whom if he is found disobedient, they must proceed according to the rule of Christ, as after shall be declared.

If the crime is public, and such as is heinous, as fornication, drunkenness, fighting, common swearing, or execration, then ought the offender to be called into the presence of the minister, elders, and deacons, where his sin and offence ought to be declared and aggredged [*stressed*], so that his conscience may feel how far he has offended God, and what slander he has raised in the church. If signs of unfeigned repentance appear in him, and if he requires to be admitted to public repentance, the ministry may appoint unto him a day when the whole church convenes together, that in presence of all he may testify the repentance which before them he professed: which, if he accepts, and with reverence does, confessing his sin, and damning the same, and earnestly desiring the congregation to pray to God with him for mercy, and to accept him in their society, notwithstanding his former offence, then the church may, and ought [to] receive him as a penitent. For the church ought to be no more severe than God declares himself to be, who witnesses that, *In whatsoever hour a sinner unfeignedly repents, and turns from his wicked way, that he will not remember one of his iniquities* [cf. Ezek. 18:21-22; 33:14-16]. And, therefore, the church ought diligently to advert that it excommunicate not those whom God absolves.

If the offender called before the ministry is found stubborn, hard-hearted, or one in whom no sign of repentance appears, then must he be dismissed with an exhortation to consider the dangerous estate in which he stands; assuring him, if they find in him no other token of amendment of life, that they will be compelled to seek a further remedy. If he within a certain space shows his repentance to the ministry, they must present him to the church as before is said.

But if he continues in his impenitence, then the church must be admonished that such crimes are committed amongst them, which by the ministry has been reprehended, and the person provoked to repent; whereof, because no signs appear unto them, they could not but signify unto the church the crimes, but not the person, requiring them earnestly to call to God to move and touch the heart of the offender, so that suddenly and earnestly he may repent.

The Church – Its Discipline

If the person maligns, then the next day of public assembly, the crime and the person must be both notified unto the church, and their judgment must be required, if that such crimes ought to be suffered unpunished amongst them. Request also would be made to the most discreet and to the nearest friends of the offender to travail with him to bring him to knowledge of himself, and of his dangerous estate; with a commandment given to all men to call to God for the conversion of the impenitent. If a solemn and a special prayer were made and drawn for that purpose, the thing should be the more gravely done.

The third Sunday, the minister ought to require if the impenitent has declared any signs of repentance to any of the ministry; and if he has, then may the minister appoint him to be examined by the whole ministry, either then instantly, or at another day affixed to the consistory: and if repentance appears, as well of the crime, as of his long contempt, then may he be presented to the church, and make his confession, and to be accepted, as before is said. But if no man signifies his repentance, then he ought to be excommunicated; and by the mouth of the minister, consent of the ministry, and commandment of the church, such a contemner must be pronounced excommunicated from God, and from the society of his church.

After which sentence may no person (his wife and family only excepted) have any kind of conversation with him, be it in eating and drinking, buying or selling, yea, in saluting or talking with him, except that it be at the commandment or licence of the ministry for his conversion; that he, by such means confounded, seeing himself abhorred of the faithful and godly, may have occasion to repent and be so saved. The sentence of his excommunication must be published universally throughout the realm, lest that any man should pretend ignorance.

His children begotten or born after that sentence and before his repentance, may not be admitted to baptism, till either they are of age to require the same, or else that the mother, or some of his especial friends, members of the church, offer and present the child, abhorring and damning the iniquity and obstinate contempt of the impenitent. If any think it severe that the child should be punished for the iniquity of the father, let them understand that the sacraments appertain only to the faithful and to their seed; but such as stubbornly contemn all godly admonition, and obstinately remain in their iniquity, cannot be accounted amongst the faithful.

The Order for Public Offenders

We have spoken nothing of those that commit horrible crimes, as murderers, man-slayers, and adulterers; for such (as we have said) the civil sword ought to punish to death. But in case they are permitted to live, then must the church, as before is said, draw the sword which of God she has received, holding them as accursed even in their [very] fact; the offender being first called, and order of the church used against him, in the same manner as the persons that for obstinate impenitence are publicly excommunicated; so that the obstinate impenitent, after the sentence of excommunication, and the murderer or adulterer, stand in one case as concerning the judgment of [the church]: that is, neither of both may be received in the fellowship of the church to prayers or sacraments (but to hearing of the word they may), till first they offer themselves to the ministry, humbly requiring the ministers and elders to pray to God for them, and also to be intercessors to the church, that they may be admitted to public repentance, and so to the fruition of the benefits of Christ Jesus, distributed to the members of his body.

If this request is humbly made, then may not the ministers refuse to signify the same unto the church, the next day of public preaching, the minister giving exhortation to the church to pray to God to perform the work which he appears to have begun, working in the heart of the offender unfeigned repentance of his grievous crime, and the sense and feeling of his great mercy, by the operation of his Holy Spirit. Thereafter a day ought publicly to be assigned unto him to give open confession of his offence and contempt, and so to make a public satisfaction to the church of God. Which day, the offender must appear in presence of the whole church, and with his own mouth damn his own impiety, publicly confessing the same; desiring God of his grace and mercy, and his congregation, that it will please them to accept him in their society, as before is said. The minister must examine him diligently whether he finds a hatred and displeasure of his sin, as well of his crime as of his contempt: which, if he confesses, he must travail with him, to see what hope he has of God's mercy.

And if he finds him reasonably instructed in the knowledge of Christ Jesus [and] in the virtue of his death, then may the minister comfort him by God's infallible promises, and demand of the church if they are content to receive that creature of God (whom Satan before had drawn in his nets), in the society of their body, seeing that he declares himself penitent. Which, if the church grants, as they may not justly deny the same, then ought the minister in public prayer to commend him to God, confess the sin of that offender, and of the whole church desire mercy and grace for Christ Jesus' sake. Which prayer being ended, the minister ought to exhort the church to receive that penitent brother in their favour, as they require God to receive themselves when they have offended; and in sign of their consent, the elders and chief men of the church shall take the penitent by the hand, and one or two in name of the whole shall kiss and embrace him with all reverence and gravity, as a member of Christ Jesus.

Which being done, the minister shall exhort the reconciled to take diligent heed in times coming that Satan trap him not in such crimes, admonishing him that he will not cease to tempt and try all means possible to bring him from that obedience which he has given to God, and to the ordinance of his Son Christ Jesus. The exhortation being ended, the minister ought to give public thanks unto God for the conversion of that their brother, and for the benefits which we receive by Jesus Christ, praying for the increase and continuance of the same.

If the penitent, after that he has offered himself to the ministry, or to the church, is found ignorant in the principal points of our religion, and chiefly in the article of justification, and of the office of Christ Jesus, then he ought to be exactly instructed before he is received. For a mockery of God, it is to receive them in repentance who knows not wherein stands their remedy, when they repent their sin.

Persons Subject to Discipline

To discipline must all estates within this realm be subject if they offend, as well the rulers as they that are ruled; yea, and the preachers themselves, as well as the poorest within the church. And because the eye and mouth of the church ought to be most single and irreprehensible, the life and conversation of the ministers ought most diligently to be tried. Whereof we shall speak, after that we have spoken of the election of elders and deacons, who must assist the ministers in all public affairs of the church, etc.

APPENDIX 2

The Westminster Confession of Faith (1647) on Church Censures (Chapter 30)

1. The Lord Jesus, as king and head of his church, hath therein appointed a government in the hand of church officers, distinct from the civil magistrate.

2. To these officers the keys of the kingdom of heaven are committed, by virtue whereof they have power respectively to retain and remit sins, to shut that kingdom against the impenitent, both by the word and censures; and to open it unto penitent sinners, by the ministry of the gospel, and by absolution from censures, as occasion shall require.

3. Church censures are necessary for the reclaiming and gaining of offending brethren; for deterring of others from the like offences; for purging out of that leaven which might infect the whole lump; for vindicating the honour of Christ, and the holy profession of the gospel; and for preventing the wrath of God, which might justly fall upon the church, if they should suffer his covenant, and the seals thereof, to be profaned by notorious and obstinate offenders.

4. For the better attaining of these ends, the officers of the church are to proceed by admonition, suspension from the sacrament of the Lord's Supper for a season, and by excommunication from the church, according to the nature of the crime, and demerit of the person.

THE CHURCH

7. The Forms of Church Government

A. Introduction

1. Organised or not organised?

There have been wide differences on the matter of the organisation of the Church. It goes without saying that a Church must be organised in one way or another. Some of the forms of Church government have been more self-consciously related to Scripture and others more thirled to human traditions. Some denominations, if they can be termed such, appear to reject specific Church government altogether. That is probably true of the Quakers and the various Brethren assemblies. However, as 'Rabbi' Duncan put it concerning 'Plymouthism': "The Plymouth Brethren assert that there should be no sects, because there is no visible church; nevertheless they add one."[1] In another place he says: "It is strange that all Christendom becomes Presbyterian on an ordination day."[2] By this he means that such occasions gather people together and tacitly acknowledge the 'oneness' of the Church in relation to setting apart a man for the ministry. However, as Binnie puts it rightly: "A Church must be either organised or not organised. It cannot be both at once"[3] The question then is: How should it be organised?

The fact of organisation is written large over the Church in both Old and New Testaments. In the New Testament this is very clearly seen, for example, in Acts 15 in which there is an account of an early Assembly at Jerusalem. It is also clear in the various instructions given by the Apostle Paul in relation, for example, to the appointment of

---

[1] William Knight, *Colloquia Peripatetica*, Edinburgh and London, ⁶1907, 75.
[2] ibid., 75.
[3] Binnie, op.cit., 111.

elders in Churches (1 Timothy 5:17-28; Titus 1:5-9). Indeed, this is implicit in the very nature of the case in the New Testament letters, including those we have from the Lord Jesus to the Churches in Asia (Revelation 2 and 3).

2. Types of Church Government

Historically speaking the main forms of Church Government are:
1. Presbyterian – representative
2. Episcopalian – hierarchical
3. Congregationalist – independent

The question of the form of Church government is not a matter of indifference. It is incumbent for any Church to reflect in its organisation what it is persuaded is agreeable to the Word of God. At the same time, in all charity this does not require that bodies adhering to another form of church government or organisation will not be recognised as true Churches (for all their supposed inconsistencies). They will recognise that good Christian work has been done in Churches falling into all the differing forms of church government. Having said that, this does not mean that bodies (of whatever form of government) may not become apostate, or may not have slender claims to being considered a true Christian Church at all (such as, for example, the Roman Catholic Church). These things would be assessed on their merits, not specifically according to the forms of church government. A more important concern would be whether there is faithfulness or otherwise to Biblical doctrine within them, especially in relation to the Trinity, the Person of Christ and the Way of Salvation. Flaws in such theological or doctrinal matters may be fatal for a Church. (Some insight is given into this in Christ's letters to the Churches in Asia in Revelation 2 and 3).

The question of a Church's *polity* is not the chief end of the Church. The chief end of the Church must broadly be glorifying of the Lord in carrying out the Great Commission (Matthew 28:19-20). The truth is that that may be carried out more or less effectively under any form of Church government, as the Brethren have shown. It may be argued that

that will be *despite* inadequacies in their form of Church government. The form of Church government in itself will not *ensure* the preservation of orthodoxy in any body. However, because it may not be of *primary* importance does not mean that a Church's polity is of *no* importance. It is, to the contrary, important for a Church self-consciously to derive its polity from the Word of God and to be convinced it is "agreeable thereto."

B. The Main Forms of Church Government

1. Episcopalianism

This form of Church government, called in the older books *prelatical*, is basically a *hierarchical* form. In this form there is a visible gradation of Church offices with authority centralised in those who occupy the highest ranks. The rule of the Church is basically vested in Bishops who have authority over all the various church officers and congregations in a particular area (diocese). This is the authority exercised downwards through various strata of clergy. Diocesan Bishops are themselves subject to Archbishops whose sphere of hierarchical authority will cover several diocesan areas. This is the basic hierarchical structure of the Episcopalian system of Church government. In this category is found the Church of Rome and also Episcopal, Methodist, and Orthodox (Eastern). The exercise of the Episcopal form varies in degree between and even within Churches or denominations:

(1) *High Church*. There are those in the basic Episcopal system who maintain that Christian ordinances and ordinations are only valid if conducted by Christ and the Apostles or *those commissioned by them through Apostolic succession*. Particularly this is carried out through Bishops who are considered a higher order than presbyters (elders) or deacons. On this view, strictly speaking, no man can preach or administer sacraments unless he is ordained by a Bishop. In other words, as Binnie put it: "Where there is no bishop, there is and can be no church; and no man is a lawful bishop unless he can show that his 'orders' are derived from

the apostles in unbroken succession."[4] This is precisely the Episcopal form maintained by the ritualistic, sacerdotal and high church element in the Anglican Churches – and even 'higher' in the so-called Anglo-Catholics – as well as the Orthodox and Roman Churches. This effectively unchurches those who have not fallen in with such 'apostolic succession,' including Lutheran, Reformed and Independent Churches the world over. That factor is a significant argument against this theory of Church government.

(2) *Low Church.* There are those of a Prelatical or Episcopalian persuasion whose attachment to that form rests largely on traditional and practical grounds. It is maintained that the system lends itself to proper order and has been largely prevalent in the history of the Church from the 2nd century. That is what is maintained at any rate. The Low Church advocates do not hold to the strict 'apostolic succession' dogma. They would not hold the Episcopal form to be the only legitimate polity. They admit there may be a true Church without a Bishop. This view was reflected in prominent Anglicans at the Reformation. There have been outstanding low-church Episcopalians with whom the staunchest Presbyterians and Independents will have love and sympathy, such as Bishop J. C. Ryle (Liverpool) and more recently Archbishop Marcus Loane (Sydney).

The breakdown in the Episcopal system from a Biblical standpoint lies in the want of any such hierarchical structure evident in the New Testament and the fact that the terms 'elder' and 'bishop' or 'overseer' are used inter-changeably for the same office, as discussed below in the chapters on office in the church.[5]

2. Congregationalism

This form of Church government is otherwise known as *independency*, or congregational independency. Several prominent denominational groupings fall into this category, such as Baptists and

---

[4] ibid., 118.
[5] See the chapters on the Offices in the Church in Section E below.

Congregationalists, as also, effectively, other groups such as Christian Brethren. This form of government holds that each particular congregation has autonomy or independence from others. It is therefore maintained that no-one from outside any congregation has any authority to determine what that congregation does. In the churches of this form the congregations will be overseen pastorally by the pastor or minister set apart for that purpose. They may have deacons for administrative purposes. But the affairs of the congregations will rest on the members' meetings. The members in general meeting will exercise the discipline in a congregation and determine the forms adopted for practice and worship. This basic view of the Church is stated by John Owen thus:

> The visible church-state which Christ hath instituted under the New Testament consists in *an especial society or congregation of professed believers, joined together according unto his mind, with their officers, guides, or rulers, whom he hath appointed, which do or may meet together for the celebration of all the ordinances of divine worship, the professing and authoritatively proposing the doctrine of the gospel, with the exercise of the discipline prescribed by himself, unto their own mutual edification, with the glory of Christ, in the preservation and propagation of his kingdom in the world.*[6]

In practice much congregationalism comes quite close to a Presbyterian order in that to express the catholicity and unity of the Church associations are inevitably made and federations or fellowships of congregations holding the same faith and order are formed. They may even have Assemblies or Conferences in which the testimony or witness of the whole number of the affiliating Churches are discussed and implemented. By the same token such Independent Churches, whether paedobaptist or anti-paedobaptist, often relate to a 'denominational' magazine or hymn book representing their own 'faith and order.' Sometimes they have even taken their names from such magazines (such as 'Gospel Standard' or 'Grace' Baptists). This has a unifying influence beyond the strict application of independency in congregations.

---

[6] John Owen, *Works*, Volume 15, London 1966 (1689), 262. Italics in the original.

3. Presbyterianism

This is a *representative* form of Church government, which Presbyterians have claimed as having a 'divine right' or *Jus Divinum*. William Binnie helpfully and succinctly outlined the characteristic features of the Presbyterian Church polity:

(1) "In every congregation the stated oversight of affairs is entrusted to officers chosen by the people from among themselves."[7] Generally speaking there are three offices in the Presbyterian Church: minister or pastor, ruling elder and deacon. Some Presbyterians hold a 'two-office' view, holding that there are only elders and deacons, distinguishing in the case of the elders a *teaching* from a strictly *ruling* function. The responsibility of elders is to exercise spiritual oversight in a congregation, taking care over the life and conduct of the flock and ensuring that the ordinances are duly maintained as purely as possible. The office of deacon, however, is spiritual but administrative, attending to the 'outward business of the house of God.' These officers are elected from within the congregations by the members of these congregations. "Thus," wrote Binnie, "according to the Presbyterian system, *every congregation or local Church is a corporation capable of managing its affairs by means of representatives chosen for the purpose out of its own membership.*"[8]

(2) "There is *in every congregation a pastor*, – one at least, – who is also an elder, but whose special duty is to minister the word and sacraments."[9] The pastor or preaching elder is the officer of highest rank in the Presbyterian Church. In the Free Church of Scotland, the distinction has been made between the pastor and the elder, and the relationship of pastor to ruling elder is well stated in the *Catechism of the Principles and Constitution of the Free Church of Scotland* issued in 1882. The question is asked: '*How many kinds of presbyter are there?*' The answer is given: "Two – pastors, and ruling elders, who assist the pastor in the government of

---

[7] Binnie, op. cit., 112.
[8] ibid., 112-113. Italics in the original.
[9] ibid., 113. See Section E below on the question of office in the Church.

the Church."[10] The biblical texts provided in support of this are: 1 Timothy 5:17, 1 Corinthians 12:28, and Romans 12:8.

(3) "In all cases in which the arrangement is possible, *neighbouring congregations are associated under a common government.*"[11] Practically speaking this is arranged geographically, ministers and ruling elders being commissioned by congregations to represent these congregations and constitute a Presbytery in a given geographical location. In turn Presbyteries are grouped together in wider geographical areas to form 'Provincial Synods,' generally bodies of review. Representatives from all the Presbyteries in the whole area covered by the Church geographically will annually comprise the General Assembly, charged with the oversight of the whole work of the Church in all the affairs common to all the congregations that comprise the Church, after the pattern of the Assembly described in Acts 15. Binnie commented: "Next to its conformity to Scripture, the boast of this system is that it combines, more perfectly than any other, a jealous solicitude for the liberty of the Christian people, with due regard to the interests of effective and orderly government." He further added that "it is a fine example of popular government, tempered and guided by the official teachings of an educated ministry, and so organised, with gradations of representative assembles, as to provide for the union of many particular Churches in one ecclesiastical fellowship."[12] In other words, practically speaking it combines an element of the structures of both Episcopalian and Independent models in a happy harmony which at its best will reflect the catholicity of the Church. This, it may be said, is what might be expected of a form of church government agreeable to the Word of God

To summarise: Of the various forms of church government it is our conviction that the Presbyterian agrees most closely to the forms found in the New Testament. The essential features are:

---

[10] Question and Answer 434.
[11] Binnie, op. cit., 113. Italics in the original.
[12] Binnie, op. cit., 113.

1. The holy ministry.
2. The ruling eldership.
3. The association of neighbouring congregations under a common representative government.
4. The concurrence of popular election and official ordination in the outward appointment of office-bearers.[13]

C. Is *Presbyterianism* agreeable to the Word of God?

One of the questions put to Probationers at their Ordination in the Free Church of Scotland (and in other conservative Presbyterian churches too) states:

> Are you persuaded that the Presbyterian government and discipline of this Church are founded upon the Word of God, and agreeable thereto;...?[14]

In his *The Westminster Confession of Faith for Study Classes*, Gerald Williamson helpfully summarises the essential principles of church government, as revealed in the Scripture, by way of a table. Williamson justly concludes:

> Inasmuch as the presbyterian form of church government is the *only* form of church government which is agreeable with these biblical principles, truth requires that we testify that it alone is sanctioned by Christ, and that the other forms are without warrant from the Word of God. This does not mean that churches without presbyterian government are necessarily to be declared false churches (nor that all churches that preserve presbyterian government are true churches). But as far as government is concerned no church is pure unless it is presbyterian.[15]

Essentially this is the *jus divinum* principle, namely, the divine right of Presbytery.

In relation to that principle, John Macpherson well stated:

---

[13] ibid.
[14] *The Subordinate Standards and other Authoritative Documents of the Free Church of Scotland*, Edinburgh, 1851, 374.
[15] G I Williamson, *The Westminster Confession of Faith for Study Classes*, Philadelphia, Pa., 1964, 233. The chart in Williamson's book is reproduced in the Appendix on page 90 below.

> We hold that the characteristic principles of Presbyterianism are found in Scripture, and that other forms of church polity are, as compared with Presbyterianism, defective, inasmuch as they ignore certain of those principles to which they give exclusive attention. This claim for a full and satisfactory ground in Scripture for the characteristic principles of our church system is all that we mean to assert when we maintain, as against Prelacy and Congregationalism, the divine right of Presbytery.[16]

G. D. Henderson in his 1952 Chalmers' Lectures on *Presbyterianism* struck a necessary note of caution when he wrote:

> Dr Thomas Chalmers, in whose memory the Chalmers Lectureship was founded, said in one of his sermons that "the way to subordinate the human history is to obtain possession of the human heart." His words...serve...to remind us that it is the Gospel, and not this or that method or means of proclaiming it, that will save. Neither an old and tried and venerated constitution nor the latest Utopianism will of itself establish the Kingdom. History shows how far the effectiveness of a particular form of government has depended upon those who have operated it. Without fire, it has been said, no acceptable sacrifice. In discussing Presbyterianism as a form of Church Government we must, then, realise that apart from a truly Christian purpose, a consecrated spirit, a surrendered will, no means or methods can succeed.[17]

Further Reading:

For further study refer to the works of William Binnie and John Macpherson cited. Readers should also consult the Catechism of the Principles and Constitution of the Free Church of Scotland *produced by the Free Church of Scotland in 1847 and reproduced with a Prefatory Note by the Rev James Begg in 1882. See also J R DeWitt's* Jus Divinum: The Westminster Assembly and the Divine Right of Church Government *(Kampen, 1969).*

---

[16] John Macpherson, *Presbyterianism*, Edinburgh, 1879(?), 10.
[17] G D Henderson, *Presbyterianism*, Edinburgh, 1954, 1.

APPENDIX

The Principles of Scripture	_Hier._	_Cong._	_Presb._
1. Christ alone is head of the Church (Eph. 5:23, Col. 1:18, etc.)	No	Yes	Yes
2. Elders are chosen by the people over whom they are to rule (Acts 1:15-26; 6:1-7)	No	Yes	Yes
3. All ruling officers (ministers/elders) are equal in authority (Acts 20:17, 28; Titus 1:5, 7)	No	Yes	Yes
4. Each particular Church must have a plurality of elders (Acts 14:23)	No	No	Yes
5. Church ministering elders/pastors are ordained by the Presbytery (i.e., a large body of ministers/elders drawn from churches in Communion with one another) (1 Timothy 4:14)	No	No?	Yes
6. The right of appeal from the smaller to the wider assembly of ministers/elders (Acts 15:1-31)	No	No	Yes

THE CHURCH

8. Church and State:
(1) The Universal Headship of Christ

1. Introduction
This chapter acts only as a very brief introduction to the principle and outworking of the Headship or Lordship of Jesus Christ over nations as well as the Church. It is an implication of the fact that He has been given "all power…in heaven and in earth" (Matthew 28:18). It is an implication of the truth that he is "Lord of all" (Acts 10:36). It is an implication of His Ascension: "he that descended is the same also that ascended up far above all heavens, that he might fill [or, fulfil] all things" (Ephesians 4:10). It is not just the Church that is to be subject to Him, but all the Nations as well (Psalm 2:8). This chapter comprises just a glance over the principle of the Headship of Christ that ought to be accepted by the governments of this world.

2. Christ's Universal Headship implicit in the Bible
The assertion of the headship of Christ over the Church seems clear enough. In one place Christ says, "I will build my church; and the gates of hell shall not prevail against it" (Matthew 16:18). However, the Headship of Christ is not just seen in Scripture to apply to the Church. His Lordship is universal. Think of Psalm 2. Why do the nations rage? It is folly! Why do they set themselves against the Anointed [the Lord Jesus Christ]? It is folly! Why is such opposition to the Lord's Anointed such folly? Because He is set over the nations; He will have the ends of the earth for His possession. There is no-one, men or nations, beyond His power or sovereignty. The nations will not break Him with a rod of iron, nor dash Him in pieces like a bit of pottery. Their wisdom is to make peace with Him or He will be angry and they will perish. After all,

"we must all appear before the judgment seat of Christ; that every one may receive the things done in his body, according to that he hath done, whether it be good or bad" (2 Corinthians 5:10). That doesn't just refer to the visible Church, it is comprehensive. So, Christ is not just Head of the church, He is also Head of Nations. And therefore Nations are responsible for recognising Him as such. As Paul wrote to Timothy: "[He] … is the blessed and only Potentate, the King of kings, and Lord of lords, who only hath immortality, dwelling in the light which no man can approach unto; whom no man hath seen, nor can see: to whom be honour and power everlasting. Amen" (1 Timothy 6:15-16). He is described in one place in this way: "Jesus Christ: (he is Lord of all)" (Acts 10:36). That is comprehensive, whatever formal acknowledgement or submission may or may not be given to it by any State.

3. Christ's Universal Headship asserted in the Scottish Church

The Scottish Reformed and Covenanting Church rightly, therefore, proclaimed 'The Crown Rights of Jesus Christ.' "The Scottish Reformation under the leadership of John Knox was a thorough Reformation of the Church" (T. M. Lindsay). This was consolidated through the *First Book of Discipline* (1560), the *Scots Confession* (1560) – undertaken and completed in 4 weeks! – and later, under Andrew Melville, the *Second Book of Discipline* (1578), which was effectively the blueprint for a full-blown Presbyterianism. It is clear, however, that there were not a few convulsions after the period of Reformation, involving struggles with the State and with Episcopacy. The Scottish Church asserted the principle, which it held to be Scriptural, of two spheres in which the State was concerned with the temporal interests of its citizens and the Church the spiritual. That was not taken to mean that the State was conceived of as being merely a secular institution with no regard for the spiritual or Christian good of its citizens. But such interest would be one of support for and not power over the Church. Both in their individual spheres were seen to be answerable to Christ as Head. There were struggles at various times between the Reformed Church and a Civil Magistrate which was inclined to exercise authority over the affairs of the Church(es). The Church frequently was called to assert its Spiritual Independence, such as in the run-up to the Disruption in the Church of Scotland in 1843. But that did not mean that they denied in any shape or form the Headship of Christ over the Nation, or the Nation's responsibility to maintain the true Christian faith as answerable to Christ as Head of Nations. The struggles recounted so often had to do with the question of faithfulness to the Lord Jesus Christ and the dogged maintenance of His rights and claims upon both men and nations, Church and State. And Christ's 'crown rights' were asserted for both arenas of social life.

In the face of all denials of this the church will affirm the Headship of Christ in church and state. As we read in Ephesians in a passage which is a crux: "he hath put all *things* under his feet, and gave him *to be* the head over all *things* to the church, which is his body, the fulness of him that filleth all in all" (1:22-23). This teaches that Christ is not just to be thought of as having authority over the Church, but also over the Nations. After all, He is Lord over Creation itself (Colossians 1:15-18). He has claims upon the nations whatever they may think or however they may act. They are answerable to Him and will finally submit to Him, one way or another, for good or woe (Psalm 2; Revelation 2:26; 15:3-4; 19:15; 21:24-26).

The *warrant* for a 'National Christianity' – the civil powers confessing the Christian religion – has usually been considered to be established by the Great Commission.[1] But how a nation will rightly confess the Christian faith without being *sectarian* is an issue. That is a question of balance, and the power of true spiritual biblical religion prevailing in a land and not just nominality. That in a sense is at the heart of the commission to "make disciples of all the *nations*, baptizing them in the name of the Father and of the Son and of the Holy Spirit, teaching *them* to observe all things that I have commanded you" (Matthew 28:19-20, NKJV).

---

[1] For an excellent treatment of this subject see George Smeaton's *National Christianity and Scriptural Union*, Edinburgh, 1871. This is a volume of 116 pages but long out of print.

4. Christ's Universal Headship denied in Enlightenment and Secular thought

In the course of time shadows appeared which undermined the notion of 'Christendom.' The shadows of sceptical and enlightenment thought appeared, even in a Scottish society so strongly influenced by Reformation thought. The momentum for such attitudes and ideas alien to the gospel received a particular fillip towards the end of the 18th Century with the French Revolution (1789). This tended to establish the notion of an autonomous State, independent of Christ or Christian principles. Progressively the West has veered towards merely naturalistic and secular characteristics.

Some of the main figures in enlightenment and revolutionary developments were:

- John Locke in England (1632-1704). He taught that the mind was a 'tabula rasa' (blank state). He therefore denied the basic principle of Christian faith that man is born in a lost and sinful state with a propensity to evil. His philosophy was therefore based on a false premise.
- David Hume in Scotland (1711-1776). He has been described as "the first philosopher of the modern era to produce a thoroughly naturalistic philosophy." His ideas therefore flew in the face of the biblical revelation of creation, providence, predestination, and the supernatural.
- There were also Voltaire (1694-1778) and Jean-Jacques Rousseau (1712-1778), the moving lights of the European 'Enlightenment' leading up to the French Revolution.

Mark Noll makes the telling comment: "…the enormous shift underway among European intellectual elites by the early eighteenth century did not have a widespread general impact until considerably later."[2] Owen Chadwick in his *The Secularisation of the European Mind* (1975) suggests that the years between 1650 and 1750 – the years of

---

[2] Mark A Noll, *Turning Points. Decisive Moments in the History of Christianity*, Grand Rapids, Michigan, ²2000, 253.

Locke, Voltaire, Baruch Spinoza and 'the Scottish skeptic' David Hume – "were seminal years of modern intellectual history."[3] Says Noll: "…for the results of these ideas to affect the broader European society it took another century and a half."[4] "That is why," Chadwick explains, "the problem of secularisation is not the same as the problem of Enlightenment. Enlightenment was of the few. Secularisation is of the many,"[5] This was all a programme of "violent de-Christianisation carried out in the French Revolution…whereby temporal realities began systematically to displace Christian realities as the centre of European loyalty, preoccupation, and civilisation."[6] As a consequence the evangelical churches had to contend with deviations such as Deism and Unitarianism, which were essentially compromises to the enlightenment thought. Besides, this involved a throwing off of an acknowledgement of the sovereign Lordship of Christ over Nations and denial of the responsibility of the State to maintain Christian principles of action within its bounds.

5. Reformed Church/State relations: two jurisdictions, separate but inter-related

There was a struggle against what has been called Erastianism. This scheme was named after *Thomas Erastus* (1524-1583) a Swiss philosopher who argued that the sins of Christians should be punished by the State and not by the Church withholding the sacraments. His idea assumed the supremacy of the State in Christian matters. From the time of the Reformation the Church in Scotland resisted this idea and asserted spiritual independence, albeit alongside the responsibility of the State [Civil Magistrate] to maintain Christianity within its bounds and encourage it among its citizens, in acknowledgement of the universal Headship of Christ.

---

[3] Owen Chadwick, *The Secularisation of the European Mind in the Nineteenth Century*, Cambridge 1975, 5.
[4] Noll, op. cit., 253.
[5] Chadwick, op. cit., 9.
[6] Noll, op. cit., 253.

Though often misinterpreted as teaching that the Church should have priority over the State, the *Second Book of Discipline* (1578) [and later the *Westminster Confession of Faith* (1647)] in fact is perfectly clear on the two jurisdictions, separate but inter-related. "They be both of God and tend to one end if they be rightly used, to wit, to advance the glory and to have godly and good subjects" (1:9). Churchmen were subject to magistrates in civil matters and magistrates were subject to the church in spiritual matters (1:14, 23). The ideal relation would be this: "The civil power should command the spiritual to exercise and do their office according to the word of God; the spiritual rulers should require the Christian magistrate to minister justice and punish vice, and to maintain the liberty and quietness of the kirk within their bounds" (1:17).

This is seen to be a Scriptural principle, whatever acknowledgement may be made of it in the Churches or by the civil powers, and however impractical it may *appear* to be, even though at any given time a state may be dominated by humanistic or Hindi of Islamic influences. The Headship of Christ is inviolable – it is a universal truth.

6. The Testimony of the Free Church of Scotland as to the Headship of Christ

The Free Church, in common with the Reformed National Church affirmed "that nations and their rulers are bound to own the truth of God, and to advance the kingdom of His Son."[7] They affirmed very strongly the Headship of Christ in Church *and* in State in maintaining the *Claim, Declaration, and Protest* of 1842 in which is stated among other things:

> Whereas it is an essential doctrine of this Church, and a fundamental principle in its constitution, as set forth in the Confession of Faith thereof, in accordance with the Word and law of the most holy God, that "there is no other Head of the Church but the Lord Jesus Christ" (ch. xxv. sec. 6); and that while "God, the supreme Lord and King of all the world, hath ordained civil magistrates to be under him over

---

[7] *The Subordinate Standards and Other Authoritative Documents of the Free Church of Scotland*, Edinburgh, 1851, vi.

the people, for his own glory, and the public good, and to this end hath armed them with the power of the sword" (ch. xxxiii. sec. 1); and while "it is the duty of people to pray for magistrates, to honour their persons, to pay them tribute and other dues, to obey their lawful commands, and to be subject to their authority for conscience' sake," "from which ecclesiastical person are not exempted" (ch. xxiii. sec. 4); and while the magistrate hath authority, and it is his duty, in the exercise of that power which alone is committed to him, namely, "the power of the sword," or civil rule, as distinct from the "power of the keys," or spiritual authority, expressly denied to him, to take order for the preservation of purity, peace, and unity in the Church, yet "The Lord Jesus, as King and Head of his Church, hath therein appointed a government in the hand of Church officers distinct from the civil magistrate" (ch. xxx. sec. 1); which government is ministerial, not lordly, and to be exercised in consonance with the laws of Christ, and with the liberties of his people.

The *Formula* signed by ministers and elders in the Free Church of Scotland derives from 1846 and positively disavows Popish, Arian, Socinian, Arminian and *Erastian* tenets and opinions.[8]

It is interesting that William Cunningham in his magisterial *Historical Theology* says that from 1711 the Formula actually had 'Bourignian' instead of Erastian and that it was in view of the Church/State issues and in particular the violation of the spiritual independence of the Church by the Civil authorities leading up to the Disruption of 1843 that led the Free Church to replace Bourignian by Erastian.[9] The origin and nature of 'Erastian' has been explained above. But what about Bourignian? Where did that come from? It came from the views of one *Antionette Bourignon* (1616-1680). An *Encyclopaedia* entry explains how this impacted upon the Church in Scotland:

> The General Assembly of the Church of Scotland in 1701, 1709, and 1710 passed deliverances against Bourignonians in which their views are thus described: I. They denied (1) the divine permission of sin and that divine vengeance and

---

[8] ibid., 374.
[9] William Cunningham, *Historical Theology*, Vol. II, Edinburgh, 1960 [³1870], 584.

eternal damnation were inflicted upon it; (2) the decrees of election and reprobation; and (3) the doctrine of the divine foreknowledge. II. They asserted (1) that Christ had a twofold human nature, one produced of Adam before the woman was formed, and the other born of the Virgin Mary; (2) that in each soul before birth are a good and an evil spirit; (3) that the will is absolutely free, and there is in man some infinite quality which makes it possible for him to unite himself to God; (4) that Christ's nature was sinfully corrupt, so that by nature he was rebellious to the will of God; (5) that perfection may be attained in this life; and (6) that children are born in heaven.

Notwithstanding these deliverances, the views of Antoinette Bourignon continued to exist in Scotland and in 1711 Bourignonianism was put among the heresies which candidates for the ministry were required formally to disown when applying for ordination.[10]

On the question of the civil magistrate, William Cunningham states that "when any civil magistrate assumes such jurisdiction or authoritative control in the regulation of the affairs of Christ's Church, he is guilty of sin; and when the Church submits to the exercise of such jurisdiction, she too becomes a partaker of his sin, and is involved in all the guilt of it."[11]

The issue faced by the contendings for Christ's Headship in Scottish Church history must therefore be an encouragement to Christian communities everywhere to give Christ's claims the place that is their due in Church *and* Nation. It is worth pointing out that there can be no neutrality, not when it comes to the claims of the Lord Jesus Christ. "He that is not with me is against me; and he that gathereth not with me scattereth abroad" (Matthew 12:30). This is true for individuals. It is also true for governments and nations.

This, then, is a prominent note in biblical revelation and church history. It goes without saying that the principle of the Headship of Christ and His sovereign claims applies within the Church and will have

---

[10] This is from the *Christian Classics Ethereal Library* at Calvin College:
http://www.ccel.org/s/schaff/encyc/encyc02/htm/iv.v.ccl.hrm.
[11] Cunningham, op. cit., 586.

its implications for its government and worship. It also applies in its own place to the civil authorities, which are *not* bound to be secular and neutral towards Christ or Christianity. The Christian will pray for the powers that be as 'ordained of God' (1 Timothy 2:1-3) and not least that they come to affirm Christianity just as it might rightly be expected that a family will do when its members come to acknowledge Jesus as Saviour as Lord. This will have far-reaching implications for any area of the State's actions and legislation, including education at every level, to the degree to which the State authorities may be involved in such a sphere in the nation. The Nations, too, must pass before the judgement of the One by whom they will be judged (Revelation 19:11-16).

THE CHURCH

9. Church and State:
(2) The Relationship between Church & State[1]

1. Introduction

This subject has been a matter of controversial discussion since the time of Constantine. When the emperor professed himself a Christian, he expressed the new relationship which was to subsist between the Church and state, by saying to certain bishops, "God has made you the bishops of the internal affairs of the Church, and me the bishop of its external affairs." This saying approximates to what William Cunningham called 'the golden mean' between the extremes of clericalism (church domination) on the one hand and Erastianism (state domination) on the other. The former is to be seen in the medieval (*ultramontane*) papal claims, and the latter in the Byzantine control of the Eastern Church. However, as Constantine understood it, the statement expressed a kind of modified Erastianism rather than true ecclesiastical independence from state control (for which the Covenanters contended). It asserts that to the church belongs the right to choose her officers, regulate all matters relating to doctrine, administer the Word and sacraments, order public worship, and to exercise discipline. And to the state, to provide for the support of the ministry, to determine the sources and amounts of their incomes, to fix the limits of parishes and dioceses, to provide places of worship, to call together the clergy, to preside in their meetings (which Constantine did at Nicea), to give the force of law

---

[1] For this chapter the writer is indebted to the late Rev Ronald Mackenzie (Inverness), sometime lecturer in Church History and Principles at the Free Church of Scotland (Continuing) Seminary in Inverness. This chapter is largely his work in connection with his course at that Seminary which he served from 2002 to 2008.

to their decisions, and to see that external obedience at least was rendered to the decrees and acts of discipline.

2. Church/State relationship according to the *Westminster Confession of Faith*

The teaching of the *Westminster Confession of Faith* (1647) on Church/State relations is as follows:

(1) *Chapter 23:1 – Of the Civil Magistrate*: "God, the supreme Lord and King of all the world, hath ordained civil magistrates to be under him over the people, for his own glory, and the public good; and to this end, hath armed them with the power of the sword, for the defence and encouragement of them that are good, and for the punishment of evil-doers."

(2) *Chapter 23:3 – Of the Civil Magistrate*: "The civil magistrate may not assume to himself the administration of the word and sacraments, or the power of the keys of the kingdom of heaven; yet he hath authority, and it is his duty, to take order, that unity and peace be preserved in the church, that the truth of God be kept pure and entire, that all blasphemies and heresies be suppressed, all corruptions and abuses in worship and discipline prevented or reformed, and all the ordinances of God duly settled, administered, and observed. For the better effecting whereof, he hath power to call synods, to be present at them, and to provide that whatsoever is transacted in them be according to the mind of God."

(3) *Chapter 30:1 – Of Church Censures*: "The Lord Jesus, as king and head of his church, hath therein appointed a government in the hands of church-officers, distinct from the civil magistrate."

(4) *Chapter 31:2 – Of Synods and Councils*: "As magistrates may lawfully call a synod of ministers, and other fit persons, to consult and advise with about matters of religion; so if magistrates be open enemies to the church, the ministers of Christ, of themselves, by virtue of their office, or they, with other fit persons upon delegation from their churches, may meet together in such assemblies."

(5) *Chapter 31:5 – Of Synods and Councils*: "Synods and councils are to

handle or conclude nothing but that which is ecclesiastical; and are not to intermeddle with civil affairs, which concern the commonwealth, unless by way of humble petition, in cases extraordinary; or by way of advice for satisfaction of conscience, if they be thereunto required by the civil magistrate."

(6) *Chapter 20:4 – Of Christian Liberty, and Liberty of Conscience*: "And because the powers which God hath ordained and the liberty which Christ hath purchased, are not intended by God to destroy, but mutually to uphold and preserve one another; they who, upon pretence of Christian liberty, shall oppose any lawful power, or the lawful exercise of it, whether it be civil or ecclesiastical, resist the ordinance of God. And for their publishing of such opinions, or maintaining of such practices, as are contrary to the light of nature, or to the known principles of Christianity, whether concerning faith, worship or conversation; or to the power of godliness; or such erroneous opinions or practices; as either in their own nature, or in the manner of publishing or maintaining them, are destructive to the external peace and order which Christ hath established in the church; they may lawfully be called to account, and proceeded against by the censures of the church, and by the power of the civil magistrate."

(7) *Chapter 23:2 – Of the Civil Magistrate*: "It is lawful for Christians to accept and execute the office of a magistrate, when called thereunto; in the managing whereof, as they ought especially to maintain piety, justice, and peace, according to the wholesome laws of each commonwealth; so, for that end, they may lawfully, now under the New Testament, wage war upon just and necessary occasions."

(8) *Chapter 23:4 – Of the Civil Magistrate*: "It is the duty of people to pray for magistrates, to honour their persons, to pay them tribute and other dues, to obey their lawful commands, and to be subject to their authority for conscience' sake. Infidelity, or indifference to religion, doth not make void the magistrates' just and legal authority, nor free the people from their due obedience to them from which ecclesiastical persons are not exempted, much less has the Pope any power and jurisdiction over them in their dominions, or lives, if he shall

judge them to be heretics, or upon any other pretence whatsoever."

3. Comment

William Cunningham stated the matter of the obligations of the civil magistrate thus: "Under the general head of the civil magistrate, or of the civil magistracy, – that is, in the exposition of what is taught in Scripture concerning the functions and duties of the *supreme* civil authorities of a nation, whatever be its form of government, – the Reformers were unanimous and decided in asserting what has been called in modern times the principle of national establishments of religion, – namely, that it is competent to, and incumbent upon nations, as such, and civil rulers in their official capacity, or in the exercise of their legitimate control over civil matters, to aim at the promotion of the honour of God, the welfare of true religion, and the prosperity of the church of Christ...Men who concur in asserting the general duty or obligation [of civil rulers] as a portion of scriptural truth may differ from each other about the measures which it may be lawful or incumbent to adopt in discharging it."[2]

Cunningham wrote further, that some Erastians "have confounded altogether the members of the Church and the State, and have virtually denied that the church is a distinct independent society; others, admitting that it is in some sense a distinct independent society, have denied that this society has a distinct government, or an independent power of judicial decision in ecclesiastical matters, according to the word of God; while others, without formally denying a distinct government altogether, have set themselves to curtail the sphere or province within which this government is to be exercised...And many more, who might with perfect justice be called Erastians, have abstained wholly from the discussion of general principles, and have confined themselves to an attempt to palliate and gloss over the interferences which the civil authority might happen at the time to be making, and opposition

---

[2] *Historical Theology*, London, 1960 [1870], Vol. II, 559-561.

The Church – Its Relationship to the State (2)

to which might have proved inconvenient or dangerous."[3]

James Bannerman for his part argued that "the state and the church are essentially different in regard to their origin...in regard to their primary objects for which they were instituted...in regard to the power which is committed to them respectively by God...in regard to the administration of their respective authorities..."[4]

Cunningham further wrote that: "...the equality and independence of the civil and ecclesiastical powers, – the independent supremacy of each in its own proper sphere, and within its own peculiar province; is...in entire consistency with the preservation of their proper distinctness and independence...they may enter into a friendly alliance with each other upon terms of equality, retaining all their own proper and inherent rights and prerogatives, the unfettered exercise of their own functions, and yet may afford to each other important assistance...that nations as such, and civil rulers in their official capacity, are entitled and bound to aim at the promotion of the interests of true religion, and the welfare of the Church of Christ; that there are things which they can lawfully do, which are fitted to promote these objects; and that thus a connection may be legitimately formed between Church and State...the one principle on the subject of which the advocates of national establishments of religion feel which it may be lawful or incumbent to adopt in discharging it. And errors in regard to the particular way in which the duty ought to be discharged ought not, in fairness, to prepossess men's minds against the general truth that such a duty is binding'."[5]

Referring to the limitations of that duty, Cunningham remarked: "Though the Scripture imposes upon civil rulers an obligation to promote the interests of true religion and the church of Christ, it does not invest them with any jurisdiction or authoritative control in religious or ecclesiastical matters; though to use a distinction in frequent use among the old Presbyterian writers in opposing

---

[3] *Historical Theology*, London, 1960 [1870], Vol. I, 401.
[4] *The Church of Christ*, London 1960 [1869], Vol. I, 97-100.
[5] *Historical Theology*, Vol. I, 391-5.

Erastianism, it gives them a power *circa sacra*, it gives them none *in sacris*...The scriptural view of the origin and character, constitution and government of the Christian church, are necessarily and obviously exclusive of the idea of its being subordinate to the State, or of civil rulers having any jurisdiction or authoritative control over the regulation of its affairs...the Church is a divine institution established by Christ, placed by Him in a condition of entire independence of any secular or foreign control, and invested by Him with full powers of self-government and complete sufficiency within itself for the execution of all its functions." 6

In his *Discussions on Church Principles* Cunningham provided us with the following definition: "The fundamental principle of the doctrine of the Scottish Presbyterians in regard to the proper relation of the civil and the ecclesiastical authorities, has been correctly described as that *of a co-ordination of powers and a mutual subordination of persons*."7 In dealing with the National Establishment of religion, he noted "in order to uphold the principle of National Establishments of religion, it is not indispensable to establish any particular views of what is implied in civil government being an ordinance of God, or to show that the promotion of religion is one of its proper objects or ends. For, even though the possession of civil authority were regarded merely in the vague and general aspect of a talent or means of influence, the Establishment principle might be shown to derive some countenance from the general obligation attaching to all men, in all circumstances, to employ all their talents for the promotion of God's glory and the advancement of His cause. And if it were conceded that the proper direct end of civil government is only the temporal and not the spiritual welfare of the community, it would still be quite competent to argue, and not difficult to prove...that civil rulers are called upon to aim at the promotion of religion as the best and only certain means of advancing

---

6 *Historical Theology*, Vol. I, 403-4.
7 *Discussions on Church Principles*, Edinburgh, 1863, 153.

the temporal welfare of their subjects."[8]

In discussing the ends or objects of the two societies he went on to say that: "Since the general ends or objects of the two societies, though different, are not only not opposed to each other, but harmonious and accordant – since they are both fitted and intended, in their respective spheres, to promote the glory of God, and the welfare of the community, there is no reason why they may not enter into a friendly union or alliance with each other, provided it is not a union or alliance of such a kind as to destroy or supersede their distinctness. It has never been proved that all union or alliance between them must necessarily possess this character or produce this result; and on the contrary, it has been shown that the very differences between them afford important facilities for their affording each other mutual assistance without encroaching upon one another's province and functions, abandoning their own proper position, or neglecting their appropriate objects."[9]

Again, concerning the civil magistrate he stated that: "the matters with which it appears from this passage that the civil magistrate has something to do, are – the preservation of unity and peace in the Church, – the promotion of the truth of God – the suppression of blasphemies and heresies, – the reformation of corruptions and abuses in worship and discipline, – and the right administration of all the ordinances of God; and there is manifestly, from the very nature of the case, no rule or standard by which these matters can be determined, – by which men can be guided in aiming at the promotion of these objects, – except the sacred Scriptures [i.e. the only rule]. Whatever the civil magistrate may be warranted to do in these matters, he must, – unless he is to be invested with absolute and uncontrolled lordship over the conscience, and to be wholly exempted from any regard to God's authority, – form his opinions and regulate his conduct by the rule which God has prescribed...it is

---

[8] ibid., 198-9.
[9] ibid., 204-5.

manifest that the civil magistrate is not here authorised to do anything about the church of Christ until he has made up his mind as to what is the will of God upon the point; and that whatever he does must be, professedly at least, in accordance with the standard of the sacred Scriptures."[10]

He continued: "If the Church and State come into collision upon any matter which either party considers to be settled in the word of God, they must either, by consultation and discussion, come to an agreement upon Scriptural grounds, or else they must separate from each other...these are objects which he [the civil magistrate] is entitled and bound to aim at...and that to interpret them as going beyond this, and as ascribing to the magistrate jurisdiction in these things...is to make the confession to contradict itself and the known views of its authors and of the Church of Scotland at the time when it was adopted; and that therefore the true, real, and intended import of the passage, is just to declare the great fundamental principle of national establishments of religion, – namely, that the civil magistrate is bound to exercise his lawful authority in civil things, with a view to the promotion of the interests of religion and the welfare of the Church of Christ, and for the purpose of securing these great results...The exercise of any ecclesiastical jurisdiction – the assumption of any right to decide authoritatively ecclesiastical questions – cannot be supposed to be one of the means which he is to employ for promoting these ends, for there is no statement here that sanctions this idea; while it would flatly contradict those parts of the Confession which assert Christ's appointment of a distinct government for His church in the hands of ecclesiastical office-bearers, and forbid the assumption by the civil magistrate of the power of the keys...The civil magistrate is, just like men in general, to use the authority and power competent to him as such – and what that is must be ascertained from other sources – for promoting the interests

---

[10] ibid., 216-7.

of religion, and the purity and prosperity of the church."[11]

James Bannerman argued for the duty of a friendly connection between church and state, at least to the extent of public recognition, and, if possible, to the extent of pecuniary endowment on the basis that both church and state are moral parties accountable to God. He set down five propositions:

(1) "Both the state and the Church are to be accounted moral parties responsible to God."[12]

(2) "Both the Church and state, in consequence of this responsibility to God, are bound to own and recognise His revealed word."[13]

(3) "The state, by a regard to itself, and to the very objects for which it exists as a state, is bound to recognise the true religion, and, so far as it is in its power, to promote its interests."[14]

(4) "The state is bound, by a regard to the Church, as God's ordinance for good, to countenance it, and, as far as it is in its power, to advance its interests."[15]

(5) "The duty of the state thus to recognise, and, in so far as circumstances permit, to endow the Church, is undeniably countenanced by the whole tenor of Scripture."[16]

Bannerman maintained that this was countenanced, (a) by the only form of civil polity framed by God; (b) by approbation given in Scripture to the countenance shown to the Church by heathen magistrates; and, (c) by the predictions made concerning the future or millennial state of the Church. He also argued for the necessity of this connection on the basis that the ordinance of God was designed for the temporal well-being of the community, that the ordinance of God was intended for the spiritual well-being of the community, and that these were, from their essential character, so related to each other, that

---

[11] ibid., 219-226.
[12] *The Church of Christ*, Vol. I, 126.
[13] ibid., 128.
[14] ibid., 130.
[15] ibid., 131.
[16] ibid., 133.

there must unavoidably be a connection, either friendly, or otherwise, between them. It seemed clear that the civil element and the religious element are so interwoven in the very constitution of human society, that they must necessarily tend either to establish or destroy each other; and that unless the Church and state are to be regarded as enemies, hostile to each other's existence, they must be united as friends, aiding and promoting each other's welfare. There can be no such thing as neutrality between the two.

Bannerman highlighted several specifics illustrative of the interrelationship between the jurisdictions of Church and state, or at least the Christian religion and the civil authorities:

(1) The case of the lawful oath, which, he wrote, "is the bond and seal of human society."[17]

(2) The right inherent in the Church of Christ "to propagate the Gospel, and make disciples in every country and nation under heaven."[18]

(3) The law of marriage "as another of those cases which illustrate the general position, that the civil and religious elements are so connected together in human society, that they do not meet and unite in friendship and mutual co-operation, they must inevitably tend to the serious or fatal injury of one or the other."[19]

(4) The case of the Sabbath. On this matter "when religion and the civil government do not meet and act in harmony, the difference must to the fatal injury of the one or other."[20]

4. Conclusion

"The power that was given to Christ as Mediator for the complete fulfilment of the mediatorial scheme is unlimited and universal," said William Cunningham, "there is nothing which is not put under Him;– He administers God's providence over the affairs of men,– He exercises

---

[17] ibid., 137.
[18] ibid., 140.
[19] ibid., 144.
[20] ibid., 145.

The Church – Its Relationship to the State (2)

a special superintendence and control over all the actions of all His creatures,– the hearts of all men are in His hands, and He turneth them whithersoever He will;– the riches and the power and the glory and this world are placed under His sovereign control, and He disposes of them according to His own good pleasure. He is the King of kings and the Lord of lords,– by Him kings reign and princes decree justice;– it is His right to reign, and the kings of this world exercise authority only so far and so long as He is pleased to permit."[21]

More recently John Murray summed up the relationship of the church to the state as follows: "The church is not subordinate to the state, nor is the state subordinate to the church. They are both subordinate to God, and to Christ in His Mediatorial dominion as Head over all things to his body the church. Both church and state are under obligation to recognise this subordination, and the corresponding co-ordination of their respective spheres in the divine institution...The principle that defines this unity is the sovereignty of God, and the obligation emanating from it is the requirement that both church and state must promote the interests of God."[22] By contrast, in the U.S.A., where the *Constitution* forbids a national establishment of religion, we find Charles Hodge expressing the contrary *voluntary* position that "we have reason to rejoice in the recently [?] discovered truth, that the Church is independent of the state, and that the state best promotes her interests by letting her alone."[23] This position is, it need hardly be said, at odds with the

---

[21] William Cunningham, *Sermons from 1828 to 1860*, Edinburgh, 1872, 244. This is from a sermon based upon Ephesians 1:22.
[22] *Collected Writing of John Murray*, Volume one, Edinburgh, 1976, 254.
[23] When the *Westminster Confession of Faith* was adopted by the American Presbyterian Church in 1729, section 3 of Chapter 23, 'Of the Civil Magistrate', was excepted, or ' adopted' only in a qualified manner; and in accordance with the 1789 Constitution, it and the corresponding passages in the *Larger Catechism* were omitted, unnecessarily in our view.

ecclesiology of such Scottish Reformed theologians as William Cunningham and James Bannerman.

THE CHURCH

10. The Antichrist: A Biblical and Confessional View

1. The Confessional statement

The *Westminster Confession of Faith* in its chapter 'Of the Church' makes a very specific identification of the 'Antichrist':

> There is no other Head of the Church but the Lord Jesus Christ; nor can the Pope of Rome in any sense be head thereof; but is that antichrist, that man of sin, and son of perdition, that exalteth himself in the church against Christ, and all that is called God.[1]

Texts used in support of this are: 2 Thessalonians 2:3, 4, 8, 9, and Revelation 13:6. This is a dogmatic statement. But it is a clear one, and it is one that is affirmed by those who adopt the *Confession of Faith* in an unqualified way. Some maintain that it is 'exegesis' or 'interpretation' and not 'doctrine,' and therefore not really binding on those who affirm "the whole doctrine contained in the Confession." Many think, too, that it is a step too far for a Confession to go. How do we answer that?

It is the case that this statement is exegesis/interpretation. That, however, is not necessarily an argument against it. After all, all Church dogma or doctrine is arrived at by such means, including the doctrine of the Trinity or justification by faith. The question is: is it supportable by biblical teaching and history, seen in the light of such teaching?

It is true that many Reformed Confessions do not contain such a teaching. Yet almost all Reformation theologians and Puritan preachers and divines made the self-same identification the *Confession* does, understanding this to be the implication of 2 Thessalonians, chapter 2.

---

[1] Chapter 25, section 6. See also the *Catechism on the Principles and Constitution of the Free Church of Scotland*, Edinburgh, 1882 [¹1847], 47-50.

The question may be raised: Would anything be missed if this section were not in the *Confession*? The answer to that question is, yes and no.

- *It is a contentious identification.* Good theologians, orthodox men, have denied it, and it is omitted from other Reformed/Reformation Confessions and creeds. In itself the exclusion of it would not indicate heterodoxy or denial in any way of the Headship of Christ in His Church. Yet, it can be seen as an *important identification* given the responsibility upon the Church to affirm Christ's sovereign Headship in the Church throughout history *over against rival claimants*. After all the Antichrist in Scripture is seen as a significant challenge to Christ's exclusive headship over the Church through the greater part of its history.
- *It is clearly a matter of prediction in the New Testament.* That is to say, there are passages in Scripture which invite the Church in every age to identify the Antichrist who would more or less throughout history, in some measure, usurp Christ's authority (2 Thessalonians 2:1-13; 1 John 4:3). It becomes, therefore, not only important but necessary to identify the predicted Antichrist, given the damage that can be done to the Church through its agency.

However, this obviously raises an all-important question:

2. Is the identification of the Papacy as the Antichrist supportable?

2.1 *Initial factors to consider*

- The rise and continuing significance of the Roman Catholic Church is highly significant in the history of the Church and is arguably accompanied by much potentially soul-destroying error
- The Roman Catholic system is an authoritarian and hierarchical one, calling itself 'universal' (=catholic) and essentially claiming precedence over all else that claims to be

Christian. The claims to primacy of the Roman Catholic Church renders its leaders – or over-all leader – as vested with peculiar influence, such authority in the Pope being recognised as in some respects 'infallible.'[2] Thus the position, historically, of the Bishop of Rome.

- The Church in the East (Eastern Orthodox) has nowhere near the same universality, nor claims, nor leader invested with such authority.

2.2 *Importance of a focus on Roman Catholic history*

- Familiarity with the history of the Roman Catholic Church and its dogma in general is important in order to identify it as an influential force for error within the umbrella of the Christian Church (as it purports to be) and as a religious body claiming a continuity right back to the apostles in a direct succession.

- The position of the Papacy in particular as a continuous office or leader in a defective theological and ecclesiastical system must always be recognised as the most influential *single office* in Christian Church history. Therefore, it has marks which *prima facie* invite it to be regarded as a strong candidate for the Antichrist of 2 Thessalonians 2, despite the ostensible Christian aspect.

2.3 *Specific identification of the Papacy as the Antichrist.*

It is necessary in considering the identification of the Antichrist to look at the passage in Scripture in which it is most explicitly dealt with, 2 Thessalonians 2:1-13. That is not the only reference to the matter of antichrist or antichrists. There is also 1 John 2:18-19 and 1 John 4:1-3, as well as Daniel 7, 8 and 9, and Revelation 13, 17 and 18.

(A) *1 John*

In 1 John 2, John predicts that antichrist would come, but states

---

[2] This doctrine was finally defined dogmatically in the First Vatican Council of 1870.

that already many antichrists had come. He identifies these as including those who once had seemed to be with them, but went out from them and, presumably, apostatized (vv18-19).

The passage in 1 John 4 is different. This reads: "and every spirit that confesseth not that Jesus Christ has come in the flesh is not of God: and this is that spirit of the antichrist, whereof ye have heard that it should come; and even now already in the world" (v3). It might be said that John here simply mentions "the spirit of antichrist" being evident in various situations. It is interesting that such a spirit appears to be manifested *within* the Christian world. Someone might say that the Papacy hardly shows the character of one who "confesseth not that Jesus Christ has come in the flesh..." However, it could be argued that such a phrase may not necessarily mean denial of the incarnation, but usurpation of some distinct aspect or aspects of Christ's *office and authority*. It is interesting that there is a note in the 1599 *Geneva Bible* that says on this point:

> He giveth a certain perpetual rule to know the doctrine of Antichrist by, to wit, if either the divine or human nature of Christ, or the true uniting of them together be denied: or if the least jot that may be, be derogate from his office who is our only King, Prophet, and everlasting high Priest.[3]

On such an understanding the possibility is opened out in this text of application to such an *office* as the Papacy.

(B) *2 Thessalonians 2*

Three important questions arise from this chapter, presupposing that it is the Antichrist that is being referred to in the first 13 verses:

(1) *What is the "restraining power" ("till the manifestation of the lawless one") (vv5-7)?*

- Paul had often spoken of the matter (v5), that is, the restraining power (vv6-7, "what withholdeth", KJV). They would know what he meant. It was something at work in their own day that made it easier to speak about than write

---
[3] *1599 Geneva Bible*, Tolle Lege Press, White Hall, WV, 2006-2007, 1298.

about (in case the writing was used against them). Because Paul was speaking of a political power of the day, some unnecessary persecution might be averted from Christians by not putting explicitly in writing what that power was.

- The restraining power he spoke of could not have been the power of God for Paul would have had no qualms about writing about that. Chrysostom wrote that "if he had meant the Holy Spirit when he speaks of the power that restrained, he would have spoken clearly, and said so."

- Was there any tradition in the early Church about who or what the 'restraining power' was? Tertullian suggested it was the Roman state. Iranaeus maintained that Paul in describing the revelation of the lawless one was describing what would take place upon the dismemberment of the Roman Empire, which he took to be the fourth Empire spoken of in Daniel 7:23. Jerome wrote (on Daniel 7): "Let us therefore say, – what all Ecclesiastical Writers have delivered to us, – that, when the Roman Empire is to be destroyed, Ten Kings will divide the Roman World among themselves, and then will be revealed the Man of Sin, the Son of Perdition, who will venture to take his seat in the Temple of God, making himself as God."[4] The 'restraining power' which would be removed was seen to be *the heathen power of Imperial Rome*.[5]

(2) *Has the 'restraining power' been removed out of the way (v7)?*

The answer here, presupposing the strong argument in identifying it as the Roman Empire, is 'yes.' Though its power was much diminished before the 5th century, the Roman Empire finally crumbled when Alaric stormed the walls of Rome and pillaged the city on 24th August 410, the so-called 'sack of Rome.' This spelt the end of the Roman Empire in the west. In 476 the barbarian King Odoacer

---

[4] Quoted in, Bishop Christopher Wordsworth, *Is the Papacy Predicted by St. Paul?*, first published in 1880 and reprinted by the Harrison Trust, Ramsgate, in 1985, page 10.
[5] For support of this view see Wordsworth, op. cit., 11-14.

deposed the last Roman Emperor. That was the immediate cause of the decline of the Roman Empire. Underlying were other weaknesses. Through immorality and diminishing human and material resources the decline had been happening for two to three hundred years before the final *coup de gras*.[6] This is what the Church would be looking for as a fulfilment of the prophecy of 2 Thessalonians 2:7.

(3) *Who is the 'lawless one,' the 'man of sin' (vv8-12)?*

- He, or it, will be particularly revealed after the removal of the restraining power (v8). Things had been working up to this even before the 'removal' (v7; also 1 John 4:3).
- Therefore the 'lawless one' or 'man of sin' has long since been revealed.
- Since the influence of the lawless one/man of sin will be of long continuance, right up to the end when he/it will be "destroyed with the brightness of his [Christ's] coming" (v8) and therefore far exceeding the life of any one individual, he or it cannot be a single person, but must be an *office* or *official position* throughout the period. This clearly narrows the options.
- The *restraining power* cannot be one individual either, but must be a succession of single persons, in this case Roman Emperors acting for the Empire.
- The man of sin, therefore, has a corporate existence, continued by a succession. This must be the case since the character is prophesied to remain till Jesus returns at the end of history (v8ff).
- The *time* of the revelation of the man of sin is the removal of the restraining power. This is something that would arise early in the history of the Church rather than far

---

[6] See, Richard A Todd, "The Fall of the Roman Empire," in, *The History of Christianity*, Lion Publishing, 1977, 179-186. This is found in pages 160-168 in the new revised edition of this enormously helpful history produced in 2013 under the editorship of Tim Dowley and with the title *Introduction to the History of Christianity* (Lion Hudson, 2014).

into the future, otherwise there would have been scarce any reason for Paul providing such an 'immanent warning.'
- The *place* of the revelation of the man of sin would be the place from where the restraining power would be removed; its former centre of operations.
- The conclusion is inevitable: the one 'office,' time and place that fits here is the Papacy in Rome. Nothing otherwise seems remotely to fit, historically speaking.

But this raises a fourth question:

(4) *Does the Papacy really fit the marks of the 'man of sin'?*

Many people have considered this improbable, given that the Roman Catholic Church is widely considered to be part of the Christian Church. However, the answer must be 'yes,' for the following reasons:

- What about the reference in verse 3 to a "falling away" first? Yet there was a falling away very quickly from the primitive apostolic faith after the close of the age of the Apostles. In any case this phrase must refer to a professing Christian Church rather than any pagan or false religion, concerning which falling away would be rather meaningless.
- So, identification of the man of sin (=Antichrist) will be expected to arise *from within the broad Christian framework* and among the claimants to Christianity. Over the time-scale envisaged only the Roman Catholic Church fits the bill.
- What about the "Son of Perdition"? Such a term really is only applicable within the Christian context and will refer to a professed Christian leader who in one way or another betrays Christ or in some way usurps His prerogatives in the Church. This may well be applied to the Bishop of Rome.
- The system in question is called a "mystery" (v7). This indicates that we will not be looking for an 'infidel system', such as Islam or some other ethnic religion, or political entity. Infidel systems and political entities are 'open' and hardly 'mysteries.' This is something then – the rise of the

- Antichrist (the lawless one, the son of perdition, the man of sin) – which will apply to some corruption in the professed Church through history.
- But what about the "lawlessness" mentioned in verse 7? Does this really apply to such an authoritarian body as the Roman Catholic Church? The answer, again, must be 'yes,' for there has been within that body such a development and purported deployment of both human and divine authority. But how was this working in the days of the Apostles (2 Thessalonians 2:7; 1 John 4:3)? Well, it was, as may be detected in the various letters to the Churches in Revelation 2 and 3.
- But what about "exalting himself against all that is called God" (v4)? Can that be attributed to the Papacy? But we are told simply that the man of sin exalts himself *against* or *above* all that is called God. That is tied in with his taking his seat in the "Temple of God." And that phrase shows that something from within the Christian Church is meant. The style and veneration of the Papacy and of St Peter's in Rome fits as nothing else does, that particular expression. When one sees the ceremonials involving the Papacy and how exalted he is, in a temporal and spiritual sense in the Church, what with claims of infallibility and description as 'Vicar of Christ' and 'Holy Father,' it is not so far-fetched to fix the identification of the Papacy in 2 Thessalonians 2.[7]
- *Anti*-Christ may rightly be taken in this context as involving a usurper of divine authority; arrogating authority belonging only to Christ as the great Head of the Church, involving displacement of the simplicity of apostolic faith, sacraments, worship etc.
- Even the claims of the Roman Catholic Church in respect

---

[7] See Wordsworth, op. cit., 21ff, for details.

of the miraculous fit into the picture described in verses 9 and 10.[8]

3. Conclusions

(1) There are strong arguments for the teaching of the *Westminster Confession*, chapter 25, section 6. Nothing else in Church history can compete against the identification of the Papacy with the Antichrist. It is clear that in the nature of the case Antichrist will arise within the Church. This is part of the power to deceive that there will be in that office down the millennia of Church history. The deception lies in the mixture of truth and error in the *system*, and the huge plausibility inherent in the Papal *office* as purporting to represent Christ and Christianity.

(2) Though the Reformers pretty uniformly made the identification the *Confession* subsequently did, nevertheless they did not hold that it was *impossible* for someone to be saved in the Roman Catholic Church. After all there is a fair degree of genuine Bible truth among them. There is an orthodox view of the Person of Christ; and there are sound views of the doctrine of God in general and the Trinity in particular. It would be thought that a really enlightened soul would soon abandon the system, but no doubt many do not. This, however, does not mitigate the spiritual dangers in being within the system headed up by the Papacy.

(3) Though a passage such as 2 Thessalonians 2 warns of the rise of a 'Man of Sin' (who is to be taken as the Antichrist), this is not inconsistent with the rise of other 'antichrists' with damaging doctrines and practices, as indicated by John (1 John 2:22; 4:3) and Paul (2 Timothy 3:1-9) and Peter (2 Peter 2). In such cases there are dangerous developments and movements to beware from *within* the professed Christian Church, including the rise and prevalence of

---

[8] Consult the books in the *Further Reading* list at the end of the chapter for details in support of this point.

modernism and theological liberalism within Protestantism itself.[9]

---

[9] See, for example, J Gresham Machen's *Christianity and Liberalism*, first produced in 1923. In this book Machen's thesis is that "The chief modern rival of Christianity is 'liberalism.' An examination of the teachings of liberalism in comparison with those of Christianity will show that at every point the two movements are in direct opposition" (page 53).

Further Reading:

Bishop Christopher Wordsworth (1807-1885), Is the Papacy Predicted by St. Paul? *The Harrison Trust, Cambridge, 1985 [1880]. This is a brief exegetical and theological study of 2 Thessalonians 2. It is a remarkable and concise booklet by a high Churchman who was Bishop of Lincoln. It shows that not all discussions identifying the Papacy as the Antichrist are from Presbyterian sources. For details in obtaining a copy of this see:* http://reformationfaith.com/2008/08/02/is-the-papacy-predicted-by-st-paul/.

J. A. Wylie (1808-1890), The Papacy is the Antichrist, *Edinburgh, 1888. This book can be found on the web:*
http://www.historicism.net/readingmaterials/thepapacy.pdf .

David Silversides, The Antichrist: A Biblical and Confessional View, *The James Begg Society, 2002. An excellent discussion of the issues. This is the substance of an address given at a meeting of the James Begg Society and is available from that Society (www.jbeggsoc.org.uk).*

In addition to the above there is material to be found in the works of John Calvin (e.g. The Institutes of the Christian Religion, Book IV, Chapter II, Section 12; Book IV, Chapter VII, sections 25 to 30; *and his Commentary on 2 Thessalonians which provide a flavour of the arguments generally used by the Reformers on this topic).*

For a Puritan view, contemporaneous with the Westminster Confession, *consult Thomas Manton, who has an extensive discussion in Sermons on 2 Thessalonians, as found in Volume 3 of* The Works of Thomas Manton, *re-issued by the Banner of Truth Trust in 1993 from an 1871 edition of the complete works of Manton.*

SECTION B

THE CHURCH
ITS CREEDS & CONFESSIONS

CREEDS AND CONFESSIONS

1. General considerations

1. Introduction

A Church's creed or Confession is a crux. How does the Church understand the teaching of Scripture? What is its doctrinal 'hermeneutic'? What standards are to bind its office bearers, and define the Church, in dependence upon the Word? These are all-important matters. They have exercised Churches throughout history, not least the Churches of the Reformation heritage. Decline from orthodoxy can be tracked by changes in the relation of the Churches to their creeds. There is always pressure to loosen subscription to allow a bit more leeway to liberal theological scruples, or secular influences of science and philosophy, or changes in the understanding of the normative nature of the Bible itself. In his *A Constitutional History of the Presbyterian Church in the United States of America* [[1]1839] Charles Hodge said this:

> The controversies which have so long agitated the Presbyterian Church have, at length, resulted in separation. It would not be easy to state, in a manner satisfactory to both parties, the points of difference between them. It may, however, be said, without offence, that the one party is in favour of stricter adherence to the standards of the church, as to doctrine and order, than the other (I:1).[1]

It is usually the case that reservations and lack of conviction about certain truths expressed in the Church's Confession are entertained by ministers and/or other office-bearers in a Church *before* any moves for

---

[1] Quoted in Gary North's *Crossed Fingers: How the Liberals Captured the Presbyterian Church*, Texas, 1996, 99. North's book of 1086 pages is a powerful, thorough and critical examination of the rise and conquest of the mainline Presbyterian Churches in America from the mid-to-late 19th Century. It is a fascinating and in many ways invaluable work in which there are parallels to be drawn to the take-over of mainline Protestant Church throughout the west in contemporary church history.

formal changes to confessional statements, or qualifications of it. It is like a leaven working away and not dealt with. Churches have down the years adopted qualifying statements, such as happened in the United Presbyterian Church of Scotland in 1879 and the Free Church of Scotland in 1892. Such statements have usually led to the loosening of strict adherence to the doctrinal position of such Churches.

Another alternative is found in Churches which recognise that there are widespread reservations about certain particulars in its Confession but wishing to retain what may be considered a strict subscription, they may agree to allow certain 'exclusions' from particular statements of the Confession, always provided they are not on 'fundamentals.' This, however, has a considerable disadvantage of 'institutionalising' within the same Church diversity of opinions on specific confessional truths and will almost inevitably lead to internal tensions within the Church or a 'Church within a Church' phenomenon. It may also raise the question of how 'fundamentals' are defined, especially since what may be considered as 'lesser' truths – for which 'exclusions' may be allowed – may nevertheless be argued to be Biblical by others.

It has also been the case that Churches, in which there has been traditionally a strict subscription, may come to accept in an unwritten way that there are different sorts of things within its Confession which do not have all the same binding effect. It may be said, for example, that there is doctrine, and that there is explanation or comment, and also exegesis. It may be maintained by some that, for example, it is only the undeniable 'doctrine' that is binding. The problem here is: Who says what is what? Where are the grounds for the idea that such distinctions act as a qualification of ordination vows? If they are not themselves explicit in the ordination vows or subscription formula what force can this have? What are the criteria for distinguishing these things?

2. A matter of interpretation?
This does raise the question of the degree to which there is scope for differences of opinion on matters addressed in a Church's Confession.

It may be, for example, that in certain statements things are not entirely explicit or unambiguous. No doubt there is an element of 'interpretation' or 'exegesis' involved, no matter how careful and explicit or comprehensive the Confession may be on the whole. No doubt there are truths or 'doctrines' of any Church Confession intrinsically less important than others. That is true of the Bible as a whole. There is a very considerable difference in content between the letter to the Romans and the letter to Philemon, for example. Yet all established facts and truths are important in their place. This is not to deny that men may have different perceptions of the importance of the various chapters and sections of the *Confession*. In that connection some scope will be allowed for differences of opinion on certain issues in which the *Confession* may be considered not to be decisive, or not well expressed. In relation to the *Westminster Confession of Faith*, for example the visible church is defined as consisting of "all those throughout the world that profess the true religion; and of their children" (25:2). Is that a wholly accurate definition of the visible Church? Can the church as visible be *defined* in terms of mere profession? It is debatable.[2] There is also to be taken into account areas which may not be covered specifically or explicitly in a Confession. Again, in the case of the *Westminster Confession* it is arguable that more could be said about regeneration, the preaching of the gospel and eschatology in general. This no doubt raises the matter of *revision*.

3. Power to revise?

It is not illegitimate for a Church to consider seriously the revision of its subordinate standards. This might theoretically and practically involve alteration, addition or deletion. No creed is beyond revision, however highly it may be regarded. Professor John Murray's comments are warranted, speaking of the *Westminster Confession*:

> To appraise [the Confession] as perfect and not susceptible to improvement or correction would be to accord it an estimate and veneration that belong only to the Word of

---

[2] This takes us into the debate about 'marks' of the visible Church discussed above.

God. This would be idolatry and would be a denial of that progressive understanding which the presence of the Holy Spirit in the church guarantees.[3]

It goes without saying that it is an extremely serious matter to change any part of a well-established Confession which in the nature of the case throughout showed a high degree of faithfulness to the Word of God and extremely careful drafting. Three real concerns would arise:

- What are the motives behind any move for revision?
- Are the revisions really necessary?
- Does the whole Church approve?

There would also be the question of expediency. As John Murray put it well: "Would that the genius for confessional formulation possessed by the divines at Westminster were present in the church today!"[4]

Though the *Westminster Confession of Faith* itself has never been revised in the Scottish Presbyterian Churches, there have been changes to the form of subscription down the years. For the greater part these were motivated by liberalisation – to modify or diminish the historic consistent Calvinism of the *Confession*. That was true of the Declaratory Acts of the United Presbyterian Church (1879) and the Free Church (1892), as well as changes to the form of subscription following the unions of 1900 (UPC and FC to form the United Free Church) and 1929 (the UFC with the Church of Scotland). The minister's relationship to the Church as an office-holder under Christ involves a solemn vow by which he is bound to the stated Confessional position of the Church.[5] Any alteration in subscription will inevitably raise questions of the sincerity and honesty of the vows taken in the first place, and, furthermore, imply or involve a change in the nature of the position of the Church more or less significantly. In Scotland such

---

[3] John Murray, "The Theology of the Westminster Confession," in *Scripture and Confession* (ed. J H Skilton), Presbyterian and Reformed Publishing Co., 1973, 145.
[4] ibid., 148.
[5] We are here equating the 'Questions and Formula' with taking a solemn vow to uphold the doctrine, worship, government and discipline of the Church. This would therefore come into the category 'Of lawful Oaths and Vows' in Chapter 22 of the *Confession of Faith*.

changes have been a harbinger of decline from past attainments doctrinally and has resulted in the institutionalisation of broad Churchism with its ambiguities and ambivalence in doctrine and practice, and therefore in clarity of witness to truth.[6]

Not all such changes are thus motivated. It was the case, for example, in the days following the Disruption of 1843, that the Free Church did see fit not only to change the form of subscription to exclude Bourignianism and substitute Erastianism, but also issue a formal clarification of the teaching of the *Confession* on the subject of the Civil Magistrate declaring that the Church whilst firmly maintaining Scriptural principles as to the duties of nations and rulers in relation to Christian faith and the Christian Church, disclaimed "intolerant or persecuting principles" which some may, wrongly, impute to the *Confession* (Act XII, 1846).[7] These sorts of things *may* be happily done, but – and it is a big 'but' – they would require to be approved, or acquiesced in, by the *whole* Church. Otherwise in the interests of honesty and integrity office-bearers taking issue with any of the *existing* form of adherence or subscription would have no alternative but to leave the church and adhere to a Church consistent with their new or deviant views.

4. Is the Confession beyond improvement?

Though the *Westminster* Confession, for example, is not beyond improvement as a Confession which is not vested with infallibility, there is nothing with which any wholehearted Calvinist would take issue. The danger always is that suggested amendments have invariably been intended to *detract* from the historic Calvinism it states so beautifully and explicitly. James MacGregor (1830-1894) was Professor of Systematic Theology in New College Edinburgh (1868-1881). In an article on 'On the Revision of the Westminster Confession of Faith,' in

---

[6] For a stimulating essay on the subject of 'Broad Churchism' see, Robert L Dabney's discussion of that subject in *Discussions: Evangelical and Theological/2*, London, Banner of truth Trust, 1967 [1891], 447-463.
[7] See, William Cunningham, *Historical Theology*, Vol. 2, Edinburgh, 1960 [³1870], 583-7.

the *British and Foreign Evangelical Review* in October 1877, MacGregor addressed the idea of relaxing the form of subscription. Rather than subscribing the "whole doctrine" of the *Confession* some apparently thought it would be easier simply to subscribe to the "substance" or "system" of the *Confession*. But (wrote MacGregor) why should an honest man scruple about the whole doctrine if he can hold the substance or system? He is frankly suspicious that "those vague expressions ["system" or "substance"] are liable to most formidable abuse." His conclusion is that what is intended by the prescribed form of adherence should be provided for "by a form which admits no misapprehension."[8] John Murray states something along the same lines, lines which commend themselves to those exercised to maintain inviolate the whole doctrine contained in the Confession of the Church's faith:

> When a Confession is examined carefully in the light of Scripture and in relation to the demands of confessional witness in the church today, the amazing fact is that there is so little need for emendation, revision or supplementation. And of greater importance than the fact that justifiable or necessary amendments do not affect the system of truth set forth in the Confession. In other words, the *doctrine* of the Confession is the doctrine which the church needs to confess and hold aloft today as much as in the seventeenth century.[9]

5. Why adopt a Confession of Faith?

The purpose of a Confession adopted in a Church is to summarise the Christian faith from the Biblical data. This will cover (1) the *substance* of the Biblical faith; and (2) the *system* of the Biblical truth. This will *clarify* the faith in terms of seven main areas:

---

[8] James MacGregor, 'On Revision of the Westminster Confession of Faith,' *The British and Foreign Evangelical Review*, October, 1877, 711.
[9] "The Theology of the Westminster Confession," op. cit., 146.

- Theology – the doctrine of God
- Genesiology – the doctrine of origins
- Christology – the doctrine of Christ
- Soteriology – the doctrine of salvation
- Pneumatology – the doctrine of the Spirit
- Ecclesiology – the doctrine of the Church
- Eschatology – the doctrine of the last things

All this would be set within a particular view of the place and proper interpretation of Holy Scripture as a revelation of God. The place of Scripture is all-important. It will make all the difference in the world what view of Scripture is adopted. In the Reformed Confessions, such as the *Westminster Confession of Faith*, it is clear that the framers had a high view of Scripture as utterly normative and God-breathed (2 Timothy 3:16). This is crystal clear from the fact that the *Confession* opens with a Chapter on Scripture, and that it deals with the position of Scripture so thoroughly (see *Westminster Confession of Faith*, 1:1-10).

6. What *use* are Confessions?

Some people object to such Confessions on the basis that there should be 'no creed but Christ.' But even that raises doctrinal questions: Who is Christ, and what did He do? What is His significance? Others might question whether such a Confession doesn't come to take precedence over the Bible itself. As a subordinate standard any such Confession is not invested with infallibility, as we have already stated. However, it is not only important but also necessary to summarise revealed truth in the interests of clear witness-bearing to the truth. It is true that creeds and confessions have value in relation to the extent that they are agreeable with the Word of God. But men and churches after all *must* interpret Scripture. It is therefore a folly to ignore the reflections of the Church in history on a right Biblical understanding of the faith and its implications, fully recognising where that has been accomplished. There is strength in a godly consensus, as reflected in sound Confessions, such as the *Westminster Confession of Faith*.

We may summarise the *uses* of a sound Confession, agreeable to Scripture teaching:

- It is useful as a bond of union between Christian believers, affirming a consensus about the truth of the Word of God
- It is a means of affirming a unified testimony to the world concerning the true doctrine of God's written revelation
- It serves as a test for parties holding office within the Church
- It may act as a basis of fellowship and co-operation between individuals and Churches
- It is useful as a means of instruction within the Church
- It is a standard by which to judge the orthodoxy of individuals or Churches

In connection with the use of Confessions the more detailed it is on clearly fundamental matters of Christian faith and life the better placed it will be to act as a 'bond' of fellowship. A brief Confession which provided wide scope for differences of opinion would likely give occasion for either a measure of tyranny or constant dispute; the tyranny relating to the resistance to 'making things more explicit,' in the interests of keeping things vague and broad; the constant dispute relating to inevitable areas of disagreement in areas not explicitly stated in the limited creed. More of this will be covered in the next chapter.

CREEDS AND CONFESSIONS

2. The Place and Usefulness of Confessions of Faith

1. What are we to believe?

In relation to the matter of Church creeds or confessions there are some who may say: 'We have no creed but Christ'; or, 'We have no creed but the Bible.' We know – or think we know – what is meant by such statements. They are thinking: 'We are not beholden to any creed or confession of faith. After all, these things are just divisive.' No doubt in a perfect world such statements would be sufficient. But in truth they raise more issues than they solve. They would have to answer such questions as these:

- What is God?
- Who is Christ?
- What makes Him so important?
- Who or what is the Holy Spirit?
- What is the Trinity?
- What is the Bible?
- What is sin?
- How is a person saved?
- What is the incarnation?
- What is the meaning of the cross?
- How is the Church to be organised?
- How is such organisation determined?
- Who has authority in the Church?
- What are the limits of that authority?
- How are we to worship God?
- What about the end of the world?

These are searching questions. How is the Church, or how are Christian believers, to make these things clear to the world? Many people might say their creed is Christ, or the Bible, who would have very different views on such questions. In the end of the day such over-simplification would be destructive of Church in any meaningful sense.

Having said this, the element of truth in such statements is that whatever a Church believes, whatever it believes concerning God and Christ, whatever worship it adopts or church government it applies, these things ought to be agreeable to the Bible – the Scriptures of the Old and New Testaments – properly understood and conscientiously worked through. It will readily be seen, therefore, how vitally important it is for any body of Christians to have a clear Confession of what the Church believes, and how it is organised. It will readily be recognised that this will involve careful, devout and prayerful effort, and that the resultant Confession will be seen to summarise faithfully and in a balanced way the teaching of Scripture. It is surely of primary importance to highlight the most important truths in relation to God, Christ and personal salvation, and yet also confess truths in relation to morality, Church order, worship forms, Church discipline and so on. It seems reasonable as well as desirable if there is not to be uncertainty or theological chaos that such a Confession should be as thorough as possible. The world, as well as the Churches themselves, should be perfectly clear what a Church stands for; what it believes.

There is more to this than simply the 'Confession of Faith' a Church adopts. The whole position of a Church is determined also by how it defines its doctrine, worship, government and discipline. There will no doubt be reference to such things in the 'Confession of Faith.' But there will also be other 'Subordinate Standards and Authoritative Documents,' some of them historical in nature, subscribed by the Church. And most crucially there will be *questions* to be asked of office-bearers, and a *formula* to sign which commits the office-bearer (minister, elders and deacons) to the doctrine, worship, government and discipline defined in the 'Subordinate Standards and Other Authoritative Documents' of the Church. But subscription to the *Confession* is a central pillar in a Church.

In this chapter we will focus upon the *Confession of Faith* and its significance for the health and soundness of a Church. But bear in mind the wider issues.

2. What is the place of Creeds and Confessions in history?

Historically speaking from the period of the Apostles the Church has expressed its belief through creeds or confessions. There are simple statements in the Scriptures themselves which indicate this. They amount to a warrant for the formulation of statements affirming Bible truth in doctrine and practice.

James Bannerman suggested three examples from within the post-Apostolic Church:

(1) In the Johannine writings (Gospel and 3 Letters of John the Apostle) there is clearly a desire to determine the orthodox view of Jesus Christ as the divine Son (see John 1:14; 1 John 4:2-3);

(2) In the Pauline writings there is a clear concern to state and defend truth, as, for example, in 1 Corinthians 15 in the case of the matter of the resurrection of Christ in particular and the general resurrection in consequence, but not least the letter to the Romans which provides an apostolic outline of gospel truth;

(3) In the Acts of the Apostles chapter 15 there is the case of the 'Jerusalem Assembly,' which convened to establish doctrine and practice in the apostolic church.[1]

In addition to this the early church formulated creeds both in the interests of positive statements of truth and out of a concern to counteract unbiblical heretical ideas. We have, for example, the 'Apostles' Creed' (in the early post-apostolic period). Then there was the Nicene Creed (325) which resolved the issue of the Trinity, and the Chalcedon Creed (451) which resolved the issue of the two natures of Christ. As time went on there was an increased necessity for statements of faith to clarify just exactly how the Church collectively understood the teaching of Scripture on central issues for faith.

However, not only were creeds/confessional statements compiled by the orthodox, there were also statements issued by the heterodox.

---

[1] James Bannerman, *The Church of Christ* (1869), 291ff.

Often the Orthodox confessions were compiled to counter heterodox ones. This was true, for example, of the *Canons of the Synod of Dort* in the Dutch Reformed Church (1618-19). These comprised a fundamental affirmation of the doctrines of grace, commonly called Calvinism designed as a riposte to the 1610 'Remonstrance' of the Arminians. The time of the Reformation in the 16th century was a great era of Confessions of Faith.[2] Thus, we have the famous *Scots Confession* of 1560 (partly prepared by John Knox). This was displaced in the Scottish Church the following century after the production of the *Westminster Confession of Faith* (1647).

3. What is the *purpose* of adopting a Confession?

A Church has both a right and a necessity to declare the truth. In pursuit of this it has the power and the duty to adopt a summary of its doctrine in a form of a Confession as a standard, subordinate to Scripture as the Church's supreme standard. In this way the church establishes the standard of orthodoxy and terms of communion for office-bearers and members. Not that *members* in a Church will be expected to affirm the creed *directly*. But *indirectly* the creed will act as a standard of Christian faith and life, and therefore a general standard for admission to ordinances will be established. Any confession that they make ought to be in line with the Church's doctrinal standards. And the more the 'people in the pew' are acquainted with the Church's confessional standard the healthier that Church will be. They ought to know what the Church believes and to confess it and defend it in the world!

Although a creed or Confession is not in itself an infallible document and cannot be given a place on a par with Scripture, nevertheless the content of the Confession adopted, and the strictness and sincerity of the adherence of office-bearers in the Church to it, are of the utmost significance for the strength and health, spiritually and in

---

[2] For example: *Scots Confession* (1560); *Belgic Confession* (1561); *Heidelberg Catechism* (1563); *39 Articles of the Church of England* (1563).

terms of biblical orthodoxy, of the church, given that the Confession adopted is a clear declaration of Scripture truths. That is certainly the case with the *Westminster Confession of Faith* adopted in the Scottish Church.

But *why* adopt a Confession of Faith? The purpose of a Confession is to summarise the Christian faith from the Biblical data. This will cover

(1) the *Substance* of the Biblical faith; and

(2) the *System* of the Biblical truth.

The adoption of a detailed Confession – such as the *Westminster Confession of Faith* – is not to be taken as implying that all who do not receive the Confession are heretics or Christians of doubtful standing. That may be the case! But that is not a judgement in adopting a specific Confession. Those who do not accept the whole doctrine of the Confession may be wholly in agreement with the doctrine of Christ and of sin and salvation, but may differ in, say, sacramental theology, or Church/State relations, or the Last Things.

It is not a requirement of membership that a person must accept all that is in the Confession, though it will be a requirement for all office-bearers, and the nature of their acceptance of the Confessional doctrine will be expected to be knowledgeable, sincere and whole-hearted. If it is not they ought to renounce such office, leave the Church to take office with a Church whose Confession and constitutional position is more agreeable to them, or they will ultimately be subject to discipline, if they are found to be guilty of views not in conformity with the Church's Confession of Faith.

The Confession will therefore *clarify* the faith across a range of theological and practical concerns, as confessed by the Church and its office bearers. All this is set within a particular view of the place and proper interpretation of Holy Scripture as a revelation of God. *The place of Scripture is all-important.* It will make all the difference in the world what view of Scripture is adopted. In the Reformed Confessions like the *Westminster Confession of Faith* it is clear that the framers had a high view of Scripture as utterly normative and God-breathed (John 10:35; 2

Timothy 3:16). This is crystal clear from the fact that the *Confession* opens with a chapter on Scripture, and that it deals with the position of Scripture so thoroughly (see *Westminster Confession of Faith*, 1:1-10).

It is in this area that there has been a weakening in the Scottish Church from the later years of the 19th Century and throughout the 20th century, what with qualifications made in the mainline churches on teaching of the Confession and of specific adherence to it. The core issue was the nature and authority of Scripture as the inspired, infallible and inerrant Word of God. It is precisely in that area that the mainline Scottish churches, and some of the smaller ones too, have seriously failed in recent times. The Free Church that continued as such after 1900 was not party to such qualifications.[3] It saw its responsibility to "hold fast the form of sound words" and to "strengthen the things that remain." That is a responsibility especially to be felt by office bearers, but also by people in the pew, if the Church is to be doctrinally sound and spiritually healthy. It is beautifully summed up in the opening article of the *Belgic Confession* of 1561: "We all believe with the heart and confess with the mouth…" (Article 1). This reflects the teaching of Romans 10:9.

In connection with the use of Confessions the more detailed it is across the whole range of Christian faith and life the better placed it will be to act as a 'bond' of fellowship. As we have previously stated, a brief Confession would simply provide wide scope for differences of opinion and would give occasion in all likelihood either of tyranny or constant dispute; the tyranny relating to the resistance to 'making things more explicit,' in the interests of keeping things vague and broad; the constant dispute relating to inevitable disagreement in areas not explicitly covered by such a limited creed. Meantime we are thankful to have such a comprehensive Confession (with the Catechisms) and with a good conscience are to assert, maintain and defend the doctrine, humbly and enthusiastically.

Having said this, it may be recognised that the Confession of Faith

---

[3] Nor has the Free Presbyterian Church of Scotland.

is not a perfect document. Though we cannot here go into specifics, it can be said that the Confession does not say everything that can be said about Biblical truth or even the doctrine it does expound, nor does it necessarily put things in the best way at all points. We must never think it is beyond improvement in some respects, by amendment or addition. However, the truth is that even where in one place it may not be as clear as it might be usually this is compensated for by the teaching in the Catechisms (and vice versa). There is a remarkable consistency in the teaching of the Confession and the Catechisms, as one might expect. If any changes, additions or alterations were to be ever contemplated (and they have been from time to time) one would expect them to *build on past attainment* and not subtract, detract or dilute.

4. What is the *usefulness* in adopting a Confession?

As we mentioned at the beginning, some people object to Confessions on the basis that there should be 'no creed but Christ.' Truly a major focus of a Church's confession must be the person and work of the glorious Mediator. We have already suggested that the 'no creed but Christ' sort of position raises doctrinal questions, as we have already noted. Others have questioned whether such a Confession doesn't come to take precedence over the Bible itself. As a subordinate standard any such Confession is not invested with infallibility. However, it is not only important but also necessary to summarise revealed truth in the interests of clear witness-bearing to the truth. It is true that creeds and confessions have value in relation to *the extent that they are agreeable with the Word of God*. But men and churches after all *must* interpret Scripture. It is therefore a folly to ignore the reflections of the Church in history on a right Biblical understanding of the faith and its implications, fully recognising where that has been accomplished. There is strength in a godly consensus, as reflected in sound Confessions, such as the *Westminster Confession of Faith*.

So what use are such Confessions? There are several clear advantages of a strong and clear confessional position for any Church seeking to be faithful to Christ and His Word:

(1) *It is useful as a bond of union between Christian believers, affirming a consensus about the truth of the Word of God.*
In a sense the primary use of a confession relates to the existence of the Church itself. The Church is at its basic level a gathering of those who profess to be true believers; who profess to be led by God's Spirit and Word. It is inevitable that this will of necessity be expressed in some clear and lucid way: "Here is what we, unitedly, profess that we believe to be the teaching of Holy Scripture rightly understood for faith and life, the person and work of the Saviour, sin and salvation, heaven and hell." A commonly held and sincerely believed confession demonstrates the union between believers on the teaching of Scripture.

(2) *It is a means of affirming a unified testimony to the world concerning the true doctrine of God's written revelation*
It seems obvious that a Church which embraces all sorts of views would have no unified message for the world; it would be rent with all sorts of disputes, debates and disharmony; the right hand wouldn't know what the left hand was doing spiritually or theologically; it would be confusion, as we can see with broad Churches in the West today. In other words, it would give an 'uncertain sound', as, indeed is the case in mainline Churches such as the Church of Scotland in Scotland, the Church of England in England, and denominations like the Methodist Church and the United Reformed Church. Churches which have qualified or adjusted their adherence to an Evangelical Confession in reality have no *clear* doctrinal position.

(3) *It serves as a test for parties holding office within the Church*
It goes without saying that if the Church is to be unified in its testimony to the gospel truth, and if its message is going to be clear in the world, there needs to be a commitment to the Church's confession which will bind, voluntarily but with sanctions for denial, the leadership of the Church, the office-bearers, ministers, elders and deacons. This is the purpose of 'subscription' to the confession: a clear affirmation of *personal* attachment to the doctrinal and practical position of the Church as stated in its Confession. Historically, the Reformed Churches have required a wholehearted (*ex animo*) commitment without qualification.

That has the virtue of making a test of confession for office-bearers. It also has the advantage of maintaining standards within a Church of which the members and adherents can have confidence.

(4) *It will act as a basis of fellowship and co-operation between individuals and Churches*

For Churches which adopt the Confession of Faith and have a genuine concern to promote its teachings as agreeable to the Word of God there is a good basis in the common understanding of the Confession to enjoy fellowship and co-operation. It may be that for historical reasons orthodox conservative Scottish Churches wholeheartedly holding to the Confessional teaching remain separate, such as the Free Church (in both its manifestations), the Free Presbyterian Church, the Associated Presbyterian Churches and the Reformed Presbyterian Church. Common commitment to the Confession in such cases at the very least is a basis for fellowship and co-operation, though that may be more limited in situations where there has been a division in a Church. Yet when a Church considers what fellowship it can practically have with other Reformed Churches, adherence to a Reformed Confession is an obvious criterion.

(5) *It is useful as a means of instruction within the Church*

We normally think of the Shorter Catechism as a means of instruction in our Churches. We can readily see how well adapted the Catechisms are for instructing young and old in the tenets of the Reformed faith. However, we ought to see the Confession of Faith as a primary study source for a summary of Bible teaching. Earnest Christians will benefit greatly from personal study of the Confession, together with some of the useful study guides available (such as those of Robert Shaw, A. A. Hodge, G. I. Williamson, etc.[4]). It is something that might well come into the ministry, for example through expositions at midweek meetings

---

[4] There are several sound expositions of the Confession which have been produced, most of which are readily available: David Dickson, *Truth's Victory over Error* (c1650); Robert Shaw, *An Exposition of the Confession of Faith* (1877); A A Hodge, *The Confession of Faith* (1869); G I Williamson, *The Westminster Confession of Faith for Study Classes* (1964); Joseph A Pipa, Jr, *The Westminster Confession of Faith Study Book* (2005).

or separate series. A people familiar with the teaching of the Confession will be a well taught people knowledgeable of the teaching of the Scriptures and what the Church stands for. They will not be blown about by winds of doctrine.

(6) *It is a standard by which to judge the orthodoxy of individuals or Churches*
The creeds and confessions developed to counteract error in one form or another. They developed to establish Biblical orthodoxy and provide criteria by which a person's or Church's orthodoxy may be tested. In this sense the Confession acts as a basis for determining who stands square on purity of doctrine. Consider the Bereans, who, after hearing the Apostolic message "received the word with all readiness, and searched the Scriptures daily to find out whether these things were so" (Acts 17:11). Given that the Confession is a faithful exposition of the Word of God, it is a means of establishing what is true and right and orthodox.

5. Are there dangers to avoid?
It is only fair to say that although our emphasis has been on the usefulness of the Confession to the individual and the Church, there are things of which we are to be wary:

1. It is perhaps easy to assume or presume familiarity with the Confession and yet give it little thought or study. We should constantly test our doctrine with the Confession and catechisms.
2. It is also possible to have a judgemental or superior spirit by feeling we have the truth because we adhere in an unqualified way to the Confession whereas so many others are looser and therefore theologically suspect. They may be looser and suspect, but for our part we must beware a merely superior or judgemental spirit.
3. It is possible to be proud in our orthodoxy. We are the people and wisdom ends with us because after all we hold to the Confession wholly. Yes, we should gladly adhere to the whole doctrine contained in the Confession, but with humility and thanksgiving that it has been given to us in the Lord's gracious providence to have such a grand exposition of the Reformed truths.

4. It is possible to think that knowledge of the teaching of the Confession is the important thing. Let us not forget that doctrine/theology that does not touch the heart is sterile. Doctrine that does not stir in us a desire to know Christ and touch our experience of the life of God in the soul falls short of what it is to be Christian and Reformed.

6. Conclusions

1. There is a responsibility resting upon all office-bearers in the Church to be acquainted with the 'whole doctrine' contained in the Confession, to know its teaching and to be convinced that it reflects accurately the teaching of the infallible Word of God. The office-bearer – minister or elder or deacon – is bound in this responsibility by the form of subscription which is affirmed at ordination and induction. There are two aspects to this:

(1) The teaching of the Confession is to be subscribed *ex animo*, that is to say, "from the heart." "I...do own the same as the confession of my faith..." In addition,

(2) There is the matter of *honesty*. W. G. T. Shedd put this strongly but fairly:

> Honesty is as important in theology as in trade and commerce, in a religious denomination as in a political party. Denominational honesty consists, first, in a clear unambiguous statement by a Church of its doctrinal belief; and, second, in an unequivocal and sincere adoption of it by its members. Both are requisite...Heresy is a sin, and is classed by St. Paul among the "works of the flesh," along with "adultery, idolatry, murder, envy, and hatred," which exclude from the kingdom of God (Gal. 5:19-21). But heresy is not so great a sin as dishonesty...A heretic who acknowledges that he is such, is a better man than he who pretends to be orthodox while subscribing to a creed which he dislikes, and which he saps under pretence of improving it and adapting it to the times. The honest heretic leaves the Church with which he no longer agrees; but the insincere

subscriber remains within it in order to carry out his plan of demoralization.[5]

2. There ought to be a concern to teach the confessional doctrine in the ministry of the Church. This requires a clear assertion of the pre-eminence of the teaching of Scripture as the infallible and inerrant word of God. Again, the form of subscription requires the office-bearer to "own and believe the whole doctrine contained in the Confession of Faith…to be the truths of God…founded on the Word of God, and agreeable thereto…" There need be no apology in teaching this doctrine, whether by midweek studies, or other such study groups. Our people ought to be familiar with the truths of our Confession, and exemplars of the spirituality and piety based upon such an understanding of the truth.

3. The Westminster Confession and Catechisms are a treasure in the Church. All who have the interests of the Church at heart ought to have a concern to familiarise themselves with the Confessional teaching. As with ministers and other office-bearers, it ought to be something frequently used and studied, both individually and in groups. This way the people will be, as they can and ought to be, well versed in the Christian faith and its application for their lives in this world as witnessing people, sanctifying their hearts and "be ready always to give an answer [defence] to every man who asketh you a reason for the hope that is in you with meekness and fear" (1 Peter 3:15). This cannot but have the benefit of being a help to others, being discerning of error, and advancing assurance of faith and stability in the Christian life.

---

[5] W G T Shedd, *Calvinism: Pure and Mixed* (1893), 152.

CREEDS AND CONFESSIONS

3. The Westminster Confession of Faith

1. The origin of the Confession

The Westminster Confession and other documents: the Larger and Shorter Catechisms, the Form of Church Government, and the Directory for Public Worship, as well as a translation of Metrical Psalms, were produced by an Assembly of Divines at Westminster, London, between 1643 and 1649, though meetings were held up to 1652. The Assembly was set up by the so-called 'Long' Parliament in 1643 with a view to settling the Government and Liturgy of the Church in England in part by clearing the doctrines of the Church from false accusations and interpretations. Initially the thought was that the Assembly should revise the *39 Articles* of the Church of England (1571 in their final form). They did this by using Archbishop Ussher's *Irish Articles* (1615).

The Assembly essentially was English in nature, and comprised 139 divines, several of whom (including all the Episcopalians, such as Archbishop Ussher) did not actually attend any of its meetings. There were also 15 peers, 30 members of the House of Commons; and four scribes or Clerks. Though it was English in nature there were 6 Scottish ministers who were appointed commissioners, and 9 Scottish elders.[1] The commissioners from the Scottish Church played an influential role in the Assembly, though they had no vote. The six ministers appointed were: Alexander Henderson (Edinburgh), Robert Douglas (Edinburgh) (who never took his seat), Samuel Rutherford (St Andrews), Robert Baillie (Glasgow), George Gillespie (Edinburgh), and Robert Blair (St

---

[1] There are details of all the Commissioners to the Assembly, together with the composition of the three standing committees, in Robert Paul's *The Assembly of the Lord* (Edinburgh: T & T Clark, 1985), Appendix I, 546-556.

Andrews) (who replaced Douglas). Many of the commissioners have subsequently become well-known in recent times through the reprints of their writings, such as: William Bridge, Jeremiah Burroughes, Thomas Goodwin, and Edward Reynolds.[2]

Through 1644 the revising work was abandoned in favour of work on a new Confession. This was completed in 1647. In the Scottish Church the following was the order in which the various documents produced by the Assembly were approved:

- The Directory for the Public Worship of God, February 3, 1645
- The Form of Presbyterial Church Government, February 10, 1645
- The Confession of Faith, August 27, 1647
- The Larger Catechism, July 2, 1648
- The Shorter Catechism, July 28, 1648
- The Scottish Metrical Psalter, November 23, 1649[3]

The Confession, then, was completed in 1647. It was adopted both in England and in Scotland. In England it was the Church's Confession up to the Restoration of 1660, when the monarchy and Episcopacy were re-established in England. It was in the final quarter of the 19th century that there was a decisive movement away from the Confessional teaching in the mainline denominations in Scotland. It is still, however, the unqualified Confession of the Free Church of Scotland (Continuing) as well as other smaller Scottish Presbyterian Churches: the Free Church of Scotland, Free Presbyterian Church of Scotland, Associated Presbyterian Churches and the Reformed Presbyterian Church of Scotland.

---

[2] For a goldmine of information about the Westminster divines and others of the English, Scottish and Continental 'Puritans' see the volume of Joel R Beeke and Randall J Pederson, *Meet the Puritans*, a volume of 896 pages produced by Reformation Heritage Books, Grand Rapids, in 2006.

[3] The 'Scottish Metrical Psalter' was largely based on the metrical translations produced by the Assembly at Westminster. See Millar Patrick's *Four Centuries of Scottish Psalmody*, Oxford University Press, 1949, Chapter 9: "Francis Rous and the Scottish Psalter." See also *The Practice of the Free Church of Scotland*, Knox Press, [8]1995, 121. The Scottish Metrical Psalter, as it became known, came into authorised use from May 1st, 1650.

2. The sources of the Confession

We have already mentioned that the original intent was to revise the English *39 Articles* and the Irish *19 Articles*. It soon became clear that there was a concern to produce documents of a more comprehensive nature. The Westminster divines did not attempt to cover every head of doctrine comprehensively. They were selective in the *Confession* of those things that were considered of the first doctrinal and practical importance. The *Catechisms* were masterly productions. The *Larger Catechism* was intended for those who had some 'proficiency' in the grounds of the Christian faith. It is a monumental work of what might be described as Puritan Moral Theology, and as such it is at once instructive, edifying and challenging. It amounts to a through application of the law of God, understood as a basis for Christian living. The *Shorter Catechism* was designed by contrast for 'such as are of weaker capacity.' However, it is the latter which has had more influence in the Churches than the *Larger*.[4] It remains a manual of doctrine without real rival among the Reformed churches.

It goes without saying that the framers of the *Confession* drew upon the attainments of the past in the understanding of sound Biblical and Reformed faith. Since the Lutheran Reformation there had been 150 years of theological reflection. Without question the most influential of these influences was John Calvin (1509-1564), not least through his *Institutes of the Christian Religion* (^{1}1536). Calvin himself was greatly influenced by 'giants' upon whose shoulders he stood, such as Augustine (354-430). But in the Puritan era (roughly the first half of the 17th century) there were in England and Scotland a large company of men capable in linguistics, patristics, and reformed theology. This all added up to the Westminster standards representing the high-watermark of the great Reformed creeds. Though the fallible productions of fallible men, there are few things in any of the

---

[4] On the *Larger Catechism's* teaching see the superb study by Johannes G Vos (1903-1983) edited by G I Williamson and published by Presbyterian and Reformed Publishing in 2002.

documents with which anyone with a reverent view of Scripture could seriously object.

3. The doctrinal position of the *Confession of Faith*[5]

Even a cursory acquaintance with the *Confession* indicates that it is at once biblical, reformed, and Calvinistic. It represents what is called *federal theology*. What that means is this, in the words of George Smeaton:

> It is due to the federal theology to state, that it was only meant to ground and establish the undoubtedly scriptural doctrine of the two Adams (Rom. v. 12-20; 1 Cor. xv. 47)...No one can doubt, who examines the federal theology, that the design of those who brought that scheme of thought into general reception in the Reformed Church for two centuries, was principally to ground, and to put on a sure basis, the idea of the two Adams; that is, to show that there were, in reality, only two men in history, and only two great facts on which the fortunes of the race hinged.[6]

"What this means," wrote Ronald Shillaker, "is that when Adam sinned and fell, soon after his creation, the result was passed to all humanity because he was their representative. Christ, the second Adam, who was the other federal representative in the scheme, remedied the situation through the incarnation and his atoning work on the cross."[7]

It is Reformed, rather than Lutheran, in that it represents the theology of the Calvinistic Reformers in exulting the sovereignty of grace. It is 'federal' in that salvation is understood in relation to the covenant of grace and the representative headship of the Lord Jesus Christ acting on behalf of His elect people. However, it also contains

---

[5] See, for example, David Dickson, *Truth's Victory over Error* (c1650); Robert Shaw, *An Exposition of the Confession of Faith* (1877); A A Hodge, *The Confession of Faith* (1869); G I Williamson, *The Westminster Confession of Faith for Study Classes* (1964); Joseph A Pipa, Jr, *The Westminster Confession of Faith Study Book* (2005).

[6] George Smeaton, *The Doctrine of the Atonement as taught by Christ Himself*, Edinburgh ²1871, 439.

[7] R M Shillaker, "The Federal Pneumatology of George Smeaton (1814-1889)," PhD thesis, Highland Theological College, 2002, 1. 'Federal' is from the Latin *foedus*, covenant. 'Pneumatology' is from a Greek word *pneuma* which means (among other things) 'Spirit' and thus *pneumatology* refers to the doctrine and work of the Holy Spirit.

teaching on the Church and its sacraments, religious worship and the relationship of Church and State, as well as the last things.

4. The fundamental basis of the Confession

The *Confession* begins with a lengthy chapter on *the doctrine of Scripture*. This sets out the stall for the proper basis of theological reflection. It must be based upon an accurate doctrine of Scripture as the Word of God. Therefore, the framers of the *Confession* spent considerable care in framing these sections. Several important questions are answered:

1. *Is Scripture necessary?* The answer is, Yes! (sec. 1). It is necessary because (1) there is an insufficiency in natural revelation; and (2) supernatural revelation has ceased. Nature can tell you about the power of God but not the salvation of God. For that, Scripture revelation is necessary. Special revelation ensures that what we have written is exactly what God intended us to have. It is infallible. Anything outside special revelation is fallible. The emphasis in sec. 1 that God's way of revealing Himself formerly have ceased has implications for the question of the charismatic special gifts. It has an implication of the cessation of such charismata.

2. *What is the nature of Scripture?* It is defined in terms of the Old Testament and the New Testament as we now have them. This is made perfectly clear by the listing of the canonical books accepted as the Protestant Scriptures (sec. 2). These are the inspired Scriptures (secs. 2, 8). The Bible is not to be treated as any other type of human literature, for it is perfectly distinguishable from all other human literature (sec. 3). This, incidentally, was one of the serious flaws in the changing attitudes to the Scriptures in the 19th Century Presbyterian Churches. It sounded very plausible that the Bible books should be approached with the same critical apparatus as the literary criticism of secular literature. That was fatal. It undermined the very foundation of the theological enterprise. The Higher Critics especially were like George slaying the

dragon through its heart. That is what they did with the Bible. The 20th century, on the continent – where the Higher Critical views were spawned – and in Britain and America, has consequently and not surprisingly seen the rapid demise of the outward visible Church which became dominated by liberal views based upon a deconstructed Bible. That was a departure from the solidity and stability of the *Confession's* doctrine of Scripture, the only bulwark against such deviant views as emerged trough the Higher Critics (Charles A. Briggs in the USA and A. B. Davidson/William Robertson Smith in Britain were decisive influences in that downgrade). "William Robertson Smith," wrote Edward Young, "...sought to accomplish the impossible task of reconciling the newer views of Wellhausen...with the doctrine of inspiration stated in the first chapter of the Westminster Confession of Faith."[8] The battle ground for orthodoxy has most certainly been the doctrine of Scripture.[9] As R. L. Dabney aptly commented: "No fair man doubts but that the *Confession of the Free Church*, Chap. 1, sec. 2, means to assert what Mr. Smith distinctly impugned touching the Old Testament canon. It is no new thing, indeed, in church history, to find the advocates of latitudinarian views raising this false issue"[10]

3. *What are the characteristics of Scripture?* First of all, there is the matter of (1) *Authority* (sec. 4). There are 4 aspects to the

---

[8] E J Young, *Thy Word is Truth*, London, 1963, 194. Perhaps this is not so self-evident. The *Confession* does not specifically state, for example, the Mosaic authorship of the Pentateuch. There is no doubt, however, that the Mosaic authorship of the first five books is a crux, given what the New Testament states (see Matthew 19:8; Luke 16:31; 24:27, 44; John 1:17; 5:46; Acts 28:23; Romans 10:5; 2 Corinthians 3:15).

[9] Reference may be made to the interesting books of Eta Linnemann who wrote a couple of devastating critiques of the Higher Critical methodology: *Historical Criticism of the Bible* (Kregel, 1990), and *Biblical Criticism on Trial* (Kregel, 1990). See also Nigel Cameron's *Biblical Higher Criticism and the Defense of Infallibilism in 19th Century Britain* (Edwin Mellen, 1987), and the recent brief 'essay' of Peter Barnes, *A Handful of Pebbles* (Banner of Truth, 2008).

[10] R L Dabney, *Discussions: Evangelical and Theological*, London, 1967, Vol. I, 401.

authority of the Bible according to the Confession: (a) there are *external* evidences (incomparable excellencies and entire perfection); (b) there are *internal* evidences (its heavenliness of matter, doctrine, style, consistency, scope and perfections); (c) there is the witness of the Holy Spirit; and (d) there is the testimony of the Church (an important factor in *confirming* the canon of Scripture). This makes the Word *self-authenticating*. Scripture testifies its own divine origin. There is internal coherence and excellence (sec. 5). Secondly (2) *Completeness*. There is a full sufficiency in Scripture for faith and worship (sec. 6). It is therefore a protection from mere human standards and philosophies and teachings. Thirdly, (3) *Perspicuity*. Scripture is clear (sec. 7). Especially is this important in relation to salvation itself. No doubt there is a range of styles and literature in Scripture – the Lord did use men as His penmen – so that some places are harder to understand than others, as Peter himself concedes about Paul's writings (2 Peter 3:16). However, no special priestly function is necessary, albeit there is a role for preaching, as expounding the truth of Scripture in a direct and challenging way. After all, the Holy Spirit is promised as helper, not least in enabling understanding of the truth.

4. *How do we use Scripture?* In sec. 8 the Confession addresses the question of the justification for translations, but it also makes statements about the original languages. In connection with the original texts it maintains that "by His singular care and providence" the texts were "kept pure in all ages." This was no doubt something they attributed to the New Testament 'received text.' It seems to have passed notice that this principle has been rather overturned by the textual theories developed concurrently with the Higher Critical ones in the 19th century

(principally by Westcott and Hort[11]). Though the two issues are not the same, there is still a subjectivism in the 'lower' criticism not altogether dissimilar to the subjectivism of the 'higher' criticism.[12] In the opening chapter the *Confession* also lays down some basic steps in interpreting Scripture. Scripture is to interpret Scripture. To elucidate the meaning of any one part the student will compare Scripture with Scripture. This principle arises from the basis of Scripture as non-contradictory (sec. 9). The Scriptures in addition are to be the basis for the resolution of controversies in the church (sec. 10). We have focussed on the opening chapter of the *Confession* because it is so crucial to the whole issue of theological reflection as well as authority in the Church.

5. The Question of adopting a Confession

A Church has both a right and a necessity to declare the truth. In pursuit of this it has the duty and power to adopt a summary of its doctrine in a form of a Confession as a standard, subordinate to Scripture as the supreme standard. In this way the Church establishes the standard of orthodoxy and terms of communion for office-bearers and members. Not that members will affirm the creed directly. But indirectly the creed will act as a standard of Christian faith and life, and therefore a standard for admission to ordinances will be established. There are good Scriptural grounds for a Church to do this. James Bannerman suggested 3 examples which warrant such action by the post-Apostolic Church:

---

[11] Modern textual theories were pioneered by B F Westcott (1825-1901) and F J A Hort (1828-1892) in the last quarter of the 19th century. These Anglican scholars were essentially the architects of the modern critical text and the departure from the traditional text which had hitherto been the basis of Bible translations since the Reformation.

[12] Dr Jakob van Bruggen's *The Ancient Text of the New Testament* (Premier Publishing, 1976) provides a scholarly and stimulating 'corrective' to the predominant anti-textus receptus position that has almost completely dominated textual critical studies in the period since the mid-19th century.

1. In the writings of the Apostle John there is clearly a desire to determine the orthodox view of Jesus Christ as the divine Son (see John 1:14; 1 John 4:2-3);
2. In Paul's writings there is a clear concern to state and defend truth, as, for example, in 1 Corinthians 15 in the case of the matter of the resurrection of Christ in particular and the general resurrection in consequence;
3. In the Acts of the Apostles chapter 15 there is the case of the 'Jerusalem Assembly' which convened to establish doctrine and practice.[13]

These instances show the necessity to state or re-state truth over against error, something motivating the best Creeds and Confessions. It is important to do this, although not now infallibly it is true, because many Churches will claim to believe the Bible though their positions are greatly at odds with one another, e.g., the evangelical Arminians or Wesleyans, and even Roman Catholics. Therefore, the Church has a duty to state the truth of Scripture doctrine as an assurance to its members in maintaining the unity of the body of those having the same convictions. In addition, this arises from the necessity of a church to bear clear witness to the world of just what it believes, and that what it believes derives from Scripture teaching.

6. The Question of Subscription and adherence to the Confession

The maintenance of orthodoxy in Churches relates to three particular concerns:

1. The adoption of a soundly Biblical and Reformed subordinate standard with due emphasis on the nature, authority, and sufficiency of Scripture as the supreme standard;
2. The adoption of a form of subscription which is clear and unqualified; and,
3. The willingness to apply sanctions to any evident deviation from the doctrine, worship, and government of the Church through properly applied Church discipline.

The movement of a Church in a liberal direction occurs either (1) through revision of the standards to modify the teaching to make it

---

[13] James Bannerman, *The Church of Christ*, Edinburgh 1960 [1869], 291ff.

more acceptable to prevailing opinion; or (2) through relaxation of ordination vows to allow 'liberty of opinion' on major (or minor) teachings of the standards. It is conceivable for there to be a revision of a creed in order to tighten up certain truths or elaborate on things thought not to be adequately dealt with in the standards. It is also conceivable to change the ordination position with a view to making it tighter. The latter is rarer, however, than the pressures for relaxation.

In Scottish Presbyterianism there never has been any revision of the *Westminster Confession of Faith* itself. The pressures for change in Scottish Presbyterianism have come from two angles:

1. Changes to the ordination vows or forms of subscription; and/or,
2. Adoption of official declarations which have effectively relaxed subscription and taken the sting out of any trials for doctrinal heresy.

The vital things in maintaining faithfulness to the creed is an unqualified subscription and an honesty and sincerity on the part of all ministers and elders in affirming the Church *Confession* subordinately to Scripture as an expression of their own faith. Trials in Churches have invariably arisen when reservations arise and are allowed to remain unaddressed.

In the smaller conservative Presbyterian Churches in Scotland such as the Free Church of Scotland, the Free Presbyterian Church of Scotland and the Free Church of Scotland (Continuing), the form of subscription is both *unqualified* and *personal*. The probationers at their licensing and all office-bearers at their admission affirm that they "do hereby declare, that I do sincerely own and believe the whole doctrine contained in the Confession of Faith, approven by former General Assemblies of this Church to be the truths of God; and I do own the same as the confession of my faith; as likewise I do own the purity of worship presently authorised and practised in the Free Church of Scotland, etc."[14] The phrase about owning the same as the confession

---

[14] *The Practice of the Free Church of Scotland*, [8]1995, 153-4. It may be noted that the wording of the question put to *Probationers* before licensing in the Free Church of Scotland is:

of personal faith is an important one in committing the minister and other office-bearers in a personal way to the Church's Confession as their own. The implication is that there ought to be no reservations about any of the doctrine of the Confession.

7. The Erosion of Confessional Subscription in Scottish Presbyterianism

This form of subscription, or 'Formula,' is what was adopted in the Scottish Church in 1711 (Act X). It involves no liberty to depart from the Confessional standard, allowing no verbal or written qualifications. In the history of the Scottish Church there were, however, pressures to modify this, but invariably with a view to relaxation, or allowing some qualifications to be held without threat to the minister's standing in the Church. Though erosion of commitment to the Westminster standards was evident in the Secession Churches of the late 18th Century in Scotland it was not until the Union of the two Associate Synods of the New Light Burghers and Anti-Burghers in 1820 that real change in subscription was engineered.

(1) On the one hand, an article of the union stated disapproval of statements in the subordinate standards that taught or may be thought to teach, "compulsory or persecuting and intolerant principles of religion."[15] This appeared to have reference to the Confession's teaching on the Civil Magistrate.[16] However, that was not specified and it may be understood how some might apply this qualification to Confessional matters such as God's eternal decree which spoke of the predestination of some to eternal life and the foreordination of others

---

"Do you sincerely own and believe the *whole doctrine of the Confession of Faith* &c." omitting the words 'contained in' (ibid, 151). This is probably a typographical error, though it perhaps indicates that the inclusion of 'contained in' is not intended to make any substantive difference to the meaning of the requirement. The form of the question ('whole doctrine of') is found in the earliest post-1843 copies of the Free Church Standards.

[15] Reference may be made to Ian Hamilton's useful historical study of creed subscription, *The Erosion of Calvinist Orthodoxy*, Edinburgh 1990 (²2010).

[16] See Chapters 23 and 31:2.

to everlasting death (3:3); or the implication of limited atonement (8:8); or the reference to 'elect infants, dying in infancy' (10:3).

(2) More serious, on the other hand, was the part of the new formula which asked: "Do you acknowledge the Westminster Confession of Faith, with the Larger and Shorter Catechisms, as the confession of your faith, expressive of the sense in which you understand the Scriptures." This was a shift from the former adherence to the "whole doctrine" contained in the Confession. Because office-bearers could take it in this way: that they were not obliged to believe the 'whole doctrine' contained in the Confession, but only regard it as "an exhibition of the sense in which the Scriptures are to be understood."[17] In a real sense, as Hamilton maintains in his study of 'Seceders and Subscription in Scottish Presbyterianism,' this was a 'toe in the door' of relaxation. By the Union of the United Secession and Relief Churches in 1847 (to form the United Presbyterian Church of Scotland) the question was: "Do you sincerely acknowledge the Westminster Confession and the Larger and Shorter Catechisms as an exhibition of the sense in which you understand the Holy Scriptures." This was quite far removed from an unqualified subscription and was an indicator of theological downgrade which came to fruition in the Declaratory Act adopted in that Church in 1879.[18]

In both the Declaratory Acts of 1879 in the United Presbyterian Church, and 1892 in the Free Church the relaxation of ordination vows was consummated in the now infamous terms (more or less the same in both cases), "That while diversity of opinion is recognised in this Church on such points in the Confession as do not enter into the substance of the Reformed Faith therein set forth, this Church retains full authority to determine, in any case which may arise, what points fall within this description, and thus to guard against any abuse of this liberty to the detriment of sound doctrine, or to the injury of her unity

---

[17] Hamilton, op. cit., 18.
[18] Ian Hamilton in Appendices 'B' and 'C' respectively provides the content of the Declaratory Acts of the United Presbyterians (1879) and the Free Church (1892). See, *The Erosion of Calvinist Orthodoxy*, 192ff.

and peace." This is as wide a concession as can be imagined given that there is no definition of what exactly enters into the substance of the Reformed Faith. Nor is there any clear statement of what exactly 'sound doctrine' is to be taken to be. Basically, what became accepted was authoritarianism in Church law: the Church arbitrarily determines what is and what is not acceptable.

This was a huge step in the take-over by modernism in the Church. Such a take-over usually takes the same route:

- (1) establish a solid base for liberal scholarship in the divinity faculties;
- (2) plead for toleration of 'diversity' in order to avoid sanctions for deviations from doctrine or practice so that 'heresy trials' become impossible; and
- (3) by adopting a basically authoritarian principle of Church law and focussing on the 'unity and peace' of the Church the way is open eventually to *exclude* conservatives.

That is how a Church is destroyed as a spiritual force from within. In the sad subsequent history of the mainline Presbyterian Churches in Scotland (and elsewhere[19]) the result has been ambiguity and uncertainty about exactly what the Church believes. This has consequently had an impact on standards for membership. Membership invariably becomes nominalised in the wake of the downgrade of Biblical authority through the acceptance of critical processes and the downgrade of historic and experiential Calvinism. Such Calvinistic orthodoxy will only be substantially retained through an honest unqualified adherence to the whole doctrine contained in the Confession (as still found in the smaller conservative Presbyterian Churches): Confessional subscription is a crux in maintaining orthodoxy.

---

[19] See e.g. Gary North's monumental *Crossed Fingers* (Tyler, Texas, 1996) on 'How the Liberals Captured the Presbyterian Church' (i.e. in the United States of America).

Further Reading:

James Benjamin Green, A Harmony of the Westminster Presbyterian Standards, *Collins World, 1976 [1951]*

J R De Witt, Jus Divinum. The Westminster Assembly and the Divine Right of Church Government, *Kampen, J H Kok, 1969*

Robert S Paul, The Assembly of the Lord, *Edinburgh: T&T Clark, 1985*

John L Carson and David W Hall (editors), To Glorify and Enjoy God (A Commemoration of the Westminster Assembly), *Edinburgh: Banner of Truth, 1994*

Ian Hamilton, The Erosion of Calvinist Orthodoxy, *Fearn, Ross-shire: Christian Focus, 2010*

Carl R Trueman, The Creedal Imperative, *Wheaton, Ill: Crossway, 2012*

J V Fesko, The Theology of the Westminster Standards, *Wheaton, Ill: Crossway, 2014.*

SECTION C

THE CHURCH
ITS WORSHIP

WORSHIP

1. The Regulative Principle[1]

1. Introduction – What regulates a Church's forms of worship?

All Christian Churches are regulated in one way or another. It might be expected that all Churches would at least claim to be regulated by the Scriptures. In many instances, however, Churches have deviated from the Scriptures as their rule of doctrine and practice. In the history of the Church this has become a particular focus of discussion and differences. What requires to be examined is how Churches have developed and applied a 'regulative principle,' particularly on the question of worship.

Most Churches would hold to some sort of Biblical authority behind their government and practice. However, under various social and secularist pressures the application of Biblical authority in Church life has diminished or been modified in most 'main-line' Churches. The higher critical movement, which arose in the mid-nineteenth century, produced considerable pressure for a change in the Church's view of Biblical authority, a pressure continued through the twentieth century and into the twenty-first century both in Old Testament and New Testament studies. Consequently, the Bible was reckoned not to be sufficient to provide an exclusive source for doctrine and government in the Church. If a Church does not accept the full inspiration and sufficiency of the Bible as God's Word, this will have a profound effect on how it will regulate its affairs. The regulative principle thus adopted will be influenced by man-centred considerations and perhaps even by largely social or political concerns.

---

[1] This chapter, and the two that follow, are taken from the author's *Sing the Lord's Song* (1994, 2003). The material has been slightly edited.

2. Is this a matter of indifference?

At the same time there are some who do accept the inspiration and authority of the Bible in an orthodox sense and yet do not consider that the Bible provides sufficient materials for the regulation of worship and government in the Church. Many churchmen of a conservative evangelical standpoint maintain that the Church is largely to be left to its own discretion in these areas of Church practice. They may even point to a section of the *Westminster Confession of Faith* for support: 'there are some circumstances concerning the worship of God, and government of the Church, common to human actions and societies, which are to be ordered by the light of nature, and Christian prudence, according to the general rules of the Word, which are always to be observed' (1:6).

What is referred to there, however, are circumstances *common to human actions and societies*. The worship of God, and most specifically its content, the form of Church Government, and the offices and sacraments of the Church, are, however, the *distinctives* of the Church and hardly 'common to human actions and societies'! The *Confession* at that point simply refers to some outward circumstances, such as times and places of services, Church records and buildings, Church finances and the like. So the question of a Church's stated, or implicit, regulative principle is of far-reaching significance, not least in the matter of determining the content of praise, an area in which denominational peculiarities, distinctives or prejudices will find expression, as the variety of Hymn Books produced reflecting denominational distinctives demonstrates.

3. What 'regulative principle' is found in Scripture?

The question, therefore, needs to be asked: What is the Church's regulative principle? Is it sound? Is it Biblical? What are the practical implications of this for the Church's government and worship? The Churches of the Old and New Testaments were to be regulated in their government and worship, as well as in their doctrine. They were regulated by God's express will. To go beyond the revealed will of God was found to be perilous, as Nadab and Abihu found (Leviticus 10:1-3); as King Saul found (1 Samuel 13:13-14); as King Solomon found (1 Kings 11:9-11); as Israel found (Ezekiel 5:5-8; Malachi 2:1-17); as the Pharisees in Jesus' day found (Mark 7:6-13); as Dives found (Luke 16:19-31, especially vv 29-31); and as so many of the Churches spoken of in the Book of Revelation found (Chapters 2 and 3). The particular law in focus, expressive of the word and will of God, was the Decalogue – the Ten Commandments. The common factor was the violation of the will of God in connection with His worship. It was violation, essentially, of the second commandment (Exodus 20:4-6). Worship was not to be set up according to man's desires, but according to the express commandments of God. That this is not a strange principle in the New Testament context is sufficiently shown in a passage such as Matthew chapter 15, verse 9, in which Jesus draws on the prophet Isaiah in dealing with the hypocrites who subverted the commandments of God through their additions. Paul, similarly, in his letter to the Colossians, contrasts the commandments of God and the commandments of men in relation to the devotional life (see Colossians 2:20-23). The word and will of God, then, are to be paramount! That is the consistent message of Old and New Testaments. In the older covenant the principle was 'keep my commandments' (Exodus 20:4-6). 'Whatever I command you, be careful to observe it; you shall not add to it nor take away from it' (Deuteronomy 12:32). There were blessings attaching to obedience: as Moses found (Deuteronomy 4:1-2, 39-40); as Noah found (Genesis 6:22; 7:5-7; cf. Hebrews 11:7); as the Children of Israel found (Jeremiah 7:23-24). The last chapter of the book of Exodus is a model of the Old Testament regulative principle.

In the New Testament, too, we find a similar attitude. In His teaching on prayer the Lord Jesus Christ includes the petition 'Thy will be done, on earth as it is in heaven' (Matthew 6:10; Luke 11:2). Furthermore, Jesus gives commission to His disciples to go into the world with the gospel message. He spells out their task: "teaching them to observe *all things whatsoever I have commanded you*" (Matthew 28:20). He says, "if ye love me, keep my commandments" (John 14:15; cf. John

15:14; 1 John 5:3). In other words, the regulative principle of the New Testament Church is very much of a type with that of the Old Testament. The New Testament Church is to comply with the Saviour's stated wishes. To help in this the Holy Spirit was sent to the Church, to represent Christ, to extend the Kingdom (John 3:3, 5), to ensure the completion of the Scriptures, and to enable subsequent generations to understand and comply with them (cf. John 14:26; 16:7-8; Acts 2:33). It is significant that at the close of the canon of Holy Scripture there is a warning, a regulative principle (Revelation 22:18-19; cf. Deuteronomy 4:1-2). The New Testament contains clear principles and regulations governing the life of the Christian Church. There are principles and regulations, for example, in connection with office bearers (Acts 6:1-7; 1 Timothy 3:1-13 [cf. 4:11 and 5:21]; Titus 1:5-9 &c.); in connection with the Lord's Supper (Matthew 26:26-30; 1 Corinthians 11:23-34); in connection with Paul's teaching (see 1 Corinthians 2:12-16; Galatians 1:12). The over-riding concern is to know and do the will of the Lord.

4. How does this principle apply today?

The responsibility of the Christian Church today, no less than in the first century of the Christian era, is to conform to the revealed will of God. It is intended that the Church be based upon "the foundation of the apostles and prophets, Jesus Christ himself being the chief cornerstone" (Ephesians 2:20). Therefore, the will of Christ is paramount. It is true that the Bible requires to be properly interpreted and that differences can arise in that connection. It is necessary that the principles of the Scriptures be grasped as clearly as possible, with sincerity and a good conscience (Romans 14:5). A Church's regulative principle in Christian faith and life by and large will be determined by a combination of the following factors: (1) the perceived *authority* of the Bible; (2) the acceptance of the *sufficiency* of Scripture; and (3) the application of a sound Biblical *method of interpretation*.

5. What regulative principle should apply in the Church?

A Church or body of professing Christians with a weak view of the authority of the Bible and its sufficiency, or a liberal and critical approach to Scripture, will have a very different pattern of doctrine and worship from a Church or body of professing Christians which has a high view of Scripture and its sufficiency. What interests us here is how such views have affected the development of praise materials adopted within Churches. Two main views have arisen, at least within evangelical Protestantism.

(1) *The Lutheran or Anglican view*. The view of the regulative principle associated with the Lutheran or Anglican outlook is one which basically maintains that anything may be admitted to the worship or practice of the Church provided it is not *forbidden* or *proscribed* by the Word of God. In one form or another this is the predominant view in the Church today. This broader or looser view is expressed, for example, in Article XX of the *39 Articles of the Church of England* (1571) which states that: 'The Church hath power to decree Rites or Ceremonies, and authority in Controversies of Faith: And yet it is not lawful for the Church to ordain anything that is contrary to God's word written.' In other words, anything may be admitted provided it is not prohibited. It will be recognized how far-reaching this principle might be. For example, as Professor Petticrew put it in 1902, accepting this idea would allow such things as, "the sign of the cross in Baptism ... bowing to the East, the wearing of symbolical vestments, the lighting of wax candles in churches in the daytime, the ceremonial use of incense, holy water ... the elevation of the host, &c, &c, for *none* of these things is *expressly forbidden* in Scripture."[2] One can see how this broad principle could be the occasion, not only of the addition of all sorts of things not commanded in the Bible, but also of a serious imposition on people's consciences. No one can be bound by anything which is not entirely Biblical. This do-what-is-not-forbidden approach really states that what the Church says, either as a denomination, or for that matter as a local

---

[2] Professor Petticrew, *Psalm Singers' Conference*, Belfast, 1903, 68.

congregation, goes. It is hard to see how this does not amount to the imposition of commandments of men (cf. Matthew 15:6, 9; Mark 7:6-13; Colossians 2:18-23).

(2) *The Reformed or Calvinistic view.* This view states that only what is *prescribed* in the word of God is warranted. This was the approach of the Reformed Churches. It maintains that the Church is bound by what God has been pleased to reveal in the Holy Scriptures. Needless to say this implies a high view of Scripture and its sufficiency and application in all matters of faith and worship. The *Westminster Confession of Faith* (1647) expresses this well, when it declares that, 'it pleased the Lord, at sundry times, and in divers manners, to reveal Himself, and to declare that His will unto His Church; and afterwards, for the better preserving and propagating of the truth, and for the more sure establishment and comfort of the Church against the corruption of the flesh, and the malice of Satan and of the world, to commit the same wholly unto writing: which maketh the Holy Scripture to be most necessary; those former ways of God's revealing His will unto His people being now ceased' (1:1). The implication of this, as it applied to worship, was seen to be that, 'the acceptable way of worshipping the true God is instituted by Himself, and so limited by His own revealed will, that He may not be worshipped according to the imaginations and devices of men, or the suggestions of Satan, under any visible representation, or any other way not prescribed in the holy Scripture' (21:1). This is in perfect agreement with the regulative principle evident in the Scriptures themselves and outlined above. The principle is well stated by the outstanding Scottish Reformed theologian, William Cunningham (1805-1861): "The Calvinistic section of the Reformers...were of the opinion that there are sufficiently plain indications in Scripture itself, that it was Christ's mind and will, that nothing should be introduced into the government and worship of the church, unless a positive warrant for it could be found in Scripture. This principle was adopted and acted upon by the English Puritans and the Scottish Presbyterians; and we are persuaded that it is the only true and safe principle applicable to this matter." As far as the implications of this principle are concerned,

Cunningham goes on to point out that, "if it were fully carried out, [it] would just be to leave the church in the condition in which it was left by the apostles, in so far as we have any means of information; a result, surely, which need not be very alarming, except to those who think that they themselves have very superior powers for improving and adorning the church by their inventions."[3]

6. What about freedoms allowed in the New Testament?

There are two points raised by advocates of non-canonical praise materials which are felt to qualify the more rigorous application of the regulative principle.

(1) *The analogy with prayer and preaching.* It is maintained by some that as there is freedom allowed in the New Testament in preaching and in prayer, by analogy freedom ought to be allowed also in the use of suitable songs of human composition. Each element, however, must have its own warrant from the Word of God. The requirements for these different elements of worship services are not identical. What distinguishes the singing of praise from prayer and preaching is this: (1) there is clear precedent (and therefore warrant) for 'free' prayer and preaching[4]; and, (2) as in its nature the singing of praise is something that engages *all* the worshippers it therefore must involve a form (or 'canon') of material in which *all* can engage without any violation of conscience. This is implicit in Paul's reference to materials of praise in Ephesians 5:19 and Colossians 3:16, i.e., he is referring to a specific body of songs.

In a 'Memorial' in answer to a Report in favour of the introduction of uninspired hymns presented to the General Assembly of the Free Church of Scotland in 1869 at the height of the 'hymns controversy' in that Church, Professor James MacGregor effectively deals with the argument based on the analogy with prayer and preaching. The

---

[3] W. Cunningham, *The Reformers and the Theology of the Reformation*, London, 1967 (1862), pp.31-32.
[4] See, for example, 1 Timothy 2:1-2 and Acts 20:36 in relation to prayer, and 2 Timothy 4:2, Hebrews 4:2, and Acts 17:1-4 in relation to preaching.

'analogy' of praise with prayer and preaching, maintained MacGregor, merits the *opposite* conclusion to the one given in the *Report*. How so? Well, for one thing, because if they really are parallel, then it would follow that if we have a *form* for hymns (from outside the canon of Scripture), then we should have a form for public preaching and praying, so that our public praying and preaching may be of a piece with our congregational song. For another thing, in any case the functions can in fact be contrasted. After all, 'free' prayer and preaching are possible in their nature, whereas 'free' praise is not possible because everyone has to sing from some source book all at the same time. Unlike prayer and preaching praise can thus *never* be 'free' in the sense *they* are or can be! There is also a contrast, it has to be said, in *Scriptural warrant*. Of warrant for man-inspired song there is no evidence, though for prayer and preaching there is abundant warrant. There is a contrast in these exercises in terms of Biblical provision. Material for congregational praise is provided for. This is not the case with prayer or preaching, albeit there are recorded prayers and sermons in Scripture (or at least parts thereof). Prayer and preaching will always be adapted to the changing exigencies of man's experience, whereas the praise materials relate to the God who is worshipped, who is the same, yesterday and today and forever.[5]

Whatever the merits of non-inspired materials, they are after all not immediately inspired by the Lord. One can never say, 'these were given by the Lord for the use of all Christian worshippers'. The fact is that God has given a manual or Book of Praises in the Psalms. Is it not presumptuous to impose some other 'canon' of sung praise which in the final analysis is not God's Word? In their nature prayer and preaching are 'free.' The praise, however, is akin to the reading of Scripture. In its nature it must be a fixed manual. Just as we would not expect Scripture reading in Public Worship to be supplanted by

---

[5] The 'Memorial' of Professor MacGregor was reprinted under the title *Professor MacGregor on Hymns*, in *The Watchword*, a periodical edited by James Begg, August 2, 1869, 210-215. MacGregor was Professor of Systematic Theology at New College, Edinburgh, 1868-1881.

readings from the works of mere men, by the same token we should not expect the congregational songs to be other than God-given songs.

(2) *The demands of the expansion of revelation.* Some will say that the expansion of revelation in the New Testament justifies the extension of praise beyond what we have in the Old Testament. However, as John Murray pointed out: "We have no evidence either from the Old Testament or from the New that the expansion of revelation received expression in the devotional exercises of the church through the singing of uninspired songs of praise. This is a fact that cannot be discounted."[6] It is suggested that some hymns can express truth better than the psalms, especially in relation to the themes of the gospel.[7] This implies that somehow man has to make up what God has left out, namely, produce song based on New Testament material. But who decides which of such materials are, and which are not, to be used by the whole Church? This is not only potentially destructive of uniformity of worship, but also of unity in worship. The giving of the Spirit at Pentecost did make a profound difference in the Church. But it is presumptuous to imply from this that there is thus a competence given to the Church to add non-canonical materials for congregational song. There was new revelation, inscripturated in the New Testament, though, significantly, *no separate manual of praise.* It is interesting that in the post-resurrection appearance of Christ to the disciples on the road to Emmaus (Luke 24:13-35) Jesus at one point rebukes them as "O fools, and slow in heart to believe all that the prophets have spoken: ought not Christ to have suffered these things, and to enter into his glory?" (vv25-26). To this is added: "And beginning at Moses and all the prophets, he expounded unto them in all the scriptures the things concerning himself" (v27).

---

[6] J Murray and W Young, *Minority Report of the Committee on Song in the Public Worship of God,* Orthodox Presbyterian Church, 1947, 19.

[7] See, for example, I H Murray, *The Psalter – The Only Hymnal?* Edinburgh, 2001, 24-27. For a review article of this work see, J W Keddie, 'The Psalter – The Only Hymnal?' in, *Free Church Witness,* December 2001, 6-7.

The New Testament is, of course, very necessary. The Spirit's coming did shed light on the meaning of the Old Testament. But this does not mean we have to resort to uninspired materials of praise in congregational song. The Spirit will most certainly enable the people of God not to be 'slow in heart' to understand Christ in all the Psalms! Properly understood the Psalms do, we maintain, constitute a sufficient volume for praise for the Christian Church. The Psalms were given by Christ, and may all be understood to speak of Him and His works. It is maintained, therefore, that Churches holding to the authority and sufficiency of the Bible as God's Word written, should apply the principle that 'what Scripture does not prescribe, it forbids.' This in turn will encourage the Church to look for warrant and provision in the matter of the content of its praises, and to be circumspect concerning anything that arises from mere human invention or taste. If the Church confined itself to what derives from Scripture precept or example it would have a perfectly adequate directory for worship and government. That is the sphere of its discretion. It is the consistent application of this principle which is the basis of our appeal – our regulative principle – for the use as song in public worship only of the songs of praise found in Holy Scripture.

WORSHIP

2. The Singing of Psalms: (1) General Principles

A. The Bible Psalms in Worship

The singing of praise to the Lord has been a feature of Church life from Old Testament times. Before even the specifications of the Tabernacle were revealed, there was an outpouring of inspired song to the Lord. The Exodus from Egypt drew out the Song of Moses (Exodus 15:1-18) and the Song of Miriam:

> Sing ye to the LORD,
> for he hath triumphed gloriously;
> the horse and his rider
> hath he thrown into the sea! (Exodus 15:21).

Through to the last book of the New Testament the redeemed of the Lord have a song to sing in His praise. Indeed, the song of the redeemed in glory is the song of Moses and the song of the Lamb (Revelation 15:3-4). In this way a link is forged between the first inspired song recorded in Scripture and the last! It can readily be recognized that song has always played an important part in the life of the Church of the Living God.

1. The Position of Psalms in Worship

Until relatively recently the inspired Psalms of Scripture enjoyed a position of prominence in the praises of the Church. These Songs of Zion in one form or another have encouraged, uplifted, instructed and inspired generations of earnest Christians. The Reformation of the sixteenth century saw a renewal in congregational Psalm singing, restoring a practice which prevailed in the early Church. Subsequently, especially in Presbyterian Churches, Metrical Psalms were more or less exclusively used in services of public worship. Today the situation is very different. The Psalms of Scripture have been largely displaced in modern Church worship. Patterns of worship are changing with baffling rapidity. Songs and hymns entirely of man's devising and composition have proliferated. It appears that anything goes in today's worship, in which there is a constant desire for something new. Worship services and evangelistic programs devote a significant amount of time to hymn and chorus singing. The Psalms of Holy Scripture seem to have been left well behind. Churches which have maintained Psalm singing are under pressure to change on the grounds that such praise today is regarded as a hindrance to people coming in to the Church.[1] Perhaps such praise may even be considered as 'restrictive' by some, or as not encouraging 'real' worship.

2. The situation in worship today

In all this flux in the area of the public worship of God it is easier to recognize what *men* deem desirable than to establish Biblical answers to such questions as: 'What does the Lord *warrant* in His worship?' 'Is the Bible clear on what we are to use in worship?' 'Do we really have to rely upon what is "modern," however that is to be measured, or by whomever it is to be determined?' To some degree it will be unavoidable that the *style* of a people's music will be moulded by cultural factors. But will that be true also of the *content*? Has the Lord not provided a manual of praise? These are important questions to ask. They will be considered briefly in this chapter and the one that follows. It is our conviction that Christian Churches should willingly adopt a God-centred, Scriptural 'regulative principle' applying to all aspects of

---

[1] An example here is the change that took place in the Free Church of Scotland in an Assembly of November 2010 in which liberty was given to congregations to sing hymns and use instrumental music in worship services. The relevant statement was given in the Free Church web-site: http://www.freechurch.org/index.php/scotland/news events item/worship statement/ (accessed 1st August 2014). Despite this 'permission' in 2010, the Free Church neither changed its ordination vows, which formerly committed its office bearers to 'purity of worship', nor did it adopt an authorised hymn book! Hitherto, in line with the position of the Church in 1843 as reaffirmed after 1900, the Free Church had been committed exclusively to inspired materials of praise, unaccompanied.

public worship, so that among other things materials used in sung praise have positive divine sanction.

3. A case for using only inspired materials of praise

The concern here is to demonstrate that in public worship there is warrant for the use in congregational song only of materials of direct divine inspiration. By 'materials of direct divine inspiration' is meant those writings which derive their content, thought, detail, truth and authority from the fact that they are the Word of God written, and are part of the canon of Holy Scripture, infallibly and inerrantly produced under the inspiration of the Spirit of God (cf. Hebrews 1:1; 2 Peter 1:21; 2 Timothy 3:16; Revelation 22:18-19). In other words, presupposed here is a high doctrine of Scripture and of the canon of Holy Scripture, as expressed for example in the *Westminster Confession of Faith*, Chapter 1. By 'uninspired' is meant all writings not part of the canon of Holy Scripture, however true to the Scriptures they may claim to be. It is our conviction that there is warrant for the use of the Book of Psalms in sung praise in the public worship of God. But what about other songs found in Scripture outside the Psalter?

4. The status of songs outside the Psalter

On the face of it, the use of other songs in Scripture outside the Psalter does not seem objectionable as the principle of adopting only inspired song is not violated. Yet our concern should be to use only what has divine sanction and approval. There is clear sanction for the Book of Psalms. Such sanction is not clear in connection with other songs found in Scripture. These may have been intended for a temporary or personal or national use, and in any case are found scarcely to express truths not already found in the Psalms. On this question the conclusion of John Murray in his *Minority Report of the Committee on Song in the Public Worship of God*, presented to the General Assembly of the Orthodox Presbyterian Church in 1947, is relevant on this point: "In view of the uncertainty with respect to the use of other inspired songs, we should confine ourselves to the Book of Psalms."

5. The question of Scripture Paraphrases[2]

It is granted that even within the Reformed tradition Bible materials other than the 150 Psalms, such as Scripture Paraphrases, have been used occasionally in Psalm-singing Churches. To this writer there are two main objections to the adoption of such materials. (1) *There is no clear warrant in Scripture for putting into verse for singing parts of the Bible not originally recorded in the form of song*; and (2) *it is rather presumptuous for any person or group of people to take upon themselves the responsibility for selecting passages to be adapted for singing*. After all, since the Lord has not caused such passages to be expressed in the form of songs nor indicated that such passages should be paraphrased for singing, by what authority do men take on such a responsibility?

In a comment on the continuing tradition of "unevangelical Moderatism" into the 19th Century, Principal John Macleod made a suggestive historical observation when he wrote with reference to the attitudes of the 'moderates' to the teaching of the Church's Confession [*Westminster Confession of Faith*]: "The Moderates had killed it largely by means of the Paraphrases." He adds: "These had helped to set aside the old metrical Psalter as the matter of public praise."[3] Paraphrases thus became a lever to dislodge commitment to exclusively and undisputed God-inspired and appointed items of praise. Once merely human compositions have been admitted into Church praise, historically the Psalms have tended to be displaced. Whatever else this may produce, it will tend radically to alter religious experience and piety from something God-centred to something directed by the fallible notions and experiences of men not immediately inspired by the Holy Spirit.[4]

---

[2] See John Keddie, 'The Paraphrases – An Historical Perspective,' in, *The Monthly Record of the Free Church of Scotland*, September 1983, 198-9, for a brief discussion of the issues involving the collection of 'Scottish Paraphrases' of 1781.

[3] John Macleod, *Scottish Theology in Relation to Church History since the Reformation*, Edinburgh, ²1946, 266. Macleod's reference is to the 'Scottish Paraphrases' finalised in 1781 in the Church of Scotland. The General Assembly, however, never did give them its full and formal authority. See Thomas Young, *The Metrical Psalms and Paraphrases*, London, 1909, 150.

[4] Between 2004 and 2010 there were discussions on worship in the Free Church of Scotland, the majority party in the division which occurred in the Free Church in 2000,

B. Controversial issues

In addressing the issue of what materials are appropriate vehicles for praise in the Christian Church many questions arise in people's minds, especially when the predominant position on the use of uninspired materials is questioned. At this point we will deal with some possible misunderstandings that arise, or objections that are often raised against confining the praise materials to Biblical Psalms.

1. Isn't this just a minority opinion?

Someone might say: 'This is a minority opinion nowadays. There must therefore be a presumption against this view. The vast majority of Christians surely can't be wrong.' What can one say about this argument? Obviously, there is no special virtue in holding a minority opinion. By the same token, however, minority opinion or practice is not necessarily wrong. It was a majority opinion in Israel that there should be a king to rule. Yet that did not seem to be right in God's eyes, nor good for the nation in the longer term (see 1 Samuel 8:1-22; 10:17-27; 15:10-35)! Majority opinion in Church history has often occasioned oppression or even tyranny. Majority opinion itself, therefore, and likewise any minority view, is to be subjected to the overriding consideration: What does God say? What is Scriptural (cf. Romans 4:3: Galatians 4:30)?

The truth is that Old Testament prophets and New Testament apostles were often called to counter majority opinion or practice. Mention of the prophet Jeremiah is sufficient to prove this point. Again

---

in relation to the use of uninspired materials of praise and of instrumental music. The issue was determined by a plenary Assembly held in Edinburgh on 18th and 19th November 2010, in which the dramatic decision was taken to depart from the previous practice and admit, according to the initiative of Kirk Sessions, both uninspired materials of praise and instrumental accompaniment. In this way the Acts anent Worship of 1905 and 1910 were repealed and enabling permissive legislation was introduced. The Free Church of Scotland (Continuing), the smaller party in the division of 2000, continued to be committed to the purity of worship principle formerly held in the Free Church of Scotland. Paraphrases are not used in any Free Church of Scotland (Continuing) congregations.

and again these men found themselves in a minority and frequently seemed to be standing alone for the claims of truth. Even the Lord Jesus Christ in His days on earth did not command majority support. Yet He was completely right. We should not make too much of where the majority stand. Nor should a minority practice be discounted simply because it may have little support. At the same time, it has to be said that the practice of congregational Psalm singing was itself once widespread, at least in the Reformed Churches. A review of modern hymnals reveals just how the praise materials of the modern Church largely date from the late eighteenth century. Whatever else may be said of this it is clear that by and large the praise materials of the majority of Churches today are neither apostolic in origin nor specifically commanded by God in his Word. In our estimation this raises serious questions for the modern hymn singer.

2. Were the hymn writers all wrong?

This question may then be raised: 'Are you saying that all these hymn writers, whose hymns have been so blessed among Christians, were wrong and out of step with the Lord?' The answer to this is an emphatic 'No!' The argument is *not* about whether it was right or wrong for this or that person to compose hymns and religious songs. It is not disputed that there are many hymns of outstanding poetic quality, doctrinal soundness and devotional sweetness. It is not disputed that hymns have been greatly blessed to many souls over the years. What is questioned is the warrant to use such hymns and songs of merely human composition in the formal and public worship of the Church. Although such compositions may contain excellent sentiments even the best of them fall short of being immediately inspired by God. In this connection 'inspired' refers specifically to what is canonical Scripture. It is true that some people will say that this or that hymn writer has surely been 'inspired' and has produced inspiring song. In a sense that may be correct, but not in the sense that there has been divine inspiration, an inspiration attributable only to the writers of the Holy Scriptures. This is a far more significant point than is usually recognised.

3. What about the question of blessing?

'If Psalm singing is so right, why aren't Churches maintaining that position more obviously blessed?' The matter of the praise materials of a Church is only one aspect of that Church's responsiveness to the Lord. There are many other important aspects of a Church's life and witness in which there must be obedience to the word and will of the Lord. Blessing will certainly be hindered where people or a Church fail to obey the Lord. Care has to be taken in claiming a particular cause and effect in the matter of blessing enjoyed within a Church or denomination. What can be said is that there is a relationship between the Lord's blessing and a people's faithfulness. We see this reflected, for example, in the call of Abraham (Genesis 12:1-3), when the Lord tells him to move to another land and adds a promise of blessing for himself and for the world as he responds to this call. But we have to be cautious here. For it may be that whilst a remnant is faithful, the Lord's displeasure against a generation is such that He refuses to bless, despite the presence of a Noah or a Daniel or a Job (cf. Ezekiel 14:12ff).

It can be maintained that the Church has enjoyed blessing and revival in periods when only Biblical Psalms were used in praise. A Psalm-singing Church will not lack the blessing of the Lord because it confines its praise materials to the Biblical Psalms. Lack of blessing in any Church will arise from deficiency somewhere in the work and outlook of that Church, perhaps even on account of a doctrinally diffuse and devotionally unbalanced hymnody.

4. Isn't this an unnecessarily divisive issue?

'Are there not far more important issues to be concerned about than arguing about psalms and hymns?' There is no doubt that there are other matters of serious and far-reaching importance confronting the Church. It is undeniably a priority within the Church to present the gospel to sinners that they might be saved and avoid a lost eternity. Mission must be in the forefront of the Church's task in the world: "Go therefore and make disciples of all the nations, baptizing them in the name of the Father and of the Son and of the Holy Spirit" (Matthew

28:19, NKJV). But there is more. The Great Commission itself does not end there. Jesus goes on to say: "teaching them to observe all things whatsoever I have commanded you: and lo, I am with you alway, even unto the end of the world" (v20). The Church is charged not only to evangelize, but also to instruct; to keep the word of Christ; to conform to His teaching and not, knowingly and willingly, to step beyond it, however much people may consider themselves competent to add to or improve upon what is there.

5. Is this not a relatively unimportant matter?
Whenever the question of the content of the Church's praise is raised it is not uncommon for people to suggest that it is a secondary matter. But is that right? The truth is that the great priority of the Christian Church in the broadest sense is the worship of God. What could be more important? Is it not the case that the order of the Church's priorities is this: first of all, the worship of God, secondly, the building up of the body of Christ, and thirdly, the proclamation of the gospel to those outside? These should *all* be found in significant measure in a living Church or congregation. But it stands to reason that if the first two elements mentioned are not right then there will be little effectiveness in the third. At the same time as it calls sinners to come faith in Jesus Christ, the gospel is calling people back to the true worship of God (cf. Revelation 14:6-7). In view of this it is a mistake to reckon the content of praise a matter, even relatively speaking, of indifference for the confessing Church.

It is also common for people to maintain that there is a hierarchy of priorities in the Scriptures. Some feel, for instance, that the demands of evangelism take precedence over such concerns as the principles or practices of worship. It is true no doubt that there are some things relatively more important than others in the life of the Christian Church as it is guided by the Word of God. But it is a mistake to think that there are demands in the Word of God so relatively unimportant that we can dispense with them, as if we can put aside certain things simply because we perceive them to be not so important in the Church's work or witness. It is dangerous for mere men to decide which parts of Scripture are necessary and sufficient, and which we can safely ignore or treat with relative indifference. It is for the Church, rather, to come *under* the teaching of Scripture as fully sufficient in all matters of faith *and* practice (cf. 2 Timothy 3:14-17). As the *Westminster Larger Catechism* puts it, in answer to the question, 'What is the word of God?' (Q3): "The holy scriptures of the Old and New Testament are the word of God, the only rule of faith and obedience." The *Confession of Faith* is explicit on this: "The whole counsel of God concerning all things necessary for His own glory, man's salvation, faith and life, is either expressly set down in Scripture, or by good and necessary consequence may be deduced from Scripture: unto which nothing at any time is to be added, whether by new revelations of the Spirit or traditions of men" (I:6).

It is all too easy to say that the matter of the specific praise materials is not central or foremost in the Church's concerns. Yet the Holy Scriptures contain a Book of 150 Psalms, clearly intended for praise among the people of God. It is an irony, no doubt, that in modern patterns of worship the praise element does tends to loom large as a matter of considerable significance. Nowadays worship services are increasingly taken up with praise and singing, and decreasingly with the proclamation of God's word. In all this people are being asked to engage in the worship of God! The words that are being taken up on people's lips ought to be pleasing to the Lord. That must, therefore, be a central concern. Consequently, it is important to enquire about the sufficiency of Scripture in the matter. Jesus put the Church's task in proper perspective when He said in the parable of the unjust steward that "he that is faithful in that which is least is faithful also in much: and he that is unjust in the least is unjust also in much" (Luke 16:10).

6. Isn't this a matter of the heart?

Someone may object: 'Does it matter so much what we're singing as long as it is not positively unsound? Isn't it the spirit that is important and not the letter?' There is some plausibility in this argument. Dead formalism in singing even the best materials is scarcely superior to singing with spiritual fervour songs not drawn from the Scriptures. A right attitude of worship cannot be automatically assumed simply because Bible songs are used. The Lord clearly desires the spiritual attitude expressed by the writer to the Hebrews: "By him [i.e. by Jesus] therefore let us offer the sacrifice of praise to God continually, that is, the fruit of our lips, giving thanks to his name" (Hebrews 13:15).

The issue, however, is not the attitude of the worshipper's heart. It is not doubted that people singing hymns of merely human composition may have a good spirit of worship and a real earnestness. The issue here is this: What materials for praise does the Lord desire His Church to use? What songs unquestionably have His approval, his sanction and his seal? An example from the Bible illustrates the point, that the spirit or heart of the thing is not the only, or even the primary consideration. When Aquila and Priscilla encountered Apollos at Ephesus they found him to be a man instructed in the way of the Lord and "fervent in spirit." He even taught accurately the things of the Lord, though, we are told, "he knew only the baptism of John." So what did Aquila and Priscilla do after they heard him preaching? "They took him aside and explained to him the way of God *more accurately*." They did not question his sincerity or fervency or even his general soundness. But they did make good his deficiencies in Christian ordinances (Acts 18:24-28; see also Acts 19:1-7 for a similar incident involving the Apostle Paul).

7. Doesn't the New Testament give greater liberties in the elements of worship?

It is true that there is relatively little said in the New Testament of the precise patterns of worship. It is also true that there is a certain continuity and discontinuity between the Testaments which is not easy to define. However, are there grounds for maintaining that differences between the Old and New Testaments might allow for the adoption of elements into our worship which the Lord has not prescribed in

Scripture? There are two passages of Jesus' teaching that bear powerfully on this question.

(1) First of all, in Mark 7 there is record of a debate between Jesus and the Pharisees. At issue were laws which the Pharisees superimposed upon the Biblical commandments, laws which they laid down for everybody simply on their own initiative and authority. In response Jesus quotes Isaiah 29:13: "This people honoureth me with their lips, but their heart is far from me. Howbeit in vain they worship me, teaching for doctrines the commandments of men" (vv6-7). In countering the attitudes and actions of the Pharisees, Jesus goes on to state that they were 'making the word of God of no effect' through their tradition which they had handed down – their tradition which had *no warrant from the word of God*! (v13). "In vain they worship me, teaching for doctrines the commandments of men." This shows rather clearly that, (i) Jesus was aware of *continuity* in this respect at least with the Old Testament; and, (ii) for the elements of the worship of God sanction is required from the word of God. There is no scope, according to the principle stated by the Lord here, for the introduction of elements of worship simply on the initiative and authority of men.

(2) The second passage in question is in John 4 in which there is recorded a conversation between the Lord Jesus Christ and an unnamed woman at the well of Sychar in Samaria. John 4:21-24, together with Jesus' general discussion with the woman, stress the need for *inwardness* in worship. However, in the terms Jesus states here, such worship is to be consonant with the nature of God: "the hour cometh, and now is, when the true worshippers shall worship the Father in spirit and truth: for the Father seeketh such to worship him." It must be inward, spiritual worship – from the heart; but it must also be according to truth: "God is a Spirit: and they that worship him must worship him in spirit and in truth." It must be consistent with His revealed will rather than according to the judgments of men, points powerfully made also in Colossians 2:18-23 and Romans 1:21-25. Incidentally, in this discussion at Sychar, Jesus is clearly aware of an element of *discontinuity* with the Old Testament, as he implies the disappearance or abrogation

of the Temple and its services, including the sacrifices, the priesthood, and the musical instrumentation associated with the Temple and its worship.

From this it can be maintained that in passing from the Old Testament to the New Testament, whatever discontinuity was involved, there is no evidence whatsoever that God has surrendered the right to determine acceptable worship. For the New Testament Church, too, the concern must be: What is sanctioned in the word of God?

8. Aren't you at odds with Christendom?

As an argument against using only materials of divine inspiration in congregational song it has been said that "the fact that it puts us out of step with the rest of Christendom and makes our praise sectarian."[5] What can one say about this argument? It is a remarkable statement. However, 'Christendom', a nebulous undefined entity, in reality has no uniformity of practice and can be said to represent a diffuse or confused picture. But 'Christendom' is not the standard in any case. The most important issue surely is: what is acceptable to the Lord? What is agreeable with the Word of God? What 'Christendom' thinks or practices is subordinate to these questions. Indeed, what 'Christendom's' practices and principles *are* may require wholesale reformation in the area of worship, or doctrine, as has often been the case in the past. Logically, the issue of being "out of step with Christendom" would have precluded the 16th Century Reformation! But the over-riding question is: Who is 'in step' with Scripture?

---

[5] Donald Macleod, "The Highland churches today," in, James Kirk (ed.), *The Church in the Highlands*, Scottish Church History Society, Edinburgh, 1998, 160.

Further Reading:

Besides the books listed in the Selected Reading List, there have been numerous books produced which in one way or another encourage the use of the Bible Psalms in the contemporary scene. The first three advocate a Psalms only position. The following may be noted:

Michael Bushell, Songs of Zion. The Biblical Basis for Exclusive Psalmody *(Norfolk Press, ⁴2011)*

Michael LeFebvre, Singing the Songs of Jesus *(Christian Focus, 2010)*

Joel R Beeke and Anthony T Selvaggio, Sing a New Song. Recovering Psalm Singing for the 21st Century *(Reformation Heritage Books, 2010)*

C Richard Wells & Ray Van Neste (Editors), Forgotten Songs. Reclaiming the Psalms for Christian Worship *(B&H Publishing, 2012)*

Gordon Wenham, The Psalter Reclaimed *(Crossway, 2013)*

Bruce K Waltke and James M Houston, The Psalms as Christian Worship *(Eerdmans, 2010)*

Bruce K Waltke, James M Houston & Erika Moore, The Psalms as Christian Lament *(Eerdmans, 2014)*

It may be noted, significantly, that these books were produced by six different publishers!

WORSHIP

3. The Singing of Psalms: (2) Scriptural Basis

A. Psalm Singing Commanded

Singing praise to the Lord is a distinct element in the worship of God. Naturally the question has to be asked: What does the Lord require of His Church in this regard? What has He commanded? What has He provided? Does this matter? At least in one respect there does not seem to be any doubt about what the Lord has provided and commanded in the matter of His praise. The Psalms of Scripture are to be sung by His people. There is ample evidence for this in the Psalms themselves, but also and not least, in the New Testament. We review the evidence briefly here:

1. There are the implications of the titles of the Psalms

There is no reason to believe that these titles are not of considerable antiquity and perfectly authentic. They appear to have been included with the Psalms during the time the Old Testament was in the making.[1] Thirty-four Psalms in the Hebrew text do not have a title, though in the Septuagint (or LXX) – the Greek translation of the Old Testament which was completed about 180 B.C. – only two lack titles. Whether or not these titles are to be considered part of the original inspired text is a matter of dispute, but as Edward J. Young points out, they "are to be regarded as trustworthy and of great value in determining the Psalm in question."[2] The New Testament writers would certainly have been familiar with the various Psalm titles. The fact that no fewer than 55

---

[1] D Kidner, *Psalms 1-72* (TOTC), Leicester, 1973, 32-33.
[2] E J Young, *An Introduction to the Old Testament,* London, 1964, 307.

Psalms are addressed 'to the Chief Musician' points eloquently to the purpose of the Psalms.

2. There are implications from the form of the Psalms.

For the greater part the poetry of the Psalms is characterized by a parallelism and rhythm of sense, rather than by the type of rhyming metres distinctive of Western poetry. However, the rhythmic structure of the Psalms was no doubt designed to be consistent with an underlying musical form. Derek Kidner explains that, "the poetry of the Psalms has a broad simplicity of rhythm and imagery which survives transplanting into almost any soil. Above all, the fact that its parallelisms are those of sense rather than of sound allows it to reproduce its chief effects with very little loss of either force or beauty. It is well fitted by God's providence to invite 'all the earth' to 'sing the glory of his name'."[3] This is a point, incidentally, which answers the problem some have with the translation of the Psalms into a metrical form for singing within our Western musical tradition.

3. There are the direct statements in the Psalms, and also from elsewhere in Scripture.

In Psalm 95: "Let us come before his presence with thanksgiving, and make a joyful noise to him with psalms" (v2). In Psalm 105: "Sing unto him, sing psalms unto him: talk ye of all his wondrous works" (v2). Besides this, in many Psalms there is encouragement to sing to the Lord with the words of the Psalms. Such encouragement is to be found in at least 37 Psalms.[4]

But even outside the Psalter there are clear enough indicators of the use of the Psalms by the worshippers. In 1 Chronicles 16 we find Psalms being sung when David placed the Ark of God in the Tabernacle. In Nehemiah 12, Psalms of thanksgiving were sung after the restoration and rebuilding of the walls of Jerusalem. These Psalms

---

[3] Kidner, op. cit., 4
[4] See, for example, Psalms 9, 30, 47, 68, 75, 81, 96, 104, 108, 138, 147, i.e., all sections of the Psalter are represented.

were led by appointed singers (see vv8 and 27). In the New Testament, too, there is clear encouragement to sing Psalms (cf. Ephesians 5:19; Colossians 3:16).

4. There are the implications of New Testament teaching.

The book of Psalms is frequently cited in the New Testament. To a significant degree New Testament theology and experience are derived from the Psalms. Jesus himself claimed this. He said when He appeared to His disciples after His resurrection: "all things must be fulfilled which were written in the Law of Moses and the Prophets and the Psalms concerning me" (Luke 24:44). This is how it can he said with truth and conviction that Christ is in all the Scriptures. Christ Himself did not just begin to exist at His conception in the womb of the virgin. He said of Himself: "Before Abraham was, I am" (John 8:58; cf. Colossians 1:15-18). It may be argued that some Psalms more directly and explicitly point to the Messiah or are more specifically applicable to Him.[5] Yet, as Professor Edmund Clowney, formerly of Westminster Theological Seminary, reminds us, "In their theological depth the psalms are songs of God's covenant and of the hope of the covenant. Since God's great work of salvation will be accomplished by the Son of David, the psalms are explicitly messianic."[6] Writing in 1859, Andrew Bonar was to say this about Christ in the Psalms: "Now, in the early ages, men full of the thoughts of Christ could never read the Psalms without being reminded of the Lord. They probably had no system or fixed theory as to all the Psalms referring to Christ; but still...they found their thoughts wandering to their Lord, as the one Person in whom these breathings, these praises, these desires, these hopes, these deep feelings, found their only true and full realization. Hence Augustine (Psa. lviii.) said to his hearers, as he expounded to them this book, that

---

[5] William Binnie, *The Psalms: Their History, Teachings, and Use*, London, 1886², 176ff. Binnie has a helpful discussion on the classification of what may be considered more specific Messianic Psalms.

[6] E P Clowney, 'Preaching Christ from all the Scriptures', in S T Logan, Jr. (Editor), *Preaching*, Welwyn, 1986, 188-189.

'the voice of Christ and his Church was well-nigh the only voice to be heard in the Psalms.'"[7]

There is no reasonable doubt that the Psalms are themselves essential Biblical praise – the song book of the Church, provided and inspired for that purpose. They were rich in their contemporary significance to Israel, as songs of history, inspiration and hope. But they are in a real sense even richer in Christological significance for the New Testament Church, which is, indeed, why they are so often quoted. In a real sense they are timeless. They are songs designed to be sung by God's people in every age and it must he counted a tragedy that so many Christian Churches today fail to use these canonical and covenantal songs of Scripture in the worship of God.

B. Textual Material

By textual material is meant those passages or verses of Scripture which have a bearing on the issue of Biblical praise. In looking at this material we have to ascertain which words and passages are perceived to be relevant, and why.

It must surely be agreed that the Lord has provided in the book of Psalms a song book, at the very least for the Church of the Old Testament. It also must surely be agreed that the Psalms, in view of the place given to them in the New Testament, continue to be appropriate materials for the worship of the Church of the New Covenant. But the question arises: Is there a command to sing songs of merely human composition? Is there *divine authority* to sing the hymns of Isaac Watts (1674-1748) or John Newton (1725-1807) or Charles Wesley (1757-1834) or Horatius Bonar (1808-1889), or other such hymn writers?

Advocates of non-canonical song will seek to find warrant for their songs somewhere in Scripture. A number of passages are appealed to in support of the use in congregational song of materials other than those

---

[7] Andrew Bonar, *Christ and His Church in the Book of Psalms*, London, 1859, ix.

found in Scripture itself. Passages claimed as hymn fragments in the New Testament are also cited by way of collateral support. We shall look at these passages of Scripture and our chief concern will be to ask whether they really do warrant the expansion of praise beyond the confines of the Bible's own praise book.

It should perhaps be said in this connection that there are several words in the Greek New Testament, which in English translation can give rise to misunderstandings. For example, the word translated 'hymn' does not necessarily mean in the New Testament context what the word has come to mean in common English usage. The relevant Greek words found in the New Testament in relation to song are the nouns *psalmos, humnos* and *ōdē,* and the verbs *humneō* and *psallō*. We will examine the New Testament references in which these words or their derivatives appear.[8]

1. Matthew 26:30; Mark 14:26 (ὑμνήσαντες, *humnēsantes*)

The disciples are gathered with Jesus for the Last Supper in the Upper Room. It is the Jewish Passover. We read that when they had sung a hymn *(humnēsantes)* they went out to the Mount of Olives. What was this 'hymn?' Commentators agree that this would have been one of the Hallel Psalms, from that group of Psalms from 113 to 118 commonly sung at the Passover.[9] *Humnēsantes* is an aorist active participle, which here indicates simply an action in the past. In this case the meaning is, roughly, 'having hymned.' It is from the verb *humneō,* which means simply 'to sing a hymn' or 'to sing praise.' Any of these Hallel Psalms would have been appropriate to Jesus on the threshold of His crucifixion. It is as if Jesus takes these words as His own prayer in the gathering storm of His final days and hours on earth. He pledges to keep His vows in the presence of all the people (Psalm 116:12-19); He

---

[8] Cf. G W Bromiley (Translator), *Theological Dictionary of the New Testament* (abridged in one volume), Exeter, 1985, 1225ff.
[9] Cf. R V G Tasker, *Matthew* (TNTC), London, 1961, 252; R A Cole, *Mark* (TNTC), London, 1961, 216; R T France, *Matthew* (TNTC), Leicester, 1985, 370; D Hill, *The Gospel of Matthew* (NCBC), London, 1972, 340; W L Lane, *The Gospel of Mark* (NLCNT), London, 1974, 509.

calls upon the Gentiles to join in God's praises (Psalm 117); and He concludes with a song of triumph: "I shall not die, but live, and declare the works of the LORD" (Psalm 118:17). William Lane commented that, "When Jesus arose to go to Gethsemane, Ps. 118 was upon his lips. It provided an appropriate description of how God would guide his Messiah through distress and suffering to glory."[10] So here, at least, this reference to 'hymn,' rather than pointing to any uninspired song of praise, points to the Psalter.

2. Acts 16:25; Hebrews 2:12 (ὑμνέω, *humneō*)
Paul and Silas have taken the gospel to Europe. There is encouragement (Acts 16:11-15). But there is also opposition. They are imprisoned in Philippi (vv16-24). Are they downcast? Not a bit of it! After all, Jesus had encouraged rejoicing in just such situations (Matthew 5:12). At midnight, with their feet in the stocks in an inner prison, Paul and Silas are heard 'praying and singing hymns *(humnoun)* to God' (v25). This word *humnoun* is an imperfect of the verb, *humneō*; indicating continuing action. What were they singing? We do not know for sure. But the suggestion of Addison Alexander commends itself: "*Praying, hymned* (or *sang to*) *God*, seems to express, not two distinct acts…but the single act of lyrical worship, or praying…by singing or chanting, perhaps one or more of the passages in the Book of Psalms peculiarly adapted and intended for the use of prisoners and others under persecution."[11]

Clearly whatever Paul and Silas sang that night was something they knew by heart. "The explanation doubtless is," says Professor William Binnie, "that they had been taught to say and sing the Psalms in their childhood; and that their habitual attendance in the Synagogue and participation in its services had prevented the early familiarity with 'the praises of Israel' from being lost or impaired."[12]

---

[10] Lane, op. cit., 509.
[11] J A Alexander, *The Acts of the Apostles*, London, 1963 (1857), Volume Two, 121.
[12] Binnie, op. cit., 372.

This understanding of *humnoun* here is strengthened by the reference in Hebrews 2:12 – the only other place in the New Testament where this verb is found. This is in fact found in a quotation from a Psalm! Speaking of Jesus' brotherly relations with believers the writer quotes Psalm 22:22: "I will declare your name to my brethren; In the midst of the congregation I will sing praise [*humnesō*] to you."

3. 1 Corinthians 14:26 (ψαλμὸν, *psalmon*)

The word *psalmon* is found in 1 Corinthians 14: "How is it then, brethren? When ye come together, every one of you hath a psalm (*psalmon*)..." (v26). C. K. Barrett suggests that this may be "a fresh, perhaps spontaneous, composition, not an Old Testament psalm."[13] However, it would most likely be 'charismatic' – the question of the 'charismata' is an issue in that chapter. Besides this, Paul is speaking of the utterances of *individuals*. It is not likely that these would be *congregational* songs and in any case they would be directly Spirit-inspired. In addition, as Ralph Martin has observed, "nothing...is known of the content or form of such spontaneous creations"[14] – assuming, that is, that they were not Bible Psalms, which in fact they may well have been. In other words, it would be unsafe to read too much into this reference.

4. Ephesians 5:19; Colossians 3:16 (ψαλμός, *psalmos*, ὕμνος, *humnos*, ᾠδή, *ōdē*)

We come now to the passages most commonly used in support of a warrant for the adopting uninspired hymnody. 'Look,' someone will say, 'surely these verses indicate that we can use more than the Old Testament Psalms!' The nouns, *psalmos, humnos* and *ōdē* are found together in both these passages. In an article written some years ago, Robert Morey claimed that "the mention of 'hymns' and 'songs' clearly reveals that we can sing other materials than the Psalms."[15] This is a

---

[13] C K Barrett, *A Commentary on the First Epistle to the Corinthians*, London, ²1971, 327.
[14] R P Martin, *Colossians and Philemon* (NCBC), London, 1981, 115.
[15] R A Morey, 'Reformation in our Singing', in *Reformation Today*, March/April, 1977, 9.

common view. But does it give any such warrant? Is it sustainable? Let us see.

In these verses Paul is certainly concerned with worship. He is also speaking of the believer's inward life. He exhorts the Ephesian Christians to "be filled with the Spirit" (5:18). To the Colossian believers he says: "let the word of Christ dwell in you richly in all wisdom" (3:16). The infilling of the Spirit brings the word of Christ to the heart, for it is the Holy Spirit's task to "take the things of Christ" and declare them to the disciples (John 16:15). Paul puts this so tellingly to the Romans: "if the Spirit of him that raised up Jesus from the dead dwells in you, he that raised up Christ from the dead shall also quicken your mortal bodies by his Spirit that dwelleth in you" (Romans 8:11). A consequence of the indwelling Spirit is praise. So, Paul enjoins the Ephesian and Colossian Christians to 'speak' or 'teach and admonish' each other through the medium of "psalms, and hymns and spiritual songs", singing and making melody to the Lord with grace in their hearts (Ephesians 5:19; Colossians 3:16).

The question is: what exactly are these 'psalms, hymns and spiritual songs'? It goes without saying that every Christian will be happy to sing the songs to which Paul is referring here. It is reasonable to assume that these were *existing* compositions, otherwise the Ephesian and Colossian readers would simply he bemused by the reference. But to what compositions could he be referring? To the end of his ministry Paul had a high view of Scripture (cf. 2 Timothy 3:14-17). Would compositions of men, not immediately inspired by the Spirit of God, qualify as the 'word of Christ' with which the believers were to be filled? It surely stretches credulity to maintain that they were non-inspired materials or that the Apostle was giving a free hand to post-apostolic writers to go ahead and compose their own hymns for use in worship.

To be sure, we cannot be certain about how Paul's hearers would have understood him. Commentators are by and large agreed that there is no general agreement about the meaning of this threefold description! Nor is there general agreement as to whether the adjective

Worship – Singing Psalms (2)

pneumatikais ('spiritual') qualifies only *ōdē* ('song'), or all three terms.[16] F. F. Bruce's comment is representative: "It is unlikely that any sharply demarcated division is intended, although the 'psalms' might be drawn from the OT Psalter (which has supplied the chief vehicle for Christian praise from primitive times), the 'hymns' might be Christian canticles, and the 'spiritual songs' might be unpremeditated words sung 'in the Spirit,' voicing holy aspirations."[17] We cannot fail to notice how this paragraph of Bruce's is so replete with 'mights.' and vague suggestions. There is no positive evidence in these verses to warrant the conclusion that Paul was referring to three distinct groups or types of compositions, although no doubt the words had their distinctive meanings indicating the variety and richness of the songs Paul has in mind. There is simply no warrant for taking Ephesians 5:19 and Colossians 3:16 as justification for adopting uninspired hymnody in the worship of God. That would have these verses support far more than sound exegesis of them can sustain.

It seems perfectly reasonable, however, to take the references to psalms, hymns and spiritual songs as referring collectively to the Psalter. The various Greek words would be familiar to the New Testament Church as being found in the Old Testament Greek translation (the Septuagint or LXX) which was commonly in use. In the Septuagint the Psalm titles frequently contained these terms. In many cases more than one of the terms is used in a title, and in at least one instance all three terms are found in the title (Psalm 76)!

• *Psalmos* occurs 87 times in the Greek Old Testament, 67 times in the Psalm titles. In the New Testament this word occurs seven times: in each of the verses presently being considered, four times with reference to the book of Psalms (Luke 20:42, 24:44 and Acts 1:20,

---

[16] Cf. E K Simpson and F F Bruce, *Commentary on the Epistles to the Ephesians and Colossians*, (NICNT), Grand Rapids, 1957, 125, 284-285; W. Hendriksen, *Ephesians,* Edinburgh, 1972, 161-163; W Hendriksen, *Colossians,* Edinburgh, 1971, 240-241; R P Martin, *Colossians and Philemon* (NCBC), London, 1973, 115-116; C L Mitton, *Ephesians,* (NCBC), London, 1973, 191.
[17] Bruce, op. cit., 284-285.

13:33) and once in 1 Corinthians 14:26, where the reference is either to the Biblical Psalms or perhaps to a charismatic utterance, in which case the song would be individual and Spirit-inspired.

• *Humnos* occurs 17 times, 13 times in the Psalms, six of which are in the titles. In the New Testament this word only occurs in the verses under examination.

• *Ōdē* occurs 80 times, 36 in Psalm titles and many other times within the Psalms themselves.[18]

As we have seen, the word *humneō* is used of the Book of Psalms (cf. Hebrews 2:12). *Ōdē* can also be used of the Psalms, although in the New Testament, apart from the texts in Ephesians and Colossians, the word is only found in the Book of Revelation (5:9; 14:3; 15:3), where the 'new song' refers neither to modern hymns nor any uninspired compositions. In connection with the passages in Ephesians and Colossians, Heinrich Schlier commented: "It is 'spiritual', i.e., has a measure of inspiration (Eph. 5:19). Hence it is not an expression of personal feeling or experience but a 'word of Christ' (Col. 3:16)."[19]

There is weight, therefore, in the interpretation that understands Paul as using these three terms, *psalmos, humnos* and *ōdē*, with reference to the Book of Psalms. These would correspond broadly to the Hebrew terms *mizmorim, tehillim* and *shirim* – the types of composition found in the Old Testament Psalter. As Thomas Manton (1620-1677) wrote: "In Col. iii. 16, and Eph. v. 19, Paul biddeth us 'speak to one another, ψάλμοις καὶ ὑμνοις καὶ ὠδαις πνευματικαις, in psalms and hymns and spiritual songs.' Now these words (which are the known division of David's psalms, and expressly answering to the Hebrew words *Shurim, Tehillim*, and *Mizmorim*, by which his psalms are distinguished and entitled), being so precisely used by the apostle in both places, do plainly point us to the Book of Psalms."[20] No doubt the terms do

---

[18] For the information in this section the writer is indebted to John Murray and William Young: *Minority Report of the Committee on Song in the Public Worship of God*, Orthodox Presbyterian Church, 1947, 16.
[19] Bromiley, op. cit., 24.
[20] Thomas Manton, *An Exposition on the Epistle of James*, London, 1968 (1693), 443.

reflect different types of Psalms and Paul would be implying, what we know to be the case, that there are Psalms which relate to the whole range of our spiritual needs. It is interesting that in other places in the Old and New Testaments threefold descriptions of similar things are given. For example, in Exodus 34:7 we find "iniquity and transgression and sin." In Deuteronomy 5:31 and 6:1 we find "commandments and statutes and judgments." In Acts 2:22 we find the phrase, "miracles, wonders, and signs." This general perspective finds support in some older writers like the Puritan Thomas Ford (1598-1674), a member of the Westminster Assembly of divines, and William Binnie (1823-1886), and in more recent years has been ably expounded by Professor John Murray and William Young in a *Report* they produced for the Orthodox Presbyterian Church in 1947.[21]

Someone might still object that this interpretation is somewhat speculative and less than conclusive. But Paul is clearly saying *something*, and the case seems to be much stronger for the view which sees reference to the Psalter in these verses. At any rate, it can be seen that these texts do *not* provide any positive warrant for the adoption of non-inspired extra-scriptural materials of praise as congregational song. Neither these texts, nor any other related New Testament passages, provide any support for the introduction of uninspired human hymns into Christian public worship. Furthermore, let it be said that no Christian is *bound* to sing any songs which the Lord, in His wisdom, has not *commanded* them to sing or *provided* for their singing, however good such songs may appear to be on a human level.

---

[21] Thomas Ford, *Singing of Psalms the Duty of Christians*, Presbyterian's Armoury Publications, Burnie, Tasmania, 2004 (1659); William Binnie, *The Psalms: Their History, Teachings, and Use*, London, ²1886; Professor James Harper (Xenia) (in his *Psalm-Singers' Conference* paper at Belfast, 1902) cites a comment of Jerome on Ephesians 5:19: "The difference between the psalms and hymns and spiritual songs is best seen in the Book of Psalms" (*Psalm-Singers' Conference*, Belfast, 1903, 108). This was a common view among the Early Church Fathers.

5. James 5:13; Romans 15:9 (ψάλλω, *psallō*)

The last word we shall look at is the verb *psallō*, 'to sing psalms, or praises.' James encourages those who are suffering to pray. He encourages those who are cheerful to 'sing psalms' (*psalletō*). What has James in mind here? Well, this word, *psallō*, appears 56 times in the Septuagint, predominantly in the Psalms. It came to mean, generally, a song of praise. This cannot be shown conclusively to refer to Biblical Psalms. However, as the Puritan writer, Thomas Manton, suggests: "In the original there is but one word, ψαλλετω, let him sing; but because the apostle is pressing them to religious use of every condition, and because this is the usual acception of the word ψαλλετω in the church, it is well rendered 'let him sing psalms'."[22]

The use of *psallō* in another New Testament context indicates that Manton's interpretation is a sound one. In Romans 15:9, the only other place in the New Testament where this word appears, Paul finds Biblical support for the Gentiles to praise God. Where? Well, in the Psalms! Jesus Christ came, says Paul, "that the Gentiles might glorify God for his mercy, as it is written: 'For this cause I will confess to thee among the Gentiles, and sing [*psalō*] unto thy name' [Psalm 18:49]." There is simply no advocacy of the use of uninspired songs of praise in public worship in any of the references which either refer to worship itself, or use the language relevant to the content of biblical praise.

6. New Testament 'Christian Hymns'

There are some songs in the New Testament. In Luke's gospel, for instance, there are the songs of Mary (1:46-55), Zacharias (1:68-79) and Simeon (2:29-32). These are Spirit-inspired songs, and whilst there does not seem to be any objection in principle to their use in public worship, it is not altogether clear that even these songs were intended by the Lord for such a purpose, so personal are they to those who uttered them.

---

[22] Manton, op. cit., 439.

There are, however, other passages which some have suggested are fragments of hymn-type compositions. These 'fragments', it is felt, bear witness to a developing liturgical tradition in the early Church. Ephesians 5:14; Philippians 2:6-11; Colossians 1:15-20; and 1 Timothy 3:16 are appealed to as illustrating this point. What are we to make of such claims?

(1) *The procedure is speculative.* However confident the claims may be that there are hymn-citations in the New Testament, there is no uncontradicted proof that this is the case. Binnie rightly called such claims 'precarious.'[23] Much ingenious and careful research has been done. Despite this there is still a lack of universal agreement amongst scholars on the precise nature of these verses. It cannot be shown that they were ever sung and it would seem that no two New Testament writers quote from the same 'hymn' fragment and no one writer quotes from the same 'hymn' fragment twice![24] Commenting on the subject, the "songs of Primitive Christianity", Gerhard Delling made the significant observation that, "Attempts have been made to distinguish Christian hymns in the NT but these are hypothetical in the absence of discernible laws." He also makes the obvious point that "...the mere presence of lofty speech or integrated structure does not have to denote a hymn."[25]

(2) *The procedure is inconclusive.* Even supposing that it could be proved conclusively that hymn fragments were to be found in the New Testament, that would still not prove that these items were part of a developing liturgical tradition. For one thing, the providence of God is against it. In this way: none of the items of which the various verses in the New Testament are taken to be fragments has come down to us. The writers might indeed have gleaned these 'fragments' from contemporary songs, but why then did these songs not come down in their entirety if they were to be used by the Church, or if they were to

---

[23] Binnie, op. cit., 377.
[24] Cf. G B Caird, 'Hymns in the New Testament', in *Expository Times,* February 1972, Volume LXXXIII, Number 5, 153.
[25] Bromiley, op. cit., 1227.

be part of a liturgical tradition? What sort of tradition is it that fails to retain such items whole and entire? If the Holy Spirit had meant the Church to use them, it is inconceivable that He would simply have left fragments here and there, and not ensured that the compositions (if they were such) were preserved in their entirety.

There is no evidence that these passages were either songs or part of a developing liturgical tradition. But even supposing the passages were found to be songs or parts of songs, it does not follow that this provides some sort of warrant for the use of uninspired hymns in worship or demonstrable proof that they were ever used in worship services. This whole area of New Testament studies is marvellously imaginative, but entirely inconclusive as far the question of New Testament praise is concerned.

WORSHIP

4. The Singing of Psalms: (3) The Imprecatory Psalms

1. A sensitive issue

One issue in the use of the Psalms for singing is the matter of imprecations in the Psalms. These are thought by some to be contrary to the spirit or ethic of the gospel. There are various Psalms which in large measure or in part invoke the wrath or curse of God against the enemies of the people of God. How can it be right to desire or pray for the destruction or doom of others? Naturally the *use* of any such expressions or imprecations would require to be very carefully considered. But is it right for us to hold that, (a) the spirit of such passages is contrary to a Christian spirit; and, (b) such passages should be avoided in the sung praise? How should one approach, or answer this perplexity?[1]

2. Defining the terms

'Imprecation' has been defined as "an invocation of judgement, calamity, or curse uttered against one's enemies who in these special cases are also simultaneously the enemies of God."[2] They are a prayer or cry to God, containing a desire for God to punish certain people who are considered His enemies.

3. Keeping the issue in perspective

The difficulties should not be overstated. The imprecatory elements in the Psalms are relatively limited in number. Of the one hundred and

---

[1] For an excellent study of this sensitive subject see Michael LeFebvre's *Singing the Songs of Jesus*, Christian Focus Publications, 2010, 113-132. See also David Searle, 'The Imprecatory Psalms Today,' in, David Wright and David Stay (Editors), *Serving the Word of God*, Christian Focus Publications, 2002, 169-179.

[2] Walter C Kaiser, Jr, *Towards Old Testament Ethics*, Grand Rapids, Michigan, 1983, 294.

fifty Psalms only three are mainly or totally imprecatory: 35, 69, and 109. Other Psalms at least partly of an imprecatory nature are: 5, 7, 10, 28, 31, 40, 55, 58, 59, 70, 71, 79, 83, 137, 139, and 140. Walter Kaiser has pointed out that apart from the more frequently quoted Psalms of a strong Messianic nature (1, 22, 110, 118), Psalms 35, 69 and 109 are the next most frequently quoted Psalms in the New Testament. The 18 Psalms referred to here have a total of three hundred and sixty-eight verses, of which only sixty-five have imprecatory elements.[3] The imprecatory passages are therefore relatively limited in number. This is the first point to be made in facing this issue.

4. The perceived difficulty faced

The question remains concerning the appropriateness of using in a Christian context, the cursings and imprecations which are found in the Psalter. Take Psalm 10, for example:

> Break thou the arm of the wicked and the evil man:
> Seek out his wickedness till thou find none. (Verse 15).

Other instances of such imprecations are found in Psalm 58:6-8, or Psalm 140:9-10.

How does one respond to the objections raised about the moral tone of the imprecatory elements in the Psalms and thus consider them inappropriate for sung praise in the Christian Church? The following points may be made:

(1) In relation to the suggestion that imprecatory portions of the Psalms are inappropriate for sung praise in public worship in the Christian Church, due weight requires to be given at the outset to the statement of the Apostle that "all scripture is given by inspiration of God [God-breathed], and is profitable for doctrine, for reproof, for correction, for instruction in righteousness, that the man of God may be perfect, thoroughly furnished unto all good works" (2 Timothy 3:16-17). If the

---

[3] ibid., 293. Kaiser's reference to Psalms of a strongly Messianic nature should have cited Psalm 2 rather than Psalm 1, which is not directly quoted in the New Testament. This is presumably a typing error.

imprecatory passages are deemed unsuitable for *sung praise* in the Christian Church, does that mean that they are also to be taken as unsuitable for *reading* or *teaching* in the Christian Church? However, if such passages express truths found in the New Testament, properly understood, they cannot be inappropriate for singing, reading or teaching in the Christian Church.

(2) David was the author of most of the imprecatory Psalms. Psalms 79 and 83 are attributed to Asaph, and Psalm 137 is an Exilic Psalm. Yet when we think of David's reaction to King Saul, and to his son Absalom later, it cannot be said that he was wont to take matters into his own hand mercilessly. Even within the imprecatory Psalms we find kindly thoughts being expressed towards his enemies. Take, for example, Psalm 35:12-14, or Psalm 109:4-5. There does not appear to be a personal vindictive spirit with the Psalmist.

(3) It is not only in the Old Testament that we find imprecatory elements. There are imprecations also in the New Testament. Take, for example Jesus' own pronouncing of 'woes' against the scribes and Pharisees in Matthew 24. Paul speaks of his desire that those who troubled the Galatians would "cut themselves off" (Galatians 5:12, NKJV), and against Alexander the coppersmith who had done him much harm, he says: "the Lord reward him according to his works" (2 Timothy 4:14). "For the wrath of God," wrote Paul to the Romans, "is revealed from heaven against all ungodliness and unrighteousness of men, who hold the truth in unrighteousness, etc." (1:18ff.). In the Book of Revelation, it is recorded that the cry of the martyrs is this: "How long, O Lord, holy and true, dost thou not judge and avenge our blood on them that dwell on the earth" (6:10).

(4) The context of the imprecations, consistently, is that of righteousness in the eyes of God. There is an assumption that God will triumph over all that opposes Him and righteousness will be vindicated. Derek Kidner sees in the *substance* of the imprecatory elements in the Psalms "the plea that justice shall be done and the right be vindicated", and he adds that "this is a concern which the New Testament warmly

upholds."[4] We see this "warmth", for example, in Luke 18:1-8.

(5) The imprecations reflect the zeal of God's people for the Kingdom of God and His truth. Those who utter the imprecations in the Psalms (or in the New Testament) are representatives of God. The imprecations are not directed towards *private enemies*, but against the enemies of God Himself. Though the tone of the imprecations ranges from the plaintive to the ferocious (as Kidner put it), "it is only fair to point out that the words wrung from these sufferers as they plead their case are a measure of the deeds which provoked them."[5] At the same time, "horror may be piled on horror more to express the speaker's sense of outrage than to spell out the penalties he literally intends."[6] That is to say, in such cases we detect men speaking with holy passion.

(6) The apparent harshness of the cries of God's saints against their enemies is a measure of their abhorrence of sin and evil. We must remember that those who rise up against the Lord are essentially anti-God and anti-Christ, and anti-truth. "Doeg, Cush, and Ahithophel are not your average criminal or hostile types: they are the culmination and final fruit of all falsehood, greed, hate, cruelty, and treachery aimed against the very means of their own salvation."[7]

(7) The imprecations amount to humble request to the Lord to carry out what he threatens on the ungodly who persist in opposition to the offered mercy of the Lord through the Saviour and His work. We must remember that the consistent teaching of both the Old and New Testaments is that the Lord will punish those who oppose Him, spurn His mercy and refuse to repent and believe the truth. In all this there is a realism in the Scriptures in relation to people's sin and destiny. Part of that realism is expressed in the imprecatory Psalms and is perfectly consistent with New Testament teaching.

---

[4] Derek Kidner, *Psalms 1-72*, Leicester, [1]1973, 26.
[5] ibid, 27.
[6] ibid.
[7] Kaiser, op. cit., 296.

5. What about Psalm 137, verses 8 and 9?

Psalm 137 is clearly a Psalm deriving from the Exile in Babylon (586-539BC). The last two verses are among the most notable imprecations in the Bible. How are we to understand these, consistent with our high view of Biblical inspiration and the merciful and forgiving spirit fundamental to a Christian outlook?

> O daughter of Babylon, who art to be destroyed;
> happy shall he be, that rewardeth thee as thou hast served us.
> Happy shall he be, that taketh and dasheth
> thy little ones against the stones [rock]. (Verses 8 and 9).

(1) The first thing to notice here is the *judicial background*: "Remember, O LORD, against the sons of Edom…" (v7, NKJV). The divine judge is presented with evidence against the wickedness of those who have oppressed the people of God. In this Babylon is seen to be the chief offender (vv8-9).

(2) The concern is strict *justice* (v8b). We discern here the principle of divine retribution, a principle that is applicable in every age of human history. As such it is perfectly righteous. It is clearly stated in Deuteronomy 19:19-21, and Proverbs 24:29. That it is not just an Old Testament matter, however, is clear from what Paul wrote in Romans 12:19 and 2 Thessalonians 1:4-10.

(3) We need to remember that apart from souls coming under the redemptive merit of the Saviour's blood and righteousness, they will be exposed to the righteous judgement of God who "will render to every man [each one] according to his deeds [Psalm 62:12; Proverbs 24:12]" (Romans 2:5-10).

(4) Though verse 9 may well refer, literally, to what the Babylonians did in sacking Jerusalem in 586BC, the heart cry of the Psalmist – and of the Church – although a plea for *divine retribution*, can be taken in a metaphorical sense of simply desiring the ungodly persecutors to be brought down. We have such a sentiment also in Psalm 141: "their judges are overthrown by the sides of the cliff…", a judgement we note which will cause people to reflect and heed the sweet words of God's grace (v6, NKJV).

(5) With reference to verse 9, Derek Kidner has commented: "To cut this witness out of the Old Testament would be to impair its value as revelation, both of what is in man and of what the cross was required to achieve for our salvation."[8] In summarising the place of the 137th Psalm in Scripture, he further wrote:

> So this psalm takes its place in Scripture as an impassioned protest, beyond all ignoring or toning down, not only against a particular act of cruelty but against all comfortable views of human wickedness, either with regard to the judgement it deserves or to the legacy it leaves; and not least, in relation to the cost, to God and man, of laying its enmity and bitterness to rest.[9]

6. Christian use of the Imprecatory Psalms?

(1) The imprecatory Psalms must be used with care. It is wise for those who conduct services to explain any imprecatory element in a Psalm portion used in song, or in a Bible reading. As William Binnie commented: "As powerful witnesses for the truth that sin is hateful to God and deserving of His wrath and everlasting curse, – a truth which the world would fain forget, – the Imprecatory Psalms must be accounted worthy of their place in the divine Manual of Praise."[10]

(2) In the New Testament we have a wonderful revelation of the accomplishment of salvation, and that Christ has brought "life and immortality to life through the gospel" (2 Timothy 1: 10). Yet there is to be a continuing sense of the justice and holiness of God in His demand upon the sinner, and of a concern for righteousness and an abhorrence of sin on the part of the believer.

(3) It is not without significance that the very fact of Christ's coming for the accomplishment of His work brings even greater culpability upon those who refuse the offered mercy. After all, Christ Himself taught that for the people who will not receive His words or His messengers "it shall be more tolerable for the land of Sodom and

---

[8] Derek Kidner, *Psalms 73-150*, Leicester, [1]1975, 461.
[9] ibid.
[10] William Binnie, *The Psalms: Their History, Teachings, and Use*, London, [2]1886, 289.

Gomorrha in the day of judgement, than for that city" (Matthew 10:15). (4) There are *sorer punishments* revealed in the New Testament even than in the Psalms. We can see this, for example, when we compare Psalm 6:8 and Matthew 7:23. The words "depart from me, ye that work iniquity" (Psalm 6:8) are transformed from a cry for relief on David's part to a sentence of eternal death on Christ's use of the phrase. The matter of punishment for sin far from being minimised in the New Testament is stated with even greater clarity and explicitness than is the case in the Old Testament.

(5) It is notable that there are in the New Testament frequent quotations from imprecatory Psalms, without any reserve or qualification.[11] When Peter spoke to the other disciples in the upper room after the Ascension of the Lord he quoted from both Psalm 69 and 109. The verses quoted are taken as prophecies concerning Judas. We note also how Paul in Romans 11:9-10 cites Psalm 69:22-23 in relation to the blindness to Christ as Messiah of the (non-elect) of Israel at that time.

(6) We must recognise that ultimately Christ is speaking through the Imprecatory Psalms as He is in all the Scriptures.

7. Conclusions

(1) Christians are to love their enemies and bless those who curse them and spitefully use them (Matthew 5:43-44). They will desire the spiritual good of their neighbours (verse 45). Nevertheless, they will desire at the same time the downfall of every evil way, and the overthrow of all who practice a lie (2 Corinthians 10:4). They will cry out to God for such. It will not be *personal* vindictiveness, but rather an expression of righteousness and an abhorrence of sin that ought to characterise the believing soul. "If these passages in the psalms open our eyes to the depths and just deserts of evil, they have done their work."[12]

(2) People require to face the fact that "it is a fearful thing to fall into

---

[11] See, for example, Psalm 2 referred to in Revelation 2:27, 12:5, 19:15; Psalm 110:5 referred to in Romans 2:5; Psalm 79:6 referred to in 2 Thessalonians 1:8.
[12] Kidner, *Psalms 1-72*, 32.

the hands of the living God" (Hebrews 10:31) and that "our God is a consuming fire" (Deuteronomy 4:24; Hebrews 12:29). The imprecations are one thing, but what people who know not God must face is eternal punishment. For all who will not repent of sin and come to Christ that they might have life, and for all who persist in deceiving themselves about their relation to God, the dread words will be heard: "Depart from me, ye cursed, into everlasting fire, prepared for the devil and his angels" (Matthew 25:41).

(3) The fact of imprecations in the Psalms, and elsewhere in Scripture, must provide for the Christian Church a strong motive to press upon the lost the free offer of Christ in the gospel. It will also surely provide an incentive for the unsaved person, confronted by the awfulness of sin and judgement, to repent and turn to Christ alone. Thereby they will "flee from the wrath to come" (Matthew 3:7) and find peace with God. After all, it is a distinctive ministry of the Holy Spirit to "reprove [convince, convict] the world of sin, and of righteousness, and of judgement" (John 16:8).

(4) We are bound to conclude that there are in fact no expressions in the Imprecatory Psalms which are inconsistent with the high standard of holiness required of the people of God in the Old or New Testaments, or are inappropriate in the Christian Church's sung praise.

WORSHIP

5. Instrumental Music

1. Introduction

Very little thought is given these days to the question of the propriety of using instrumental music in public worship services. It is not questioned. The fact that instrumental accompaniment was more or less unknown in Presbyterian Church in Scotland up to the end of the 19th Century comes as a surprise to people, as does the knowledge that the great Baptist preacher of the Victorian era, Charles Haddon Spurgeon, never used instrumental accompaniment in the Metropolitan Tabernacle in London. To this day the Eastern (Orthodox) Church by and large eschews the use of instruments. In the Scottish context only a few of the smaller conservative Presbyterian bodies have maintained unaccompanied praise in their services in recent times, though the prohibition of instruments in worship was recently abandoned in the Free Church of Scotland.[1] The Free Church of Scotland (Continuing), the minority group which arose from the division in the Free Church of Scotland in 2000, still requires this statement to be made at all ordinations of ministers:

> It is my duty to explain to you, and also to the Congregation here present, with reference to that part of the question which will be put to you as to 'Purity of worship as presently practiced in this Church' that, in 1910, the General Assembly reaffirmed the legislation of the Church as to

---

[1] This was changed in the Free Church of Scotland by an Act of a plenary Assembly in November, 2010 [Act 1, Class 2, November 2010]. By this Act the practice eschewing the use of instrumental music in the Church was abandoned. The Free Church of Scotland (Continuing) still affirms the position of the post 1900 Free Church as reflected in the relevant Act in 1910 on the matter of the use of inspired materials of praise without instrumental accompaniment [Act anent Public Worship (No. 1 of Class I), Edinburgh 31st May 1910].

uniformity in public worship going back to the year 1707; and that in accordance with that legislation, it is the present practice of the Free Church to avoid the use, in public worship, of uninspired materials of praise, as also of instrumental music. Such present practice determines the purity of worship to which the maintenance of which the Ordinand pledges himself.[2]

For much of the history of the Reformed Church in Scotland the matter of unaccompanied praise was therefore seen to be part of the Church's principles or purity of worship. The question is: Is there a biblical principle here? Is there a sound argument for the exclusion of instrumental accompaniment in public worship services? The burden of this chapter is to provide some basis in Scripture for this position.

2. The Basic Approach

For all elements of worship – as argued elsewhere, with reference to the singing of Psalms[3] – it is incumbent upon any Church to establish that its practice derives from divine appointment and not merely the wit and wisdom of men. In connection with instrumental music there are certain things, superficially, that appear to be in its favour, and these have to be addressed:

(1) Instrumental music was appointed to be used in Old Testament times. Why should that not apply also for the New Testament?

(2) Instrumental accompaniment greatly aids the singing by keeping the pace up and providing a perfect pitch

(3) The use of an instrument provides the potential for a wider variety of musical forms for the songs that may be sung

(4) In any case the use of a mere instrument, or instruments, doesn't encourage or spread error, as the words of songs admittedly might do. Is it not a thing 'indifferent'?

---

[2] Act V, Class 2, 1932. See, *The Practice of the Free Church of Scotland*, Edinburgh, [8]1995, 150. This was repealed by the Free Church of Scotland (not the Free Church of Scotland (Continuing)) in November 2010 as noted above.

[3] See chapters above on the Singing of Psalms.

Worship – Instrumental Music

The most ardent advocate of the 'no instrumental accompaniment' position has no bone of contention with instrumental music *per se*.[4] Musical *appreciation* is not the issue. The potential of instrumental music for example to stir emotions is not questioned, nor are the God-given talents of those who compose music or play instruments. But the question is: Is it warranted positively in the New Testament and are there sound reasons for *not* employing such accompaniment *in public worship services*?

3. The Old Testament experience
1. The earliest references to instruments in relation to praise are found in connection with the Exodus from Egypt under Moses. In Exodus 15 after the Red Sea deliverance we have the instance of Moses' sister, of whom we read: "Miriam the prophetess, the sister of Aaron, took a timbrel in her hand; and all the women went out after her with timbrels and with dances. And Miriam answered them, 'Sing ye to the LORD, For he hath triumphed gloriously; the horse and its rider he hath thrown into the sea!'" (Exodus 15:20-21). There is here, however, no specific reference to public worship, but simply spontaneous or 'patriotic' praise from among the women. After all, it was men alone (Levites) who were appointed to lead the entire worship of the Tabernacle service (Numbers 3:5-11). It was only later, indeed, that the whole form of worship that the Lord required of His people in the wilderness was revealed to Moses at Sinai (Exodus 25:40; Hebrews 8:5).
2. In Psalm 81 it is doubtless a call to celebrate the Passover or Feast of Tabernacles that is spoken of. The Psalm refers back to the Exodus period but clearly relates the praise to what God Himself appointed: "Sing aloud unto God our strength: make a joyful noise unto the God of Jacob. Take a psalm, and bring hither the timbrel, the pleasant harp with the psaltery [lute]. Blow up the trumpet in the new moon, in the time appointed, on our solemn feast day. For this was a statute for

---

[4] See the interesting book of Percy A Scholes on *The Puritans and Music in England and New England* (Oxford University Press, 1969 [¹1934]) by way of illustration of this point.

Israel, and a law of the God of Jacob. This he ordained in Joseph for a testimony, when he went out through the land of Egypt: where I heard a language that I did not understand" (1-5). However, the actual reference to the instruments was contemporary Temple worship.

3. It was by the command of God that Moses appointed trumpets to be blown in certain circumstances, such as at times of burn offerings, and other sacrifices and special occasions (Numbers 10:1-10). These were to be blown by the sons of Aaron (Numbers 10:8; 1 Chronicles 15:24). In the nature of the case the trumpets, whether straight (silver) or curved (rams), were not intended to accompany sung praise. Other instruments were introduced also (2 Chronicles 7:6; 29:25-26) and these too were played by the Levites. They were not used for the accompaniment of psalm-singing at the morning and evening sacrifices.

4. In the period of the Exodus and subsequently before settlement in the land of Canaan the centre of worship was the Tabernacle. It had no fixed place of residence until some time after the conquest of Canaan. In Solomon's time it was replaced by the Temple. In both cases the specifications for the structures and their functions and services were specifically appointed and determined by the Lord, in great detail. There is no evidence that instrumental music was common in the Tabernacle when it was not fixed in one position. When the Levites were no longer required for moving the Tabernacle they were deployed to various duties, including 4,000 to praise the Lord with stringed instruments (1 Chronicles 23:4-5; see also 1 Chronicles 25 for further details). The arrangements latterly in the Tabernacle clearly carried over subsequently to the Temple worship. The following should be noted of the use of instrumental music in the Tabernacle and Temple:

1. The instrumental music employed in the Tabernacle was divinely ordained and not just a whim of King David (or any of the priests or Levites) (1 Chronicles 28:11-13, 19).
2. When the Temple was built and the order of services instituted, it was also a matter of divine commandment (2 Chronicles 29:24-26).

3. Instrumental music would not have constituted an element in Temple worship without the express authority of God (2 Chronicles 5:13-14; 8:14).
4. When the burn offerings began the song to the Lord began with trumpets accompanied by the instruments. This is what we read: "when the burnt offering began, the song of the LORD began also with the trumpets, and with the instruments ordained by David king of Israel. And all the congregation worshipped, and the singers sang, and the trumpeters sounded: and all this continued until the burnt offering was finished. And when they had made an end of offering, the king and all that were present with him bowed themselves, and worshipped" (2 Chronicles 29:27-29). The musical accompaniment lasted as long as the burn offering, and so what we read in verses 29 and 30 in relation to sung praise was unaccompanied. We can understand therefore that all the elements associated with the offerings, including the instrumental music were typical or symbolic.
5. There is no evidence for instrumental music accompanying praise outside the Tabernacle/Temple worship. And *all* the worship of the Tabernacle and Temple was necessarily in types, symbols and shadows, pointing forward to fulfilment in the later work of Christ and the Holy Spirit. This is clear from Hebrews. The priests simply "served the copy and shadow of the heavenly things" (8:5, NKJV). The worship was "symbolic for the present time" (9:9, NKJV). The sacrifices were limited and merely pointed forward to a once-for-all perfect sacrifice offered by Christ: "For the law having a shadow of the good things to come, and not the very image of the things, can never with those sacrifices which they offered year by year continually make the comers thereunto perfect. For then would they not have ceased to be offered? because that the worshippers once purged [purified], would have had no more conscience of sins. But in those sacrifices there is a

remembrance [reminder] again made of sins every year. For it is not possible that the blood of bulls and goats should take away sins" (10:1-4). What takes away sin? The sacrificial work of Jesus: "this man, after he had offered one sacrifice for sins for ever, sat down on the right hand of God" (10:12).

6. All this indicates that instrumental music, being appointed and ordained for the typical, symbolical and shadowy worship of the Old Testament, would also be an element, like the priesthood, and the sacrifices, which would be fulfilled in the New Testament and therefore serve no further purpose.

7. Mention is often made of the content of Psalms such as Psalm 150 which make references to all sorts of musical instruments. These references may be understood, however, perfectly well in relation to the elements of the instrumental music which were typical or symbolical of their New Testament fulfilment. Thus, on the supposition that the use of musical instruments pointed forward to the work of the Holy Spirit in the New Testament era (principally), then such Psalms in fact become far clearer to the Christian Church than it would have been even to the Old Testament Church.

4. The New Testament position

1. We have spoken already of the passing of the Old Testament ceremonies, types, symbols and shadows with the work of Christ and pouring out of the Holy Spirit. It stands to reason – and is agreeable with Biblical revelation – that those things which anticipated the New Testament era must of necessity be abolished (Matthew 27:51). It also stands to reason, however, that there will be an element of continuity or at least evident replacement of elements of the Old Testament services. This applied, for example, to the sacraments, baptism replacing circumcision as a sign of the covenant (Matthew 28:19-20),[5] and the

---

[5] See chapters below on Baptism.

Lord's Supper replacing the Passover (Matthew 26:17-30; 1 Corinthians 11:23-34).[6]

2. Thus, the positive sanction for the instruments in the Tabernacle or Temple does not carry over to the New Testament any more than the priesthood or sacrifices did. That is not to say that there will not be aspects of the Temple services which will have their analogy in New Testament worship. We have that, for example with the singing of Psalms (Ephesians 5:19; Colossians 3:16) and the offerings (2 Corinthians 8). But it is the fruit of the lips that praises Him, not the sounds of instruments in His worship: "by Him let us continually offer the sacrifice of praise to God, that is, the fruit of our lips, giving thanks to His name" (Hebrews 13:15).

3. The principal question is whether or not there is any direct and express warrant in the New Testament for the accompaniment of sung praise. If the Temple and its services must be recognised as fulfilled and therefore obsolete; and if the instrumental music was expressly appointed as a type or symbol of something fulfilled in the New Testament age, then it is unwarranted simply to adopt such instrumental music without having a clear warrant to do so from the Lord's Word in the newer testament.

4. Whatever the origins of the local Synagogues may have been as meeting places for the worshippers under the older testament, it was clearly consistent with the application of the 2nd and 4th commandments and the basic need of people to devote time on the weekly Sabbath to public praise, as exemplified by the Lord Himself (Luke 4:16). There is every reason to believe that there were no instruments in the Synagogues. There appears to be the simple elements of prayer and praise and preaching. This much is suggested by the several instances in the gospels and Acts in which we have glimpses into the worship patterns within the Synagogues. It is clear from the Acts that Synagogues became the first centres for collective Christian congregational worship (Acts 17:10-12).

---

[6] See chapters below on the Lord's Supper.

5. There is no question that the Old Testament with its elaborate system of ritual and sacrifices presented a more carnal, outward aspect of religion than what we find in the New Testament. It is clear that in the New Testament a veil was lifted (2 Corinthians 3:14-15) and the worship was more simple, spiritual and experiential than visual. This is understandable, given the uniqueness of the giving of the Spirit at Pentecost (Acts 2). Jesus Himself indicated this contrast in speaking to the woman at the well in Samaria: "Woman, believe me, the hour is coming when you will neither on this mountain, nor in Jerusalem, worship the Father. You worship what you do not know; we know what we worship, for salvation is of the Jews. But the hour is coming, and now is, when the true worshipers will worship the Father in spirit and truth; for the Father is seeking such to worship Him. God is Spirit, and those who worship Him must worship in spirit and truth" (John 4:21-24).

6. In a sense this answers an obvious question: If all the worship that was adopted in the Tabernacle/Temple were typical or figurative of a fulfilment in the New Testament era, what was it specifically of which the instrumental music was typical? We can understand all the sacrifices and the priesthood as being fulfilled in Christ and His work. This much seems very clear in the letter to the Hebrews. But what in the Old Testament points forward to the Holy Spirit's work, conjointly with Christ's? We read in Hebrews: "if the blood of bulls and goats, and the ashes of an heifer sprinkling the unclean, sanctifieth to the purifying of the flesh: how much more shall the blood of Christ, who through the eternal Spirit offered himself without spot to God, purge [cleanse] your conscience from dead works to serve the living God?" (Hebrews 9:13-14).

Southern Presbyterian theologian of the 19th century, John L. Girardeau suggested that, "the elements in the temple service, which were not embraced in that of the synagogue, were typical; that some of these were typical of the Holy Ghost and the effects to be produced by his grace in New Testament times; and that among them instrumental music must be classed."[7] There seems good reason for affirming that it is precisely the instrumental music element of the Temple worship that pre-figured the work of the Holy Spirit in the New Testament era.

5. Conclusions

1. It must come as no surprise that Churches of the Reformed and Presbyterian tradition, conscientiously seeking express commandment and appointment, directly and by good and necessary consequence from Scripture, generally came to the conviction that instrumental music was inappropriate and without divine warrant for New Testament worship. The adoption of instruments, mostly organs, but more recently a whole range of instruments and styles of music, derives for the greater part from the mid-to-late 19th century, certainly in Scotland. Typically, legislation was passed of a permissive sort. Thereafter in local congregations its introduction and development depended largely upon mere supportive majorities. The Free Church of Scotland allowed instrumental music in 1883 though after little or no discussion of the principle. The legislation that allowed instrumental accompaniment was repealed and repudiated by the post-1900 continuing Free Church between 1905 and 1910.[8]

2. Initially the motive for the adoption of instrumental music lay in the desire to improve praise. The preference was for organs, the so-called 'queen of instruments.' However, as we have argued, Biblical warrant for such a thing is weak in the extreme. What is more, once it is admitted there is little prospect of restricting the types or numbers of instruments used. There are simply no Biblical criteria to say what instruments may – or may not – be adopted. It may be said to be retrogressive in worship in that the use of instrumental music radically shifts the focus of worship from the individual engaged in praise from his own heart and lips to the 'music' as that which drives it all along and

---

[7] John L Girardeau, *Instrumental Music in the Public Worship of the Church*, Richmond, VA, 1888, 74.
[8] But see the notes 1 and 2 above for changes in worship in the Free Church of Scotland in November 2010.

may so readily become an element in itself as a 'performance' or merely producing ambient noise before, during or after services. This is not to excuse poor singing or carelessness about the leading of the unaccompanied praise. Nor does it involve accusations of heresy. But there is an argument for eschewing musical instruments in New Testament worship because of the evident want of direct warrant and the concern there ought to be to avoid that which smacks of being essentially the "doctrines and commandments of men" (Colossians 3:22).

Further Reading:

James Begg, "Musical Instruments in Public Worship," in, The Watchword, *January 1, 1872, 435-445, and February 1, 1872, 491-503. [This James Begg was the Church of Scotland minister in New Monkland, Ayrshire, and the father of James Begg the Free Churchman. The 'Treatise' was published first in 1808 at the time of an 'organ' controversy in the Church of Scotland]*

John L Girardeau, Instrumental Music in the Worship of the Church, *Richmond, VA, 1888. Classic study from a Southern Presbyterian USA theologian.*

Gerald I Williamson, "Instrumental Music in Worship: Commanded or Not Commanded?" in, The Biblical Doctrine of Worship, *Reformed Presbyterian Church of North America, c1973, 338-349. This was a contribution to a useful Symposium produced by the RPCNA and covering a wide range of exegetical, theological and historical issues in relation to Worship.*

John Price, Old Light on New Worship, Musical Instruments and the Worship of God, a Theological, Historical and Psychological Study, *Simpson Publishing Company, 2005. This is the work of a Reformed Baptist. A book of 256 pages it is a comprehensive modern study of the issue of the use of musical instruments in public worship and why it should not be adopted in Christian worship.*

WORSHIP

6. Posture in Public Prayer

1. First Impressions

Possibly the first thing that struck visitors to Free Churches in Scotland — apart perhaps from the absence of instrumental music — at least until the recent past, was the practice of standing for prayer, and correspondingly sitting for praise. Towards the end of the 20th century, however, that was changing with more congregations sitting for prayer and standing for the singing.[1] Again, the practice of standing to pray had been widely accepted in Presbyterian Churches and changes took place for pragmatic reasons rather than on any principle. The majority of evangelical Christians today would view such a practice – or any concern for *postures* in worship – as a matter of indifference, or perhaps even a mere eccentricity. As the practice of standing to pray is admittedly out of step with most Christian communions today it is right to ask whether there is any real Biblical basis for the position. Is this any more than merely a tradition in a matter of indifference? Are there *any* considerations raising it above matters of mere tradition or temperament? It is the purpose of this chapter to explore such questions and bring out some considerations in support of a distinctive position in relation to postures in worship.

2. Preliminary Points

(1) Some may say that this is such an *unimportant subject* that any settled conviction on the matter would simply tend to make an unnecessary difference between Churches. This is a serious point. We must be sensitive to anything that unnecessarily divides Churches. There are

---

[1] Standing to pray remains the practice of the Free Church of Scotland (Continuing) and the Free Presbyterian Church of Scotland.

certainly more important issues in Church life to engage our energies, such as evangelism and the defence of the Faith. However, without majoring on minors, it must be desirable as far as possible to bring all our practices to the Word of God. Our desire should be "to hold forth such things as are of divine institution in every ordinance."[2] We remember, too, the words of our Lord: "he that is faithful in that which is least is faithful also in much" (Luke 16:10).

(2) As regards the *nature* of prayer, no doubt the principal thing is the *inward disposition of the heart towards God*. We are well aware that "man looketh upon the outward appearance, but the LORD looketh upon the heart" (1 Samuel 16:7; cf. 2 Corinthians 10:7). Nevertheless, this should not inhibit enquiry about the *outward* behaviour or appearance of men and women in worship. After all, it is the nature of Christian discipleship and Church practice that there are outward aspects to them. Christian disciples – and the Churches – are to be a "doers of the word," as James emphasises in his 'practical' epistle. It is suggested that we have to be careful not to dismiss what we might imagine are just 'small' principles. This can so easily lead to carelessness or indifference in practice. Because the outward appearance may deceive, that does not give us warrant to be unconcerned about the outward appearance altogether. As Samuel Miller commented: "This is not essential. A prayer truly spiritual and acceptable may be offered up in any posture. And yet this is, undoubtedly, a point by no means unworthy of consideration and inquiry."[3]

3. The Biblical Material

Do the Scriptures give us any guidance on the appropriate *posture* in public prayer? What does the Bible set down as appropriate in our approach to God in prayer? A survey of relevant biblical material indicates that there are basically two postures adopted as appropriate in drawing near to God in prayer corporately: standing and kneeling.

---

[2] *The Subordinate Standards and Other Authoritative Documents of the Free Church of Scotland*, Edinburgh, 1851, 289.
[3] Samuel Miller, *Thoughts on Public Prayer*, Philadelphia, 1849, 116.

(1) *Standing.* An early indication of the appropriateness of standing before the Lord is to be found in Abraham's intercession with God on behalf of the righteous in Sodom. We are told that "Abraham stood yet before the LORD" (Genesis 18:22; cf. 19:27). When Hannah brought Samuel to Eli at the Temple she reminds the Priest that she had been the woman he had observed on an earlier occasion standing in the Temple precincts "praying unto the LORD" (1 Samuel 1:26). The same testimony is found in the New Testament in the parable of the Pharisee and the publican (Luke 18:9-14). The scene here again is the Temple and the attitude adopted in prayer is standing: "The Pharisee stood and prayed..." "The publican, standing afar off..." Clearly standing to pray was normative in such circumstances. Other instances in which we have evidence of standing for prayer are to be found, firstly, in Jehoshaphat's prayer in 2 Chronicles 20 (vv5-13), secondly, on the occasion when "the seed of Israel separated themselves from all strangers, and stood and confessed their sins, and the iniquities of their fathers" (Nehemiah 9:2; cf. v3ff.), and, thirdly, in Solomon's prayer at the dedication of the Temple (see 1 Kings 8:22. Verse 54 of that chapter indicates that Solomon must have assumed a kneeling posture in the course of his prayer, but note v55ff.). The fact that standing to pray was an appropriate posture in prayer before God is indicated also in the words of the Lord recorded in Mark's Gospel: "And when ye stand praying..." (Mark 11:25; cf. Matthew 6:5).

One other point should be made in connection with this posture. It is this: that there is a theological and reverential significance in standing before the Lord. For example, in the Book of Revelation we read that "a great multitude, which no man could number, of all nations, and kindreds, and peoples, and tongues, stood before the throne, and before the Lamb, clothed with white robes, and palms in their hands..." (Revelation 7:9; cf. 8:2ff. where the Angels are described as standing before God among other things offering prayers of the saints on the altar (v3)). The case of Elijah the Tishbite also offers us an illustration in this respect (cf. 1 Kings 19:11-13, with which cf. 1 Kings 17:1; 18:15; 2 Kings 3:14; 5:11 and 16. See also Psalm 134:1; 135:2;

Nehemiah 8:5; Exodus 19:17; Deuteronomy 4:10 (cf. Hebrews 12:18, 19); Leviticus 9:5, etc., for biblical examples illustrating this same point). There is also significance in this posture in connection with the making of a covenant with the Lord (cf. 2 Kings 23:3; 2 Chronicles 34:32; etc.). There is therefore a very strong argument from *precedent* for standing in public prayer.

(2) *Kneeling*. Kneeling is frequently referred to as an appropriate posture in prayer in God's presence. There are numerous examples of individuals assuming such a posture in prayer: There is Solomon (2 Chronicles 6:13; cf. 1 Kings 8:54), Daniel (Daniel 6:10), Ezra (Ezra 9:5), Jesus (Luke 22:41), Peter (Acts 9:40), and Paul (Acts 20:36). There are also several texts pointing to the appropriateness of such an attitude in a congregational context: In the Psalms we are enjoined: "Let us worship and bow down: let us kneel before the LORD our maker. For he is our God" (Psalm 95:6-7). In the New Testament we have the example of Paul and his company, when taking leave of the disciples at Tyre, "they all brought us on our way," says Luke, "with wives and children, till we were out of the city: and we kneeled down on the shore, and prayed" (Acts 21:5; cf. 20:36). Again, this attitude indicates theological and reverential significance, as the texts cited illustrate. (See also 1 Kings 19:18, Romans 11:4; Philippians 2:10, Isaiah 45:23, Ephesians 3:14, Romans 14:11, etc.).

It can thus be seen that both standing and kneeling are acceptable postures in public prayer, there being clear biblical *precedent* in these cases. It is true that other postures are found, such as, for example, complete prostration (cf. 2 Samuel 12:16 and 20; Leviticus 9:24; Numbers 14:5; 16:22, 45; Joshua 5:14; 7:6; Matthew 26:39; and Revelation 11:16 etc.) and clearly prayer may be made in any (physical) circumstances. However, we have no scriptural *precedent* supporting the sitting position in public prayer. In one or two instances, where there are overtones of humility or fasting (or mourning – cf. Job) there are references to sitting. For example, in Judges it is stated that "all the children of Israel, and all the people, went up, and came unto the house of God, and wept, and sat there before the LORD, and fasted. ..."

(Judges 20:26; cf. Lamentations 2:10.). In 2 Samuel 7:18 we are told that David "sat before the Lord" and spoke to Him. However, it appears that, besides the fact that this is not public prayer, the Hebrew word translated "sat" (*vashev*) should strictly speaking be rendered "remained" (thus Berkeley Version) or "abode with" (thus Genesis 24:55; Genesis 29:19).

(3) *Sitting*. As far as *sitting* in public prayer is concerned, then, Samuel Miller correctly stated that "The posture of sitting in public prayer has no countenance either from Scripture, from reason, or from respectable usage, in any part of the Church's history. It was never allowed in the ancient Church, and was universally regarded as an irreverent and heathenish mode of engaging in public devotion. True, if there be any worshippers so infirm from age, or so feeble from disease, that standing erect would really incommode or distress them to a degree unfriendly to devotion, let them sit; not in a posture of indifference or indulgence; but with bowed heads, and fixed countenances, as becomes persons reluctantly constrained to retain such an attitude, and who are yet devoutly engaged in the service."[4]

Thus, we seem to be closed in by the biblical evidence and example, and by particular theological and reverential considerations, to the propriety of standing and/or kneeling at public prayer. As the arrangement of our Churches best allows the former, it is right that on balance a standing posture should be adopted in public prayer.

4. Some Historical Considerations

Standing at public prayer appears to have been prevalent in the first few centuries of the Christian Church. The *Council of Nicea* (A.D. 325) enjoined that worshippers in the Churches on the Lord's Day stand for prayer. The 20th Canon of that Council ordered that "all persons shall offer up their prayers on Sundays and Pentecost standing."[5] In the early Church the significance of standing for prayer was closely related to the

---

[4] Samuel Miller, *Thoughts on Public Prayer*, 127-128.
[5] Edward H Landon, *A Manual of Councils*, London, 1846, 436.

resurrection. Thus, Augustine stated that, "We pray standing, which is a sign of the resurrection."[6] The Princeton historian, Samuel Miller, summarised the position thus: "...in the second, third, and following centuries, it was accounted unlawful even to kneel on the Lord's day; this posture being reserved for days of fasting and humiliation. This is asserted by Tertullian; and the Council of Nice passed a solemn decree to the same amount, because on that day is celebrated the joyful remembrance of our Lord's resurrection. This posture, both of public prayer on the Lord's day, and of receiving the communion, was invariably standing."[7]

At the time of the Reformation the practice of kneeling at public prayer was more evident, though there was a shift to the standing posture, principally arising from the disapproval felt of the anti-Protestant practice of kneeling to receive communion, and desire to give no countenance to such a Roman Catholic practice.[8]

One final consideration is the position of the Free Church of Scotland in the 20th century. Act VII, 1910 anent *Postures in Public Worship* stated that "The General Assembly...declare that the posture in public prayer sanctioned by Scripture and authorised by this Church, and the reverence due to the professed worship of God, is that of standing; and inasmuch as there is no guidance in the matter of praise, it is expedient, having regard to the comfort of worshippers, that the position in praise be that of reverent sitting in the pew."[9]

5. Some Practical Applications

Bear in mind that we are here seeking simply to encourage a practice which is patterned on the Word of God for *public worship*. We are not saying that people are not or cannot be praying if they are seated. We are not saying either that it is wrong to stand for sung praise. However,

---

[6] Ep. 55 ad. Jan. Cited by H C B Bazeley, *Standing to Pray*.
[7] Samuel Miller, *Manual of Presbytery*, Edinburgh, 1842, 147.
[8] Cf. Charles G M'Crie, *Public Worship of Presbyterian Scotland*, Edinburgh, 1892, 447ff; and Samuel Miller, *Manual*, 146-148.
[9] *Free Church of Scotland Acts of Assembly*, 1910, 374.

it is our conviction on the balance of Scriptural teaching that standing for prayer in public worship is warranted by the Word of God. People and Churches must answer for themselves before the Lord. Without making this a term of communion with other Christians and Churches we may well with a good conscience continue to observe the standing posture in our public prayers, as previously held to, for example, in the Free Church of Scotland.

It is good to remind ourselves of the significance of our practice of standing for prayer in its reverential aspect. Standing for public prayer, as we have sought to show, does not arise from mere caprice or indifference, but derives from deep consciousness of the holy character of God, and is revealed as an appropriate manner in which people approach His throne in public prayer. This practice at least has the sanction of Scripture and is properly reverential in its nature. It would be strange if we were not to stand to address the Queen if she came into our presence. That seems all the more reason to maintain this practice when we think that in prayer we approach Almighty God to address the King of kings!

WORSHIP

7. The Wearing of Head coverings by Women during Public Worship Services[1]

1. The issue stated

Paul uses some important theological arguments when he exhorts the women in the congregation of Corinth to cover their heads and men not to cover their heads during public worship. As the majority of Bible commentators from the past and some of from the present (e.g. R. C. Sproul[2]) explain, the wearing of an appropriate head-covering by women during public worship is not optional. Paul teaches in 1 Corinthians 11:1-16 that this is divinely mandated, and that failure to do so is an act of disobedience toward God's revealed will.

Some state, however, that Paul teaches in verse 15 that the woman's hair is her covering, and that therefore no physical covering is required. Others claim that Paul says in verse 16 that the wearing of a physical head-covering is only a custom, and that we have no such custom in the church of God.

2. Flaws in arguments against the use of physical head coverings by women

These interpretations are seriously flawed for the following reasons:

- First, such an interpretation of verses 15 & 16 ignores what Paul has written in verses 1-14. To hold to such a view would

---

[1] This exposition from the Rev Bartel Elshout and the Heritage Reformed Church Consistory of Chilliwack, British Columbia, first appeared in *The Banner of Sovereign Grace Truth*, Volume 20, Number 6, July/August 2012, pages 158-161, and is used with the authors' kind permission.

[2] Sproul's exposition of 1 Corinthians 11:1-16 is to be found on-line under 'Principle or Custom?' in his *Table Talk* web-site at http://www.ligonier.org/learn/scripture/1-corinthians_11/

create the impression that Paul has been arguing about something that does not really matter and that in verses 15 and 16 he apologizes for any confusion he may have created. Such an argument would mean that 1 Corinthians 11:1-13 has little or nothing to say to the New Testament Church today. This obviously cannot be the case! Paul, who so brilliantly lays out his points, being inspired by God, in all of his letters, is not suddenly theologically inept here by contradicting in verses 15 and 16 what he has convincingly stated in verses 3-13. He makes it clear in verse 2 that he wants the Corinthian Church to keep the (apostolic) ordinances he has delivered unto them, and then proceeds in verses 3 to 13 to explain that the wearing of the head-covering by women (and not wearing a head-covering by men) is one of these ordinances. In other words, verses 15 and 16 can only be properly understood by taking into account that which has been stated in verses 3 to 14. To explain verses 15 and 16 completely divorced from the context in which they are found is to be guilty of taking Scripture out of context.

- Second, if one believes that a woman's hair is her covering, and if one would consistently apply that interpretation to verses 3 to 7 and 13, it would render these verses ludicrous. What happens if we substitute "hair" for the verb "to cover" or the noun "covering"? The passage would then read as follows:

> But I would have you know, that the head of every man is Christ; and the head of the woman is the man; and the head of Christ is God. Every man praying or prophesying, having *hair on his head*, dishonoureth his head. But every woman that prayeth or prophesieth *without hair on her head* dishonoureth her head: for that is even all one as if she were shaven. For if the woman *have no hair on her head*, let her also be shorn: but if it be a shame for a woman to be shorn or shaven, let her *have hair on her head*. For a man indeed ought not to *have hair on his head*, forasmuch as he is the image and glory of God: but the woman is the glory of the man...Judge in

> yourselves: is it comely that a woman prays unto God *without hair on her head?*

Thus, the insistence that hair is equivalent to head-covering would render what Paul is saying in these verses nonsensical. This leads to one conclusion: Paul, as the divinely inspired writer of 1 Corinthians 11:15-16, cannot possibly negate and/or contradict what he has argued so compellingly in verses 3 to13.

Also, if 1 Corinthians 11 simply meant that women should have long hair and men short, there would be no need to specify that this should be when they meet for public worship (to pray and prophecy) as this command would apply to all times, not just to church worship services.

Therefore, before we address what Paul is saying in verses 15 and 16, we must address what he is teaching in verses 3 to 13. In order to examine this passage in its proper context, we need to understand the following:

- First, in the larger context of 1 Corinthians 11, Paul is dealing with issues that pertain to public worship. Specifically, he is addressing two problems that had surfaced in the public worship of the Corinthian church:
  1. Insubordination of women to divine (male) authority in public worship (that is, when the congregation is engaged in public prayer and public teaching); and the
  2. Abuse of the sacrament of the Lord's Supper.
- Second, Paul deals with the female insubordination problem by addressing a sin that reinforced this insubordination, namely, the failure of the Corinthian women to wear a head-covering in public worship – the visible symbol of submission to divine authority in public worship. Paul recognizes that addressing the head-covering issue will go a long way in resolving this insubordination, for the wearing of the head-covering will be a visible and physical reminder to the women of their divinely appointed place in public worship. He addresses this issue also in 1 Corinthians 14:35-36, when he writes: "Let your women

keep silence in the churches: for it is not permitted unto them to speak; but they are commanded to be under obedience, as also saith the law. And if they will learn any thing, let them ask their husbands at home: for it is a shame for women to speak in the church."

- Third, when Paul uses the words "cover" or "covering," he uses a Greek word that means "veil" – a word that refers to a cloth covering. It is noteworthy that in verse 15 he uses a different Greek word for the word "covering," referring to a much more generic type of covering. He does this for the simple reason that he is talking about two different kinds of covering. In other words, when he talks about the hair being a covering in verse 15, he is talking about something very different than the veil or cloth covering he is referring to in verses 3 to 13.

3. Theological arguments stated

Let us now consider the theological arguments Paul uses to convince the Corinthian women that by refusing to wear a head-covering in public worship they are disobedient to God's revealed will for public worship. Paul, consistent with his position and skill as the master theologian of the New Testament church, advances three weighty theological reasons why women must have their heads covered during public worship. Here they are:

Argument 1:
The wearing of the female head-covering in public worship visibly reinforces God's authority structure in the community of the church - a community that recognizes and submits to Divine authority. Paul teaches us here that there is a divine hierarchy that must be observed. That hierarchy looks as follows: God is the head of Christ, Christ is the head of the man, and the man is the head of the woman. Or to put it this way, the divine order is God, Christ, the man, and then the woman.

As the inspired penman, Paul tells us in verses 3 and 4 that if a man engages in public worship with his physical head covered (his hair is *not* the issue!), he dishonours his spiritual head, Christ. In a sinful way he would be challenging God's established hierarchy.

However, to emphasize that the woman's place in this divine authority structure is not the same, but that her place is one of subordination to the man, she must cover her head in public worship, for in not doing so she would place herself on the same level as the man, and thereby would challenge and defy God's hierarchy. Thus, Paul is teaching that it is God's revealed will that the woman's head be covered in public worship as a visible reinforcement of His, the Creator's, established hierarchy. It was the failure of the Corinthian women to understand this divine hierarchy that led them to engage in what only men may do in public worship: engage in public teaching and prayer. To counter this serious problem, Paul goes to great length in explaining why the head-covering must be worn, for he viewed it as the divinely appointed antidote for such disobedience to God's revealed will.

Paul reinforces this argument in yet another way in verse 7 when he emphasizes that the man's head may not be covered since he is "the image and glory of God"; that is, he is the divinely appointed bearer of authority in the church. He is God's appointed representative to exercise His authority in the church. Since the woman is the glory of the man, that glory must be veiled, so that only God's glory be visible in His house. Since that glory is symbolized by her long hair (verse 15), this glory must be veiled or covered in public worship. In public worship only God's glory (reflected in the man) must be visible, and man's glory (reflected in the woman) must be veiled.

Therefore, when a woman engages in public worship with her head uncovered, it is a symbolical statement that she views herself as being on par with the man in terms of God's hierarchy. Paul teaches us here, as he does elsewhere in the New Testament, that such equality is contrary to God's created order.

As we read these verses, let us keep in mind that it is the Holy Spirit who moved Paul to address this issue in detail. He (the Spirit) did so in anticipation of the resistance there would be to this divine hierarchy in the New Testament Church – including the church today.

Argument 2:

Recognizing that his argument would meet with resistance, Paul now advances another argument that is rooted in creation itself. In theology an argument that is rooted in God's original creation order is always the most powerful argument that can be made, for it recognizes that in redemption God restores and enhances His original created order.

To reinforce that in God's created order and hierarchy the role of the woman is subordinate to that of the man, Paul stresses the following:

- The woman was made from the man; not vice versa (verse 8).
- The woman was created for the man; not vice versa (verse 9).

And so, Paul is emphasizing that the woman's position in God's order of things, also in the church, is rooted in the order in which God created the man and the woman—and in His purpose in creating them in this order. God created the woman to be the man's helpmeet (i.e. a help suitable for him) and his "completer." Therefore, to allow women to have a position of equality in public worship is contrary to God's creation ordinance. This challenge to God's order cannot be permitted in the public activity of the church, for it is nothing less than a defiance of God's revealed will. Also, in 1 Timothy, 2:11-14 Paul uses the creation argument to establish this position when he writes, "Let the woman learn in silence with all subjection. But I suffer not a woman to teach, nor to usurp authority over the man, but to be in silence. *For Adam was first formed, then Eve. And Adam was not deceived, but the woman being deceived was in the transgression.*"

This is what Paul is also teaching in 1 Corinthians 11:8-9. Here he presents the theological argument as to why women must cover their heads in public worship, and why men may not. The observance of this divine precept becomes all the more important in a culture that rebels at all levels of society against God's created order and authority structure.

Lest there be men, however, who would abuse their God-given position of headship, Paul hastens to add in verses 11-12 that in their status before God, men and women are equal and are fully dependent upon each other. And yet they are not equal in the roles which God has assigned to each of the sexes. In God's order the woman's role is one of subordination rather than leadership, and to challenge that order is an abomination to God. In recognition of that, Paul therefore spends a great deal of time explaining why women must have their heads covered in public worship.

Argument 3:

As Paul presents his argument from creation, he inserts another supporting thought. In verse 10 he says, "For this cause (that is, the woman being created for the man) ought the woman to have power on her head because of the angels." The Greek word translated here as "power" is the word frequently translated as "authority." We find this word in the well-known words of Christ when He says to His disciples, "All power is given unto me in heaven and in earth" (Matthew 28:18). With equal justification this could be translated as "All authority is given unto me in heaven and in earth." The connection is obvious: authority is inextricably linked to power. One who has authority over others can exercise power over them.

What Paul is therefore telling us in verse 10 is that in order to reinforce God's creation order, the woman must have authority on her head, thereby confirming what we have already concluded: the head-covering is a symbol of divinely instituted authority. It is by wearing the head-covering that the godly woman confesses her willing submission to this divine authority, and that she knows her proper place in God's hierarchy. Therefore, the wearing of the head-covering in public worship is a public statement by the church, as well as by the woman who wears it, that they willingly submit to God's authority structure.

Why does Paul mention the angels in this connection? In the context of verses 8 to 12, he does so to reinforce his logical and theological argument.

First of all, the angels themselves are the perfect example of willing submission to divine authority. They know and honour their proper place in God's order, being ministering spirits who are ever ready to do God's bidding. We read of this in Psalm 103:21: "Bless ye the LORD, all ye His hosts; ye ministers of his, that do his pleasure." That is why Christ teaches us in the Lord's Prayer that we should pray that God's will may "be done in earth *as it is in heaven.*" In other words, we should be as ready to do God's will as the angels are ready to do God's will in heaven. And thus the angels are set before us here as the ultimate example of unquestioned and unconditional submission to God's will. Consider also the sin of the angels that fell; they were not content with their God-appointed position.

Second, Calvin comments as follows on verse 10: "But it is asked, why it is that he would have women have their heads covered *because of the angels* – for what has this to do with them? Some answer: 'Because they are present on occasion of the prayers of believers, and on this account are spectators of unseemliness, should there be any on such occasions.' But what need is there for philosophizing with such refinement? We know that angels are in attendance, also, upon Christ as their head, and minister to him. When, therefore, women venture upon such liberties, as to usurp for themselves the token of authority, they make their baseness manifest to the angels. This, therefore, was said by way of amplifying, as if he had said, 'If women uncover their heads, not only Christ, but all the angels too, will be witnesses of the outrage'" (Calvin's Commentaries).

Thus, Calvin argues that the angels are always present when God's church worships. They are the unseen guests. Since they are the ultimate example of whole-hearted submission to God's authority, they are most pleased when the church in her public worship displays her submission to this authority – a submission that is also visibly displayed by women veiling their heads in public worship.

4. Implications of the arguments used

Having supported his teaching that it is God's revealed will that women cover (or veil) their heads in public worship by way of three compelling theological arguments, he then asks this question to his readers, "Judge in yourselves: is it comely (that is "proper") that a woman pray unto God uncovered?" (He is obviously *not* talking about women praying without hair.) In light of his arguments, there is only one logical answer: It is not proper for women to pray in public without their heads being covered.

It is only at this point, after Paul has rested his case, that he refers to the woman's hair. After having made his point theologically, he now uses an argument from nature for any who might still not be persuaded. Paul is saying in verse 15 that not only is there a theological difference between men and woman, but there is even a visible difference – a difference reinforced by the length of hair. It is the long hair of the woman that sets her apart from the man, and Paul here argues that this natural difference simply underscores that there is a well-defined theological difference. It is as though Paul is saying, "If God has given the woman a natural covering (*not* the word "veil" or "cloth covering" of verses 3-7), then I should not have to argue about the fact that in public worship God requires a physical covering whereby her glory is veiled." Therefore, verse 15 is really Paul's fourth argument in support of the divine mandate that women cover their heads in public worship.

Only now will we be able to understand what Paul means in verse 16. He is saying, "If any man, after all the solid arguments I have advanced, still wants to argue (be contentious) about something that is God's revealed will, we (the churches) have no such custom; that is, we do not debate endlessly about something that is taught in Scripture. In the churches, God's truth is not up for debate." In other words, Paul is saying, "If anyone still wants to argue about this, I will not be a party in this debate. I have made my point, and I now move on to the next issue."

Elsewhere Paul also warns against such a contentious spirit toward biblical teaching, when he writes, "If any man teach otherwise, and consent not to wholesome words, even the words of our Lord Jesus Christ, and to the doctrine which is according to godliness; He is proud, knowing nothing, but doting about questions and strifes of words, whereof cometh envy, strife, railings, evil surmisings, perverse disputings of men of corrupt minds, and destitute of the truth" (1 Timothy 6:3-5).

And so it is with apostolic (and thus divine) authority that Paul teaches that one of the ways in which godly women display their godliness is by willingly covering their heads in public worship. Failure to do so is disobedience, and therefore dishonouring to God and grieving to His Spirit.

5. Significance of the stated practice

It is for this reason that there are a growing number of churches in evangelical North America that have reinstated the biblical practice of women wearing a head-covering in public worship. It is being rediscovered that Paul's use of theological arguments in support of this position makes it clear that godly women wearing a head-covering in public worship is a divine ordinance taught in God's Word and not a result of legalism or tradition.

There are a number of Reformed denominations in North America and the Netherlands who now endorse women in church offices. The disturbing fact is that the pathway toward this unscriptural position began with the rejection of the teaching of 1 Corinthians 11:1-16 regarding the divinely mandated use of the woman's head-covering in public worship. Once the symbol of the head-covering was rejected (along with all of its theological implications), it was only a relatively smaller step toward teaching that women should also be permitted to hold positions of authority in the church as office-bearers.

This down-hill trajectory underscores the fact that the head-covering issue is more important than some deem it to be. A careful study of 1 Corinthians 11:1-16 teaches that God's precept regarding head-coverings is binding for the New Testament Church until Christ returns. Therefore a disregard for this divine precept governing public worship will inevitably produce will-worship – a worship of God according to our notions rather than the teaching of His Word.

The words of Christ in His Sermon on the Mount are therefore also applicable in regard to this issue, "Verily I say unto you, Till heaven and earth pass, one jot or one tittle shall in no wise pass from the law, till all be fulfilled. Whosoever therefore shall break one of these least commandments, and shall teach men so, he shall be called the least in the kingdom of heaven" (Matthew 5:17-18).

And thus, also regarding this issue we are to remember that we are forbidden to add to or subtract from Scripture (Revelation 22:18-19), for in doing so we will make the Word of God of none effect.

6. Conclusion

In conclusion, what is at stake here with this head-covering issue is the teaching of God's Word in 1 Corinthians 11:1-16 regarding God's revealed will for public worship. To deny that Scripture here requires that women wear a head-covering in public worship and men do not, has serious implications; it would mean that:

1) 1 Corinthians 11:1-16 is such an ambiguous passage of Scripture that it cannot be determined with certainty what the Holy Spirit is teaching here.
2) Paul in this passage writes as a very inept theologian, who uses various important theological arguments, and then basically tells us to ignore what he just said.
3) We cannot know with certainty which portions of Paul's writings are applicable for the church today. If 1 Corinthians 11:1-16 is only applicable to the Corinthian setting, then it can also be argued that other portions of Paul's writing are only applicable to the circumstances of his day.

Given the fact, however, that Paul expresses himself in a clear and logical fashion (as he does in all of his epistles), devotes one half of a chapter to this subject, and supports his argument with fundamental biblical principles, the only sound conclusion is that Paul's explicit insistence that women wear a cloth covering in public worship is because in God's wisdom the head-covering represents biblical truths that are of fundamental importance.

And it also needs to be understood that this instruction was not merely intended for the Corinthian Church. The opening words of this first epistle to the Corinthians make it abundantly clear that Paul's instruction was intended for the entire New Testament Church. He writes, "Unto the church of God which is at Corinth, to them that are sanctified in Christ Jesus, called to be saints, *with all that in every place call upon the name of Jesus Christ our Lord*" (1 Corinthians 1:2).

We conclude therefore that it is indeed important to take a stand on head-covering issue. We need to do so in order to defend:

1) The integrity of God's Word;
2) The integrity of Paul's writings;
3) A component of public worship that visibly reinforces God's authority structure and created order in His Church.

May God give us the courage and steadfastness to take every part of His inspired Word seriously – also 1 Corinthians 11:1-16!

Note:

The above exposition was the predominant position and practice in the Christian Churches up to the 20th Century. The reason for changes in practice have arguably arisen from the social pressures of the so called 'women's liberation' movement of the 1960s and the subsequent feminism which became so widespread in the West. An interesting implication from this passage relates to the propriety of Christian women having 'long hair' to preserve a distinction from men, who should not have 'long hair.' Though the precise length of hair is not specified, the general tendency in recent times of women having hair length more or less indistinguishable from men also arguably breaches the apostle's teaching here. For further reading readers are invited to consult David J. Lipsy's, The Headcovering in Worship, *Word-Based Publishing, Pompton Plains, New Jersey, 2005.*

WORSHIP

8. Collections and Offerings

A. Introduction

In the Reformed Confessions little if anything is to be found about 'collection', 'giving', 'offering' or 'tithing' as an aspect of Christian devotion or responsibility. The situation has not really changed much since William Binnie wrote over a century ago:

> This [i.e., giving to the Lord] also is a divine ordinance. This ordinance, moreover, has received a larger and more honourable place in the Bible than has ever yet been conceded to it in our books of divinity.[1]

For some reason it has been a subject to shy clear of, and yet a subject, one way or another, which can become for a Church a preoccupation, causing much tortuous heart-searching. This may arise because the Church, and its people are losing touch with a living faith in the risen and ascended Lord. Essentially this is, after all, a matter of devotion, and the uncomfortable truth is that where a financial 'problem' exists for a Church the fundamental answer is not to be found in the pocket, but in the heart. The early disciples seemed to have a freedom from the anxieties of financial provision. To the lame man at the Beautiful Gate at the Temple Peter was to say: "Silver and gold have I none; but such as I have give I thee..." (Acts 3:6). It seems impossible to us to go through life, including Church life, without financial anxieties. The uncomfortable truth is, that it is not a 'problem' when the priorities and spiritual state of a Church are right. We must never lose sight of this spiritual dimension.

However, this said, finance is nonetheless of real importance for a Church, not least for the maintenance of ministry. As William Binnie

---
[1] William Binnie, *The Church*, Edinburgh, c1882, 94.

pointed out, giving to the Lord looms large in the Bible. Clearly, giving to the Lord's cause is a vital spiritual matter within the Church. The focus is on the responsibility of the Christian as a steward. This should therefore always be in the forefront of the professing Christian's life before the Lord. We may have a lot, we may have little, either way, this is an important aspect of Christian discipleship as an indicator of a person's real estimation of the Lord and His cause on earth (Luke 21:1-4).

In looking at the question of giving to the Lord, we will in this chapter consider some general principles governing giving to the Lord. In this we will be speaking primarily of giving of our financial substance. That will be a token – a token based, hopefully, on Biblical guidelines – which simply reflects a total commitment of time, talents, and resources to the Lord. The trouble is, we so readily 'hold back' (Acts 5:1-11). Practically speaking, our reference point will be the giving of our financial substance to the local congregation. It is recognised that a Christian's giving to the Lord's cause may extend beyond the local Church. It is assumed, however, that the fundamental concern of the Christian as steward will be towards the local congregation, or the wider Church of which it is a part, for the maintenance of its gospel ministry and missions, church fabric and charitable work. We consider the principles applicable in this matter.

B. Principles

1. Why we give to the Lord

(1) First of all *we give because all we have is from God*. Human beings were made in the image and likeness of God. Though seriously defaced by the fall into sin, they still have the imprint of their Maker upon them, whether they acknowledge it or not. The Biblical doctrine of creation alerts us to the basic reality that our lives are from Him, and all we have or receive are from Him. Says Paul to the Corinthian Church: "who maketh thee to differ from another? And what hast thou that thou didst not receive? now if thou didst receive it, why dost thou glory, as if thou

hadst not received it?" (1 Corinthians 4:7). Clearly this applies to material as well as spiritual blessings. This may seem commonplace, this implication of creation. But it is after all a powerful fundamental perspective in our attitude to our possessions. David in his expression of praise in connection with the collections for the (future) building of the Temple, cries out: "But who am I, and what is my people, that we should be able to offer as willingly after this sort? for all things come of thee, and of thine own we have given thee." He goes on: "O LORD our God, all this store that we have prepared to build thee a house for thine holy name cometh from thine hand, and is all thine own" (1 Chronicles, 29:14, 16). So, principle number 1 is this: we give because all we have we have received from our gracious God!

(2) Further, the Christian gives *because he or she has submitted to Jesus as Lord*. If Jesus is a person's Lord, then he should be Lord of all; of our talents, our time, and also our money. Paul encourages the Corinthian Church to excel in giving (2 Corinthians 8:1-7). What is our pattern in this? Well, surely it is Jesus Himself: "For you know the grace of our Lord Jesus Christ, that, though he was rich, yet for your sakes he became poor, that ye through his poverty might be rich" (v9). He then goes on to encourage their giving and concludes by quoting Exodus 16:18: "As it is written, He that had gathered much had nothing left over; and he that had gathered little had no lack." We give as Jesus our Lord gave (of Himself).

(3) Another motive for giving is found in this: *we give because our spiritual welfare is advanced by our giving*. Perhaps we should say that this is a *consequence* of our giving to the Lord. In Acts 20, as Paul gives his parting counsel to the Ephesian elders, he affirms that he has not coveted anyone's money or clothes, and he says: "I have shewed you all things, how that so labouring ye ought to support the weak, and to remember the words of the Lord Jesus, how he said, It is more blessed to give than to receive" (v35). More blessed to give? Yes, there is spiritual blessing in giving, not least in giving to the Lord, for His cause.

(4) One other motive for giving to the Lord is simply this: *we give because He desires it*. This is written so large over both Old and New Testaments

that it scarcely needs any 'proofs' here. There are tithes and offerings (e.g. Leviticus 27; Numbers 18; Deuteronomy 14; Nehemiah 10; Malachi 3); talents (e.g., Exodus 38; Matthew 25); and collections (1 Corinthians 16; 2 Corinthians 8) all clearly desired by the Lord. The Lord desires us to give. It is our privilege, and our duty to respond accordingly.

2. What we give for

Basically, Christian giving is for the Church's ministry. In this connection there are at least three financial priorities. The first of these is this:

(1) *Christian giving is for the support of the ministry of the Word.*

It is for the support of those who will be engaged in the full-time ministry of preaching, pastoring and praying. This was the reason behind the appointment of the first deacons in Acts 6 (if they were deacons in the strictest sense of the term[2]): to allow the apostles to give themselves continually to prayer and to the ministry of the word. A full-time paid ministry is perfectly consonant with that principle. "The labourer is worthy of his hire", taught Jesus (Luke 10:7). Writing to the Corinthians, Paul put it this way: "the Lord ordained that they which preach the gospel should live of the gospel" (1 Corinthians 9:14), by which we take it that just as the priests in the Old Testament lived out of the Temple revenues (Numbers 18:25-26), the New Testament preachers are to derive their personal and family subsistence from their ministry. This is implicit also in what Paul writes to the Galatian Churches: "Let him that is taught in the word communicate unto him that teacheth in all good things" (Galatians 6:6). The Christian is basically giving for the maintenance of a ministry which is as 'full-time' as possible.

---

[2] See the chapter on the diaconate in Section E below.

Worship – Collections

(2) *Christian giving is also directed towards the ministry of mercy.*
That is to say, it will be partly also directed towards the relief of the poor (see Acts 3; Deuteronomy 14:28-29). Again, what Professor Binnie wrote more than a century ago is still valid, even in our era of the Welfare State:

> Where there is a legal provision for the relief of the poor, the need for Church action in this matter is considerably mitigated. Still, the hand of this kind of charity is a cold hand at best...(and) there is much room left for the kindly attentions to the godly poor on the part of their brethren in Christ."[3]

No doubt the Church and its courts – and members and adherents of local Churches – might be far more aware of needs within the professing Christian community than is the case currently. There is an assumption of a State safety net. But for sure this does not absolve the Churches from responsibility for a ministry of mercy.

(3) *Christian giving is for the support for missionary endeavour.*
In a sense this is hardly distinguishable from the first priority mentioned, but it is worth focussing on separately. Christian giving should be directed most specifically towards the extension of the cause of Christ at home and overseas. This is to say that giving is to be towards the support of ministry not only in this or that given congregation – 'our' congregation – but also generally towards the support of the gospel as it is spread abroad by those whom the Lord raises for that task. Clearly New Testament collections were also for just this sort of purpose (Philippians 4:10-20).

3. What we should give

Perhaps this concerns people more than anything: Practically speaking, what am I to give? What does the Lord require of me? Here I have a certain income (from all sources), what amount(s) should I be giving for the Lord's work? What should I be 'putting in the plate'? As we look at the Biblical material we need to look first of all at the

---

[3] Binnie, op. cit., 95

prominence given in the Old Testament to the tithe and the practice of tithing.

(1) *The Old Testament tithe.* The first thing to be said is that the Lord did not simply leave it to the whim of the people what they should give for the support of the ministry. He established the tithe as the norm. This is clear from the law of Moses (Leviticus 27:30-32). The tithe was a tenth part of one's resources – produce or 'income'. That tenth was to be holy, that is, 'separated to the Lord.' It was precisely from this 'tithe' that the priestly, Levitical, families were to be supported (Numbers 18:25-26). The children of Israel frequently failed to observe this law once they settled in the land. That was a mark of declension. Interestingly, at periods of spiritual revival, this ordinance came back into the picture. For instance, at the time of Hezekiah there was a revival. This involved, as all genuine revivals will, a return to the teaching of the Scriptures. So, the Temple is cleansed (2 Chronicles 29:3ff.); the Temple worship is restored (2 Chronicles 29:20ff.); the Passover is kept (2 Chronicles 30:1ff.); and then this: "Moreover he commanded the people that dwelt in Jerusalem to give the portion of the priests and the Levites, that they might be encouraged in the Law of the LORD" (2 Chronicles 31:4). What contribution? Well, "as soon as the commandment came abroad, the children of Israel brought in abundance the first-fruits of corn, wine, and oil, and honey, and of all the increase of the field; and the tithe of all things brought they in abundantly" (v5, and also v6). A similar situation occurred in the days of Nehemiah in a restored Jerusalem (Nehemiah 10:34-37). Yes, a time of spiritual awakening brought a restoration of responsibility also for the 'tithe', and thereby the support of the ministry of the 'Law of the LORD.' Even the very last book of the Old Testament revelation brings out the significance of the tithe in connection with spiritual responsibility and blessing: The people had "robbed God" (Malachi 3:8). How? Withholding "tithes and offerings." What does the Lord say? "Bring ye all the tithes into the storehouse, that there may be meat in mine house, and prove me now herewith, saith the LORD of hosts, if I will not open for you the windows of heaven and pour you out a

blessing that there shall not be room enough to receive it" (v10). In all these cases the relationship between tithes and blessings is clear. Surely no lesser standard is to be expected of the New Testament Church.

One further point may be made about the Old Testament tithe. It is often used as an argument for the perpetuity of the Sabbath, not only that it is contained in the Mosaic moral law, but that it is found in practice *before* the law was given formally. This is also true of the tithe. We read of the tithe *before* the law given by Moses. It is first found in Genesis 14 in the meeting of Abraham with Melchizedek as Abraham returns from the rescuing of Lot from captivity. Significantly, this 'giving' is discussed in Hebrews 7 in the context of Melchizedek being considered as a 'type' of Christ. "What does this passage tell us about tithing?" asks Fred Catherwood.

> It tells us that since Christ's order of priesthood preceded and succeeded the Mosaic priesthood, the tithe, which illustrates the argument, must also precede and succeed the law.[4]

The conclusion is this: "If Abraham gave a tithe to Melchizedek, can we give any less to Christ?" Again it comes into Jacob's vow at Bethel after his vision of the Lord in a dream there (Genesis 28:22). The tithe, then, was clearly the norm for giving in the Old Testament Church, though it clearly was not just a matter of Jewish law. But what about the New Testament practice?

(2) *The New Testament practice.* First of all it could be argued that Jesus gave His approval in an indirect way to the Old Testament tithing system when He reproaches the Pharisees for neglecting the weightier matters of the law whilst being so careful about their tithing (Matthew 23:23). The implication is that their tithing was quite proper, but it was an anomaly to be proper about that whilst negligent of bigger spiritual issues. As the Lord said on another occasion: "These ought ye to have done, and not to leave the other undone" (Luke 11:42).

It may be argued that there is no formal advocacy of tithing in Christian giving in the New Testament. Does this mean that we can

---

[4] H F R Catherwood, *God's Time, God's Money*, London, 1987, 143.

leave aside tithing as a principle for the New Testament Church, or that people may just give as they are 'led' or can 'afford'? The answer to these questions must be, No! Whilst tithing is not specifically stated as mandatory 'law' for the New Testament believer, it is scarcely arguable that a lower standard of commitment in giving would be expected of a New Testament Christian than was required or expected of the Old Testament believer. The New Testament teaching surely confirms this.

It has to be said that the Christian believer's commitment is seen to be total. The claims of Christ are total. Take the case of the rich young ruler. He asked what he should do to have eternal life (Luke 18:18). He reckoned he had kept all the commandments, but Jesus identifies an 'Achilles heel': "Sell all that thou hast and distribute to the poor..." (v22). The issue was the attachment of the young man to his material possessions. In some way, like so many people today, he was putting his trust in his affluence. There is also the sad case of Ananias and Sapphira in Acts 5. Ananias "kept back part of the proceeds" of the sale of a possession, a fact his wife knew well about. They were both judged for lying to the Holy Spirit. It wasn't that the keeping back a part was the serious thing – it was their possession, they were entitled to do with it as the liked. The serious thing was giving the impression that it was the whole of the proceeds. The point is, that this passage indicates just how great the commitment of some was, an implication of the behaviour of the first converts, something clearly linked in with the blessing being enjoyed (Acts 3:40-47).

Jesus demands wholeheartedness in discipleship. This does not mean applying *all* one's resources to the work of the Church. But it does mean maintaining the Old Testament standard at least, *developed in terms of liberality*. Christian giving will transcend tithing! Specifically, notice:

1) *Christian giving will be proportionate*. This is clear from 1 Corinthians 16. Collections are to be laid aside "as God hath prospered him" (v2), that is to say, it is to be a proportion of your total income.

2) *Christian giving will be sacrificial.* Is this not clear from what Paul wrote of the giving of the Corinthian Church?: "in a great trial of affliction the abundance of their joy and their deep poverty abounded unto the riches of their liberality. For to their power, I bear record, yea, and beyond their power [ability] they were willing of themselves" (2 Corinthians 8:2-3).
3) *Christian giving will be substantial.* Returning to Acts, this is clearly the implication of the practice of the first converts at Pentecost: "Now all who believed were together, and had all things in common, and sold their possessions and goods, and divided them among all, as anyone had need" (Acts 2:44-45). Whatever else this demonstrates, it certainly indicates that giving was substantial.

4. How we should give

The practical question then arises as to how Christian giving is to be done. Again, the New Testament gives clear guidelines:

1) *Christian giving will be systematic.* "Upon the first day of the week let every one of you lay by him in store, as God hath prospered him" (1 Corinthians 16:2). There should be a systematic weekly collection each Lord's day. A weekly envelope scheme is a great help to systematic giving and should be encouraged amongst all givers. The collection in the plate is indeed the first act of worship in our services on the Lord's day.
2) *Christian giving will be cheerful.* It will be "cheerful." The Lord loveth such a giver (2 Corinthians 9:7). It will be out of love for the Lord, for his Church, for the ministry of the Word. It will be Freely and willingly (2 Corinthians 8:3). Christians should give freely, out of a spirit of devotion and love for the Saviour. Remember the widow's mite (Luke 21:1-4)!
3) *Christian giving will be discreet.* In the Sermon on the Mount Jesus teaches about alms – or, "charitable deed." He warns His followers not to blow their own trumpet about their giving, but rather observe discretion, not letting the right hand know what

the left hand is doing, "that thine alms may be in secret: and the Father which seeth in secret shall himself reward thee openly" (Matthew 6:1-4). The way this is usually secured is by the use of an envelope system. It may be for a Gift Aid donor that the amounts of collections must be recorded for recovery of tax. However, that should itself be done discreetly by those who handle these matters in the congregation.

Christian giving, then, basically flows from these two things: (a) A love to the Lord Jesus Christ (2 Corinthians 8:9); and, (b) The obligations of Christian stewardship (Luke 16:1-13).

5. Some practical matters.
There are however, some practical matters that are of concern to people:
(1) *If I am going to give in the region of a tenth of my income, will that be from my gross income, or net, disposable income?*
Essentially it ought to be based upon total gross income. The argument has been made that the taxes imposed by the state are applied in part at least in a way that would legitimately be part of a 'tithe', namely, taxes raised in connection with the care of the sick, the poor, and the underprivileged. On this basis it is maintained that only a tenth of net income might be considered a norm for giving by Christians. Against this it has to be said that, (a) in New Testament times the believers were required to pay both their tithe of all their income and the Roman taxes (Matthew 17:24-27); (b) the welfare support through regular taxes by no means exhausts the need, nor the Christian's responsibility in terms of a ministry of mercy; and, (c) in any case, if a person is a tax-payer this matter is happily resolved by Gift Aid Declarations so that the tax relative to the actual contribution made may be recovered from the Inland Revenue. The recovery of income tax from such giving is perfectly consistent with the Establishment principle traditionally maintained in the Free Church of Scotland, namely, that the state has a responsibility to maintain the true Christian religion (without persecuting policies).

(2) What about the responsibility of students (or widowers or widows)?
Is their income by way of grants not too low to expect them to tithe, or to give proportionately? It is a matter of priorities, and of the confidence the Christian student has that the Lord will provide. No one will ever lose out who so trusts in the Lord, and so loves the Lord that he or she is prepared, whatever their circumstances, to give proportionately, sacrificially and substantially of their incomes. [This would not strictly speaking apply to student loans, which presumably remain to be wholly repaid].

(3) What about the question of hardship experienced?
It has to be acknowledged that there may be circumstances causing particular hardships, such as periods of unemployment, or an unexpected sudden rise in interest rates greatly increasing the burden of mortgages. There is no easy answer to these. But the believer takes all his or her problems and burdens to the Lord. The believer asks the Lord for grace, wisdom, and sufficient temporal welfare. Nonetheless, the example of the widow's mite appears to leave no room for the complete exclusion of giving, however straitened the circumstances may be, as long as there is income. There is an absolute necessity for the believer to provide for his own family (1 Timothy 5:8 and also Matthew 6:5-6). It can never be used as an excuse that one has not been able to do that because of one's givings to the Church. At the same time care needs to be taken to examine very carefully financial needs and priorities within the family sphere and to exercise proper Biblical stewardship, confident that the Lord will provide.

(4) How might I leave money to the Church?
The believer ought to ensure that a due proportion of what he or she leaves at death is also devoted to the work of the Lord. The tithe principle should be applied also when consideration is given to making out a Will.

At every stage the believer will review his or her givings to the Lord in the light of his or her present changing circumstances, and, more especially in the light of the needs that exist within Christ's visible Church.

C. Conclusion

Giving to the Lord is in a sense a test of faith – for the individual and the Church. It may no doubt involve the tithing person to some degree having less, financially speaking, than his or her non-tithing contemporary. But it will itself give rise to wonderful blessings, as it is found again and again that the Biblical proverb is true in reality: "There is that scattereth, and yet increaseth; and there is that withholdeth more than is meet, but it tendeth to poverty" (Proverbs 11:24). The "cheerful giver" loses nothing. Giving to the Lord is at once a challenge to real faith and a wonderful privilege. But in all of the Scriptures there is surely no greater challenge than these words of Jesus: "He that is faithful in that which is least is faithful also in much: and he that is unjust in the least is unjust also in much. If therefore ye have not been faithful in the unrighteous mammon, who will commit to your trust the true riches? And if ye have not been faithful in that which is another man's, who shall give you that which is your own? No servant can serve two masters: for either he will hate the one, and love the other; or else he will hold to the one and despise the other. Ye cannot serve God and mammon" (Luke 16:10-13).

Christ taught His disciples that their righteousness had to exceed the righteousness of the Pharisees (Matthew 5:20). His standards are greater than the law. This poses serious questions for our giving. Is a tenth so hard? Fred Catherwood put it this way:

> There is surely no Christian who cannot spend a tenth less than their friends and neighbours outside the church. Are there not some things which our neighbours buy that we can do without? We are not asked to cut our spending drastically, just to have a bit less heat, to spend a fraction less on food, have slightly less expensive holidays and fewer drinks, make our clothes and cars last just a bit longer and have homes which are perhaps 10% smaller.[5]

The Church has a task in the world – a ministry of the Word, and a ministry of mercy. For carrying out this task the Church has many and

---

[5] H F R Catherwood, *God's Time, God's Money*, 145.

pressing needs. There is of course *prayer*. And there is *witnessing*. There is to be a clear and passionate *belief* in the Scriptures as God's Word, and also a *commitment*, of time, talents, and money in the service of the Lord.

When it comes to our giving, then, is a tenth too much? Surely it is not, for what have we that we have not received from the Possessor of all? Besides which consider the gift of God to mankind – the "indescribable gift" of the Lord Jesus Christ (2 Corinthians 9:15; John 3:16). But is this not legalistic? How can it be, for surely our liberality will stretch further than any mere legalistic requirement!

A cautionary note must be struck in closing: It may be that in this matter of giving people may be willing to give to the local Church and yet neglect the more important matter of their soul's salvation. A person may willingly tithe their income and yet fail to come to repentance before God. Repentance and faith in Christ are the prerequisites for sinners. Giving should not be seen either as meritorious in itself before God, or as being in some way a reward to a Church or pastor, making them indebted to the giver. Giving is a privilege as well as a duty, not first of all to the Church or pastor, but to the Lord for the support of the ministry of the Word, and the ministry of mercy. It does not in any way substitute for the prior necessity for the individual to come to faith in Christ. This is the thrust of what Paul says to the Corinthians about the giving of the Macedonians, and why he was so pleased with them: because they *first* gave of themselves to the Lord (1 Corinthians 8:5)!

WORSHIP

9. Prayer, Reading and Preaching the Word and the Benediction

1. Introduction
In Public Worship considerable attention is often paid to the content of the praise and to the use or otherwise of instrumental music. Comparatively little attention is paid to other elements, such as prayer, reading the Word and the Benediction. Yet all these have their special place and prominence in the Scriptures, and these too, are elements to be governed by the regulative principle by which that only is admitted which is warranted by the Word. Admittedly, it is more straightforward to establish some unanimity among the Churches on these elements. But they are clearly of great importance in public worship and some account must be provided of what is proper in public worship in these areas in considering Church Principles in worship.

2. Prayer as part of public worship
"Prayer, with thanksgiving, being one special part of religious worship, is by God required of all men…"[1] This applies to all religious worship, whether private or corporate. Prayer as an element in public worship is clear, e.g., in the Psalms, which were intended principally for corporate praise, though they include many personal aspects of prayer. The fact that prayer is so central in all Christian religious worship is ample warrant for it to be an element in public Church worship. However, the want of any prescribed forms of prayer indicates that prayer is to be extempore or spontaneous (Philippians 4:6; Psalm 65:2; 1 Peter 2:5). That said, it is true that in the Lord's teaching on prayer in response to

---

[1] *Westminster Confession of Faith*, 21:3.

the request for help by the disciples we do have what has been commonly called the 'Lord's Prayer' (Matthew 6:9-13; Luke 11:2-4). This provides a guideline on the *manner* in which prayer may be offered. There is a notable structure, helpfully outlined by Michael Schneider:

> ADORATION: "Our Father which art in heaven, Hallowed be Thy name..."
> SUPPLICATION: "Thy kingdom come. Thy will be done in earth, as it is in heaven. Give us this day our daily bread..."
> CONFESSION: "And forgive us our debts, as we forgive our debtors. And lead us not into temptation, but deliver us from evil..."
> ADORATION: "For Thine is the Kingdom, and the power, and the glory for ever. Amen."[2]

The prayer is intended to help prayer, no doubt public prayer as well as prayer in private. The form of the prayer in using the collective 'our' is indicative of this. The *Shorter Catechism* recognises the significance of the Lord's Prayer as a help in praying. Question 99 asks: "What rule hath God given for our direction in prayer?" To this the answer is given:

> The whole word of God is of use to direct us in prayer; but the special rule of direction is that form of prayer which Christ taught his disciples, commonly called *The Lord's Prayer.*

The *Catechism* proceeds to expound the Prayer in questions 100 to 107. The prayer thus acts as a 'blueprint' for the ordering of public praying.

The importance of prayer in the Westminster standards is clear from *The Directory for the Public Worship of God*: "The congregation being assembled, the minister, after solemn calling on them to the worshipping of the great name of God, is to begin with prayer." Prayer is to be offered for pardon, assistance and acceptance in the whole service. The *Directory* sees prayer as *constituting* the public worship act.[3] The *Directory* also advocates prayer before and after the preaching. The

---

[2] A Michael Schneider, III, 'Prayer Regulated by God's Word,' in Frank J. Smith and David C Lachman, *Worship in the Presence of God*, Greenville, South Carolina, 1992, 233. Schneider's essay in that volume repays study in this matter of prayer in public worship.

[3] Somehow this was displaced in worship services by an opening Psalm. *Subordinate Standards and Authoritative Documents of the Free Church of Scotland*, Edinburgh, 1851, 289.

prayers offered will focus on various concerns for the Church. It may be wise to have a briefer prayer of adoration and invocation as the first prayer of the service and concentrate in the prayer before the sermon not only on blessing upon the Word but also supplications, praying for concerns ranging over the families attached to the Church, the congregational life and prospering of the work of the Church at large, for the young in the congregation and the sick, for the Royal Family, the Government and those in authority, and the concerns of the gospel the world over (1 Timothy 2:1-2). The minister should give time to prepare himself beforehand even though his prayer will be spontaneous and with felt dependence upon the Lord. Yet he may well note down some items for public intercession, the names of the sick and the like.[4]

3. Reading and Preaching the Word

There is a very moving instance of Bible reading in a public context in the book of Nehemiah. The walls of Jerusalem and its gates had been rebuilt subsequent to Nehemiah's coming to Jerusalem. Though it had taken 20 years to build the Temple in an earlier return from exile, after Nehemiah returned around 445BC the people were galvanised into rebuilding the walls and gates within 52 days. The events of chapter 8 take place very shortly after that. There is something very spontaneous in the gathering of the people in the square before the Water Gate. What do the people do? They tell Ezra the scribe to read the Book of the Law of Moses, which the Lord had commanded (v1). A 'pulpit of wood' is erected (v4) and the Book of the Law is read 'from morning until midday' (v3). The people are attentive (v3) and they are deeply moved (v6). Such are their feelings that they stand out of respect when the Book is read (v5). The Word is read with great care, and it is clear that the meaning was given by Ezra and those who were assisting him: "they read in the book in the law of God distinctly, and gave the sense, and caused them to understand the reading" (v8). This beautifully

---

[4] On the matter of posture in public worship see the chapter on 'Posture in Public Prayer' above.

brings together Bible reading and explanation or 'preaching.' In the reading of the Word and preaching in public worship ministers should study to speak clearly with proper pronunciation and cadence so that people are helped in understanding the reading and the message based upon it. Notwithstanding, or perhaps because of, its relatively archaic language, this is a feature of the King James Version. As Leland Ryken observed:

> By modern standards, the KJV is too heavily punctuated; the explanation is that the King James translators had in mind the oral reading and hearing of their translation, so they used punctuation to guide oral reading.[5]

By contrast modern translations tend to be less memorable and seem even banal, in public oral readings.

It is clear from the New Testament that both the Scriptures and the preached word are all-important in the life of the Church. This is true in the public ministry of the Lord, whether in the open air (Matthew 5 to 7) or in the Synagogue (Luke 4:16-21). It was also clearly a feature of the apostolic church from the Day of Pentecost in which we have a lengthy record of Peter's sermon, including many quotations from the Old Testament (Acts 2:14-36). The emphasis on Scripture, as, for example, in Paul's counsel to Timothy (2 Timothy 3:14-17), would encourage both the reading of the Word and exposition and exhortation of it in public worship. He says a few verses later: "Preach the word! Be ready in season and out of season. Convince, rebuke, exhort, with all longsuffering and teaching" (4:2). Preaching does not just involve explanation or exposition. It ought also to be hortatory, with exhortation and persuasion with passion. A good example is found in Paul's words to the Corinthians: "Knowing, therefore, the terror of the Lord, we persuade men..." (1 Corinthians 5:11).

The upshot is that great care should be taken about the reading of the Word and exposition of it. It is instructive that in 1846 the Free Church passed an Act "Anent the Public Reading of the Scriptures":

---

[5] Leland Ryken, *The Legacy of the King James Bible*, Wheaton, Illinois, 2011, 56.

> ...the General Assembly did and hereby do instruct and enjoin the Ministers of this Church to give special attention to the scope and spirit of that portion of the Directory for Public Worship which enjoins the public reading of the Scriptures, and to take order that its regulations are duly carried into effect, and in particular, that a portion of the Scriptures be read at each of the ordinary diets for public worship.[6]

4. The Benediction

The Benediction is an imparting of blessing upon the gathered Church. The warrant is found in the following:

- The Aaronic blessing, as given through him and pronounced by those who followed him in Old Testament times (Numbers 6:22-27)
- The repeated 'blessings' found in the New Testament letters (Romans 16:25-27; 2 Corinthians 13:14; Jude 24-25; etc.)

The most complete 'Apostolic Benediction' is that found in 2 Corinthians: "The grace of the Lord Jesus Christ, and the love of God, and the communion of the Holy Spirit be with you all. Amen" (13:14, NKJV). The Trinitarian framework of New Testament theology is expressed explicitly in Christ's formula in connection with baptism in the Great Commission: "Go therefore and make disciples of all the nations, baptizing them in the name of the Father and of the Son and of the Holy Spirit" (Matthew 28:19, NKJV). This Trinitarian structure is sustained in the benediction at the end of 2 Corinthians and there are good grounds for that benediction to be habitually adopted in giving the blessing at the conclusion of public worship. As William Binnie put it:

> The Benediction, in all its scriptural forms, conjoins with the declaration of the divine name *a declaration of the Lord's mercy and grace towards His people, and of the place He has prepared for them*. This declaration, since it takes place in a divinely prescribed form of blessing, may well be interpreted as signalling an invisible ministration of grace, mercy, and

---

[6] *Principal Acts of the General Assembly of the Free Church of Scotland*, Act V, 29th May 1846. See also the *Subordinate Standards and Authoritative Documents of the Free Church of Scotland*, Edinburgh, 1851, 289-290.

peace, going forwards continually within the believing Church, whereby light and comfort are shed abroad in the hearts of all true worshippers.[7]

It is a solemn thing for a minister to pronounce a Benediction. Binnie again: "To Him, therefore, the faith of the congregation ought to rise when the benediction is pronounced." As for the minister, "in the Benediction...the minister is only the instrument by whom Christ makes Himself heard...It is Christ, present in the midst of His Church according to His promise, who truly puts the name of the Lord upon the people and blesses them."[8] This is no empty thing. For this reason it seems appropriate that only ordained ministers or probationers should pronounce the Benediction. With reference to the apostolic benediction of 2 Corinthians 13, Philip Hughes commented that "the Apostles valedictory wish [was] that they may all continuously know in their daily experience the presence of the grace, love and fellowship of Son, Father, and Holy Spirit, the eternally blessed Triune God to whose sovereign goodness alone they owe their everlasting salvation."[9]

5. Conclusion

These elements of public worship, then, which often are taken as formalities or circumstantials, ought to be performed with the utmost care and seriousness. There is nothing in the whole scope of the worship of God which should be thought a formality, or thought to fall outside the demands of the 'regulative principle' for public worship, at least in a general sense of leaning upon Biblical usage and precedent. For every element of the public worship ought to reveal a Word-centeredness and reverence for what is commanded, or by good and necessary consequence may be deduced from the Word of the great Head of the Church, the Lord Jesus Christ, whose glory ought to be the focus of all our acts of worship.

---

[7] Binnie, op. cit., 92. *Italics* in the original.
[8] ibid., 92-3.
[9] P E Hughes, *Paul's Second Epistle to the Corinthians*, London, 1961, 490.

WORSHIP

10. The Christian Sabbath

1. Introduction

There is a sense in which the Christian Sabbath is a 'test case.' For whom or what? It is a test case for a nation and a church and an individual – of the presence of a vital Christianity. It is true that a perfectly quiet Sabbath does not mean that there is necessarily a vital spiritual Christianity. Yet a vital Christianity will surely be found when people do have positive attitudes to the Christian Sabbath and its observance. True, it will not do to be 'Christian' the first day of the week, and 'secular' the other days. Christian faith and life is to be reflected in every aspect and area of life. This much is implicit in the fourth commandment, which is not just about the Sabbath, but all our time. One well-known preacher of an earlier day said this about the Christian's day of rest and worship: "It is an infallible sign of the state of true religion in a land, in a church, in a family, and in a man's own heart and life...it is the sign of a standing or falling church. There is perhaps no surer sign of a falling Christian than a growing neglect of Sabbath-day ordinances, and an indolent and profane abuse of its sacred and priceless hours."[1] By this standard the state of true religion in our land is low. In that sense the Sabbath and its observance is an indicator and symptom of a malaise. It has clearly been a ploy of the evil one in his attack on Christianity to loosen, regard for the Christian Sabbath and its proper observance, not least among professing Christians. In this, no doubt Television has played a profound part, as it has in recent times on all public and private morality.

Firstly, let us notice two things in approaching the fourth commandment:

---

[1] Alexander Whyte, *A Commentary on the Shorter Catechism*, Edinburgh, c1882, 133.

(1) *It is stated positively.* In the common mind the Sabbath or Lord's day observance has negative connotations. No doubt there are negative requirements to all the commandments: "Thou shalt not..." This is inevitable in a fallen world. But the Sabbath in essence is not just 'abstention' from this or that. Rather, for the believer it is a "market day of the soul" as the Puritans used to put it. Rest is undeniably important, but the best use of the day is made in what a person does for his or her soul on that day.

(2) *'Sabbath' does not mean 'seventh.'* It means, literally, 'rest.' In other words it is not a necessity of the nature of the Sabbath that it is the 'seventh day of the week.' It will be argued that the change of day to the first day of the week was necessary through the coming and the work of the Lord Jesus Christ and of the coming of the Holy Spirit which marked the birth of the distinctively Christian Church. The Sabbath is not distinctly and only 'Jewish.' It is good for us to look at this commandment (Exodus 20:8-11) again and restate its meaning and application not least in a New Testament context.

2. Confessional teaching

The doctrine of the *Westminster Confession of Faith* is found in the chapter on 'Of Religious Worship, and the Sabbath Day.'[2] It teaches that a due proportion of man's time is to be set apart for the worship of God, who by a "positive, moral, and perpetual commandment," has given one day in seven to be kept holy unto Him. Several important points are made about the Sabbath:

(1) *It is binding on all men and all ages.* This must be evident from the fact that a commandment for a Sabbath is found in the Decalogue (Exodus 20:8-11; Deuteronomy 5:12-15) and because it is a creation ordinance (Genesis 2:1-3; Exodus 31:15-17), it is rightly understood as positively moral and universally and perpetually applicable.

(2) *The day was changed but the Sabbath preserved.* On the principle of the nature of the Sabbath and Sabbath rest as demarcating man's weeks

---

[2] Chapter 21:7 and 8.

perpetually, it is rightly taken that the New Testament did not change the obligations in relation to a Sabbath. It is clear from the New Testament, however, that there was a change in the day of worship to the "first day of the week," the change arising from the resurrection of Christ. Scripture material indicating such a change will be discussed below.

(3) *The day is called "the Lord's Day"* (τη κυριακη ἡμέρα) in the book of Revelation (1:10). It is not inappropriate, however, to describe this as a Sabbath – the Christian Sabbath – in view of the perpetuity of the application of the commandment to the end of the world.

(4) *The principles that applied to keeping the day holy in the Old Testament are seen to continue into the New*: ordering ordinary affairs beforehand as far as possible; leaving out unnecessary worldly employments and recreations (sports); and taking due time in public and private exercises of worship. Clearly there is also the matter of having this day as one allowing *physical rest* from normal weekly tasks and duties and having a concern that others on your account are not caused to forsake a Sabbath rest (consistent with works of true necessity and mercy).

3. What are the obligations attached to Sabbath observance?

As we look at the commandment the obligation is clear: *One whole day in seven is to be specially given over to the Lord in rest and in worship (albeit also in such works as may be works of necessity, mercy and piety)*. This is clear from the form of the commandment in Exodus 20:8-11. Its permanence and morality is established by the linking of the Sabbath with the pattern of the creation week. It is a 'creation ordinance.' Given its institution before the fall of man into sin, as well as its inclusion in the moral law, it is clear that this is an ordinance for man's good. It was not just 'Jewish', nor was it just "ceremonial". It is distinctly moral, and therefore of permanent application. There were ceremonial aspects in relation to the Sabbath ordinance and no doubt such aspects are referred to, for example, in Colossians 2:16.

To summarise, it is clear that the law contained in this commandment is moral and permanent for several reasons:

(a) The day of rest was instituted at creation before man's fall into sin;

(b) The arguments in the 4th Commandment are moral and not ceremonial (either in Exodus 20 or Deuteronomy 5);

(c) The other commandments in the Decalogue are certainly moral and the 4th cannot be different;

(d) The Sabbath was to be kept by 'strangers' also (see Nehemiah 13) though they had no obligations under the ceremonial law; and finally,

(e) The commandment is not abrogated in the New Testament.

The encouragement to "remember" the Sabbath indicates that it must have been established *before* the law, something that the pattern of manna gathering in Exodus 16 clearly indicates. The obligations are moral and spiritual.

4. What day is to be observed?

The Sabbath clearly demarcated man's weeks, something not astronomically fixed (unlike days and years). The principle of the Sabbath is that one day in seven is to be specially observed by all people in honour to God and in the interests of their souls. But what day of the week is to be the Sabbath? Some say, "It should be the seventh day of the week. That is what it appears to be in the Old Testament." How is it that we have a first-day Sabbath, and is that of any real importance? Let us summarise the arguments for our observing of the Christian Sabbath or Lord's day on the *first* day of the week.

(1) *There is the use of the term 'Lord's day' in Revelation 1:10.* This is at least highly suggestive, taken along with other arguments. It seems clear that this refers to the day of Christian worship. Why should that term "Lord's day" be used? It is argued that this fits well with that greatest of days for the Christian, which to the New Testament believer is surely *the day of resurrection.* After all it is by the resurrection of the Lord that we know that our faith is not in vain (1 Corinthians 15:17-20)! And the resurrection was on the first day of the week (Matthew 28:1; Mark 16:1-2; Luke 24:1; John 20:1). It is little wonder that this became the new

Sabbath for the Christian Church, indeed in a real sense it became a necessity that it should be so. It is inevitable that the Christian's Sabbath would commemorate His triumphal rising from the dead.

(2) *There are numerous indicators that the first day of the week was specially observed in the Church.* For example, there are the meetings of Jesus with the disciples after His resurrection, on the first day of the week (John 20:19, 26); there is the incident in Acts 20 when Paul 'breaks bread' and preaches (v7), and the taking up of collections specified in 1 Corinthians 16:2. The 'first day' religious activities are at the very least strongly suggestive of a change of day.

(3) *There is the coming of the Spirit at Pentecost.* This was seven weeks to the day after the rising of Jesus from the dead and again, therefore, on the first day of the week. It is not surprising that that event which was in effect the birth-date of the *Christian* Church should also be significant as the apostolic day of gathering and worship. It stands to reason, therefore, that the Christian's Sabbath would be the first day of the week, seeing Christ triumphed over death on that day, and the Spirit came to give special life to the Church on that day.

5. How is the day to be kept?
What is to be in our hearts with reference to the first-day Christian Sabbath? We assume that the Sabbath commandment is of permanent obligation. This is not to promote legalism. It is clear that keeping this commandment, or any of the commandments, saves no one. The letter to the Galatians, for example, establishes this decisively. But one of the uses of the moral law is that it is God's prescribed way of life for mankind. Certainly the spiritual person will love the law of God after the inward man (Romans 7:22). The believer will show love and loyalty to their Lord by his or her regard for the moral law in their lives. The proper observance of the Lord's day, our Sunday, is summed up as rest and worship. It is to be *remembered*, and it is to be *kept holy*. This day provides an opportunity for giving ourselves as far as possible to the concerns of our souls, as well as not giving ourselves as much as possible to what can very well be done on other days (e.g. daily work,

sports and recreations, entertainments, chores, unnecessary travel). The believer should think in *positive* terms of the benefits it affords when properly used to advance the life of God in the soul. They will say to themselves: "How can I make the best use of this day to advance spiritual religion in my life?" "How can I advance my understanding of the Word of God?" There will be as far as possible a laying aside normal duties, except such as are of mercy and necessity.

It is sad that professing Christians and Churches are not more concerned with the use of the Lord's day. After all, this is not a notable age for piety. It appears to be a day in which there is a low ebb spiritually. This seems all the more reason to emphasise the spiritual benefits of the Lord's day rather than argue against it! Let it be a day in which the people of God give attention to their souls; in which they attend the ordinances; in which they meditate on the Word; in which they pray and humble themselves before the Lord. Let it be a day of joy and gladness; a day for the Lord. Let us be clear too, that it is a day for *all* to keep. It is true that one cannot force people to observe the day. But people can be encouraged to enjoy a day of rest and worship, and give time to their families on Sundays. Besides this, it is a matter of the witness of Christians to the claims of Christ and His Word upon their lives. Professing Christians need to be bold today, like Nehemiah in his day (13:15-18). Let the right impression be given, that this is a jewel of days, a treasure, for the individual and for the family and for the nation – and, of course, for the Church. Who is so advanced in the ways of the Lord that they can do without the Sabbath in whole or in part? Let the Church and the Christian seek to limit the intrusion of distractions such as the media, and let them have a heart for this 'market day of the soul.'

6. What is the practical significance of Lord's Day observance?
(1) *It encourages a proper recognition of God* and His claims upon us. Especially in relation to our use of time. It is a day which used aright will keep a society from the corrupt influence of complete secularism.
(2) *It encourages man's relationship with Christ.* For it gives opportunity for worship in private and public not found so directly on other days.

(3) *It provides rest from weekly toil* even for people who are aged or retired. And the first-day Sabbath emphasises the priority of the heavenly over the earthy (important as the earthly is in its place in terms of the 4th commandment).

(4) *It is an index of the state of a person's soul.* The Sabbath is respected and observed by lively Christians. "There is no surer sign," says one writer, "that a young man [or older person] is declining from faith and personal religion when he [or she] begins to find his own pleasure and do his own way on the Lord's holy day."[3]

(5) Finally, *it points people forward to heavenly rest*. It will be – ought to be – treated as a foretaste of heaven. This is basically the perspective of Hebrews 4:9 (Literally, "There remains a keeping of the Sabbath – σαββατισμός – to the people of God"). Yes, an eternal Sabbath "Where congregations ne'er break up, and Sabbath's never end." And here the question may legitimately be asked: if we have little or no appetite for our earthy Sabbath, what real taste can there be for the Heavenly state? If we find the Christian Sabbath drags, as the traders in Amos's day did (8:5-6) or Nehemiah's day (13:20ff.), then we should look to our souls and seek the Lord. But someone may say, "Preacher, I do my very best to keep the Lord's day – I always have, and I deplore all the changes in attitudes to this day." We should not imagine, however, that Sabbath keeping will save one's soul. It may be possible to be as careful as any human being might be in outwardly observing the Lord's day and yet be a stranger to God and to grace. The first priority is the one thing needful – having Christ in the heart by faith. It is not a case of either/or, but both/and.

7. Conclusion

We close with the moving words of Robert Murray M'Cheyne from his tract, "I love the Lord's day":

> When a believer lays aside his pen or loom, brushes aside his worldly cares, leaving them behind him, with his week-day clothes, and comes up to the house of God, it is like the

---

[3] Alexander Whyte, op. cit., 133.

morning of the resurrection, the day when we shall come out of great tribulation into the presence of God and the Lamb. When he sits under the preached word, and hears the voice of the shepherd leading and feeding his soul, it reminds him of the day when the Lamb that is in the midst of the throne shall feed him and lead him to living fountains of waters. When he joins in the psalm of praise, it reminds him of the day when his hands shall strike the harp of God…When he retires, and meets with God in secret in his closet, or, like Isaac, in some favourite spot near his dwelling, it reminds him of the day when "he shall be a pillar in the house of our God, and go no more out."

This is the reason why we love the Lord's day. This is the reason why we "call the Sabbath a delight." A well-spent Sabbath we feel to be a day of heaven upon earth, for this reason we wish our Sabbaths to be wholly given to God. We love to spend the whole time in the public and private exercises of God's worship, except so much as is taken up m the works of necessity and mercy. We love to rise early on that morning, and to sit up late, that we may have a long day with God. How many may know from this that they will never be in heaven! A straw on the surface can tell which way the stream is flowing.[4]

This is a spirit and attitude which surely needs to be maintained conscientiously in the Churches, and amongst all professing Christians today.

---

[4] Andrew A Bonar, *Memoir and Remains of the Rev. Robert Murray M'Cheyne*, Edinburgh, ²1892, 596-7.

APPENDIX

What about the Observance of 'Holy Days'?

From an early period the post-Apostolic Church adopted 'festivals' and 'holy days' to commemorate various Saints, and events of Christ's life and ministry. These became a feature particularly of Roman Catholic, Orthodox, Lutheran and Episcopalian Churches, which tended to develop an elaborate 'Christian Year,' based on such purported dates and events. Most notable among these were the 'celebration' of Christmas, Good Friday, and Easter respectively to observe Christ's birth, death and resurrection.[5]

It may be said that the 'celebration' of these great events in the life of Christ had plausibility. The Incarnation of the Eternal Word and the physical Resurrection of Christ from the dead (as the seal on His saving work upon the cross, 1 Corinthians 15), with the Saviour's atoning work, are the most significant events in the history of the World. We could say that they deserve to be celebrated and shouted from the rooftops. Indeed, that is the responsibility and the task of any Christian Church worth its salt. In addition, it might be said that in history such events have been 'kept alive' in people's minds by such widely observed 'festivals,' albeit overlain by many pagan and secular accretions in the course of time.

In assessing the rightness of such Church 'holy days', however, there is a prior question: *is there divine warrant for them*? Has the Church been told by the Holy Spirit speaking in Scripture to institute such 'holy days'? If there is no direct divine warrant in Scripture, then the Church is right to eschew such days. The Puritan *Directory for the Publick Worship of God*, accepted in Scotland by Church and Parliament in 1645, contained an Appendix 'Touching Days and Places for Publick Worship.' This succinctly puts the position that excludes the adoption of 'holy days' not founded on direct Scriptural warrant:

> There is no day commanded in scripture to be kept holy under the gospel but the Lord's day, which is the Christian Sabbath. Festival-days, vulgarly called Holy-days, having no warrant in the word of

---

[5] The fact that the AV translates *pascha* as 'Easter' in Acts 12:4 provides no support for an Easter Festival! The translation, as in 26 other instances of the translation of the word in the New Testament in the AV, should have been 'Passover.' *Pascha* is consistently translated 'Passover' throughout the Geneva Bible (1599)(and the NKJV).

God, are not to be continued. Nevertheless, it is lawful and necessary, upon special emergent occasions, to separate a day or days for public fasting or thanksgiving, as the several eminent and extraordinary dispensations of God's providence shall administer cause and opportunity to his people. As no place is capable of any holiness, under pretence of whatsoever dedication or consecration; so neither is it subject to such pollution by any superstition formerly used, and now laid aside, as may render it unlawful or inconvenient for Christians to meet together therein for the public worship of God. And therefore we hold it requisite, that the places of public assembling for worship among us should be continued and employed to that use.[6]

What private individuals do in relation to social festivals described as Christmas or Easter is a matter for such individuals and no doubt censoriousness should be avoided. Nevertheless, it must be the concern for a Church to take care not to institute days in a Christian calendar for which there is no direct divine warrant. At the same time the Church should emphasise the claims of the Christian Sabbath as a weekly reminder of the glorious truth of the resurrection of Christ from the dead, and therefore His triumph over death and the grave, and the coming of the Holy Spirit at Pentecost. In addition, the *truths* of the virgin birth of Christ and His sacrificial death for His people, ought to receive due prominence in the Church's teaching and preaching, without becoming entangled in a 'Christian Year.' It has often been found, perhaps ironically, that politely declining to observe such religious festivals provides opportunity for clear witness to gospel facts whilst explaining that the Bible does not warrant such holy days.

Further Reading:

Samuel Miller and John G Lorimer, Manual of Presbytery, *Edinburgh, 1842. Especially the section of Samuel Miller's contribution in Chapter V, Section II: Presbyterians do not observe Holy-days (pages 126-134)*

G I Williamson, On the Observance of Sacred Days, *New Covenant Publication Society, c1975. This 11-page booklet succinctly and challengingly outlines the case for rejecting such 'Festivals' as Christmas, Good Friday and Easter.*

---

[6] *The Subordinate Standards and other Authoritative Documents of the Free Church of Scotland,* Edinburgh, 1851, 300.

SECTION D

THE CHURCH
ITS SACRAMENTS

SACRAMENTS

1. General

1. Introduction
Among the 'outward means' by which Christ communicates the benefits of redemption are the Word, the Sacraments, and Prayer. In relation to the Sacraments, the first thing to ask concerns the word, *sacrament*. Where does it come from? It is not found in the Bible. That is no disqualification as long as the word conveys truth that is found in the Bible, which this word does. We recognise Circumcision and the Passover as 'sacraments' of the Old Testament and Baptism and the Lord's Supper as the equivalent New Testament ordinances.

2. How are these ordinances, 'sacraments'?
The word, 'sacrament,' is a Latin word. Originally it meant, simply, "something sacred." It came to have a wider meaning. In law, money deposited by contending parties in a case was *sacramentum*, and when forfeited was to be used for suitably sacred purposes. In the military the *sacramentum dicere* involved swearing an oath of allegiance to the General or Army or, indeed, King. It is perhaps easy to see how this came to be adopted by the Church. In a Latin translation of the New Testament the word 'mysterium' (= secret, mystery) was translated '*sacramentum*' (e.g. Ephesians 3:3, 4). Thus, the *mysteries* designated 'sacraments' were (a) things sacred; (b) signs of loyalty; and (c) things involving mystery. In the course of time the word became somewhat debased (like 'Christian' or 'evangelical' today) so that it came to be applied to a whole range of 'signs' which in the 13th Century were adopted as 'sacraments' in the Roman Church – seven in all, including besides Baptism and the Lord's Supper, confirmation, penance, holy orders, extreme unction and marriage. The last five were not considered

sacraments by the Reformation faith. The idea of sacrament, then, has been abused, though the word itself may very properly be used of the two true sacraments of the Old Testament (Circumcision and Passover) and New Testament (Baptism and the Lord's Supper).

There has always been a fair bit of controversy in relation to the sacraments, and exactly how they work. What happens when they are observed or administered? Do they change those who partake? In what respects are they effective in a spiritual sense? Augustine called them "visible signs of invisible grace." Later, however, people began to believe that they automatically contained and conveyed grace. That is what sacramental Churches such as the Roman Catholics, and to a degree the Lutherans and High Anglicans believe to this day. So, in some quarters, the application of Baptism, for example, was taken to convey spiritual regeneration, i.e. made the subject a Christian, thus Baptismal regeneration or 'Christening.' In the Lord's Supper the issue was how the elements changed into the actual body and blood of Christ and how they therefore – so it was wrongly believed – could not but convey grace. Such teachings are not Biblical. But all this means that we must be very careful in handling such things. These false ideas were renounced by the Reformers, on whose shoulders we stand.

We have to be careful as we approach sacraments to recognise that there is use of symbolism, and figurative language, in connection with their administration. For instance, in the institution of the Lord's Supper Jesus says, "This is my body...this is my blood." He is speaking figuratively. The bread and wine are used symbolically. He speaks in a similar way in John 6 in the 'bread of life' discourse (see, e.g., vv51-57). There He calls people to eat his flesh and drink His blood. He clearly does not mean for them to do that literally. It is a figurative expression for the exercise of faith and of spiritual union with Him. This is at the heart of the benefits of the sacraments. In the case of the Supper, faith is necessary for benefit, as too in Baptism, though in some Protestant Churches there has been in general less strictness in the administration of Baptism than the Lord's Supper. There has been a tendency in some cases to allow "attentive adherents" admission to Baptism but not to the Lord's Supper. This is a looser view than the *Westminster Confession of Faith* and Larger and Shorter *Catechisms* would support. In relation to Baptism the water is used as a symbol. It does not itself cleanse the heart but it does point to such a need.

The *Catechism* asks how sacraments become effectual means of spiritual life (which is what we take 'salvation' to mean here). The answer given is:

> The sacraments become effectual means of salvation, not from any virtue in them, or in him that doth administer them; but only by the blessing of Christ, and the working of his Spirit in them that by faith receive them. (*Shorter Catechism*, Answer 91)

As we ponder at this question of the effect of the sacraments, let us consider, first,

3. What is a sacrament?

The *Westminster Shorter Catechism* has a concise definition of a Sacrament:

> A sacrament is an holy ordinance instituted by Christ, wherein, by sensible signs, Christ, and the benefits of the new covenant, are represented, sealed, and applied to believers. (*Shorter Catechism*, Answer 92).

We have already touched on this in considering the meaning of the word (a Latin word). But let us notice that for their validity such ordinances must be directly instituted by Christ. This is clearly the case with Baptism (Matthew 28:19) and the Lord's Supper (Matthew 26:26-30; 1 Corinthians 11:23, etc.). Furthermore, they are signs of a Covenant relationship between the Lord and His people through Christ (see the *Westminster Confession of Faith*, 7:9). But what are the features of sacraments?

(1) *They are outward and visible signs.* They are described in the *Catechism* as 'sensible signs.' That does not mean that they make sense according to some measure of common sense. It's just that there is something *visual* in the sacraments. They accommodate to one's senses of sight and touch. They are outward and visible; they are 'sensible' in that they are

addressed to our senses. The outward signs speak of certain realities. So, the elements of the Lord's Supper are signs of the death of Christ. The water in Baptism is a sign of the work of the Holy Spirit.

Let us illustrate 'signs.' Take a road sign. You see a sign with a symbol on it. The symbol speaks of some reality you have to look out for. When the driver sees the sign he or she will respond accordingly. It may be, for example, the sign of a hazard ahead. It may concern something the driver does not see immediately, and yet he is warned and acts accordingly (by 'faith'). The sign is a visible representation of something real. This is how it is with sacraments. They give a picture of aspects of the work of grace and speak of a real covenant relationship between God and His people.

(2) *They are inward and spiritual seals.* It is not just that they are signs of something. They also affect the *experience* of the Christian who receives them by faith. They point to the need for inward grace. In the case of Baptism it is the grace of regeneration and cleansing from sin; in the case of the Lord's Supper it is the grace of obedience and faith,

We can illustrate the sacraments as *seals* in this way: Think of a seal, say, on a Degree Certificate from a College or University. It has a seal on it. What is the seal for? It certifies and confers on the recipient a genuine qualification. Or take a seal on some document or product – it guarantees authenticity. In a sacrament the Lord certifies the genuineness of the benefits believers receive from Him. This also ties in with the covenant relation. In these signs and seals it is as if God says: "You are mine! Here is my seal."

So, the Lord brings spiritual benefits through 'sensible signs.' But the Spirit of God works by them and uses them for the benefit of those who receive them, so that as they are partaking – faithfully and prayerfully – they are helped and blessed. The sacraments are like visible sermons, representing truth in a *visible* way.

4. How are the sacraments made effective in our experience?

(1) First of all it is necessary to say in *what ways their effect is not to be understood*.

(a) *There is no inherent virtue in them.* That is to say, they do not *convey* grace. We usually say that they are not 'converting' ordinances. It is not as though an unsaved person will be saved through participation in the sacraments. That is not how they work. The sacraments are not 'converting' ordinances. The fact is that no one without real saving faith in the Lord Jesus Christ should receive the sacraments. It may be that far from doing them any good, they may incur the displeasure of the Lord. We see this in connection with the Lord's Supper in 1 Corinthians 11:27-34. We also see it in connection with Baptism in Acts 8 (13, 20, 21, 23).

(b) *There is no virtue received by reason of the person administering the sacrament.* That is to say, however godly the minister may be who administers the sacrament that will not ensure its effectiveness to those who receive the signs and seals. Ministers do not have any powers to make the sacraments effective, though, sadly, they may have power to hinder it! The story is told of a woman who heard Ebenezer Erskine (18th century Secession preacher) at a Lord's Supper. She was impressed and went to hear him in his own congregation the next Sabbath. She was not so impressed. So she went to see Mr Erskine and told him this experience. In reply he said this to her: "Madam, the reason is this – last Sabbath you went to hear Jesus Christ; but today, you have come to hear Ebenezer Erskine." This is the general truth of 1 Corinthians 3:7. There is a sense in which this works both ways: the godly minister does not give virtue to the sacrament dispensed. By the same token the *failings* of a minister – perhaps grievous failings – do not necessarily invalidate the sacrament.

(2) But *what way*, then, *may the sacraments be positively effective in the experience of those who partake?* In other words: How does blessing come for one's soul through the sacraments? The answer to this is two-fold:

(a) *By the presence and blessing of Christ with and in the sacrament.* In a sense this is no different from the benefits enjoyed through the other ordinances: the Word (read and preached) and prayer. But let us not forget *giving* to the Lord (tithing), after all, the Lord did say "it is more blessed to give than to receive." That is to say, the act of giving ought itself to be a blessed thing, when done in the right spirit it is a means of grace.

The sacrament is simply a tangible sign adapted to our senses. But it is not 'above' the Word (read or preached). We testify to this in our Church architecture. In the Reformed Churches the pulpits were always put in a central position, and the sacramental table or Baptismal font beneath them. The Sacramentalists usually have the Table central and the pulpit is shunted off to the side, and usually it is what is called a 'crow's nest.'

In the sacraments, however, we have a means of blessing. We have the promises of the presence of the Lord, for example in Matthew 18:20 and 28:20. We must believe that Christ is where His word and sacraments are faithfully observed. They do not say anything essentially different from one another, but there is a distinction to be made in the sacraments as to who partakes. The sacrament physically separates the professing people from the non-professing people, something not obvious in 'ordinary' services. But how can there be spiritual benefit from mere application of physical things – bread and wine and water?

(b) *By the inward work of the Holy Spirit blessing is received from the sacraments.* As Thomas Vincent put it: "Christ doth put life, and virtue, and efficacy into his sacraments and ordinances, without which they would be wholly dead, and altogether ineffectual."[1] It is perhaps obvious that spiritual benefit only goes on effectively in those who participate to the extent to which they are exercised in them, in faith and with prayer, seeking the Lord, asking for grace, and looking for the work of the Holy Spirit to make the sacrament effective and blessed. In this way there will be a stimulating and strengthening of faith and holiness, and of covenant love between the Lord and His believing people. Notice

---

[1] Thomas Vincent, *The Shorter Catechism Explained from Scripture*, London 1980 [1674], 242.

the phrase in the *Catechism*, "applied to believers." Sacraments are precious means of grace, *to believers*. The observing of them must therefore encourage the unsaved to seek the Lord, to seek that saving covenant relation in which a soul is right with God and a true heir of heaven, of which after all the sacraments are signs and seals.

SACRAMENTS

2. Baptism: (1) Mode and Meaning

1. Introduction

Previously we considered the nature of sacraments. Sacraments are among the "outward and ordinary means whereby Christ communicateth to us the benefits of redemption" (*Shorter Catechism*, Answer 88). We need the Holy Spirit to apply the Word and make it effective (Answer 89). Practically and pastorally the *Catechism* provides teaching as to our approach in these things. The professing people of God are to be diligent in reading the Scriptures with preparation and prayer. They are to believe what they read in the Word; and are to keep it in their mind and heart, and practice it in their lives.

In particular in relation to the sacraments, it is the blessing of Christ that is required through the Spirit, "working in them that in faith receive them." Clearly the divines were conscious that faith was required for proper admission to and blessing from the sacraments. As we approach both sacraments, faith in receiving the sacraments is all-important (*Shorter Catechism*, Answer 91). There can be no benefit enjoyed when there is no real apprehension of what the ordinances truly involve, as signs and seals of a covenant relation to God. In the nature of the case there must be a living faith in the Lord for benefit to be received. This must be borne in mind or both or either sacrament will be abused to the disadvantage of the Church that allows such abuse.

It appears that Presbyterians have more carefully understood this in relation to the Lord's Supper than Baptism. The practice of infant Baptism – proper as it is as a Covenant sign – can so tend to become a formal or nominal thing, as a former minister in Bracadale (Isle of Skye), the Rev. Roderick Macleod (1794-1868), found in his day in the

Isle of Skye, causing him no little pain and trial.

There are the two sacraments in the New Testament and faith is required for both. Baptism replaced the Old Testament rite of Circumcision and the Lord's Supper replaced the Passover. Circumcision was instituted in the time of Abraham as a Covenant sign (Genesis 17). The Lord's Supper is the commemoration of the New Covenant in Jesus' blood in place of the Passover, which celebrated the deliverance from Egypt by the redeeming power of God.

We consider two aspects of Baptism in this chapter. We will look at the *meaning and mode* of Baptism and in the next chapter consider the proper *subjects* of this rite. This is a large subject, but we are greatly helped by the *Shorter Catechism*, which deals with it in Questions 94 (meaning and mode) and 95 (subjects). In reply to the question, 'What is Baptism?' the *Shorter Catechism* answers:

> Baptism is a sacrament, wherein the washing with water in the name of the Father, and of the Son, and of the Holy Ghost, doth signify and seal our ingrafting into Christ, and partaking of the benefits of the covenant of grace, and our engagement to be the Lord's. (*Shorter Catechism*, Answer 94).

Unlike the Lord's Supper, Baptism is usually less often observed in the Church, and adult Baptisms are infrequent in paedobaptist (infant baptist) circles. Nor is Baptism usually treated with the same fullness – by contrast with the Communion "seasons" with their detailed attention to the administration of the sacrament of the Lord's Supper. This can give the impression that the one sacrament (the Lord's Supper) is somehow more important than the other (Baptism). It is necessary for us to recognise that Baptism as every bit as important as the Lord's Supper. This is readily shown by two factors:

(1) First of all, *there is the teaching of the Great Commission in Matthew 28*: "Go therefore and make disciples of all the nations, *baptising* them in the name of the Father and of the Son and of the Holy Spirit" (v19, NKJV). Baptism is mentioned there because it is, we might say, the ordinance of initiation in relation to Christian faith;

(2) Secondly, *there is its relationship to the covenant*. It "doth signify and seal our ingrafting into Christ, and partaking of the benefits of the covenant of grace, and our engagement to be the Lord's."

This indicates surely that it is every bit as vital as anything that can be said of the Lord's Supper. The importance of the ordinance lies in the fact that it speaks of *how* a person becomes a Christian – their ingrafting into Christ. And the whole symbolism of the use of water enforces this, reminding us of what Paul says to Titus: "he saved us, through the washing of regeneration and renewing of the Holy Spirit" (3:5, NKJV). The fact that we do not see this applied to adults so frequently in paedobaptist churches should not diminish the importance of Baptism for the Church. Indeed, the Church ought to ensure that the requirement of real faith in Christ as Saviour is consistently maintained. Whether the adult for himself or herself, or the parent(s) for the child, the same thing is signified and the same commitment is implied, namely, "our engagement to be the Lord's." After all, without faith it is impossible to please the Lord (Hebrews 11:6).

In an evangelical Church we dare not think of 'faith' except in a fully meaningful sense. We ought not to think of faith apart from real believing in and resting upon the Saviour alone for salvation. That, indeed, is the only faith that counts. All else is false faith and false hope. No sacrament should encourage anything but true faith exercised in those who receive the sacrament (for themselves or their child). This is not just a matter of mental assent. At stake is "partaking of the benefits of the covenant of grace and an engagement to be the Lord's." We dare not reduce these terms to formalities. In the next chapter we will deal with the relation of Baptism to "membership of the visible Church" (see *Shorter Catechism,* Answer. 95). Suffice to say, Baptism is a means of grace, not a converting ordinance, but also not a naming ceremony or any such thing. So, we do not hold to baptismal regeneration, i.e. the idea that the child is changed in relation to God through the rite. That is an erroneous view of Catholics and High Anglicans. It is from this idea that the word 'christening' (=Christianising) derives. This word has, unhappily, come into use in Presbyterian churches in recent times and is a term which should be avoided.

At this point we will focus on *the mode of Baptism*. In the following chapter we will deal with the matter of the *subjects of Baptism*.

2. Mode of Baptism

The mode of Baptism is the application of water in the name of the blessed Trinity. This has been one source of division in the Christian Church. It is partly a dispute over the amount of water to be used. Baptist brethren reckon that people should be baptised – on profession of faith – by immersion, or submersion, under water. That, to them, is the only acceptable and Biblical mode. So, they say that Baptism by sprinkling is not real Baptism, something compounded (they would say) by applying it to children. In support of their position the Baptists point, among other things, to the Baptism of the Lord by John the Baptist at the Jordan, which, they say, must have been by immersion. They may go as far as to say the word, 'baptize,' means 'immersion.'

John's Baptism was highly significant (see Matthew 3:13-17; Mark 1:9-11; Luke 3:21-22; and John 1:32-34). But it is simply not the case that the mode is determined by the record we have of John's own – or Jesus' – Baptism. Obviously, Baptisms were carried out where there was water, but there is simply no evidence that the subjects were immersed. And the word 'Baptism' does not only mean 'immerse.' There is a range of meaning in the word or words, and the important thing must be the symbolism, and not the mere quantity of water. The basic idea must be one of purification or cleansing – thus the appropriateness of the use of water.

There is abundant evidence from the Old Testament that cleansing was often symbolised through sprinkling. Take, for instance, the following passages: the case of leprosy (Leviticus 14:6-7); the case of David (Psalm 51:7); the case of defilement with a dead body (Numbers 19:11-13); the case of not eating without cleansing (Leviticus 15:11 and 11:29-44). The hands were 'baptised' by water being poured over them.

The Sacraments – Baptism, mode and meaning

In the New Testament there are a number of instances of baptisms, besides that of John the Baptist. These are strictly speaking Christian Baptism, unlike John's Baptism (though it may well be considered a precursor). For the greater part the New Testament Baptisms admittedly involved only adults. We have the converts on the day of Pentecost (Acts 2:41). There were those baptised who came to faith under Philip's preaching in Samaria (Acts 8:12). Then there are the cases of Simon (8:13), the Ethiopian Treasurer (8:36ff); Paul (9:18); Lydia (16:15), the Jailor at Philippi (16:33); and Cornelius (18:8). Among these there were households (Lydia, the Jailer and Cornelius). Not in every case is water mentioned. In the case of the Ethiopian eunuch there is water mentioned and Baptists will say that, like the Baptism of John, this proves immersion. But it does no such thing. True, the Ethiopian said, "here is water [on the way down to Gaza]; what doth hinder me to be baptized?" (Acts 8:36). Philip says, "If thou believest with all thine heart, thou mayest" (in which we see the necessity of saving faith) (v37). Upon his confession of faith, Philip baptises him (v38). All we are told is that "both Philip and the eunuch" went down into the water." Then it is said, "and he baptized him." You can picture it: they went down into the water. Presumably it was limited in quantity – it being a desert region (v26). But what is said of the eunuch is *also* said of Philip: they *both* went down into the water. The going down into the water was not the baptism as Philip was not baptised. The baptism followed and was more than likely to be by sprinkling or pouring on the eunuch's head. The same is true for John's baptism of Jesus. The account does not actually indicate submersion at all. And a small amount of water can satisfy the symbolical element of the ordinance every bit as much as a larger amount.

We have three effective indicators from the ministry and work of the Lord of how elements may be used in a partial or symbolical way to represent something wider and more comprehensive. These can be seen to have a bearing also on this question of the mode of baptism.

(1) At the beginning of Jesus' ministry, among other things John the Baptist said this about a contrast between his work and the Lord's: "I

indeed baptize you with water unto repentance, but he who is coming after me is mightier than I, whose sandals I am not worthy to carry. He will baptize you with the Holy Spirit and fire" (Matthew 3:11, NKJV). This prophecy of John was fulfilled at Pentecost when the Spirit came in power, as described in Acts 2, first among the disciples (vv1-4) and then among the attentive crowds (vv38-41). It is noticeable, however, that when the Spirit did come upon the waiting disciples, it appeared as forked tongues "like as of fire" alighting upon their heads (2:3). They were then filled with the Spirit (2:4). Thus, what was analogous to John's Baptism was not indicated by an *immersion*, but a pouring out symbolised by the tongues of fire on their heads.

(2) In John 13 there is an incident recorded of Christ washing the disciples' feet (vv1-11). Jesus in this instance is teaching servanthood. But He is indicating more than that. It is clear from the ensuing conversation with Peter (vv6-11) that it is also a symbolic act pointing to the need for spiritual cleansing. At first Peter does not grasp this. He says indignantly: "Thou shalt never wash my feet"! (v8). He is only thinking there of what to him was the unseemly demeaning action of the Lord in performing a lowly Jewish social convention. But there is more to it than that. "If I wash thee not, thou hast no part with me," retorts the Lord (v8). In other words, this is not simply a matter of some lowly etiquette, but is an action that points symbolically to the need for cleansing and anticipates how it would be effected through His own shed blood. In response Peter is concerned to be washed from head to toe (v9). But that is not necessary: "He that is washed needeth not save to wash his feet, but is clean every whit..." (v10). In other words, the symbolical application of the water to the feet is sufficient to indicate a total cleansing! We cannot help but see here an analogy with the application of water partially (sprinkling or pouring) to represent the total cleansing.

(3) We have indicated that the washing of the disciples' feet by the Lord indicated symbolic anticipation of Christ's own cleansing work through the shedding of His blood on the cross. It is interesting to note how that is spoken of elsewhere. In the letter to the Hebrews a contrast is

made between the Old Testament types and symbols, ordinances and offices which were shadowy, and the 'real' accomplishment of salvation through the coming and work of the Son. He made the world, upholds all things, and by His once-for-all sacrifice "purged our sins" and ascended to the right hand of the Father. Concerning Him it is said that He is "the brightness of his glory, and the express image of his person" (Hebrews 1:1-3). Salvation is accomplished through the shedding of His blood. Without it there is no remission of sin (9:22) and the "blood of bulls and goats" (that is, in the Old Testament ordinances and services) will not do it in any once-and-for-all way (10:4). But the bloodshed that saves is spoken of as "the blood of sprinkling" (12:24). Peter speaks in an entirely similar way right at the beginning of his first letter, where he speaks of believers as "elect according to the foreknowledge of God the Father, through sanctification of the Spirit, unto obedience and sprinkling of the blood of Jesus Christ" (1 Peter 1:2). So that the saving work of Christ as effected by the shedding of His own blood – His death – is represented, as applied to believers, in terms of "sprinkling of the blood of Jesus Christ." It may be recognised, therefore, how sprinkling in baptism will more accurately represent the application of Christ's redemption of sinners.

There is an interesting practical argument for the mode of sprinkling (or pouring) in baptism in the fact that such a mode may be adopted and applied in an unrestricted way anywhere in the world, from the Polar caps to the Equator. There must be water available for the rite, but by such a mode the application of baptism is not limited in situations where there may be little availability of water or where bodily exposure may even be dangerous, not least among the very young or elderly.

3. Meaning of Baptism

The really important thing in baptism is its meaning. The mode and the meaning are tied in with one another. The use of water indicates the need for cleansing or purifying. We have already quoted from Titus 3. Baptism symbolises the need for regeneration in this life. In Hebrews

10 we read: "let us draw near with a true heart in full assurance of faith, having our hearts sprinkled from an evil conscience, and our bodies washed with pure water" (v22). The water in a real sense represents Christ's blood (death). In Romans 6 – a text again used frequently by Baptists – we read that Christians are "buried with him by baptism into death…" (v4). In point of fact there is no reference here to water or immersion, but the practice of Baptism *will* involve an *identification* of the believer with Christ's death as the source of their cleansing and acceptance. This is why we say baptism speaks of regeneration – it is symbolical of a soul's "ingrafting into Christ."

We have an illustration in 1 Peter, chapter 3 in which the Apostle speaks of being identified with Christ's sufferings (18ff.). It was the Spirit who "spoke" to the multitude in Noah's day. There was divine longsuffering. But Noah and those in the ark were saved, all the others perished. But it was those who perished who were "submerged" and not those who were delivered! This was also true at the Red Sea after the Exodus from Egypt. Those who were delivered were at the most 'sprinkled' with the waters. But, says Peter, the deliverance of Noah and the others was an "antitype…*namely* baptism" (v21, NKJV).

Our understanding of the *meaning* of Baptism is in part to be drawn from the corresponding Old Testament rite of Circumcision which it replaced. Of what was it a "sign and seal"? It was clearly a sign and seal of a covenant relationship of the faithful to the Lord. There are at least two personal applications which may be made here:

(1) *All who have received this sign have received the sign of the Covenant.* It speaks of a special relationship between God and the subject of the Baptism. Even although a person's Baptism may in some respects be considered deficient, if they were baptised in the name of the blessed Trinity, that Baptism is not to be treated lightly. For those who do not subsequently make their "calling and election sure" and profess faith in Christ openly, this will be a source of judgement – that a person received the sign and did not fulfil its meaning, by their own believing in the saving work of Christ.

(2) *All who have been baptised have been sprinkled with water.* It speaks of cleansing and in a sense it commits those who have received the sign not only to be the Lord's openly, *but to be holy people*, serving the Lord. That is an expectation of Baptism, however young or old a person may have been when they received the sign. By it they were committed – and must see themselves to have been committed – to being the Lord's. To those not yet converted, or converted and not yet professing, their Baptism calls them to repent of sin, believe in Christ, and come openly to confess Him. It is a sin when the person baptised as an adult does not make such clear and open confession of Christ as Saviour at that time. It is also a covenant-breaking sin for the person baptised in infancy not to make clear and open confession of the Lord as Saviour in later years.

SACRAMENTS

3. Baptism: (2) Subjects

1. Introduction

Baptism is a sacrament symbolising initiation – essentially in relation to becoming a Christian and a part of the Christian Church. It does not make a person a Christian, but it does symbolise what is necessary for anyone to become a Christian. For notice how the *Catechism* describes its meaning in terms of being *a sign and seal of engrafting into Christ*. In other words, this sacrament focuses on *subjective* aspects of Christian faith, whereas the Lord's Supper focuses on *objective* aspects. In some Presbyterian Church life the requirements of admission to the two sacraments have generally involved 'professions' the other way round: an 'objective,' 'historical,' or non-contradicted 'profession' for Baptism and a 'subjective,' 'experiential,' or accredited 'profession' for the Lord's Supper. In reality *equal* care ought be taken over *both* sacraments that a true profession of faith in Christ is involved.

In this chapter we consider the question of the *subjects* of Baptism. Who should receive this ordinance? This is a controversial issue, not only in the debate with Baptist brethren, but even within some Presbyterian circles. Incidentally, it is a pity that the Baptists denominate themselves 'Baptists', because it gives the mistaken impression that those who maintain infant baptism are not Baptists. Advocates of infant Baptism are every bit as 'Baptist' as any Baptist!

The *Shorter Catechism* opens up this question in this way, in answer to the question, 'To whom is Baptism to be administered?':

> Baptism is not to be administered to any that are out of the visible church, till they profess their faith in Christ, and obedience to him; but the infants of such as are members of the visible church are to be baptized. (Answer 95).

In other words, this is an ordinance for the professing Christian Church in this world. There are two questions which arise here: (1) Which adults? and (2) Whose children?

2. Which Adults?

Clearly what is central in this connection is the matter of individuals making a profession of faith in Christ as Saviour. That will be required for admission to this ordinance. Some individuals coming into the 'visible church' will come to 'profess faith in Christ and obedience to him.' That is something also to be expected of those already *within* the Church who may also wish to receive this sacrament for themselves or their children if they have not previously been baptised.

The Church, in so far as it is truly faithful and evangelical, is a community of men and women and children *professing* faith in Christ and obedience to Him. For admission to Baptism, therefore, a profession of faith and obedience is required. Not everyone in the visible Church necessarily makes such a profession outwardly. But if there is to be admission to 'privileges' such as the sacraments, then there must be such an open profession of faith and obedience.

Admittedly the waters can get 'muddied,' as they have done in paedobaptist circles when a 'Half-Way Covenant' idea has prevailed. The half-way covenant view involves the justification for the Baptism of the infants of those who had themselves been baptised as children, even though such adults may not have come openly to profess saving faith in Christ. In relation to Baptism, in Churches in which a significant number of people have traditionally tended to remain non-communicants, there has been a tendency to allow 'diligent adherents' – non-communicants who attend services regularly – Baptism for their children. To get round the awkward inconsistency on the matter of the grounds of admission to the two sacraments it was argued that what was required for the Lord's Supper was an accredited profession, whereas for Baptism a simple non-contradicted or historical profession was considered to be sufficient. This, however, is an anomaly, because ironically it is the sacrament of Baptism that speaks of regeneration, cleansing from sin, and Covenant promise in a way that is not so directly the case in the Lord's Supper. That would seem all the more reason to ensure that a clear profession of saving faith be required for admission to the sacrament.[1]

Theologically, we may say that in terms of its *meaning* Baptism relates more directly to effectual calling, adoption and sanctification, whereas the Lord's Supper relates more directly to justification. It is a dangerous thing for a Church to ask an adherent to make some sort of profession in order to have admission to one sacrament (Baptism for himself/herself or children), which is not thought valid for admission to the other sacrament (Lord's Supper). What is the status of the profession? And what about the *Catechism* teaching about "obedience to Him" as a requirement for Baptism? The *Larger Catechism* is more explicit still: By Baptism (whether for oneself or one's child) the subjects "are solemnly admitted into the visible Church, *and enter in to an open and professed engagement to be wholly and only the Lord's*" (Answer 165). Such a profession made by an adult for themselves must surely be the same as that required of a parent for a child. No more can be sought for admission to the Lord's Supper. The matter of self-examination is mentioned in connection with partaking of the Lord's Supper. In the nature of the case self-examination will also be a pre-requisite for the ordinance of Baptism. Biblical precedent indicates this, as, for example, in the cases of the Ethiopian eunuch and the Philippian jailer (Acts 8:36-37; 16:30-34). It is noticeable that the instances of Baptism in the New Testament invariably involve just such an affirmation. Think of the thousands of adults baptised on the day of Pentecost. What did Peter say to them? "Repent, and be baptised every one of you…" (Acts 2:38). Then there is the Ethiopian Eunuch who professed Jesus and was baptised (Acts 8:36-38). Paul and Lydia and the Philippian Jailor were converted, confessed the Lord, and were baptised (Acts 9:18; 16:15; 16:33). Paul is an interesting case, because he would have

---

[1] That this was perceived to be a problem is indicated, for example in a Report to the Glasgow Presbytery of the Church of Scotland in August 1840. See the Appendix below.

received the Old Testament rite of Circumcision and now he receives the New Testament sign of Baptism, as the thousands at Pentecost did as well. It may be noted, incidentally, that no water is actually mentioned in these cases, nor is any indication given of significant depth of water nearby in which to 'dip' the subjects!

We can say quite clearly, then, that profession of being saved is integral to the appropriate admission to the sacrament. This stands to reason, as the sacrament speaks of a Covenant relation with God, of regeneration, union with Christ, and cleansing from spiritual impurities. Alas, Baptism can become such a nominal thing. Profession has often been reduced to an historical belief. No doubt many have received Baptism as adults for themselves or their children who were not really professing to be saved. They might be sincere enough. But how can an unconverted person really understand the spiritual significance of the ordinance? Why should we not think of this as being as bad as admitting the spiritually uninitiated to the Lord's table? Why should the same caution not be exercised in relation to the one sacrament as it is to the other? For a sacrament to be a source of blessing and benefit, there must be faith; there must be a Covenant relationship with God.

3. Which [or Whose] Children?

Paedobaptism – the practice of Infant Baptism – is a distinctive of Presbyterianism. Baptism is a sign and seal of the Covenant of Grace maintained between God and His people through His eternal Son. But should children may be admitted, and, if so, why? The *Catechism* takes this up in the second part of the answer to Question 95.

This is an unusual procedure because in this case the subjects of the Baptism do not speak for themselves. It therefore puts the onus on parents and on the Church in connection with what is done. Two questions arise here: (1) *Why should children be admitted to the sacrament?* and (2) *What is necessary for a parent bringing a child for the ordinance?*

3.1 Why Children?
There are several arguments:

1. There is the *analogy with Old Testament Circumcision.* This was instituted with Abraham in Genesis 17 as a sign of covenant relation between the Lord and Abraham. Notice that it was instituted before the law. It is not part of the ceremonial Mosaic law, though it did play a significant part in the profession of the Old Testament Church. It applied to males only: to adults on admission to the covenant community and to the male children of such. The application of the corresponding sacrament of baptism to females is clearly established by the incidents recorded in the New Testament in which females were baptised, as, for example, in the case of Lydia (Acts 16:15)

The Baptist argument against infant Baptism on the grounds that the *subject* of the sacrament does not in such cases speak for himself or herself, would apply also to the Old Testament rite. All one can say is that God's ways are not our ways. But it makes sense to have a covenant sign which is applicable to the seed of believers. For God blesses the line of continued generations. And it is not that Circumcision was more formal and less spiritual in meaning than Baptism, for it always spoke of a greater Circumcision – of the heart, just as Baptism speaks of a greater cleansing than the mere washing by water.

2. There are the *implications of household Baptisms* in the New Testament. There is no repeal of the principle that the children of believers are within the covenant and therefore entitled to receive the sign of it. There are several household Baptisms in the New Testament. There are Lydia's (Acts 16); the Philippian Jailer's (Acts 16); and the household of Stephanus (1 Corinthians 1). It is simply inconceivable, given the pattern in the Old, that in the New Testament the children would be excluded from the covenant sign. Undoubtedly such households would have included children.

3. It is important to recognise *that children can receive grace.* Baptism does not change a person (child or adult). It speaks of grace as it applies to believers and their seed. It emphasises that, after all, salvation is all of grace. The child may already have grace, but in any case this points to the necessity for grace and the prospect of it, according to covenant

promise. It is important to recognise that children too can receive and enjoy the grace of God. Is this not implicit in Jesus' blessing the little children (Mark 10:13-16; Luke 18:15-17)? That is not a 'proof text' for paedobaptism, but it does tell us to welcome the children as those who can receive grace and blessing. This is a precious thing in relation the children of believers dying in infancy.

3.2 Whose Children?

The answer is, the infants of "such as are members of the visible church are to be baptised." Remember that to be a 'member of the visible church' requires a profession of faith in Christ and obedience to Him. What about non-communicants? Are they 'members'? Well, how does one measure the faith and obedience of an adherent, if there is no open public profession and a strictly limited submission to church authority? Take the matter of obedience. Would obedience not include the whole matter of habitual commemoration of the Lord's death in the Supper? For after all the true believer is commanded to "shew the Lord's death till he come" (1 Corinthians 11:26). If someone is not professing so as to be obedient to *that* command of the Lord, how should they have other ordinances? This is a point rather persuasively made by William Cunningham:

> We cannot conclude without simply stating the following leading positions that ought to be maintained and set forth, in order to guard against error and delusion on the subject of infant baptism:-
>
> 1st. That Scripture, while furnishing sufficient materials to establish the lawfulness and obligation of infant baptism, does not give us much direct information concerning it, – does not furnish materials for laying down any very definite deliverances as to its proper effects in relation to individuals; and that the whole history of the church inculcates the lesson, that, upon this subject, men should be particularly careful to abstain from deductions, probabilities, or conjectures, beyond what Scripture clearly sanctions.[2]
>
> 2d. That while believers are under the same obligation to

---

[2] This is a very important point in relation to the application of a 'regulative principle' doctrine or practice.

present their infant children for baptism as to be baptized themselves, if they have not been baptized before, no infants ought to be baptized, except those of persons who ought themselves to be baptized as adults upon their own profession and who, being thus recognised as believers, are not only entitled, but bound, to be habitually receiving the Lord's Supper.

3d. That while believers are warranted to improve the baptism of their children in the way of confirming their faith in the salvation of those of them who die in infancy, and in the way of encouraging themselves in a hearty and hopeful discharge of parental duty towards those of them who survive infancy, neither parents nor children, when the children come to be proper subjects of instruction, should regard the fact that they have been baptized, as affording of itself even the slightest presumption that they have been regenerated; that nothing should ever be regarded as furnishing any evidence of regeneration, except the appropriate proofs of an actual renovation of the moral nature, exhibited in each case individually; and that, until these proofs appear, every one, whether baptized or not, should be treated and dealt with in all respects as if he were unregenerate, and still needed to be born again of the word of God through the belief of the truth.[3]

The point to be borne in mind when dealing with such ordinances as the sacraments is that they are for Christians, they are privileges of those who profess faith in Jesus and obedience to Him. All Christians ought to be 'members of the visible Church' in that sense. Those who make no credible profession ought not to presume to receive sacraments. As the American theologian, A. A. Hodge, put it:

> Some have supposed, since the church-membership of the child follows from that of the parent; that every person who was himself introduced into the Church by Baptism in infancy has an indefeasible right to have his children baptized, whether he professes personal faith in Christ or not. But this is manifestly absurd – *(a.)* Because all members of the Church have not a right to all privileges of church-membership. Thus baptized members have no right to come

---

[3] William Cunningham, *The Reformers and the Theology of the Reformation*, London 1967 [1862], 290-291.

to the communion until they make a profession of personal faith. Until they do this they are like citizens under age, with their rights held in suspension, as a just punishment for their refusal to believe. These suspended rights are those of communing and having their children baptized, *(b.)* A person destitute of personal faith can only commit perjury and sacrilege by making the solemn professions and taking the obligations involved in the Baptismal covenant. It is a sin for him to do it, and a sin for the minister to help him to do it.[4]

When adherents receive sacraments for themselves or their child this raises a question as to whether or not there has been a compromise of the nature of Covenant obligations. It also raises a question as to what constitutes a true profession of faith in Christ. The challenge to the Church is to be as consistent as possible, and for the 'adherent' to come to faith, or come openly to profess faith in Christ and obedience to Him, *before* receiving a sacrament for themselves or their children.

In relation to infant Baptism, what greater obligation can there be for parents than bringing up their children for the Lord? In connection with the Lord's Supper the responsibility is individual – the communicant, as it were, represents himself or herself alone before the Lord, albeit together with fellow believers. In the case of Infant Baptism, however, the responsibility is *representative* – the parents bring their child to receive the Covenant sign and make commitments and take vows in relation to them. In a real sense the future of the Church rests upon the parent bringing his/her/their child up for the Lord, with the blessing of the Lord. There can be scarcely anything more important in the life of the Church. Therefore, to downplay this sacrament is like the Church shooting itself in the foot!

There is one other aspect of this subject that should be addressed. It is more practical and has to do with what the standards speak of as the "improvement' of our Baptism. This is not dealt with in the *Shorter Catechism*. It is, however, challengingly dealt with in the *Larger Catechism* (Q167) and will be the subject of the next chapter.

---

[4] A A Hodge, *The Confession of Faith*, London 1964 [1869], 349.

4. Pastoral note

In relation to local Church practices or procedures, it has to be remembered that it is a Kirk Session which determines who shall be admitted to the sacramental ordinances. A difference of opinion may arise between a minister and his elders on the qualifications of applicants for admission to either sacrament. In relation to these things a minister would be wise to acquiesce with the decisions of the Court, albeit seeking the right to have his own reservations or objections minuted in connection with the allowance, say, of the baptism of an infant whose parents are non-communicants (or 'adherents'). At the same time, pastorally he will have an opportunity to encourage parents presenting a child for baptism, neither of whom have openly professed faith in Christ, to face up to the spiritual responsibilities in relation to their own position before the Lord and in relation to the raising of their child in a specifically Christian way.

In Churches where there is no fixed Book of Order for services, such as is the case in the smaller conservative Presbyterian Churches in Scotland, the minister will be responsible for the conduct of the service and the content of the vows taken by parents (for children), or adults (for themselves), in connection with baptism. Any such vows should always be determined according to the position of those receiving baptism for a child. However, the fact of different vows for different candidates is not a satisfactory solution. Ideally vows should be *personal* and *uniform* across a denomination, otherwise a 'two-tier' sort of administration would inevitably be the norm. Some of these matters are touched on in the interesting report from 1840 provided in the Appendix to this chapter.

Pastorally, this is a difficult area in a Church in which admission to the sacraments may not have been set, strictly speaking, at the same level of qualification, and great care and wisdom requires to be exercised whilst trying to come to the most consistent application of what after all is among the marks of a true and healthy Church.

APPENDIX[5]

The following is the Report of the Committee of Glasgow Presbytery, appointed at their ordinary meeting on 12th of June 1840, to inquire into the present practice of administering baptism within the bounds of the Presbytery, the evils connected with it, and the most advisable means of remedying them, where they are found to exist, and to report to a future meeting of Presbytery.

Agreeably to said appointment, your Committee met first, on the 10th of July, and again, on the 5th of August, and again, on this day, and after mature consideration, agree to the following report:-

Your Committee do not deem it necessary, at present, to enter into any statement, either of the principles of Scripture, or of the principles and laws of our Church, as they relate to the nature and ends of the ordinance of baptism, or to the mode of its administration, both because this reverend court is already perfectly acquainted with these points, and because they purpose submitting, in a subsequent part of this report, a recommendation, which, if adopted, will admit of this being done with more convenience.

Your Committee are deeply convinced, that evils of long continuance, of extensive prevalence, and of serious magnitude, attend the administration of this solemn ordinance. These evils they do not think it necessary to specify in detail, farther than to say, that they relate,

1st, To the fact that the ordinance, from various causes, is sometimes dispensed to the children of parents not Scripturally qualified.

2nd, To the fact, that it is very generally dispensed privately, and very often in circumstances inconsistent with the design of the ordinance, and the express and frequently repeated laws of our Church.

Without entering into proof of these alleged facts from specific cases, your Committee beg to recommend, in reference to the first of them, that it shall be enjoined on all ministers and elders to use the utmost diligence and care that no persons be recommended or admitted to the privilege of baptism for their children, without giving satisfactory proofs of competent knowledge and of Christian character. And though they do not believe that it is required, either by the nature of the ordinance, or the facts or declarations of Scripture,

---

[5] 'The Administration of Baptism', in, *Monthly Supplement to The Scottish Christian Herald*, Vol. VII, (1840), 103-104.

The Sacraments – Baptism, subjects

or the standards and laws of the Church, that persons receiving the ordinance of baptism for their children must first have been communicants at the table of the Lord, but that "the children of parents within the visible Church by baptism, and one or both professing their faith in Christ, and obedience to him, may be baptized," yet they hold it involved in this profession, that none be admitted to the ordinance of baptism, but such as are qualified, in the judgment of the kirk-session, to go to the Lord's table, and express their desire and resolution so to do; and if any do come a second time without having fulfilled such resolution, they must assign reasons which are satisfactory for having failed to do so, before they can be admitted, or profess their penitence where they do not. As a practical help to attain the object here recommended, the Committee would suggest the adoption of the following form, to be used in all cases without exception, and that the several sessions or session-clerks be enjoined to use it:-

---

Glasgow, this ____ day of ____

I hereby certify that the bearer, _____ resides in street, No. _____ ; that he attends _____ Church; that he is communicant; that I have made inquiry respecting his moral character and conduct; and that if otherwise qualified, so far as is known to me, he may be admitted to the ordinance of baptism for his child.

_____ *Elder.*

This certificate was presented to me on the __ day of ___

_____ *Minister.*

Admit the bearer to present his child for baptism __ day of ____

_____ *Minister.*

Mr _____ 's child's name is registered.

_____ *Session Clerk.*

It is farther suggested that, agreeable to the laws of the Church, persons from other parishes be enjoined to produce a certificate of character from the minister or kirk-session of the parish from which they come; and that they give reasonable evidence of their intention to attend public ordinances in the church to which they apply for baptism. It is also suggested that each session shall keep a record of those admitted to membership by baptism in the congregation.

In regard to the second fact mentioned above in reference to private baptism, your Committee, from a serious and mature consideration of the subject, in the light of Scripture and the standards and laws of the Church, most earnestly recommend that baptism shall be in all cases administered publicly in the congregation; and where there are any strong reasons why it is not convenient to have it so administered in any particular case, that public intimation of the intention of dispensing it be given from the pulpit, where practicable; and that ministers be enjoined seriously to remind all parents of their duty in this respect.

Your Committee would only farther suggest, that it be enjoined on all the ministers within the bounds of this Presbytery, to preach at least one sermon on this subject, on some convenient day to be agreed upon; and that a Presbyterial pastoral address on this subject be read to all their congregations, setting forth, in few words, the nature and ends of the ordinance, and the principles and laws of the Church on the points adverted to in this report; and they conclude with commending the subject to the prayerful consideration both of the office-bearers and Christian people within your bounds, and to the blessing of the Spirit of all grace.

(Glasgow, Aug. 5, 1840).

SACRAMENTS

4. Baptism: (3) Responsibilities

1. Introduction

The *Larger Catechism* – itself a much-neglected document – was completed in 1648. In it, in relation to Baptism, the divines speak of "the needful but much neglected duty of improving our Baptism." This is perhaps strange language to us. We perhaps think of Baptism as something administered and received on one specific occasion. Because most people are baptised as infants in Presbyterian Churches it is for this reason not something baptised infants subsequently think about. We realise our parents had a responsibility and we might think they did a good or not so good job in bringing us up in the faith. But as for a *continuing* meaning of our infant Baptism for ourselves, well, that is different. This can be a problem in paedobaptist Churches. To what extent do those who were baptised as infants recognise and follow through the significance and meaning of what they received, in terms of professing faith and being obedient to Christ? Presbyterians baptise infants because they believe it is right in terms of the Covenant of grace. There are covenant promises which apply to believers *and their seed*. This is implied in Peter's words on the day of Pentecost: "Repent and be baptized every one of you [i.e., who repent] in the name of Jesus Christ for the remission of sins, and ye shall receive the gift of the Holy Spirit. *For the promise is to you, and to your children*, and to all that are afar off, *even* as many as the Lord our God shall call" (Acts 2:38-9).

Practically speaking, it may be that many who were baptized in infancy and were asked what their Baptism means to them *now*, would give a puzzled or blank response. They may say: "How can I think of my Baptism now?" But just as in the Old Testament those who received the Covenant sign of Circumcision would be expected subsequently to circumcise their hearts (a continuing spiritual exercise), so too we should expect that for all adults or infants receiving the New Testament Covenant sign there ought to be a continuing spiritual 'improvement' of what was spoken of in the sacrament. This is something of which they will be reminded at least when they are present at baptismal services.

There are basically two aspects to this question of improving one's Baptism, one in terms of responsibility in connection with the sacrament and the other in terms of its practical consequences.

2. Responsibilities

In the first instance, obviously, there is a responsibility in Baptism which rests upon:

(1) *The subjects*, the persons baptised (in the case of an adult) or the parents of an infant receiving the Covenant sign. In terms of their responsibility, there will first of all, (a) be a profession of faith in Christ, and (b) a commitment taken on to follow Him, that is to say there will also be "an engagement to be the Lord's" (Answer 94). We can readily understand this. It must be said that the responsibility is the same for both. In the case of the parents bringing an infant, they will be expected to make the same profession as if they were being themselves baptised. One great Scottish theologian put it this way: "no infants ought to be baptized, except those of persons who ought themselves to be baptized as adults upon their own profession, and who, being thus recognised as believers, are not only entitled, but bound, to be habitually receiving the Lord's Supper."[1]

As regards their responsibility towards their children, they are under charge, in terms of their covenant relations to the Lord, to bring up their child "in the nurture [training] and admonition of the Lord" (Ephesians 6:4). There is wonderful promise, though, as we read in 1 Corinthian 7: "the unbelieving husband is sanctified by the wife, and

---

[1] William Cunningham, *The Reformers and the Theology of the Reformation*, London, 1967 [1862], 290.

the unbelieving wife is sanctified by the husband: else were your children unclean; but now they are holy" (v14), that is to say, 'set apart for the Lord.' This is not a reference to personal holiness, but the standing of the child because one or other parent is a believer.

Perhaps this was already something well understood among the people of God. We have, for example, in Deuteronomy this injunction: "And these words, which I command thee this day, shall be in thine heart: and thou shalt teach them diligently unto thy children, and shalt talk of them when thou sittest in thine house, when thou walkest by the way, and when thou liest down, and when thou risest up…" (6:6-9). Obviously this is part of the "improvement" of Baptism so far as the children of a home are concerned.

But it is not only the subjects of Baptism (adults or parents) who have a responsibility here, but also

(2) *The Church.* The Church carries a solemn responsibility for covenant children. And that is not something exhausted by simply the avaiability of a Sabbath School. The fact is that this is how the Church should see Baptism of infants, or adults when baptized for that matter: the infants, or adults, on profession of faith, not having been previously baptized, are welcomed in to the bosom of the Church and therefore must be taken in to the hearts of the people. They are part of the fellowship to be loved and to be prayed for, and to have practical spiritual concern for. This will be a continuing concern. No one should be isolated in a good-going evangelical Presbyterian Church, not least the baptized infants, nor any infants in the congregation, baptized or not. We think highly of our families, but we ought to think even higher of the Church fellowship or 'family.' There ought to be that comprehensive supportiveness, as we are enjoined: "As we have therefore opportunity, let us do good unto all men, especially unto them who are of the household of faith" (Galatians 6:10). This must be central to the health of the Church, and to the 'improvement' of the Baptism of any within the fellowship – in terms at least of prayer, support, and encouragement in spiritual things.

In the Westminster *Directory for the Public Worship of God* ministers are encouraged to instruct that "children by Baptism, are solemnly received into the bosom of the visible church, distinguished from the world, and them that are without, and united with believers…" In this matter all have a role: minister, elders, deacons and members. The responsibility extends beyond simply the subject of the Baptism – the whole Church is involved.

3. Practical Consequences

As we have indicated, when we think of Baptism we often think of a one-off event. It is doubtful that we think much of it thereafter, except, perhaps when we are present at a Baptism. What do we think of its on-going significance or efficacy? The *Larger Catechism* helpfully challenges us about this in speaking of the "improvement" of our Baptism (Answer 167):

> The needful but much neglected duty of improving our Baptism, is to be performed by us all our life long, especially in the time of temptation, and when we are present at the administration of it to others; by serious and thankful consideration of the nature of it, and of the ends for which Christ instituted it, the privileges and benefits conferred and sealed thereby, and our solemn vow made therein; by being humbled for our sinful defilement, our falling short of, and walking contrary to, the grace of Baptism, and our engagements; by growing up to assurance of pardon of sin, and of all other blessings sealed to us in that sacrament: by drawing strength from the death and resurrection of Christ, into whom we are baptized, for the mortifying of sin, and quickening of grace; and by endeavouring to live by faith, to have our conversation in holiness and righteousness, as those that have therein given up their names to Christ; and to walk in brotherly love, as being baptized by the same Spirit into one body.

It is interesting that this was seen as a "much neglected duty" in that Puritan era! Implicit in this ordinance is something that should be worked out all our life long, especially in times of temptation, because our Baptism will remind us of the need for engrafting in to Christ, for faith in Him and obedience to His Word. These things are pointed to in the ordinance.

It may be, as the *Catechism* tells us, that it is at the actual observance of the sacrament being administered to others that brings the truths back home to our hearts. Maybe people will then think on vows taken by them at the administration of the ordinance. It ought to be that when individuals think of their Baptism, if they have been baptized, that there will be sorrow and repentance for falling short in what they were covenanted to be before God, or of "walking contrary" to that of which their Baptism spoke. Any Baptism, adult or infant, must encourage the subject afterwards to seek the blessings held out in the sacrament. What are they? They are the benefits of the Covenant of Grace. And what are these? Essentially, they are blessings flowing from effectual calling, justification, adoption and sanctification. And what accompanies or flows from these? The answer is (*Shorter Catechism*, Answer 36): assurance of God's love, peace of conscience, joy in the Holy Spirit, increase of grace, and perseverance therein to the end. These are to be pursued, improved and sought, not least as improvement of one's erstwhile Baptism. We see this in the *Larger Catechism* too: assurance of pardon from sin, drawing strength from the resurrection of Jesus, mortifying sin, endeavouring to live by faith, and living a holy life. When these things are pursued actively and spiritually such persons are "improving" their Baptism. They understand its meaning in a deeply practical sense and they are confirming what was done. Again, our *Directory* encourages this: "that all who are baptized in the name of Christ, do renounce, and by their Baptism are bound to fight against the devil, the world and the flesh." That also applies to those who have received the sacrament in infancy. That is what they ought to be doing subsequently, coming to faith and living as a Christian. In other words, they are to live as those who have "given up their names to Christ." That is something signified and sealed in Baptism.

It goes without saying that outward water Baptism points to the Baptism with the Spirit. Such 'Baptism' is received at conversion (the new birth), but subsequently the Christian will desire to "walk in the Spirit" (Romans 8:1, 4; Galatians 5:16, 25), and enjoy fresh outpourings of the Spirit on them. In this way, too, they will 'improve' what was signified in the water-Baptism.

The efficacy is not confined to the moment of administration. It will cover a person's life, at least on subsequently coming to faith. And it is to be used as a motive to improve in devotion, grace, assurance, love to Christ and the brethren, praises and mortification of sin. There is a lot in this, then. Improving one's Baptism means there will be a moving forward in commitment and in devotion to the Lord and His Word.

It may be that some of what has been argued here is, in a sense, quite new to many paedobaptists. Some may think that "I would like to have been like that, improving Baptism etc., but I wasn't converted when I received Baptism for my children," or, "I have evidently failed because they are not professing or following (and perhaps even not attending Church). What can I do?" First of all they must *make their own calling and election sure.* They should profess the Lord openly and clearly for themselves. To those who are still adherents and who received this ordinance in infancy, it is calling them to come to Christ and confess Him and walk with Him.

What of baptized, or for that matter non-baptized, children? Well, pray for them, speak with them, and plead with them. The Lord says to the Christian that the promise is to them and to their children. They should cry out to the Lord: "Lord, I confess I have not been what I should have been nor done what I should have done, forgive me; but Lord, remember your Covenant and bless my children and open their hearts to be responsive to what they have heard and what they now see in Thy people." As for the Church, it must have a concern to pray for the children, that they be converted and kept and blessed with the benefits of the covenant of grace. In the final analysis our covenant God is our hope. May He enable His professing people to be faithful.

SACRAMENTS

5. The Lord's Supper: (1) Institution and benefits

A. Its Precursor

The Lord's Supper, as it is usually called, is the other of the two New Testament sacraments. It replaced the Old Testament ordinance of the *Passover*. It is clear from the New Testament that the Lord's Supper emerges from the Passover service. The Passover commemorated the Exodus from Egypt. By a mighty hand and outstretched arm He made a great deliverance for the people of God! The Passover clearly involved remembrance, and the Lord's Supper also involves remembrance. Jesus indicated this when He said: "This do in remembrance of me."

Central in the Supper, too, is the remembrance of deliverance – an infinitely greater deliverance – wrought by Christ through His sufferings and death for sinners. The Passover, though, clearly points forward to the Supper and in many ways is a pattern of it. There are differences of course. Consider what Paul speaks about in 1 Corinthians 5, verses 7 and 8. There is that lovely phrase there, "Christ our Passover…" That links the Old and the New ordinances beautifully.

1. The Deliverance Effected

What was central to the Passover? The lamb, the Paschal Lamb. It was to be sacrificed. But it had to be of a very special sort: spotless, flawless, first year, and male. Why was it slain? It was slain symbolically in place of the people. The blood was shed to protect the people who sprinkled it on their doorposts and lintels. There is a lamb in the Lord's Supper, too. Not literally, except in the sense that Jesus was that lamb. John the Baptist had already described Him as the Lamb of God who would take away the sin of the world (John 1:29). He is the lamb without blemish and without spot – holy, harmless and undefiled and separate from sinners. His sacrifice and blood-shedding would make atonement for sinners, for all who come under the shelter of His blood. He was slain from the foundation of the world (Revelation 13:8). That is to say, His death was part of the purpose of God from all eternity. That is what it would take to provide a sufficient sacrifice for sinners. What happened to the Lamb of God was not therefore random. This was no accidental event. It was the purpose and pleasure of God to bruise Him (Isaiah 53:10). He was led as a lamb to the slaughter (Isaiah 53:7). It had to be so, or there would be no basis for the salvation of sinners.

In both the Passover and Lord's Supper there was therefore the aspect of blood-shedding involved or spoken of. This is represented in the Supper by the symbols of the bread and the wine. We are reminded that without the shedding of blood there is no remission of sin (Hebrews 9:22). The Paschal Lamb pointed forward to the Lamb of God, especially on the cross. Without the death of the lamb there would be no covering for sin, no protection. The angel of death passed over those who had sprinkled the lamb's blood on the doorposts. Just so, those who are "sprinkled" (cleansed) by the blood of Jesus, coming to faith in Him, will avoid damnation.

There is no doubt that Paul expects the Corinthians (and us) to see how the Passover points to Jesus, the new Paschal Lamb. We consequently recognise in His sacrifice the effective basis for our deliverance. The death of the lamb was not the only element in the Passover (or, Feast of Unleavened Bread). There was also the Unleavened Bread. The bread taken with the Passover required to be of a certain sort – unleavened.

2. The Cleansing Required

Leaven in Scripture is used in more than one way. It is often, however, used to refer to sin, or as a picture of sin. Why leave out the leaven? Well, it would remind the people to deal with sin. This is how Paul takes this up: "purge out therefore the old leaven…" (1 Corinthians

5:7). Keep the feast with the "unleavened bread of sincerity and truth" (v8).

In the Passover there had to be no leaven, not only in the meal, but also in the whole home (Exodus 12:15). Remove it all! Why? It is a reminder of sin and the effects of sin. Like leaven, sin can spread so easily through our lives. One thing leads to another, one sin to another, one covering up of a sin to another covering up of a sin. Purge it out! Elsewhere he uses the term "mortify" (= put to death). Removal of leaven is like an instruction to remove sin. And when he says "purge out therefore the old leaven," Paul goes on to say, "for even *Christ our passover, is sacrificed for us.*" The believer, is to be 'unleavened.' If He died for their sin, they should die to their own sin! So, in the Passover there is not only a reminder of the safety to be found in the blood of the lamb (signifying atonement), there also was an encouragement to forsake sin, (represented by the removal of the leaven).

This can be readily applied to the Lord's Supper. In Chapter 11 of the same letter Paul encourages the matter of self-examination in relation to the Lord's Supper. Why? Lest any eat and drink in an unworthy manner, or carelessly. What self-examination is to be made? There will be enquiry about the possession of true faith in the Lord Jesus for one thing. Also, there will be examination about the spiritual exercise of "purging out the old leaven" of sin, and particularly *malice and wickedness*. These are to be replaced by sincerity and truth. The believer does not just wait for such 'cleansing.' They are to put to death the sin, just as they are exhorted to cleanse themselves (see for example, 2 Corinthians 7:1; James 4:8, and Colossians 3:5, not to speak of how Jesus speaks in Matthew 5:29-30 etc.). What are believers to be? A "new lump," cleansed, holy, God-honouring people.

As the believer approaches the Lord's Supper what better thoughts can they have in their minds and hearts than such meditations as these:

(1) *They are to think upon Christ*, sacrificed as the sacrificial lamb on the cursed cross, dying for sinners as their representative and substitute. He is the believer's Passover, their Deliverer from sin's guilt and curse.

(2) *They are to be active in purging sin* – the "old leaven" of wickedness and malice, however it manifests itself in their lives. After all, we are to be clean (holy) as He is clean (holy). They are to reflect the Master, and show Him forth in this world. How can they do that if they have the old leaven? "Therefore let us keep the feast" (1 Corinthians 5:8).

B. Its Institution and Benefits

The context of the institution of the Lord's Supper, as described in the three gospels where it is given, makes this clear. There is a smooth transition from one to the next. The institution is recorded in the first three gospels (Matthew 26:26-30; Mark 14:22-25; and Luke 22:15-20). The institution is also mentioned by Paul in 1 Corinthians 11 (23-26). What is clear is this:

(1) *It was instituted by the Lord Jesus Himself,* as any such sacrament must be.

(2) *It is to be observed, or administered, in the Church perpetually right up to the second coming of the Lord.* The reason for that is plain: it is because the Lord's death is to be 'proclaimed' in every age (1 Corinthians 11:26). The Lord's death is central in the accomplishment of redemption for sinners, and therefore this memorial is to be central in the Church to remind the Church, and the world too, of how salvation and acceptance and forgiveness have been accomplished for sinners in a way entirely acceptable to the holiness and justice of God.

(3) *It is an ordinance of great centrality and significance for the Church.* As we have already indicated, the focus of this ordinance is different from Baptism. The meaning and symbolism in Baptism points more to the *subjective* aspects of Christian faith (i.e. what God does *in* a sinner), whereas the Lord's Supper points more to the *objective* aspects of Christian faith (i.e., what God does *for* a sinner).

Like the Passover, which it replaced as the New Testament ordinance, the Lord's Supper basically commemorates a deliverance for the people of God. In the Passover service there was the killing of the lamb and the sprinkling of its blood as a 'covering' over the lintel and door posts. There was that sacrificial aspect to the Passover. And it is the sacrificial aspect that is central in the Lord's Supper. We have the connection beautifully stated by Paul in writing to the Corinthians when he says: "Christ our passover (lamb) is sacrificed for us" (1 Corinthians 5:7). It is clear even in the context of 1 Corinthians 5 that the Lord's Supper is in view, if not in the forefront, at least in the background. Paul goes on to speak there of "keeping the feast", and doing so with proper spirituality (v8). The ordinance of the Lord's Supper therefore also focuses on the matter of deliverance. In this case it is spiritual, that is to say it is speaking of deliverance from the power and dominion of sin through the sacrificial work of the Son of God.

1. The Names for this Ordinance

The Lord's Supper, like Baptism, has not been without controversy. The names by which it is known ecclesiastically indicate this. There is the Roman Catholic *mass*, which contains the notion or re-enacting the sacrifice of Christ. They wrongly see the sacrament as something that conveys grace to the partaker. They hold a view called 'transubstantiation' which involves the elements of bread and wine being taken to change into the actual flesh and blood of the Lord in the service. The Lutherans and some High Anglicans hold to a similar idea, called 'consubstantiation.' They maintain that the bread and wine stay bread and wine but at a certain point come to *contain* Christ's flesh and blood. We may illustrate these views in this way. The Catholic view would be analogous to the miracle at Cana – Jesus' first (John 2:1-11) – in which the water was changed into wine. The Lutheran/High Anglican view would be more like a bar of iron being heated up until red-hot. It remains iron, but nevertheless changes radically.

Our own view, which we believe to be entirely agreeable to the Word of God, takes issue with such deviations and maintains this: *that the elements do not change their composition at all.* Partaking is "not after a corporal or carnal manner" at all. Martin Luther (1483-1546) in a debate with another Reformer named Huldrych Zwingli (1484-1531), scratched on the table they were gathered round: "This is my body...this is my blood."[1] It was as simple as that to him. But in the institution in which Jesus used these terms it is clear that his body remained separate from the elements he used. He was sitting there, and it is clear He intended that the bread and the wine would be understood as *representing* Himself, especially in relation to the sacrifice of Himself on the cross, which was still then in the future. Jesus speaks in an entirely similar way in His 'bread of life' discourse in John 6. He says there: "I am the living bread which came down from heaven: if any man shall eat of this bread, he shall live for ever: and the bread that I will give is my flesh, which I will give for the life of the world" (v51). He goes on: "Except ye eat the flesh of the Son of man, and drink his blood, you have no life in you" (v53). Like Nicodemus and the teaching of the Lord in relation to being 'born again,' so too these people misunderstood by taking Him as speaking simply on a material level (v52). But He was not speaking on a material level. He was speaking on a spiritual level, as is clear, for example, when He says earlier: "I am the bread of life: he that cometh to me shall never hunger; and he that believeth on me shall never thirst" (v35). He speaks in a *figurative* way and about the *spiritual* experience of the proper exercise of faith in Him. And that is exactly the language of the Lord's Supper.

Another name often used is 'Eucharist.' In some ways this is an innocuous word because it is from the word *eucharistesas* (εὐχαριστήσας) in 1 Corinthians 11:24: having "given thanks…" However, this word 'Eucharist' has tended to be used in liturgical Churches and was clearly not used to describe the ordinance in the New Testament, though there are, it may be noted, aspects of 'thanksgiving' in the ordinance. The most appropriate designations to use are Lord's Supper and Communion (see 1 Corinthians 10:16). These do not have the

---

[1] T M Lindsay, *The Reformation*, Edinburgh, 1882, 31; see also, Alister E McGrath, *Reformation Thought: An Introduction*, Oxford, ³1999, 189-190.

sacramental or liturgical connotations.

There is also in Christian Brethren circles the use of the term "breaking of bread" to describe this ordinance. This is taken from Acts 2 and the description of the practice of the Church after the day of Pentecost. The converts are said to have "continued steadfastly...in breaking of bread..." (2:42). It was a feature of Apostolic Church life. The only other reference to breaking of bread is in an incident described in Luke's gospel in which the disciples who had met with a stranger on the road to Emmaus and taken him into their home for hospitality had their eyes opened to recognise the risen Lord in the "breaking of bread" (24:35). That, however, is clearly not a reference to the Lord's Supper. Although the reference in Acts 2, verse 42 (κλάσει του άρτου, breaking of the loaf) may well indicate the sacrament of the Lord's Supper, it is not clear that that is the case, especially given the absence of reference to the wine, though that may not be conclusive in itself. The description, "breaking of bread" may simply refer to a communal meal. That at least appears to be the connotation in verse 46, in which a similar expression is used (κλώντές...άρτον, breaking...bread).

So, what are *we* to make of this service? Is it just a 'memorial'? Is it simply to remind us of His death and that is it? Is there no 'real', or spiritual presence in the Supper? First of all, it does have the aspect of commemoration. Jesus does say: "This do in remembrance of me," and the ordinance is to be observed, "till He come." But it is more than that. The *Shorter Catechism* indicates this by the point that those who receive the bread and wine do not partake after a corporal or carnal manner. That has reference to any idea that the elements themselves are changed into Christ's flesh and blood. Rather, those who rightly take the elements will do so by faith, with this promise, that they will receive His "benefits, to their spiritual nourishment, and growth in grace" (Answer 96). In other words, *this is a means of grace*. It is not an empty ceremony, spiritually speaking. True *saving* faith is necessary for there to be any benefit. The benefit comes by faith through the presence of the Lord in the Supper.

But this raises the question: How, then, is Christ present? And further, How are blessings derived, and what blessings exactly?

2. The Benefits in this Ordinance

The blessings derived from the Lord's Supper must be linked to two things (one of which we will come back to in the next chapter): *faith in the one partaking*, and *Christ's own presence in the ordinance*.

(1) *The necessity of spiritual faith.* It stands to reason that there must be faith for any benefit to be received. This much is mentioned in the *Catechism* answer (96). No doubt there have always been those who have come to the table bereft of real saving faith. It reminds one of something Augustine said about Judas: "Judas ate the bread with the Lord, but did not eat the Lord with the bread"! There is no benefit from partaking without real faith. Indeed, that may even be a dangerous thing to do, given Paul's warning in 1 Corinthians 11:27-34.

The Church rightly has a responsibility to preserve the ordinance as purely as possible, without presuming to read people's hearts. Nonetheless, the Church must hear the profession of a saving interest in Christ before any take their place at the Table. The reason why faith is necessary is because there must be a "discerning" of the Lord (v29). There must be a spiritual understanding of who He is and what He has done to save sinners. There will be a believing and resting upon Christ. There will be a full acknowledgement of sinful unworthiness and the recognition of the worthiness of Jesus as substitute and Saviour. But there is something more in the sacrament.

(2) *The reality of Christ's presence.* You see, it is not as though the partakers are alone at the table of the Lord. It is *His* table, and He will be present. The elements do not change their constitution. The spiritual benefits do not derive from any such material change. However, *there is a real presence of Christ where the ordinance is faithfully observed.* The Lord sits and sups with His own (Revelation 3:20). How? Well, by the One who is described as the 'executive' of the Trinity, the Holy Spirit, whom He sent to

represent His interests in the World (John 16:5-15). The work of the Spirit in and through the Word and the sacrament mysteriously ensures the reality of Christ's presence, spiritually, in the ordinance. And this is a real source of spiritual blessing and benefit. It is, indeed, a means of grace. God acts by His Spirit in the Supper. He acts for our blessing. He conveys grace to the souls of His own even as they sit there, as they think upon their sin and Christ's glorious work to deal with sin.

In speaking of the Supper in 1 Corinthians 10 Paul refers to the wine as "the cup of blessing", and he says that the wine is the "communion of the blood" and the bread "the communion of the body" of the Lord. The language, again, is figurative and spiritual. But the idea of "communion" (κοινωνία) in this ordinance is precious. There is real "communion" with the Lord in His death. The believer realises that that is the basis for any acceptance with God. So, He "glories in the cross" (thus Galatians 6:14). That blood was shed and body broken for me, as I believe and rest upon Him. And He comes to the believer at the table. They enjoy 'communion' with Him and He "restoreth my soul." There is no communion without union, no blessing in the "cup" apart from His work upon and among those there at the table believing and resting and feeding by faith upon Him.

3. The Blessings Received from this Ordinance

The *Catechism* speaks of believers partaking of the ordinance "to their spiritual nourishment, and growth in grace," How does this come about? We have spoken already of the work of the Spirit in this. But how will this manifest itself? Well,

(1) *Believers will draw virtue from Christ's death*. This is something suggested by the Puritan, Thomas Vincent:

> Believers receive spiritual nourishment and growth in grace in and by this sacrament – 1. As they draw virtue from Christ's death, for the crucifying of the flesh, for mortifying and purging away sin, which doth hinder their spiritual nourishment and growth. 2. As the Lord doth convey his Spirit, and they do receive in this sacrament by faith, further

supplies of grace, which, by his death, he hath purchased for them, and which, in his covenant of grace (whereof this sacrament is a seal), he hath promised unto them.[2]

Believers will reflect upon what salvation cost in terms of the death of the Lord. They reckon on this: that He has made satisfaction for all their sins in a sacrifice of infinite value. They consequently are brought to see the incongruity of their sin. Meditation on Christ's death must encourage them to deal with their own sin, by grace to crucify the flesh and mortify and purge away sin. They will be determined to deal with all sin in the life that hinders spiritual advance. They determine to apply themselves more earnestly to the means of grace. They deal with issues in their life: sins of the flesh and spirit.

To take a practical instance: Suppose a believer has something against someone else, or *they* have something against a fellow-believer. These are the sorts of things to be sorted out before the sacrament. Or there may be some unmortified habit or desire. Such things will hinder spiritual advance. These must be dealt with. Such things may not only hinder godliness, but also fellowship. This may be true of every sin of which a believer is convicted. They focus on these things. They appreciate, there at the table, the wonderful truth that "the blood of Jesus Christ, God's Son, cleanseth from all sin." But that will involve seriously cleansing in a believer's own life, as James exhorts in his letter (4:7-8). This, practically speaking, is drawing virtue from Christ's death.

(2) Believers will receive grace in the ordinance. This is a service of blessing and benefit, at least potentially, and really when there is true faith. Christ is present by His Spirit. He gives grace there and then. There is a mysterious aspect of this, but this is where the ordinance is a 'seal.' Blessing is promised and blessing is gained, by the Lord's work in and through the sacrament. He will give inward grace. He will give the Holy Spirit to quicken and empower. So that there will be growth in devotion and love to the Lord. The response of the exercised soul? "Lord, I need

---

[2] Thomas Vincent, *The Shorter Catechism Explained from Scripture*, London 1980 [1674], 262.

thy presence. I need a felt sense of thy presence; I need thy grace to rest all the more on the Lord and to conquer and mortify my sins and failings. I rest upon the merits of Jesus. I appreciate that His death secured for me pardon and redemption. Help me, Lord, to proclaim His death, as the basis of all acceptance, 'till He come'."

SACRAMENTS

6. The Lord's Supper: (2) Partaking

1. Introduction

The Lord's Supper commemorates Christ's death for His own. His death is represented by tangible symbols of bread and wine, the bread speaking of His broken body, and the wine of His shed blood. The service is designed to be an aid spiritually to the people of God, in their devotion to Christ and commitment to Him. It is through His death that the believer is accepted, and so it is poignant to remember this Supper, speaking of His death, "till He come." It is a command of course. All who truly and sincerely love and own the Lord should be at the table. Perceived weakness or faintheartedness – or feelings of unworthiness – in themselves are not reasons to stay away. If Christ invites, the believer should be there! It goes without saying that this is not completely unqualified, because the Supper is not to be taken lightly. Rather it is to be approached with all due care and self-examination. This is the thrust of the answer to the 97th question of the *Shorter Catechism*: "What is required to the worthy receiving of the Lord's Supper?" The answer raises the matter of self-examination:

> It is required of them that would worthily partake of the Lord's supper, that they examine themselves of their knowledge to discern the Lord's body, of their faith to feed upon him, of their repentance, love, and new obedience; lest, coming unworthily, they eat and drink judgement to themselves.

The point of the self-examination is precisely to raise 'issues' in your life that must be cleared away so that you can go to the table in a right attitude of heart and spirit.

We have teaching on the matter of self-examination in 1 Corinthians 11:27-29. But why is preparation necessary? It is necessary because of the possibility of eating and drinking unworthily. We are to be careful not to incur the displeasure of the Lord in this. We are to "discern the Lord's body." That is to say, we are to recognise fully of what the elements speak. In dealing with the worthy partaking of the Supper we require to clear away some common misunderstandings.

2. Carelessness is to be avoided

This goes without saying. But the point of self-examination is that it be an *aid* to taking of the Supper. And people stumble over this, especially this talk of "eating and drinking damnation" (KJV). And some with a true interest in Christ (as far as one can tell) might say, "I am unworthy. I cannot partake for fear of judgement." But when Paul speaks of *unworthiness* here he is speaking not of personal feelings at all, but a profane of careless outward partaking. Paul called *himself* the "chief of sinners." And he is aware that true believers will reckon themselves unworthy. Anyone remotely conscious of the reality of indwelling sin will feel that way. Paul is speaking here *not* of general unworthiness on account of feelings of sinfulness, but a careless or unworthy *manner* of partaking of the Supper. The Supper is for those saved by grace, however unworthy they may feel. But they recognise Christ's worthiness for them, which in a sense is the point of the Lord's Supper itself. If a man or a woman appreciates the meaning of the symbols and the significance of the Supper as, (a) a commemoration of the death of the Saviour for them, and, (b) as a commanded duty from the Lord, the matter of unworthy *manner of partaking* does not apply. Charles Hodge beautifully explains what is not meant by unworthy partaking:

> It is not to eat and drink with a consciousness of unworthiness, for such a sense of ill-desert is one of the conditions of acceptable communion…Nor is it to eat with doubt and misgiving of our being duly prepared to come to the Lord's table, for such doubts, although an evidence of weak faith, indicate a better state of mind than indifference or false security…To eat and drink unworthily is in general to come to the Lord's table in a careless, irreverent spirit, without the intention or desire to commemorate the death of Christ as the sacrifice for our sins and without the

> purpose of complying with the engagements which we thereby assume...All that is necessary to observe is, that the warning is directed against the careless and profane, and not against the timid and the doubting.[1]

But what, then, is this "eating and drinking damnation" to oneself? Will a person be damned for unworthy partaking? The word translated 'damnation' (κρίμα) here, however, does not mean eternal punishment. In this context it means that careless participation will expose one to judgements or 'chastenings' from the Lord.[2] The nature of such chastenings is clear in verse 30 and following where Paul speaks of sicknesses and other unspecified chastenings. Whoever fails to approach the supper conscious that it speaks of the sufferings and death of the Saviour is obviously disrespectful to the One who instituted the Supper. This acts as an incentive to all the people of God to have the right attitude to the Supper, lest the displeasure of the Lord be incurred. It has to be said that preparatory services and explanations will lend themselves to a clear and proper understanding of what the Supper is about and ought to serve as a discouragement of any carelessness in approach.[3] This is the negative side as we approach the Supper. Carelessness is to be avoided.

3. Self-Examination to be pursued

Spiritual self-examination is something that should be going on in the life of the true believer all the time. It is not just for the Lord's Supper. By the same token, those who make no profession of faith in Christ must examine themselves. In a sense, when the gospel goes out to all

---

[1] Charles Hodge, *Commentary on the First Epistle to the Corinthians*, Grand Rapids, 1980 [1857], 230-231.
[2] Leon Morris, *The First Epistle of Paul to the Corinthians*, London, 1958, 164: "*Damnation* is too strong a translation for *krima*, which means rather 'condemnation'. Paul does not mean that a person who communicates wrongly incurs eternal damnation, but that he comes under the measure of condemnation appropriate to the act."
[3] See the Appendix to this chapter in which an explanation is given and a format set out of the 'Communion Seasons' which were once widespread in Scottish Presbyterian Churches though are now largely observed only by some of the smaller conservative Presbyterian denominations.

and sundry it is inviting people to consider where they stand in relation to Christ and eternity. This matter of self-examination among the people of God is no doubt especially appropriate in approaching the Lord's Supper. *Communicants should not partake without it.* When a person is admitted into the communicant membership of a congregation, as it should be at least, they are examined as to their profession of faith and assessment is made of the consistency of the life with the profession. Are these people attentive at all the means of grace? Is their life showing the character of the Saviour? Is there graciousness? Do they evidently love the Lord and His worship and His day and His people? Do they love the brethren? This examination is very much an *outward* one. It is to be expected that the outward will reflect the inward grace. Self-examination, however, is principally an examination of thoughts and *inward* desires and knowledge. I look at my life and my heart and ask: Do these give evidence of really loving the Lord and seeking to keep His word? Am I trusting in Christ? Am I dying to sin? Do I have a will for the work of the Lord? Is my knowledge and love for Christ and the gospel growing? Am I loosened more to the things of the world than I was before? "Examine yourselves," says the Apostle, "whether ye be in the faith" (2 Corinthians 13:5). Obviously, that is of first importance. "Test yourselves…" What about the fruit of the Spirit? – love, joy, peace, long-suffering, kindness, goodness, faithfulness, gentleness and self-control (Galatians 5:22-23). Believers examine themselves in relation to the worship of God, in relation to communion with God, in relation to prayer and godly works. They examine themselves as to sin, confession of sin, and repentance for sin. Here is the experience of the Psalmist: "I have considered the days of old, the years of ancient times. I call to remembrance my song in the night: I commune [meditate] with mine own heart: and my spirit made diligent search" (77:5-6). This self-examination will reveal, as it is intended to reveal, what may be lacking in the warmth of a believer's love and commitment to the Lord Jesus and/or His people, His Church. But then they are helped to identify what needs to be made good, and seek the Lord for the grace to make good their deficiencies. It will produce humility and penitence – and correction. Perhaps this will involve a relationship with another believer which has broken down in some way. These things must be put right, or at least everything possible to do so, preparatory to the Lord's Supper.

But this examination is not morbid introspection, as if it were simply an indulgence in self-accusation, or encouragement of doubts and fears. It is not to the end of concluding unworthiness to partake of the Supper. No. Rather, the purpose of this self-examination is *inclusion* and not *exclusion*. "But let a man examine himself, and so let him eat of that bread, and drink of that cup." In this self-examination believers will always seek correction, the stirring up of the graces and fruits of the Spirit; an attitude of penitence and a resolve after a new obedience. Obviously, no unbelieving man or woman can partake of the Supper well. It is both futile and dangerous for them to partake, though no more so than the mere fact of their going on and sitting under the Word in a Christless state. But the point here is that the *believers* prepare themselves to come in a proper and reverent manner to the Table of the Lord. Self-examination reminds us of necessity that, after all, the Supper is for sinful people, weak Christians, feeling feeble, but believing sinners who are exercised humbly before the Lord and penitent over sin.

In other words this self-examination encouraged in relation to the Supper is to the end that people who really do trust in the Saviour as their Saviour from sin will not hold back, and certainly not on account of feelings of unworthiness. All at the Table will have feelings of personal unworthiness. But the focus of the Table is Christ's worthiness; His provision for sinners. As one writer put it:

> It is important to be clear that this self-examination is not a quest for worthiness, as if somehow to prove to ourselves that we are good enough to participate. Self-examination is not designed to measure our worthiness as much as it is to set our unworthiness in the context of the worthiness of Jesus Christ our substitute and Saviour. Being good enough is not the issue. Believing Jesus, trusting Jesus, looking to

Jesus, and coming in the obedience of faith to Jesus is the issue.[4]

Preparation for the Supper will always involve self-examination. This can be very uncomfortable. But in connection with the Supper it is to the end of partaking – partaking with the right attitude, the right disposition, the right care and reverence. It may be that many have doubts and fears. Perhaps they hold people back for long enough on that account. Feelings of unworthiness are real. The *Larger Catechism* asks a question: "May one who doubts of his being in Christ; or of his due preparation come to the sacrament of the Lord's Supper?" The answer given is this:-

> One who doubts of his being in Christ, or of his due preparation to come to the sacrament of the Lord's Supper, may have (a) true interest in Christ, though he be not assured thereof; and in God's account hath it [interest in Christ], if he be duly affected with the apprehension of the want of it [i.e., interest in Christ], and unfeignedly desires to be found in Christ, and to depart from iniquity; in which case, because promises are made, and the sacrament is appointed for the relief even of weak and doubting Christians, he is bound to bewail his unbelief, and labour to have his doubts resolved; and, so doing, he may and ought to come to the Lord's Supper, that he may be further strengthened.[5]

"But let a man examine himself." We are in an age when this is not much done. In most Churches the old Communion seasons have been on the decline or have disappeared entirely. The matter of membership, too, has often become very loose. It is needful to hold fast in the respect and reverence given to the Word and Sacraments, as well as Church membership. However, though there may be abuses on every hand, as there have been in the past, that should not be an excuse for any to hold back in coming to profess faith in Christ. Believers in preparing for the sacrament are to examine themselves. They are to rest

---

[4] Gordon J Keddie, *Experiencing the Lord's Supper*, Grace Presbyterian Church, State College, PA, 1998, 40.
[5] *Larger Catechism*, Answer 172.

on the worthiness of Jesus, upon whose blood and righteousness alone there is any worthiness for any of the sinful sons and daughters of Adam. For any who are truly the Lord's it is a deep disrespect to the Son of God to hold back and make no open profession of Him. This is a day to nail one's colours to the mast and throw in one's lot with the people of God and be not ashamed of the gospel of Christ.

4. Conclusion

We see in the Supper and its symbols the dying love of the Saviour for sinners; we see the love of the Lord displayed in giving His Son to accomplish an all-sufficient sacrifice and satisfaction for sin. It is a wonderful source of blessing and benefit for the believer. In itself it does not say anything above what we find in the gospel. But it is an occasion in which a distinction is made between the professing and non-professing persons, and so must be an occasion for care, and self-examination in preparations made. Ultimately, it is a command of the Lord to His own, and all who are His should see it as their duty to honour Him by attentiveness to the ordinance.

Further Reading:

On the subject of the Lord's Supper Robert Bruce's sermons on The Mystery of the Lord's Supper *originally published in 1589 and reprinted in recent times by Christian Focus Publications (2005) repays study. Also, the useful recent book by Malcolm Maclean,* The Lord's Supper, *(Fearn: Mentor, 2009, 272pp) is a fine study of the subject and well worth consulting.*

APPENDIX

Communion Seasons in the Scottish Reformed Tradition

At one time Communion seasons were widespread in Scottish Presbyterianism, involving preparatory services beforehand, and a thanksgiving service in the Monday following the Communion Sabbath. Though they have been increasingly discontinued, even in the more conservative Reformed Churches, they are such a strong and many would say blessed aspect of the traditions of Scottish Presbyterian practice that it is appropriate to give a brief account here of what was generally, even if not universally, involved in them.

1. Communion Seasons in the Scottish Presbyterian Churches

Communion seasons, covering preparatory services on days leading up to a Communion Sabbath and Thanksgiving services afterwards are not mandatory in the constitutional documents of the Church. They are a matter of developed tradition in parts of Scottish Presbyterianism. Often in the past such additional services have been accompanied with times of real blessing in congregations and communities. They have often been used as occasions for the encouragement of adherents to come forward and confess their faith in the Lord Jesus Christ openly. They do this by making themselves known to the local minister and Kirk Session, whose responsibility it is to examine them concerning the credibility of their profession of saving faith in Christ.

Even within the more conservative and traditional Presbyterian Churches, practices have varied in the exact number and timing of Preparatory or Thanksgiving services. There is no fixed rule, but acts of public worship for preparation and edification and encouragement have been the norm.

There is no fixed manner of admitting members except after examination by the Session. Often this examination is brief as the person may be well known to the men. The examination will not be intrusive but will tend to focus on experiential matters of the walk of faith and not merely knowledge of doctrine. Examination of those coming forward for membership, which is not confined to occasions in which the Lord's Supper is observed, should also focus on responsibilities and privileges of communicant membership, including regular attendance at all the services of worship, support practically

The Sacraments – Lord's Supper, partaking 327

for the work of the Church, and engagement to be involved in the Church's witness and outreach. However, there have generally been no services for admission of new members in the smaller conservative Presbyterian denominations.

2. Pattern of Communion seasons
Communion seasons usually have followed the following pattern, and still do in the smaller Presbyterian denominations in Scotland: the Free Church of Scotland, the Free Church of Scotland (Continuing) and the Free Presbyterian Church of Scotland:

1. *Thursday*: Fast day; focuses on confession of sin and repentance
2. *Friday*: focuses on heart searching in relation to marks of grace/fruit of the Spirit
3. *Saturday*: preparation, focussing on the preciousness of Christ for the believer ('Tokens' are usually given out at the Saturday service)
4. *Lord's day*: *Communion service* in the morning (see below for normal Order)
5. *Lord's day*: *Evening service*: call to the unconverted (usually)
6. *Monday*: Thanksgiving (traditionally this has focussed on either,
   - an anticipation of the Second coming; or
   - a call to consecration and holy living – as expression of thanksgiving to the Lord – urged in some manner).

3. Form of service in the Communion service
(1) Normal service (Psalm/Prayer/Reading/Psalm/'Action' sermon [i.e. related to the theme of Christ's sufferings and death]/Psalm), followed by:

(2) *'Fencing'* (statement of who should/should not be at the table, including a welcome to those who are communicant members who profess Him as Saviour, and any we admit as members in good standing in other evangelical churches. It is expected of 'visitors' that they be made known to the minister/Kirk Session prior to the service)

(3) *Call to come to the table*: Psalm (usually 118:15ff) is sung till (i) elements are brought to the table; and continue Ps 118 until (ii) communicants all take their place at the table

(4) *Table service*:
   o Warrant (1 Corinthians 11:23ff)
   o Prayer of blessing

- o Brief devotional address to encourage communicants in appreciating the sacrament and especially Christ Himself as set forth
- o Administration (Officiating ministers repeats words of warrant re bread and wine and distributes to fellow minister); elements are then distributed among the people by the elders, after which minister in congregation passes elements to officiating minister and elders
- o Second devotional address encouraging communicants in their on-going walk of faith and love to Christ remembered in the sacrament

(5) Psalm (103:1ff) (rising from table)

(6) Prayer and closing Psalm (72:17-19)

(7) Benediction

SECTION E

THE CHURCH
ITS OFFICERS

OFFICE IN THE CHURCH

1. Minister - Pastor

1. Introduction
The question of office in the Christian Church has often been a contentious one. In the New Testament there are references to various offices. In writing to the Corinthian Church in his first letter, Paul stated that "God hath set some in the church, first apostles, secondarily prophets, thirdly teachers, after that miracles, then gifts of healings, helps, governments, diversities of tongues" (1 Corinthians 12:28). These, however, appear to relate to the apostolic gifts in the apostolic age and would not be expected to continue after the passing of the apostles, through whom certainly miracles were wrought. But elsewhere Paul stated that "And he gave some, apostles; some, prophets; some, evangelists; and some, pastors and teachers" (Ephesians 4:11), with the purpose of "the perfecting [equipping] of the saints, for the work of the ministry, for the edifying of the body of Christ: till we all come in the unity of the faith, and of the knowledge of the Son of God, unto a perfect man, unto the measure of the stature of the fulness of Christ" (vv12-13). This more particularly refers to *offices* in the Church. Of these offices, although, strictly speaking, the offices of apostle and prophet, and arguably also evangelist, would be considered as *special* or *extraordinary* offices, that could not be said about the other categories. The categories mentioned, however (pastor and teacher, and arguably also evangelist) may well be taken as indicating *elements* (spiritually) which entered in to the continuing office of the holy ministry, rather than *separate strictly defined categories* or 'offices.'[1]

---

[1] *The Form of Presbyterial Church-Government* distinguishes 'extraordinary' from 'ordinary and perpetual' offices in the New Testament. Among the 'extraordinary' it includes "apostles, evangelists, and prophets," and among the 'ordinary', "pastors, teachers, and

It may be argued that there was a New Testament office of 'prophet' (Acts 21:10; 1 Corinthians 14:29ff). However, the later Pastoral letters provide no inkling of any such continuing office and strictly speaking it may be assumed to be temporary and related to the special *charismata*. That view appears to be sustainable in the first Corinthian letter which is so taken up with the so-called charismatic gifts. Again, these do not come into the picture in Paul's discussion of office in his Pastoral letters (1 and 2 Timothy and Titus). Furthermore, when Paul lists the 'fruit of the Spirit' in Galatians 5, there is no indication of charismata (Galatians 5:22-23). It is a similar case with all the 'armour of God' in Ephesians 6:10-20. The focus in such passages is clearly on 'ordinary' rather than 'extraordinary' gifts. At the same time it is to be expected that in a distinct office of 'evangelist, pastor and teacher,' there would be a *prophetic element*, in the general sense of forth-telling or proclaiming God's word. The true gift of prophecy related to revelation (though it might not be written down) and as there are no new revelations after the close of the New Testament canon it stands to reason that the specific office of prophet, like the office of apostle, would pass with the passing of the apostolic age. There is absolutely no indication in the New Testament of any continuing apostolic office. There is, however, evidence of a continuing function of the 'ministry of the word.' But can such an office be strictly distinguished from the office of elder which Paul deals with in his pastoral letters, and if so, how?

2. The Biblical Office of *Minister* or *Pastor*
One of the problems in sorting out the Biblical data on office in the New Testament relates to terminology. The name for the office of elder is a translation of the Greek *presbyteros*. However, this term is clearly used inter-changeably with the Greek word *episkopos*, which cannot

---

other church-governors [elders] and deacons." See, *The Subordinate Standards and Other Authoritative Documents of the Free Church of Scotland*, Edinburgh, 1851, 304.

mean 'Bishop' in the Episcopal sense, but is simply 'overseer.'[2] This is clear, for example in Paul's letter to Titus. There Paul instructs Titus to appoint elders in all the cities of Crete (1:5). However, he goes on to describe the same person as a 'bishop' (v7). It is perfectly clear that the word simply means 'overseer' with reference to individual congregations. There is no warrant for understanding any of these terms in a way that implies an Episcopal hierarchy. Elder (*presbyteros*) may be taken as the *name* of the office and overseer (*episkopos*) as the *nature* of the office.

However, the term 'elder' (or 'overseer') is clearly a term which is applied to those who rule or 'govern' in the Church and in most contexts may be taken as comprehensive of those who are teachers or preachers or pastors, and those who simply have a ruling function in the Church without possessing a particular call to pastoral or preaching ministry. The fact that the office of pastor or teacher is inclusive of ruling eldership does not mean that the ruling office of elder must be inclusive of the teaching or preaching calling. For example, in one place Peter addresses elders in his first letter and says of himself "who am also an elder" (5:1). He was also an apostle. We take it that the apostles embraced the lower offices, though that did not mean that the lower offices included the higher. Notwithstanding the close relationship between them, the teaching and governing functions of 'eldership' are distinguishable, and there are strong arguments in favour of recognising *two separate offices* within the one description of 'elder.'

(1) *There is the implication of the Offices of Christ.*

Christ is set forth in Scripture as Prophet (Acts 3:22), Priest (Hebrews 5:6), and King (Psalm 2:6; Luke 1:33).[3] The Reformation Churches understood that the offices established by Christ in the visible Church

---

[2] This word is used only 3 times in the New Testament, in 1 Timothy 3:1-2, and Titus 1:7 with reference to office in the Church. It is also used by Peter in his 1st Letter, chapter 2 and verse 25 with reference to Christ as Overseer of our souls, but with no reference to office in the Church.

[3] This is expounded very fully in the *Westminster Confession of Faith*, Chapter 8; *Larger Catechism*, Q&A 42-45; and *Shorter Catechism*, Q&A 23-26.

would reflect these aspects of His Mediatorial reign. Gerard Berghoef and Lester De Koster suggest that,

> Though not all theologians are agreed as to the exact relation of Christ's offices to those which characterize His Church, we believe that the presence of these offices identifies those congregations where they appear as vibrant manifestations of the universal Body of Jesus Christ. The true Church is found:
> 1. Where the Word of God as revealed in the Bible is faithfully preached; there functions the office of Christ as Prophet.
> 2. Where the sacraments of baptism and the Lord's Supper are truly administered; there functions the office of Christ as Priest.
> 3. Where the congregation is aptly ruled according to the Word, and discipline is appropriately exercised; there functions the office of Christ as King.
>
> These three are generally confessed, since the Reformation, as being the distinguishing marks of the true and visible Church. Those who occupy these offices are known as follows:
> 1. Prophet: the ordinary ministry, sometimes designated teaching elders.
> 2. Priest: the deacons, called collectively the diaconate.
> 3. King: the ruling eldership, sometimes called presbyters, bishops, trustees.[4]

Though not conclusive in itself, especially in relation to the analogy of deacons with a priestly office which Berghoef and De Koster draw from the aspects of service and sacrifice in the Levitical office, this is nonetheless a suggestive argument for the distinction of three offices in the post-Apostolic Church, however much in some respects these may overlap.

(2) There is the implication of the Biblical material.

There is clearly a preaching function expected. This is implied by the call of the disciples at the first to teach and preach in the name of Christ (Matthew 10:7ff; Mark 3:14; 16:15; Luke 9:2ff; 9:60; Acts 10:42;

---

[4] Gerard Berghoef and Lester De Koster, *The Deacons Handbook*, Grand Rapids, Michigan, 1980, 53-54.

14:15). It stands to reason that, (1) there is such a distinct function commanded and warranted for the Church; and, (2) that such a function will comprise a distinct office, since it involves those who are "sent" (Romans 10:15). This does not mean, as we have already suggested, that those so specially called are not within the category of 'elder' or governor in the Church. However, it must involve a distinct role. So much is implied by the very stress on that function/exercise apart from ability to rule as overseer in a congregation. It seems obvious that a preacher/teacher/minister will have a governing ability. It does not mean that those who have a governing ability have a preaching gift for ministry. This distinction is suggested, if not explicitly recognised, in the first letter of Paul to Timothy. Written within the context of outlining the qualifications for elders (3:1-7) and deacons (3:8-13), Paul writes of elders/overseers that those who rule well are "worthy of double honour" (5:17). He then adds, "especially those who labour in the word and doctrine." This clearly indicates a differentiation between ministry and ruling in the Church, though it implies that those who minister in the word will also fulfil a task of rule. As there is also a clear expectation that those who labour in word and doctrine would be maintained in their ministry by the Church (Luke 10:7; 1 Corinthians 9:14; Galatians 6:6), there is a strong inference here of a separate office, albeit within the broad category of eldership.

(3) *There is the implication of the nature of the work of ministry.*

From an early stage in the life of the Christian Church there is a clear recognition that there will be a ministry which must be sustained by the Church, if it is acting according to the divine commission. The work of ministry to which the apostles devoted themselves, would not become redundant after their passing from the scene. However, its importance is nowhere more clearly evident than in the appointment of seven godly men to supervise the "daily ministration [distribution]" in the growing Church of the day, so that the apostles might not "…leave the word of God, and serve tables," but rather "give ourselves continually to prayer, and to the ministry of the word (διακονία του λόγου)" (Acts 6:1, 2, 4). These men are not called deacons, and should not perhaps be equated with the office of deacon as described by Paul in 1 Timothy 3, particularly since their qualifications described in Acts 6 point more to governors or elders, and the setting apart of them by the laying on of hands. Point is, the work of the ministry is seen to be of primary importance in the work of the Church. This is particularly evident in the second letter to the Corinthians in which over and over Paul speaks of ministry (4:1; 5:18; 6:3; 9:13). Also, both in the letters to the Ephesians (4:12) and Colossians (4:17) Paul pointedly emphasises the distinctness and vital importance of the ministry of the word. The passage in Ephesians 4 has reference to office in the Church seen particularly to relate to ministry. It is therefore assumed that in view of the distinctness of work of ministry (preaching/teaching/pastoral work) one would expect a distinct office for that purpose, but of necessity including qualities of ruling and governing.

(4) *There is the implication of a distinct call to the ministry of the Word.*
If this understanding of a separate and distinct ministry of the Word continuing through the 'last days' is correct and biblical, one would expect a very particular calling and equipping for those upon whom that task will fall. If there is a separate call to that work – a particular person being 'set apart' for it – then there will be a presumption of a distinct *office* for that purpose within the Church. There are, indeed, clear indications of this. Most particularly we read in Romans 10: "whosoever shall call upon the name of the Lord shall be saved. How then shall they call on him in whom they have not believed? and how shall they believe in him, of whom they have not heard? and how shall they hear without a preacher? and how shall they preach except they are sent? as it is written, How beautiful are the feet of them that preach the gospel of peace, and bring glad tidings of good things!" (13-15). Paul speaks elsewhere of the Lord "putting me into the ministry" (1 Timothy 1:12). The Holy Spirit made it clear to the Church in Acts 13 that Barnabas and Paul should be separated to the work to which the Lord had called them (13:2). In relation to this very important feature of the work and life of the Church in the 'last days' it is unthinkable that any should enter upon such a work without a divine call to it, inwardly, and

from the Church, outwardly. In that incident of the commissioning of Paul and Barnabas (and remember Barnabas was not an apostle, but he was clearly a 'minister of the word') both these inward and outward aspects are found (13:2-3). This is something upon which the Church historically has made great emphasis: a divine call to the ministry of the Word.[5] With reference to who will be responsible for the conduct of divine services, William Binnie wrote: "Those who hold by the divine appointment of the holy ministry believe that these services ought to be entrusted to men set apart for the purpose, – men separated from every secular calling in order that they may give themselves to prayer and the ministry of the word, as their vocation and life-work; and this (as we have seen) is the belief of all the historical Churches without exception."[6] No man should contemplate entering the ministry of the Church without such a sense of the divine calling and a clear conviction concerning the sort of qualities found in the seven appointed in Acts 6: "men of good reputation, full of the Holy Spirit and wisdom" (6:3, NKJV), in addition to the qualifications for eldership mentioned by Paul in 1 Timothy and Titus (1 Timothy 3:1-7; Titus 1:5-9).[7] If the Holy Spirit has not called and equipped a man for this work it is folly for him to enter such a work.

(5) *There is a degree of authority invested in minister/pastor, albeit in relation to ruling or governing in the Church there is a parity to be recognised.*

In maintaining the distinction in terms of office in the church between pastor/preacher/minister and ruling elder strictly so named, it is important to recognise,

1. First of all, *a degree of authority invested in the pastor/preacher/minister*. After all, he will have the responsibility

---

[5] *The Form of Presbyterial Church-Government* in addressing "the Doctrinal Part of Ordination of Ministers" states that "No man ought to take upon him the office of a minister of the word without a lawful calling." It cites John 3:27; Romans 10:14-15; Jeremiah 14:14; and Hebrews 5:4. See, *The Subordinate Standards*, op. cit., 314, 316.

[6] Binnie, op. cit., 120.

[7] Because the office of minister or pastor is inclusive of the other offices, the qualifications outlined in 1 Timothy 3 and Titus 1 will also apply to the office of pastor/minister. See below: The Office of Ruling Elder: (2) Qualifications.

for the ordination of elders, and not vice-versa. This is implicit, for example, in Paul's letter to Titus, in which Paul commands Titus to "set in order the things that are lacking, and appoint elders in every city" (1:5). When Paul seeks to encourage Timothy in the exercise of the ministerial office he writes: "Neglect not the gift that is in thee, which was given thee by prophecy, with the laying on of the hands of the presbytery (πρεσβυτερίου)" (1 Timothy 4:14). This is very similar language to the commissioning of Barnabas and Paul earlier (Acts 13). Yet for simply ruling elders, it is sufficient for Titus whom we take to be set apart as a minister of the word, to appoint elders in every city. However, it is also important,

2. Secondly, *to recognise a certain parity among ministers and elders in their ruling or governing responsibilities.* This much is indicated, for example, in the Jerusalem Assembly described in Acts 15 in which both apostles and elders (πρεσβυτερων, verse 4) met together and deliberated on contentious issues, apparently with perfect parity among them. Therefore, whilst the special calling and office of the minister/pastor/preacher is to be respected, this does not justify the minister lording it over the flock or simply imposing his own will when it comes to rule, including disciplinary matters in a congregation. In Church courts there is parity in such matters, but not when it comes to teaching/preaching and the conduct of services. Having said that, it may well be, because the elder is to be "apt to teach" (1 Timothy 3:2) he will be able to 'stand in the breach' in reading services in a minister's absence. It goes without saying that none of these offices are open to women (see 1 Corinthians 14:34-35; 1 Timothy 2:8-15).

3. The historical and constitutional development of the offices

It is clear from what has been argued above that there is for New Testament Christianity a three-office view of offices: minister – elder –

deacon.[8] It is recognised that this has been contradicted by some sound theologians who hold to a 'two-office' view of office: elder (teaching and ruling) and deacon.[9] There are strong arguments, however, from the New Testament, and from the Standards of the Church and elsewhere, to maintain a three-office position as the norm in New Testament office and government in the Church.

(1) *The Books of Discipline, 1560 and 1578*
At the time of the Reformation in Scotland a Book of Discipline was commissioned from the Scottish Parliament and completed in a short time in 1560, by, among others, John Knox (c1515-1572). Among the burdens in this *First Book of Discipline* was the provision of ministers for the Kirk, the means of supporting a full-time ministry in every parish of the land and the proper exercise of discipline in the Church. The 'First Book' may be said to be implicitly rather than explicitly Presbyterian, though already there is a clear distinction drawn between the minister and other ruling offices. The distinction in the offices became more explicitly stated in the *Second Book of Discipline* produced in 1578 under the driving leadership of Andrew Melville (1545-1622). In terms of office in the Church, this Book identified four: "There are four ordinary functions or offices in the kirk of God: the office of pastor, minister or bishop; the doctor; the presbyter or elder; and the deacon."[10] The *Book* adds: "These offices are ordinary, and ought to continue perpetually in the kirk, as necessary for the government and policy of the same, and no more offices ought to be received or suffered in the true kirk of

---

[8] We shall deal specifically with the offices of ruling elder and deacon in the following five chapters.
[9] For example, John Murray, 'Office in the Church,' in, *Collected Writings of John Murray, 2: Systematic Theology*, Edinburgh, 1977, 357ff. John Macpherson sees "no difficulty in recognizing a threefold distribution" as far as continuing offices in the New Testament are concerned. At the same time, he comments: "Under Presbyters must be included ministers, teachers and exhorters, and rulers; and it is a mere wrangle over names whether we shall call both simply Presbyters, or call one a Teaching, and the other a Ruling Presbyter." *Presbyterianism*, Edinburgh, 1883 (?), 34, 35-36.
[10] *The Second Book of Discipline (1578)*, Chapter 2, section 6.

God established according to his word."[11] Though this seems to advocate a four-office view, the reality was that the 'office' of 'doctor' was essentially the same as the elder (he had to be an elder), but was seen as a teacher (but not a preacher), not least within the context of a School system. In that respect it is a contentious and debatable office. By the time of the Westminster Assembly's deliberations on the *Form of Presbyterial Church-Government* an 'office' of 'Teacher' or 'Doctor' is seen to be rather a species of Pastor than ruling elder.[12]

In an overview of the 'polity' of the kirk, the *Second Book of Discipline* states that it "consists in three things: viz., in doctrine, discipline, and distribution. With doctrine is annexed the administration of the sacraments. And according to the parts of this division arises a three-fold sort of office-bearers in the kirk: to wit, of ministers or preachers, elders or governors, and deacons or distributors."[13] The *Book* proceeds to expound the Church order or 'polity' according to this three-fold division of offices and the various functions they embrace. It is assumed that each according to the various offices will be raised up by God and made able for the work to which they are called.[14]

(2) *The Form of Presbyterian Church-Government* (1645)
Subsequently in the Scottish Church, the *Second Book of Discipline* was superseded by *The Form of Presbyterial Church-Government* agreed upon by the Westminster Assembly of divines in 1645 and adopted by the Scottish Church the same year. It was adopted as part of the Church's standards (and later [1843] in the Free Church) though it was more like a 'blueprint' than something absolutely binding upon the Churches that adopted it. In relation to the 'Officers of the Church,' it quite clearly holds to a three-office view, though again four are mentioned: pastors, teachers, and other church-governors, and deacons. In the case of the *Form* the function of 'teacher' it identifies from the New Testament

---

[11] ibid., Chapter 2, section 7.
[12] See, *The Form of Presbyterian Church-Government (1645)*, in, *The Subordinate Standards &c.*, op. cit., 307.
[13] *The Second Book of Discipline (1578)*, Chapter 2, section 2.
[14] ibid., Chapter 3, section 7.

Offices in the Church – Minister

(Ephesians 4:11) it links with the pastoral office rather than 'church-governors' (or elders). The passage on 'Pastors' is as follows:

> THE pastor is an ordinary and perpetual officer in the church, prophesying of the time of the gospel.
>
> First, it belongs to his office,
>
> To pray for and with his flock, as the mouth of the people unto God, Acts 6: 2, 3, 4, and 20:36, where preaching and prayer are joined as several parts of the same office. The office of the elder (that is, the pastor) is to pray for the sick, even in private, to which a blessing is especially promised; much more therefore ought he to perform this in the publick execution of his office, as a part thereof.
>
> To read the Scriptures publickly; for the proof of which,
>
> 1. That the priests and Levites in the Jewish church were trusted with the publick reading of the word is proved.
>
> 2. That the ministers of the gospel have as ample a charge and commission to dispense the word, as well as other ordinances, as the priests and Levites had under the law, proved, Isaiah 66:21. Matthew 23:34, where our Saviour entitleth the officers of the New Testament, whom he will send forth, by the same names of the teachers of the Old.
>
> Which propositions prove, that therefore (the duty being of a moral nature) it followeth by just consequence, that the publick reading of the scriptures belongeth to the pastor's office.
>
> To feed the flock, by preaching of the word, according to which he is to teach, convince, reprove, exhort, and comfort.
>
> To catechise, which is a plain laying down the first principles of the oracles of God, or of the doctrine of Christ, and is a part of preaching.
>
> To dispense other divine mysteries.
>
> To administer the sacraments.
>
> To bless the people from God, Numbers 6:23, 24, 25, 26. Compared with Revelation 1:5, (where the same blessings, and persons from whom they come, are expressly mentioned,) Isaiah 66:21, where, under the names of Priests and Levites to be continued under the gospel, are meant evangelical pastors, who therefore are by office to bless the people.
>
> To take care of the poor.

And he hath also a ruling power over the flock as a pastor.[15]

This is a fairly full and careful summary of the functions of this separate office (as the *Form* understands it) of Pastor or Minister. Subsequently there have been no addenda or amendments to this statement of office and government in the Church. It remains part of the subordinate standards of the Presbyterian Churches in Scotland, although all that the licentiate or ordinand or other office-bearer in the Presbyterian Church is held to is that they "own" the Presbyterial government and discipline of the Church as "founded upon Holy Scripture, and agreeable thereto."[16]

4. Some practical observations

Is there any real difference, practically speaking, between the 3-office view (minister, ruling elder and deacon) and the 2-office view (elder [teaching and ruling] and deacon) of Church offices? It is our conviction that there is.

1. In our estimation a view of the preaching and pastoring function in the Church that does not consider it to be an office involving a separate special and distinct calling from the Lord but simply a sub-set of the general office of elder albeit with a teaching-preaching role, will inevitably diminish the distinctiveness of the pastoral-ministering-preaching office. There will inevitably be confusion as to the question, for example, of where the authority lies in the different roles of 'elder' and why a *Presbytery* should have the sole disciplinary authority over 'pastors' ('teaching' elders) whereas a local Kirk Session can exercise authority over the 'ruling' elder(s).[17]

---

[15] *The Form of Presbyterial Church-Government*, in, *The Subordinate Standards, &c.*, op. cit., 304-5.
[16] *The Subordinate Standards &c.*, op. cit., 373.
[17] Robert Rayburn, for one, does not like the description 'teaching elder' which has become so commonly used. With special reference to the practice of his own Church, the Presbyterian Church of America, he writes of what has become "a virtual shibboleth," namely, "the insistence on the atrocious nomenclature 'teaching elder' and 'ruling elder'." He calls this "the PCA's own contribution to the modern assault on the English language by the sacrifice of euphony in the interests of propaganda." Robert S Rayburn, "Ministers, Elders, and Deacons," in, Mark R Brown (editor), *Order in the*

2. In addition, the question arises as to why, if the *office* is indistinguishable between minister and ruling elder, a ruling elder entering the ministry requires to be re-ordained, or why the *ruling* elder should not require the same, or at least some, theological education as is usually required for the preaching elder-pastor? Such concerns fall away with the 3-office view.

3. The diminishing of the office of pastor-minister-preacher may also raise questions of who really has authority for the conduct of services and the administration of sacraments. By what authority should the administration of sacraments lie only with the pastor-minister-preacher? And if there is no distinction in *office* what would prevent a 'ruling' elder from administering sacraments? After all, if the sacraments are not 'higher' than the word and its preaching, why should the administration of the sacrament fall only on ordained ministers? It is the teaching of the *Westminster Standards*, that only "ministers of his word," which we take to be ordained ministers, rightly administer the sacraments.[18] Men *ordained* to the ministry of the Word are appointed by Christ to preach, pastor, administer sacraments and pronounce benedictions in local congregations *by virtue of their ordination*.[19] Unlike non-ordained supply they have *charge* of congregations, under Christ. From time to time ordained elders or other non-ordained men may *supply* in congregations but that does not give them the right to administer sacraments, or pronounce benedictions. They have not been set apart for the ministry in a congregation. They simply stand in the breach by keeping services from time to time. They are not set over a congregation and therefore are not entitled to administer sacraments or pronounce benedictions in

---

Offices, Classic Presbyterian Government Resources, 1993, 222. Rayburn clearly thinks that using such a term as 'teaching elder' diminishes the office which is one of 'minister' and 'pastor' and not just 'teacher.'

[18] See, *Westminster Confession of Faith*, 29:3; and *Larger Catechism*, Answer 176. Proof texts supporting this are given as follows: John 1:33, Matthew 28:19, 1 Corinthians 11:23, 1 Corinthians 4:1, and Hebrews 5:4.

[19] See the *Form of Presbyterial Church-Government*, in the section 'Pastors' (*The Subordinate Standards and other Authoritative Documents of the Free Church of Scotland*, Edinburgh, 1851, 304-6).

congregations.[20] There are no such issues in these areas with the 3-office view.

4. With the widespread acceptance of the 2-office view today the minister's position can easily become practically insecure to the extent that he may come to take a relatively minor role in the congregational worship, in some cases even sharing the conduct of services with other elders (or 'worship leader') and having limited influence, for example, in determining the musical content of the praise. Maintaining the 3-office view, however, besides being considered fully in accord with Scripture teaching, clarifies such issues and ensures that the worship of the Church is conducted decently and in order.

Further Reading:

For further reading see particularly the volume edited by Mark R Brown: Order in the offices. Essays Defining the Roles of Church Officers, *Classic Presbyterian Government Resources, Duncansville, PA, 1993, for a robust exposition of the three-office view of offices in the Church.*

For a comprehensive view of office in the Reformed tradition see also the volume of James L Ainslie, The Doctrines of Ministerial Order in the Reformed Churches of the 16th and 17th Centuries, *T. & T. Clark, Edinburgh, 1940.*

---

[20] The right to administer sacraments and pronounce benedictions will be enjoyed by all ordained ministers, whether or not settled over a congregation, as, for example, retired men.

OFFICE IN THE CHURCH

2. Ruling Elder: (1) Calling

1. Introduction
The Church should be clear on just how it is ruled. It is important for the local membership to be clear on their responsibility in considering men for office. It is also important for eligible men, too, to examine themselves about the matter of office in the Church. We are conscious that Paul says in one place that "if a man desire the office of a bishop ['overseer', or 'elder'], he desireth a good thing" (1 Timothy 3:1). But the Church must be satisfied that under Christ, the man or men in question are right for such rule.

2. What about rule in the Church?
It is clear that every congregation requires oversight. There need to be men on the ground as it were who will rule over the affairs of the congregation under God. Obviously that is an extremely solemn thing, given that they are answerable to the Head of the Church, the Lord Jesus. The Lord has also provided for that in His Word. From the New Testament it seems clear that there are three offices: pastor (or minister), elder and deacon.[1] The minister preaches and pastors, and shares in the rule. The elders rule the spiritual affairs of the congregation with the pastor. The deacons have a ministry of mercy and administration in the congregation. Theirs is not a ruling office, but is a spiritual one nonetheless. The distinct office of pastor or preacher is found in Ephesians 4:11: "And he gave some, apostles, some, prophets, some, evangelists, and some, pastors and teachers, for the perfecting [equipping] of the saints for the work of the ministry, for the

---

[1] See the previous chapter in relation to the distinct office of Minister-Pastor, and the chapter below on the distinct office of Deacon.

edifying of the body of Christ." This distinction is also found in 1 Timothy 5:17 where Paul distinguishes the elders who rule from those who "labour in the word and doctrine." Though the office of apostle is gone, the preacher-pastor principally undertakes these apostolic duties. We see this in Acts 20 where Paul speaks of his own preaching and teaching and speaks to the elders of their duties of oversight. When we come to look at the duties of the ruling elder we shall see that this does not exclude their taking a service now and again. But that is not their principal role at all. It is the principal role of the minister (see verses 24 to 27). The distinct role of the elder is *oversight*, as we will see, something the minister as pastor will clearly share in. The elders will have a crucial role in upholding the preacher-minister, but do not have authority over him. He only has authority over them as one whose role under Christ is to declare the whole counsel of God and feed their souls. It is particularly in what we call the Pastoral Epistles – 1 & 2 Timothy and Titus – that we have details about the offices of elder (1 Timothy 3:1-7; Titus 1:5 9) and deacon (1 Timothy 3:8-13). The distinctive of the pastoral/preaching office (also an eldership) is found in 2 Timothy 4:1-5, where Paul outlines to Timothy certain duties of that office which he had. These are our Biblical warrants for the offices, in brief.

3. What about the calling of the elder? (Acts 20:28)

We lay great stress on the calling of a man to the ministry, and that certainly is a *special* calling. It is clear, e.g., in what Paul says in various places to Timothy. We do not speak so often of such a calling of the elder. Yet we should. It is obviously tied in with the recognisable gifts that a man has, spiritual gifts. We are going to consider the 'qualifications' and fitness for duties later on. But from Acts 20 we should notice a remarkable statement of the Apostle's. He has called for the elders to be gathered (v17). It is clear that in his travels as and when suitable men were found (and only men) they were elected to office (14:23). He was obviously gathering the elders from all the churches in the area to give them exhortation (v28ff). But notice how he describes them: "take heed therefore unto yourselves, and to all the flock, over the which the Holy Spirit hath made you overseers, to feed the church of God, which he hath purchased with his own blood." We know that elders are elected by congregations. But this must always be a priority: to recognise that they must be men of God, men of the Spirit, men in whom the Spirit is inclining and equipping for that onerous office. That is all-important if the congregation is going to be prospered and ruled to its spiritual good. The people in other words are to choose those whom the Holy Spirit is raising up among them. It has nothing to do with progressing from one office to another; it has nothing to do with status in the community; it has nothing to do with period of time a man has been a professing man (though they should not be novices – 1 Timothy 3:6). It has everything to do with evidencing spiritual qualities and fruit. Here are men commended by their spiritual graces. For this ruling office there is a divine mandate, for this is a vital office for the advance and health of a gospel Church. That much is clear from Paul's exhortations to these elders in Ephesus. Perhaps another thing might be added here from Acts 20. And that is, the affection the elders ought to have for the pastor/preacher. We are all moved by what we read in verses 37 and 38. It was, it goes without saying, mutual.

4. Conclusion

Here is the basic truth about eldership that comes out of Acts 20:28: *God makes elders!* There are two major consequences of this:

(1) Because it is such a serious office with far-reaching spiritual implications it ought to be something men should *aspire* to – because it is such a 'good thing' (1 Timothy 3:1). At the same time it involves great heart-searching, because it involves spiritual qualities (which we will consider in detail below). Nobody is asked to do anything for which they are not equipped. Men, however, should not opt out of responsibilities (of membership or office) for self-centred reasons. It is rule, but it is rule by service. There will be an aspiring to 'service' and not to 'authority.' And it is rule answerable to Christ, the Head of the Church. What the ruling elders do in the Church is to be for Him and in obedience to Him.

(2) It stands to reason that a congregation should take great care in choosing elders. Therefore, they are to pray earnestly that God's men may be evident and meantime that they may be given the spiritual gifts, as well as any needed boldness not to shrink from the task. Therefore wisdom, prayer and guidance are the prerequisite in any such election.

OFFICE IN THE CHURCH

3. Ruling Elder: (2) Qualifications

1. Introduction
We have noted a three-fold distinction reflected in the New Testament between minister (preacher/pastor), ruling elder ('overseer') and deacon. We pointed out that for all these offices the office-holders must be men of God. That is the primary qualification naturally. Paul speaks that way to the elders from Ephesus region whom he gathered to say a farewell to, as recorded in Acts 20: "Therefore take heed to yourselves and to all the flock, among which the Holy Spirit has made you overseers, to shepherd the church of God which he purchased with his own blood" (v28, NKJV). That is the first 'qualification' – the Holy Spirit makes elders. Clearly, that places such a great onus on the membership to have in mind that basic criterion as they contemplate the election of office-bearers. However, in the NT we have very explicit descriptions of the qualifications required of overseers: ministers (2 Timothy especially), elders (1 Timothy 3:1-7; Titus 1:5-9), and deacons (1 Timothy 3:8-13). We will consider here the *qualifications* outlined in Timothy and Titus. So, with reference to 1 Timothy 3:1-7 and Titus 1:5-9 we can make clear the qualifications (qualities?) required of the elders.

2. Who is the eldership for? (1 Timothy 3:1-2; Titus 1:6)
This has been made a controversial issue with the moves in recent times in many Churches to ordain women to offices. There is no argument, however, about what the Bible teaches. The admission of women to office cannot be argued from the Bible. It is argued simply from social pressure and a humanistic view of the equality of the sexes. The author remembers Professor J. S. Stewart argue in the Church of Scotland

Assembly around 1966 that Paul certainly taught that only men should be in office in the Church, but went on to say that nowadays we are wiser than Paul (more or less). But this is a matter of pure revelation. The Bible does speak of the leadership of men and functional differences in the roles of men and women (see, e.g., 1 Corinthians 11), but it never makes women chattels. Indeed, it is clear that women do have a vital part to play in the work of the Kingdom of God, whether wives and mothers or not. We think of the prophetesses in the Old Testament (Miriam, Deborah, Huldah etc). We think of the important role of women in the New Testament, and not only in encouraging children and other women (though that is a vital role, as is clear, e.g., from the case of Timothy [2 Timothy 1:5] and the teaching of Titus 2:3-5). Think of Prisca and Aquila, mentioned frequently in Acts and Paul's letters. Priscilla is in one or two places mentioned *before* her husband. They were equally involved in teaching Apollos about the way of the Lord. It would be wrong to think there was not a major role in the Church for women. There is a role with their husbands or brothers – encouraging them to come to Church, have family worship, instruct the children and follow the Lord. There is a role with their children or grandchildren. With other women (and men too). There is a vital role in prayer. Certainly women should get together and pray together, like Lydia at the waterside in Philippi. However, as far as office in the Church of ruling is concerned, that is for men. That is clear not only from the limiting of the Old Testament priesthood to men, and the limitation of the Apostles of the Lord to men, but also what is taught here in 1 Timothy 3 and Titus 1. This is a rather 'minor' aspect of qualification for eldership, but obviously it has been made controversial in recent times. Suffice to say, if we are going by Scripture, the office is for men. "If a *man* desires the office of an overseer [minister/elder], he desires a good work" (1 Timothy 3:1, NKJV).

3. What are the positive requirements? (1 Timothy 3:2-7; Titus 1:6-9)

How many qualifications are mentioned in the New Testament which are required (at least in some degree) in elders? In 1 Timothy 3:2-7 there are 16 different aspects mentioned! Of these 10 are positive and 6 negative. This may all seem overwhelming. Who could possible manifest all these? we may ask. Yet Paul was as aware that there is no perfection possible. These qualities will not be found in perfected degrees, or all equally among men suited to the office in the Church.

One man may excel in one or more and have the others in some degree 'in place' as it were. This is one of the reasons why what we call a plurality of elders is preferable, i.e., more than one and as many as are requisite. However, let us notice that these are all a *'must'* in some measure. We will deal first with the positive qualities:

(1) *The elder must be blameless.* This does not mean sinless. It simply means that here is a man evidently walking by the rule of God's word. If he wrongs someone he will not be slow to make it right. If he gives place to anger he will not let the sun go down on his wrath. Here is a man who prays that people will see Jesus through him. A man without reproach.

(2) *The elder must be the husband of one wife.* Does an elder need to be married? Not necessarily. Paul says this to make clear the requirement of monogamy in a situation in which Churches were being planted in areas in which there was polygamy practiced. What about a divorced person? Many men may have been married and divorced before they ever became Christians. If they have been divorced for reasons allowed in Scripture and they were the 'innocent' party, there would be no bar to election to office subsequently, otherwise not. A man married for a second or third time where his wives have died may be an elder. The broader requirement here is moral purity according to the 7th commandment.

(3) *The elder must be vigilant, sober and of good behaviour.* 'Temperate' might refer either to the use of drink or indeed to the control of anger. Intemperate behaviour will not do in an elder. That is not the same as

having a just righteous indignation. But, as we know from Jesus' teaching, anger without a (just) cause is akin to murder (Matthew 5:21-26). Sober-mindedness has to do with seriousness. That is not to say the elder will be humourless. It is just that there will be a tenor of seriousness about life and issues rather than shallowness and flippancy. He will have a sound mind and exercise self-control. Good behaviour applies to his management of the outward affairs of life. He handles his affairs well. The elder must be a fair-minded man and not be full of prejudices or go to pieces under pressure. Is this man ordering his affairs aright?

(4) *The elder must be hospitable.* Hospitality is extremely important in the life of the Church. If the Church is to be a 'fellowship' then hospitality must prevail and the elder is to be at the heart of it. His house is to be open to any. We see this spirit represented, e.g., in the case of Abraham at Mamre in Genesis 18 when he is visited by three strangers. A man who is not interested in entertaining people in his house is not fit for the eldership. But hospitality is rather more than that. It also involves *visiting* others. It is a giving and receiving thing. This tends to have broken down in recent times with the individualism created by 24/7 Television. There is less coming and going, and therefore less fellowship, and the church suffers. This is why a quality of the elder is that he is "given to hospitality." In the New Testament this was seen as a necessity for *every* Christian, and therefore all the more to be exemplified by the elder.

(5) *The elder must be able to teach.* This is a distinct feature of the minister/pastor. It is the primary thing for a preacher. But this qualification of an elder is not quite the same. The point here is that the elder must know the apostolic Biblical doctrine. He must be able to give to those who ask a reason for the hope that is in him. He must be able to explain the Bible knowledge to members and adherents of the congregation and community. Yes, they may have to stand in the breach to take a service now and again, and they ought to be able to do that. But this is why the commitment of the elder at ordination to the doctrine worship and government of the Church is the same as for the

minister. Apt to teach. A measure will be: their ability to teach in a Sabbath School, traditionally a role of the elders (see Titus 1:9).

(6) *The elder must be able to rule* (vv4-5). He shows suitableness for the office by how he rules his house, not least in relation to his children. These days in our so liberal and secular society with no distinctive Christian education this is an exacting standard and one suspects that not a few ministers or elders fare none too well in this. However, are the children respectful of their father's position and authority; does the wife rule the house? These are serious questions for the man who would be elder.

(7) *The elder must be a man of good testimony in the world* (v7). It stands to reason, if a man is little thought of by his contemporaries in the world for how he manages his affairs in business or family, "how shall he take care of the church of God?" (v5).

4. What are the negative disqualifications? (1 Timothy 3:3, 6, 7)

There are characteristics he is to have, and then there are some he is definitely not to have. We have the negative things in verse 3, and verse 6. This is w*hat the elder is not to be*. We have the list in verse 3 and verses 6 and 7, with a couple of corresponding positives thrown in. Here they are: "not given to wine, no striker, not greedy of filthy lucre; but patient, not a brawler [quarrelsome], not covetous;…not a novice, lest being lifted up with pride he fall into the condemnation of the devil" (1 Timothy 3:3, 6). The use of wine (drink) is not prohibited, but there will be the strict exercise of control over it, and cutting it out if necessary. It may be that total abstinence is the best policy but this cannot be an absolute rule. "Not violent" (NKJV). That means he will not be a violent man. He should not be given to violent outbursts of temper. To be anything but 'gentle' will not do for an elder in Christ's Church. "Blessed are the peacemakers…" (Matthew 5:9). "A soft answer turneth away wrath: but grievous words stir up anger" (Proverbs 15:1). These will be his guides, though he will not be taken a loan of either, for he will be no novice and will be principled and firm in his convictions. Naturally he is not to be materialistic, though there is no bar to his having wealth or possessions. However, he is not to be covetous. We readily recognise that these are common Christian virtues which are to be found in a significant degree in the elder. If all these were found in all elders in a significant degree the Church will be well-led and overseen. For they will be gracious, selfless, firm but gentle, spiritual men concerned to teach the ways of God accurately.

These are the 'qualifications.' They are important, vital for the office-holders for one outstanding reason: It takes spiritual men of God with such a range of qualities to make positive contributions to the life of the local Church. Here are men answerable to Jesus the head of the Church. Here are men charged with the oversight and rule of souls. Here are men, in other words, upon whom the health and strength of a local Church largely depends. The role of the minister/preacher/pastor is crucial. He ought to manifest the self-same qualities. But we must notice that the election of elders – such men – is motivated by the desire to strengthen the Church (Titus 1:5). A congregation will tend to be as strong as those who have its oversight, under God. The elders do not lord it over the congregation, but oversee as under-shepherds (along with the minister). A weighty responsibility for men, though a spiritual man should desire the office and seek grace for it. A weighty responsibility for a congregation in electing men to office. This must be a matter for earnest prayer.

OFFICE IN THE CHURCH

4. Ruling Elder: (3) Responsibilities

1. Introduction

We have been looking at the nature of office according to the Scriptures and the qualifications for eldership. It is obvious that for a man to function effectively in the eldership (or diaconate) he must have the necessary gifts in exercise. They must be spiritual men, men of God, men of the Word, men of prayer. That is fundamental. They must have a concern for souls, and a desire to see the Kingdom of Christ come in the hearts of men, women and children; see them pointed heavenward and properly respond to the gospel. These things must be a burden on the hearts of men who would aspire to office in the Church and it is not fair on the men, or on the congregation, when such a spirit is evidently lacking. The gifts themselves in a sense are ordinary gifts of the Christian. But they must be in exercise. Not all men will have all the gifts in equal measure; but there must be evidence of all the qualifications mentioned in, e.g., 1 Timothy 3:1-7. The eldership properly undertaken involves the exercise of these gifts for the spiritual good of a congregation. The importance of this in the eldership is that if the duties of oversight in the congregation, spiritually, is to be carried out effectively such gifts must be evident in a man's private life in the first place.

In this chapter we will consider the *responsibilities* of the eldership. When we consider responsibilities we consider two things, firstly,

2. Personal responsibilities

(1) *The elder will be an exercised Christian.* What is the elder to be like? Clearly, he is to be a man of spirituality, a man of sound Christian faith; a man of the Word and of prayer. This is very clear from the

description we have in Titus, chapter 1: he "must be blameless as the steward of God...a lover of good men [or, things], sober[-minded], just, holy, temperate [self-controlled]; holding fast the faithful word as he hath been taught..." (1:7-9). It is only if he is thus that "he may be able, by sound doctrine both to exhort and to convict [convince] the gainsayers [those who contradict]." One would expect such men not only personally to be diligent students of the Word, but familiar with the best spiritual and doctrinal literature available. They must be men of prayer and love for souls. There is no doubt that people will take more seriously men who are recognised as men of prayer and of sincere Christian love/grace.

(2) *The elder will be exemplary at the means of grace.* Not only will the elder be an exercised Christian in those ways just mentioned, but he will be exemplary in the means of grace. It is obvious that a man who does not have an appetite for the public worship is unsuitable for office in the Church. How will a man persuade others to comply with the obligation to attend to public worship, if they are not exemplary in it themselves? They would just become an utter discouragement to that central aspect of the life of the Church. In a sense there is no 'Church' apart from such gatherings. The fact is that everyone in our communities has a responsibility to attend upon the means of grace. It is a duty before God. The fact that it is taken more lightly these days is beside the point. Anyone who can put their foot out their door has no reason to be absent from services of worship. It is understood that work (midweek) or works of necessity or mercy (Lord's day) may prevent attendance from time to time. But the question is usually not so much reasons for absence but lack of desire. This matter of public worship is a central issue for the elder, for himself and his family and his encouragement of all others. Physical infirmities, or frailties of old age, may inhibit from time to time, but overcoming such things will act as a powerful encouragement to others not to lie down under their own infirmities in relation to the means of grace.

The elder, then, is to excel in Christian character and diligence. Otherwise he will not be able to carry out the duties of oversight in the

Church effectively. The Church is to be a living spiritual body, and the office-bearers are responsible for contributing to the spiritual health and strength of the Church. "…being examples to the flock…" says Peter (1 Peter 5:3). These, then, are the personal responsibilities in relation to the lives of elders as overseers of the flock of God.

3. Public duties

We have these responsibilities stated or implied in various passages. For example, in 1 Timothy among the qualifications are aptness to teach and hospitality, as well as 'taking care of the church of God.' (1 Timothy 3:2, 5). The principal responsibility in the broadest terms is 'oversight.' We find this in Acts 20 (v28), 1 Timothy 3 and Titus 1 (the word translated 'bishop' is 'overseer' – the KJV translators were all Anglicans!), and also 1 Peter 5:2. In other words the spiritual leadership lies with the minister and the elders, all of whom exercise the oversight, the minister principally being concerned with labouring in the word and doctrine (1 Timothy 5:17).

In thinking on the responsibilities of the ruling elder it is perhaps appropriate to refer to the little known but *still applicable* outline of the duties of the elders in the Free Church of Scotland. This goes back to 1846 and may be considered as reflective of Biblical standards.[1] There are 5 things mentioned:

(1) *"That they sit in Session along with the Minister, and assist in the administration of discipline, and in the spiritual government of the Church."* This may sound a very formal sort of thing. The elders sit on what is called the Kirk Session. That is the collective ruling body for the congregation. The tone of the congregation will be set by the quality of the eldership and the minister together. The minister, being in a distinct office is always the moderator of Session and the Session cannot meet without him. But is this as commonplace as we might think? No, it is not. The Session after all determines the spiritual

---

[1] See, *Catechism on the Principles and Constitution of the Free Church of Scotland*, Edinburgh, 1882, 148-151.

tone of the congregation. After all, if these are men whom the Holy Spirit has made overseers, well, then, how are they to consider their duty on the Session? It would be very deficient if they failed to see themselves as Christ's representatives. This puts great onus on such meetings. They are not talking shops simply for the purpose of making formal decisions about sacraments and the like. They are Christ's representatives for the spiritual life of the congregation.[2] That includes discipline, making sure those who fall into error or fault are properly and fairly dealt with, corrected and (hopefully) restored. It is to be seen as a weighty thing. The outline of the duties goes on:

(2) *"That they take a careful oversight of the people's morals and religious principles, of the attendance upon public ordinances, and of the state of personal and family religion."* This is the implication of the idea of elders as 'overseers.' It will involve themselves and other members (and adherents too) of the congregation walking according to the law of Christ, spiritually and morally. It will involve being engaged with the people and encouraging them in Christian living and spiritual exercises. Also, we note, in attendance on public ordinances. It is a spiritual offence and abrogation of the duties of membership for any to be absent from public ordinances except for reasons beyond their control. This is an important concern for the elders.

(3) *"That they visit the sick from time to time in their several districts."* Visitation is crucial for ruling elders. That is implicit in oversight. Specific mention is made of the sick. Doubtless this is because of what we read in James: "Is any you sick among you? let him call for the elders of the church [πρεσβυτέρους τῆς ἐκκλησιας]; and let them pray over them ..." (5:14). The visitation will involve worship and, where appropriate, counselling.

(4) *"That they superintend the religious instruction of the young, and assist the Minister in ascertaining the qualifications of applicants for admission to sealing*

---

[2] It will be recognised that on a parity basis elders will take their part when required in Presbyteries, Synods, General Assemblies and Church Committees.

ordinances." We can understand the second part of this. Those who come forward to profess faith, to be admitted to what we call the sealing ordinances (Baptism and the Lord's Supper) will be interviewed by the minister with the help of the elders. It was said previously that an implication of the elder being 'apt to teach' may have reference to, (a) explaining doctrine to the inquirer; (b) standing in the breach for public services or prayer meetings; and also, (c) teaching the young. According to the Free Church standards the elder is to superintend the instruction of the young. This is uncommon these days. The question may be asked whether the children know who or what the office-bearers in a congregation are, and, more to the point, what difference it makes to them? If the future of the church humanly speaking depends on the spiritual development of the children, besides that being a great responsibility on the parents, this must obviously be a central concern of the overseers.

There is a fifth thing mentioned:

(5) *"That they superintend and promote the formation of meetings within their districts for prayer, reading of the Scriptures, and Christian fellowship, among the members of the Church."* This again is consistent with both an aptness to teach and being given to hospitality. It speaks for itself and must be a challenge to all elders in the present time. We can understand how this responsibility of the elder will advance the cause in any local Church, when carried out spiritually and "eagerly."

Now, let us touch on one other thing before we close. It has to do with *the manner of the oversight*. Peter guides us here (under the inspiration of the Spirit). They are under-Shepherds. Shepherding will protect and preserve, lead and gently persuade. It will also be firm lest any sheep stray. It requires care, observation, and vigilance. That is how it is to be with the flock of God. To the Ephesian elders Paul warns of savage wolves coming in not sparing the flock. "Therefore watch," says Paul, "and remember, that by the space of three years I ceased not to warn every one night and day with tears" (Acts 20:29, 31). Peter also says this oversight will be carried out "not by constraint but willingly." In other words, it will not be over-bearing dictatorial rule. It will not be for gain (e.g. the prestige or power) but "eagerly." In any case, he makes it clear that the elders are not to lord it over the people, but above all to be examples to them (1 Peter 5:3). In a real sense we have a wonderful illustration of what is involved in the 23rd Psalm. The elder represents Christ in His oversight and therefore will pre-eminently reflect His character.

A final thing: it is clear that *this is a weighty responsibility*. Of course it is. It should only be entered with the utmost seriousness. This is brought out powerfully in the letter to the Hebrews. In more than one place Paul speaks of responsibilities of those who ruled over them (he means principally in the Churches). In one place he says, "they watch for your souls, as they that must give account…" (Hebrews 13:17). However, when a man does this work well, there is promise, that "when the chief Shepherd shall appear [i.e., in His 2nd Coming], ye shall receive a crown of glory that fadeth not away" (1 Peter 5:4).

OFFICE IN THE CHURCH

5. Ruling Elder: (4) Respect

1. Introduction

We have outlined the qualities or qualifications, and the responsibilities of the eldership. Clearly their role is crucial in a Christian congregation. Under Christ's headship they are rulers in the local Church. They do not lord it over the flock, as Peter reminds us (1 Peter 5:3). Rather they are men of God, men of graciousness, men of the Spirit of God, and examples for the flock. Example can be as powerful as any words. Paul himself exemplifies that when he speaks to the Ephesian elders in Acts 20 (vv33-35). Indeed in writing to the Philippians he goes as far as to say that "those things which ye have both learned, and received, and heard, and seen in me, do: and the God of peace shall be with you" (Philippians 4:9). The role of the elders, however, is one thing. There is also a responsibility on the part of a congregation to be responsive to the elders. Why? Because they are men of God placed by the Lord Jesus to rule in the congregation (assuming a work of grace in them). With the spread of nominality in the mainline Churches it cannot be assumed that office-bearers are converted evangelical believers. It ought to be so, but it certainly cannot be assumed.

Given what the Bible says about the overseers it is clear that a deep respect ought to be given in the Churches to the faithful minister and ruling elders. They are like officers in an army under charge to the Commander of Chief. In turn the soldiers in the ranks are expected to be submissive to the officers. But what does that mean in the Church? The elders are to take their responsibilities seriously. But when they do the question is: Does the congregation take the rule of the minister and elders seriously? Obviously this becomes a big question for the spiritual health and strength of the congregation. This is not to say that the rule of elders is infallible. It does mean, however, that a congregation has a serious responsibility towards both the minister's ministry and the elders' rule. We look at three Biblical aspects of a congregation's response to their elders:

2. They are to be honoured (1 Timothy 5:17)
"Let the elders that rule well be counted worthy of double honour,..." This is the broadest reference. Due honour is to be accorded elders. Notice the qualification, "who rule well." When would an elder not be ruling well? We may assume it is when they are oppressive in lording it over the people (as Peter mentions in 1 Peter 5:3), or when they show pride or a reproach and snare (1 Timothy 3:6-7). An elder is to rule with graciousness and love and biblically, with godly concern and demeanour. Then they deserve 'honour.' The word honour means, being considered *precious*. Elders ruling well are precious to a congregation. In writing to Titus, Paul speaks about appointing elders in every city [in Crete] to "set in order the things that are wanting" (1:5). Things can only be set in order where the elders are doing their job well and the people are duly responsive, positively. But what of that "double honour"? Well, this must refer to the fact that after all these are men of God appointed by the Holy Ghost to represent the Lord Jesus in the ordering of the congregation [as it should be at any rate]. Such a role is surely worthy of double honour.

We notice this in the second part 1 Timothy 5:17: "especially they who labour in the word and doctrine." We mentioned before that we believe that there are *three* ordinary offices in the New Testament Church: minister, ruling elder and deacon. We take it that the first phrase refers to the ruling elders and the second to the minister (who also 'rules' with the others). In that case note the word "especially." It is perhaps easy for us in the day in which we live to dismiss authority, even in the house of God. We may be easily offended by what a minister says in a sermon or a Kirk Session does in its judgements. Assuming faithful Christ-centred ministry and rule, honour should be given to these offices *because they represent Christ*. They are not infallible but are due the utmost respect. Especially are we to value faithful ministry and see to it that we take it seriously as appointed by the Lord for the conversion of souls and the feeding of saints. We are unashamedly preaching-orientated, because we see how that was the case in the New Testament.

3. They are to be given obedience in the Lord (Hebrews 13:17)

In Hebrews 13, verses 7 and 17 speak of *obedience* to those who rule. Verse 17 speaks of submissiveness. This is very direct. That it has to do not with civil rule but Church rule is clear from the phrases "whose faith follow," and "they watch for your souls." This places a solemn authority on the elders and a solemn *duty* on the congregation. It is to be admitted that this is against the spirit of our age. We are in an age when people do not like authority. People want to do their own thing. They will not have people tell them what they are to do. Even in the Church, the eldership I dare say has diminished in its position. This may be because the quality and spirituality of the eldership may be low; but it also may be because the responsiveness and attitude of the congregation in resisting properly constituted authority-ministry-rule in the Church.

Again we are not speaking of rash or irresponsible or unspiritual authority-rule, or mere blind obedience. It is presumed that the rule is right and Biblical; that the elders take care not to pedal their own ideas and prejudices. It is assumed that they are not lording it over the flock in some sort of dictatorial manner. Indeed that phrase in verse 7: "whose faith follow" – indicates on the one hand that the elders are a bright example of faith (in doctrine and piety), and the other hand that the congregation will "follow" the lead. Rather it will be evident that they "watch out for your souls." The congregation can be thankful when these office-holders in the Church watch for their souls; when they have in other words such a love for them that they wish to see in them greater love and loyalty and obedience to the Lord Jesus and a careful walk in this world which is no reproach to the name of Christ. It is interesting that the elders are to be allowed to do their work for

Christ with joy and not grief. If it is a grief to them, because people will not submit to Biblical demands, that will not turn out to be profitable for those who are not submissive. Their faith is to be followed (v7). A good congregation seeking to honour the Lord Jesus Christ will not resist Biblical demands and encouragements from those whom the Lord has set over them, in ministry and rule. It is *important* to be submissive and responsive to the overseers. "They watch for your souls" [as it should be]. The elder carries a weighty responsibility for which he is answerable to the great Head of the Church. It is for that reason that the overseers are to be honoured and obeyed as they speak and act (not infallibly of course) for the Lord.

4. Their counsel is to be sought (James 5:14)
The elder's role as a visitor is mentioned by James, especially in visiting the sick. But you notice that initiative may come from the sick ones themselves. They are to *call* for the elders. This is an important role for the elders and an important responsibility of the congregation. In this context it is difficult to determine what the "anointing with oil" is about. What we would say is, that it should not merely be replicated if we are not clear why it was done in the first place. It may be that it was simply a symbolical act speaking of the Holy Spirit as One through whom the action of healing ultimately was to be found, or who at least gave needed strength in sickness of body. However, there is no doubt about the praying, or the implications of the picture of Elijah here, or the idea of calling for the elders in this context.

We are in a very mechanistic age. We are great believers in calling in the medical profession with our sicknesses. That is very sensible. What James speaks of calling for the elders in relation to sickness, this should not be taken as substituting for proper medical attention when it can be given. However, very often people leave this out altogether. Doctors are called for, minister and elders often are not. Medical attention is important. Our point here is: so too is prayer and (solemnly) the preparation for death. I wonder what thought people give these days for preparation for death. This is not to be morbid; it is simply facing a reality. Certainly, it should be a priority for a Christian who is sick to call for the minister and elders to pray for them. They must know they need the prayer of faith. People should pray for themselves in their sicknesses. However, they ought also to call for the overseers in the congregation to pray to the Lord for them. That is how it should be. The truth is that people take pills and pills and pills and medication and never actually call for the elder or elders. And they may stay away from Church because of a chronic condition, without thinking: "I shouldn't be using this as an excuse for absence, it's not like an infectious condition." These things are to be prayed about, and the elders should be called and welcome.

5. Their well-being is to be desired (Acts 14:23)
In relation to the work of the eldership in their carrying out their duties, it is not just that there is to be honour and obedience and calling on them in time of need. As the apostle repeatedly called for prayer from the Churches, so, too, a good congregation will see to it that they act well towards their minister and elders faithfully seeking to carry out their duties before the Lord, and remember them at the throne of grace. What should one pray for the elders? That they will manifest all the qualities of men of God; that they carry out their duties and responsibilities faithfully; that they do what is right in correcting the erring and encouraging the weak; that they be given the wisdom necessary in order that the work of the Lord be not hindered in the congregation, either from their side, or the side of the congregation.

From every point of view the work of the eldership requires to be highly esteemed. It cannot be underestimated just how important it is for the spiritual health and welfare of the Christian congregation. This is where the spiritual rule comes from. Where the elders will rule well, and the people respond well, and where there is prayer for the minister and his ministry, and for the elders in their work, that is a healthy situation in a Church. What can we say? May it please the Lord to raise up men for the office, who would grace the office and lead and shepherd the flock over which the Holy Spirit has made them overseers. The whole future of the Church in large measure depends upon this aspect of office and the spiritual quality of the office bearers assisting the minister in his responsible and onerous duties for the Head of the Church. The Church needs Christ-centred overseers who will care for the flock and will consequently be precious to the Church. There also needs to be in the Church a responsive people, prayerful and supportive of the ministry of the Word and spiritual oversight of those men who have been set apart to 'tend the flock' on behalf of the great Shepherd of the sheep.

OFFICE IN THE CHURCH

6. Deacon

1. What references are there in the Bible to Deacons?
The word from which we have the word 'deacon' – διάκονος – is a general word meaning 'servant.' The word is found some 30 times in the New Testament. Of itself it does not indicate that a Church office is being referred to. In Acts 6 there is a reference to seven men "full of the Holy Spirit and wisdom" being set aside for 'business' matters in order that the Apostles might be able to give themselves "continually to prayer and to the ministry of the word" (v4). Though the Greek word from which our 'deacon' derives is used to describe what these men were called to do, this does not explicitly indicate that the office of deacon is in view in their work. Indeed, there is as strong an argument that this was a setting apart of men for the eldership, but not excluding a strictly diaconal function. Two things may be argued as indicating this. One is the fact that they were set apart for their tasks by the laying on of hands (v6), something never spoken later of deacons. The other is that at least some of them became so clearly involved in ministry of the Word.[1] The development, however, of an office of 'deacon' separate from that of minister or elder is clear in a *later* period in the New Testament, especially in the Pastoral Epistles (1 and 2 Timothy and Titus).

There are in point of fact only two explicit references in the New Testament to a separate office of deacon by name:

(1) *Philippians 1:1*. Paul greets the Philippian Church in these terms: "To all the saints in Christ Jesus which are at Philippi, with the

---

[1] See with reference to Stephen, Acts 6:8-15, and with reference to Philip, Acts 8:26ff.

bishops (επισκόποις) and deacons (διάκανοις)."[2] Paul here is clearly distinguishing two offices in the Church, though at this point gives no indication as to how they are differentiated. This would, however, already have been understood in the Philippian Church.

(2) *1 Timothy 3:8.* In this chapter Paul speaks of the qualifications of both elders (vv1-7) and deacons (vv8-13). This indicates that by the time the Pastoral Epistles were written there had been a distinct development of office and administration in the Churches, and that under the revelation of the Holy Spirit to the Apostles the offices of ministry, overseer-elder, and deacon were well established.

2. What are the qualifications of Deacons according to the Bible?

The qualifications of deacons are stated in the first letter to Timothy. Distinguishing deacons from elders (or overseers) Paul writes thus to Timothy:

> Likewise must the deacons be grave [reverent], not doubletongued, not given to much wine, not greedy for filthy lucre; holding the mystery of the faith in a pure conscience. And let these also first be proved; then let them use the office of a deacon, being found blameless. Even so must their wives be grave [reverent], not slanderers, sober [temperate], faithful in all things. Let the deacons be the husbands of one wife, ruling their children and their own houses well. For they that have used the office of a deacon well purchase to themselves a good degree [standing] and great boldness in the faith which is in Christ Jesus (1 Timothy 3:8-13).

Because the qualifications of the deacons (vv8 to 13) are very similar to those listed for elders or overseers (vv1-7), it can be well understood that this too is a spiritual office and not merely administrative. That much is already clear from the appointment of the 'seven' in Acts 6, who, though not described by the designation 'deacon' were certainly to

---

[2] The word translated 'bishop' means 'overseer.' *Episcopos* is used interchangeably with *presbuteros* to indicate the office of 'elder'. See for example Acts 20:17 and Acts 20:28, both referring to the same people. Also, Titus 1:5 and 1:7, where again the same individuals are described both as πρεσβυτέρους (v5) and επισκοπον (v7).

be involved in work of an administrative nature. Therefore the principal qualification as men "full of the Holy Spirit and wisdom" (v3), and the fact that Stephen in particular is described as a man "full of faith and power" (v8), indicates clearly that such qualities would be expected of deacons. However, this is explicitly stated in 1 Timothy, in which the deacons are required to be "reverent" (3:8). This points to a requirement of Christian piety. The man respectful of the Lord and His word, and serious in disposition will invariably attract respect from others. Besides this there are six other qualifications mentioned in 1 Timothy. First of all, though, notice:

1. *Disqualifying vices*
(1) "Not double tongued." That is to say, he is not the sort of man who will say one thing to one person and another thing to another. He is honourable and honest in his speaking. He will not say things just to get out of a difficulty.
(2) "Not given to much wine." Paul does not say that he will automatically be a total abstainer, however wise such a thing might be considered to be. However, he will be a 'sober' man, one who does not lose self-control through drinking alcoholic beverages.
(3) "Not greedy for filthy lucre (money)." He wouldn't need to be, given that he might be required to handle money as part of his diaconal duties. This was clearly an issue with Judas (John 12:6). The deacon will not have a materialistic spirit and be out for what he can get.

These three dis-qualifications are negative ones: what the deacon is not to be like. Paul then turns to consider the positive traits. It perhaps stands to reason that he begins with the spiritual:

2. *Qualifying virtues*
(1) "Holding the mystery of the faith." He is a believer driven by understanding of the faith and a desire for obedience in its particulars. He understands, believes, grasps *Christian* faith and life. He knows Christ and understands what He has done and that He is exalted. He understands the gospel and holds to it tenaciously.

(2) He has a "pure conscience." A 'pure conscience' arises from knowing God's law-word and working it out, applying it conscientiously and consistently, according to his light. In other words, He will not do things he knows to be contrary to Christ and truth. He has a conscience informed by the Word of Christ.

(3) He must be found to be "blameless." Obviously, those who may be thought suitable for the office will have to be "proved." They will be proved when they show themselves "blameless." "Blameless" (ἀνέγκλητοι) literally means 'not to be called to account,' or 'irreproachable.' Upright, in other words; trustworthy; reliable.

There are other matters, too, in connection with,

3. *Social standing*

(1) "The husband of one wife." This most likely has as its context the possibility of converts coming from a polygamist situation. They will have one wife. It may also relate to the question of marriage and divorce. Can a divorced man really act as an office-bearer if, as a Christian, he has been in a situation of marital breakdown?

(2) He must rule his own house well. This applies to the sort of wife he has: "…reverent, not slanderers, temperate, faithful in all things." They rule "their children and their own houses well."

In other words, they will be shining examples in the world of Christian living and acting. It must be said that the various qualifications mentioned are by and large features of Christian living and should be evident in some degree or another in all believers. However, they are qualifications which must be found in all deacons. Not all men will have all virtues in the same measure, but they ought to have all the virtues in some measure. There is also reward in such service (3:13).

4. *Deaconesses?*

The qualification of a deacon that he be the "husband of one wife" would exclude women from this office, consistently with the exclusion from other offices as indicated in 1 Timothy 2:8-15 and 1 Corinthian 14:33-35. This does not exclude women from *service* in the Church in a general sense, something clear enough in the Pastoral Epistles and Acts (see 1 Timothy 2:10; 5:3-16; Acts 9:36; 16:13-15; 18:26; etc.). In Romans 16 Paul commends one Phoebe, whom he describes as "a servant (διάκονον) of the church which is at Cenchrea" (v1). This instance has raised the question of whether of not she was a *deaconess*. That is a fair question. It is certainly to be assumed that there were women who were especially involved in diaconal type service, not least among other women, widows and children. However, the text itself is not decisive on the matter of whether or not it refers to a specific office. Given the want of other information along these lines it is best to assume that this referred to general 'service' in the Church, as is clear from verse 2. John Murray comments that: "The services performed were similar to those devolving upon deacons. Their ministry is one of mercy to the poor, the sick and the desolate. This is an area in which women likewise exercise their functions and graces. But there is no more warrant to posit an *office* than in the case of the widows who, prior to their becoming the charge of the church, must have borne the features mentioned in I Timothy 5:9, 10."[3] The pressure in a western society strongly influenced by feminist ideology which looks askance at any exclusion from office in the Church requires to be resisted simply on the grounds of a want of Biblical warrant in the admission of women to any office in the New Testament Church.

3. What are the tasks of the Deacon in Scriptural terms?

Assuming the choosing of the seven to take responsibilities from the Apostles in Acts 6 to refer to the duties of what later became known as Deacons, though that incident may not be taken as involving the institution of the office *per se*, we have an insight there into the tasks of the diaconate. It was clearly in that context to tend to temporalities – a ministry of mercy (vv1-7). The word διακονειν as used in that context means "to supervise a meal" (v2). The word is used of 'serving' (Luke 10:40; Matthew 1:21, etc.). The word has a wider meaning, 'to serve,' as

---

[3] John Murray, *The Epistle to the Romans*, Part Two, London, 1967, 226.

used, for example, in Matthew 25, verse 42 and following. This is consistent with the tasks described in Acts 6. It is of interest that in 2 Corinthians 8, when Paul writes of the collection for the saints in Judea he speaks of it as διακονουμένη, that is to say, something 'being ministered' or administered (v19). In the same way he uses the term διακονων when he speaks of going to Jerusalem with help for the saints (Romans 15:25). As one philologist put it: "That their duties were those of administration and service may be deduced from the title, the qualities demanded, their relation to bishops [elders/overseers], and the use of *diakonia* in the NT."[4]

4. How has the office of Deacon been employed in Church History?

As far as the Scottish Reformation Church was concerned, there was recognition of the biblical office of deacon in the *Second Book of Discipline* (1578). This *Book* stated that "the whole policy of the kirk consists in three things: viz., in doctrine, discipline, and distribution. With doctrine is annexed the administration of the sacraments. And according to the parts of this division arises a threefold sort of office-bearers in the kirk: to wit, of ministers or preachers, elders or governors, and deacons or distributors."[5] It goes on to state in connection with the third of the Biblical offices, the Diaconate, the following:

> 1. The word *diakoneo* sometimes is largely taken comprehending all them that bear office in the ministry and spiritual function in the kirk. But now, as we speak, it is taken only for them unto whom the collection and distribution of the alms of the faithful and ecclesiastical goods do belong.
> 2. The office of the deacons so taken is an ordinary and perpetual ecclesiastical function in the kirk of Christ. Of

---

[4] See, G. W. Bromiley, *Theological Dictionary of the New Testament*, Grand Rapids, Michigan, 1985, 153-155 for various uses of the verb διακονέο and the noun διακονος, and their derivatives.

[5] Chapter 2, section 2: Of the Parts of the Policy of the Kirk, and Persons or Office-Bearers to Whom Administration is Committed.

Offices in the Church – Deacon

what properties and duties he ought to be that is called to this function, we remit it to the manifest scriptures. The deacon ought to be called and elected as the rest of the spiritual officers, of the which election was spoken before.

3. Their office and power is to receive and to distribute the whole ecclesiastical goods unto them to whom they are appointed. This they ought to do according to the judgment and appointment of the presbyteries or elderships (of the which the deacons are not), that the patrimony of the kirk and poor be not converted to private men's uses, nor wrongfully distributed.[6]

This understanding of the offices has been reflected in Reformed Churches in general, most notably those of Dutch origin. In his fine book on the diaconate Peter De Jong wrote:

> (1) The church is commissioned first of all to proclaim the glad tidings that in Christ is a full salvation for body and soul, for time and eternity. For this work she has received from her Glorified Head the apostles and *preachers to whom has been committed the ministry of reconciliation.*
>
> (2) Furthermore, her life must be regulated in all its details according to the teachings of His Word. To assist her in this there has been instituted *the ministry of government represented by the elders* who are to be appointed in every congregation.
>
> (3) And finally, to make more effective already in this life the law of perfect love in word and deed by ameliorating such rampant results of sin and poverty, sickness and distress, she has received *the ministry of mercy which comes to expression in the loving service of the deacons* without whose presence no congregation is completely organised according to the Scriptural pattern.[7]

This is the position also of *The Form of Presbyterial Church-Government* (1645) produced by the Assembly of divines at Westminster:

> The scripture doth hold out deacons as distinct officers in the church. Whose office is perpetual. To whose office it belongs not to preach the word, or administer the

---

[6] Chapter 8: Of the Deacons and Their Office, the Last Ordinary Function in the Kirk.
[7] Peter Y De Jong, *The Ministry of Mercy for Today*, Grand Rapids, Michigan, 1952, 13.

sacraments, but to take special care in distributing to the necessity of the poor.[8]

The Diaconate was consequently a recognised office in the Scottish Church. In the Free Church an Act was passed in 1846 which detailed the nature and responsibilities of the office:

> II. Respecting the peculiar duties of DEACONS:-
> 1. That they give special regard to the whole secular affairs of the congregation.
> 2. That they attend to the gathering of the people's contributions to the general fund for the sustentation of the ministry; and that they receive the donations which may be made for other ecclesiastical purposes.
> 3. That they attend to the congregational poor.
> 4. That they watch over the education of the children of the poor.
> III. Respecting the duties which are common to ELDERS AND DEACONS:-
> 1. That both Elders and Deacons may receive the Sabbath collections of the people, according to such arrangements as shall be made by the Deacons' Court.
> 2. That, for the better discharge of their peculiar duties respectively, as well as with a view to increased opportunities of doing good, both Elders and Deacons visit periodically the districts assigned to them, and cultivate an acquaintance with the members of the Church residing therein.
> 3. That it is competent for Elders to be employed as Deacons, when a sufficient number of Deacons cannot be had.
> 4. That Deacons may assist the Elders with their advice, whether in Session or otherwise, when requested so to do.[9]

This provides a good outline of the Deacons' duties within Scottish Presbyterianism, though some Churches, congregations and denominations, did not ordain deacons at all. It did, however, make sense as being perfectly consistent with the principles found in Acts 6.

---

[8] *The Subordinate Standards and other Authoritative Documents of the Free Church of Scotland*, Edinburgh, 1851, 308.
[9] Act VII – Act anent the Duties of Elders and Deacons, *Acts of the General Assembly of the Free Church of Scotland*, Edinburgh, 30th May 1846, Session 21.

It is clear that there are 'temporalities' involved in the administration of a congregation in gathering and disbursing funds, and the election of deacons may be seen to be perfectly in line with Biblical order in the Church.

The office of deacon, and Deacons' Courts, are still to be found in the smaller conservative Presbyterian Churches in Scotland. The diaconate is an office to which men are elected by congregations for life, in which connection they duly take vows and are ordained to the office. [10]

5. Is the office of Deacon necessary today?

Some people might argue that as the diaconal function in relation to ministering practically to the needs of the poor seem to have been taken over in modern society by state or charitable organisations. Although someone would need to be charged with taking care of collections and treasury work in a congregation, it has been argued that it does not need a deacon for that. J. L. Girardeau, writing in 1881, made some pertinent comments about such an argument:

> One of the tendencies of the age is to deify the merely human impulse of charity, and render to it the homage which is due alone to the divine principle of love – a love which was incarnated in a dying Savior, and when moving in the heart of a sinner is born alone of the new-creating power of the Holy Ghost. Societies, institutes, organizations of all sorts, founded in this earthborn sentiment of charity, spring up on every side, and flaunt their banners as the rivals of the Church in the field of benevolence. We would hinder no legitimate combination of secular agencies intended merely to alleviate the temporal woes of humanity. The fearful mass of suffering calls for massed effort to meet it. And, after all, the impression made upon it is like that which would be made upon the ocean by organized attempts to bale it out. Let the dead bury their dead: the office is indispensable. But when organisms designed to relieve the

---

[10] For details of the role of deacons and the constitution, powers and functions of Deacons' Courts in the Free Church see, *The Practice of the Free Church of Scotland*, Edinburgh [8]1995, 25-31.

secular wants of men are represented as competitors of the Church of Christ, upon the theatre of a pure beneficence flowing from love, it becomes her to look to her charities. An array of facts confronts her which she cannot afford to overlook. She must provide for her needy members, or succumb to the verdict of failure pronounced by competing secular societies, and bow her head before the judgment that she is untrue to one of her most sacred responsibilities.[11]

The matter of the temporal affairs of a congregation, coupled with the ministry of mercy that a congregation still carries as a responsibility to its own people, indicates the continuing necessity for such an office. As William Binnie put it, writing around the same time as Girardeau:

…the hand of this kind of charity [i.e. of the world outside the Church] is a cold hand at best; and after the legal guardians of the poor have done their part ever so faithfully, there is much room left for kindly attentions to the godly poor on the part of their brethren in Christ.[12]

Binnie's comment suggests also another aspect of the work of the Diaconate not really met by any state amelioration of people's poverty or temporal provision, and that is, the spiritual aspect. It should never be lost sight of that the Deacon's role is a spiritual one as well as a merely material. Real mercy involves dealing with people hurting from the effects of sin within and without, and therefore under God and in obedience to Christ the Head of the Church, the Deacon will have a concern to minister more than mere material provision.

We close with some lovely comments of Girardeau on the matter of the diaconate and its importance:

Constrained by his love, and supported by his grace, let them go on in the performance of their beneficent and important functions, satisfied with his approval and consoled by the conviction that they represent, in part, his ministry of mercy on earth. Let them use the office of a deacon well, and purchase to themselves a good degree and great boldness in the faith that is in Christ Jesus. And amidst

---

[11] J L Girardeau, "The Importance of the Office of Deacon," in, *The Southern Presbyterian Review*, Vol. XXXII – No. 1, January 1881, 10.
[12] Binnie, op. cit, 95.

the trials which must attend their service to their Lord, let them sustain themselves by the assurance that, the final conflict past, their disembodied spirits will be welcomed by the once poor, but glorified saints of Jesus, to everlasting habitations; and that in that tremendous day, when the great Minister of pity to suffering men shall take the seat and wear the crown of the Judge, he will publicly own their fidelity to him, and place an imperishable chaplet of honor on their heads.[13]

Further Reading:

For further reading on this subject readers are encouraged to refer to the book by Peter Y. De Jong cited. It is the best book available on the subject, a subject on which there is a remarkably limited literature.

---

[13] Girardeau, op. cit., 29.

QUESTIONS FOR STUDY AND GROUP DISCUSSION

Section A – The Church

1. *What variety of meaning is there in the term 'Church' in the New Testament?*

2. *How does Christ exercise headship over the Church?*

3. *By what marks is the well-being of the Christian Church indicated?*

4. *What are the main purposes of the presence of the Christian Church in the world?*

5. *Delineate the requirements for Church membership.*

6. *What commitment should be evident in the members of a Church?*

7. *Outline the intent of Church discipline.*

8. *What varied forms or applications are there of Church discipline?*

9. *Describe the different major forms of Church government.*

10. *How is the Presbyterian order of Church government most agreeable of all forms to the teaching of God's Word?*

11. *What relationship ought to prevail between the Church and the State?*

12. *How would you defend the statement that the Pope of Rome is "that antichrist, that man of sin, and son of perdition"?*

Section B – Creeds and Confessions

1. *Why should a Christian Church have a creed or confession of faith?*

2. *What are the benefits of a detailed Confession such as the Westminster Confession of Faith (1647)?*

3. How important is a clear form of subscription to a Confession on the part of office-bearers in a Church?

Section C – Worship

1. What 'regulative principle' should apply to the elements of public worship services? Why is it important?

2. What are the principal arguments in favour of adopting only inspired materials of praise in public worship services?

3. How may Ephesians 5:19 and Colossians 3:16 be understood as referring only to the Biblical Psalms?

4. How can the use of the imprecatory elements in singing the Psalms in Christian worship be justified?

5. Instrumental music was appointed in the Old Testament Church. On what grounds should the use of instrumental music be avoided in the public worship of the New Testament Church?

6. Do the Scriptures give any guidance on the appropriate posture in public prayer?

7. Discuss the main arguments used in favour of women wearing head-coverings in public worship services.

8. What should the practice and attitude of a giver be to their material contributions to the Church?

9. What is the purpose of the Benediction in worship services, and who may pronounce it and why?

10. What are the Biblical arguments for the change of day of worship and rest from the 7th day of the week to the 1st?

11. Practically speaking what does the proper observance of the Christian Sabbath indicate for an individual and a Church?

12. How would you argue that a 'Christian Year' should not be observed?

Questions for Study and Group Discussion

Section D – Sacraments

1. *What is the nature of sacraments?*

2. *Why is sprinkling with water a suitable mode in the administration of baptism?*

3. *Who is entitled to receive baptism? On what basis is this approved?*

4. *Delineate the varied responsibilities in connection with Christian baptism.*

5. *Why and how was the Lord's Supper instituted by the Lord Jesus Christ?*

6. *What preparations are needful for partaking the Communion?*

7. *How can the Lord's Supper advance spiritual nourishment and growth in grace?*

Section E – Offices in the Church

1. *How can it be rightly said that there is a distinct office of minister of the Word?*

2. *How do the offices in the Christian Church reflect the three-fold offices of Jesus Christ?*

3. *Outline the Biblical requirements for the office of ruling elder.*

4. *What are the public duties of ruling elders?*

5. *In what ways is respect to be shown to the minister and elders in a congregation?*

6. *What are the principal responsibilities of deacons?*

7. *Why will the office of deacon always be relevant for the Christian Church?*

SELECTED READING LIST

1. The Doctrine of the Church

D D Bannerman, *The Scripture Doctrine of the Church*, Baker, 1976 [1887]
James Bannerman, *The Doctrine of the Church (2 volumes)*, Banner of Truth, 1960 [1869]
William Binnie, *The Church*, T & T Clark, c1882
R B Kuiper, *The Glorious Body of Christ*, Banner of Truth, 1967
J Moir Porteous, *Jesus Christ King of the Church*, James Begg Society, 1999 [1872]

2. Church Government

John Macpherson, *Presbyterianism*, T & T Clark, [c1881]
Samuel Miller & John G Lorimer, *Manual of Presbytery*, John Johnstone [Edinburgh], 1842

> These books may be hard to come by, especially the combined volume of Samuel Miller (Princeton) and John G. Lorimer (Church of Scotland/Free Church). They are both very useful volumes for reference. The books listed in Section 1 are also relevant for this section.

3. Creeds and Confessions

John L Carson & David W Hall (eds.), *To Glorify and Enjoy God*, Banner of Truth, 1994
R Scott Clark, *Recovering the Reformed Confession*, P&R Publishing, 2008
David W Hall (ed.), *The Practice of Confessional Subscription*, Covenant Foundation, 1997
Robert S Paul, *The Assembly of the Lord*, T & T Clark, 1985
John H Skilton (ed.), *Scripture and Confession*, P&R Publishing, 1973
Carl R Trueman, *The Creedal Imperative*, Crossway, 2012

4. Christian Ordinances

Worship

Michael Bushell, *Songs of Zion. The Biblical Basis for Exclusive Psalmody*, Norfolk Press, ⁴2011

John L Girardeau, *Instrumental Music in the Worship of the Church*, Puritan Reprints [1888]

John W Keddie, *Sing the Lord's Song*, Crown and Covenant, ²2003

John McNaugher (ed.), *The Psalms in Worship*, Still Waters, 1992 [1907]

John Price, *Old Light on New Worship*, Simpson Publishing, 2005

Kenneth Stewart (ed.), *Songs of the Spirit*, Reformation Scotland, 2014

The Christian Sabbath

F Nigel Lee, *The Covenantal Sabbath*, L.D.O.S., 1972

The Sacraments

Robert R Booth, *Children of Promise, The Biblical Basis for Infant Baptism*, P&R Publishing, 1995

Malcolm Maclean, *The Lord's Supper*, Christian Focus, 2009

John Murray, *Christian Baptism*, P&R Publishing, 1962

Dwight H Small, *The Biblical Basis for Infant Baptism*, Baker, 1968

Gregg Strawbridge (ed.), *The Case for Covenantal Infant Baptism*, P&R Publishing, 2003

> *Reference should be made to commentaries on the* Westminster Confession of Faith *for discussions of the Christian Sabbath and the Sacraments, such as those of Robert Shaw, A A Hodge, G I Williamson and J G Vos (on the* Westminster Larger Catechism*).*

5. Offices in the Church

Mark R. Brown (ed.), *Order in the Offices. Essays Defining the Roles of Church Officers*, Classic Presbyterian Government Resources, 1993

David Dickson, *The Elder and His Work*, P&R Publishing, 2004 [1871]

Peter Y De Jong, *The Ministry of Mercy for Today*, Baker, 1952

> *The books listed in Sections 1 and 2 are also relevant for this Section.*

SCRIPTURE INDEX

Genesis
2:1-3	260
6:22	165
7:5-7	165
12:1-3	179
14	245
17	280, 293
18	352
18:22	221
19:27	221
24:55	223
28:22	245
29:19	223

Exodus
12:15	309
15:1-18	173
15:20-21	211
15:21	173
16	262
16:18	241
19:17	222
20	262
20:4-6	26, 165
20:8-11	260-1
25:40	211
31:15-17	260
34:7	197
38	242

Leviticus
9:5	222
9:24	222
10:1-3	165
11:29-44	282
14:6-7	282
15:11	282
19:17	64
19:18	46
19:34	46
27	242
27:30-32	244

Numbers
3:5-11	211
6:22-27	257
6:23-26	341
10:1-10	212
10:8	212
10:34-37	244
14:5	222
16:22	222
16:45	222
18:25-26	242, 244
19:11-13	282

Deuteronomy
4:1-2	165-6
4:10	222
4:24	208
4:39-40	165
5	262
5:12-15	260
5:31	197
6:1	197
6:6-7	57
6:6-9	303
12:32	165
14	242
14:28-29	243
19:19-21	205

Joshua
5:14	222
7:6	222

Judges
20:26	222-3

1 Samuel
1:26	221
8:1-22	177
10:17-27	177
13:13-14	165
15:10-35	177
16:7	220

2 Samuel
7:18	223
12:16	222
12:20	222

1 Kings
8:22	221
8:54-55	221-2
11:9-11	165
17:1	221
18:15	221
19:11-13	221
19:18	222

2 Kings
3:14	221
5:11	221
5:16	221
23:3	222

1 Chronicles
15:24	212
16	188
23:4-5	212
25	212
28:11-13	212
28:19	212
29:14	241
29:16	241

2 Chronicles
5:13-14	213
6:13	222
7:6	212
8:14	213
20:5-13	221
29:3	244
29:20	244
29:24-26	212
29:27-30	213
30:1	244
31:4-6	244
34:32	222

Ezra
9:5	222

Nehemiah
8:1-8	255
8:5	222
9:2-3	221
10	242
10:34-37	244
12	188
12:8	189
12:27	189
13	262
13:15-18	264
13:20	265

Psalms
1	202
2	91, 93, 202n3, 207n11
2:6	333
2:8	91
5	202
6:8	207
7	202
9	188n4
10:15	202
18:49	198
22	202
22:22	193
23	360
28	202
30	188n4
31	202
35	202
35:12-14	203
40	202
47	188n4
51:7	282
55	202
58	189
58:6-8	202
59	202
62:12	205
65:2	253
67:1-3	45
68	188n4
69	202
69:22-23	207
70	202

Scripture Index

71	202	15:1	353
72:17-19	327	24:12	205
75	188n4	24:29	205
76	195		
77:5-6	322	***Isaiah***	
79	202-3	29:13	183
79:6	207n11	45:23	222
81	188n4,	53:7	308
81:1-5	211-2	53:10	308
83	202-3	66:21	341
85:9	44		
95:2	188	***Jeremiah***	
95:6-7	222	7:23-24	165
96	188n4	14:14	337n5
103:1	327		
103:21	234	***Lamentations***	
104	188n4	2:10	223
105:2	188		
108	188n4	***Ezekiel***	
109	202, 207	5:5-8	165
109:4-5	203	14:12	179
110	202	18:21-22	76
110:5	207n11	33:14-16	76
113	191		
116:12-19	191	***Daniel***	
117	192	3	26
118	191, 202	6	27
118:15	327	6:10	222
118:17	192	7	115
119:11	52	7:23	117
119:33-40	52	8	115
122:1	55	9	115
134:1	221		
135:2	221	***Amos***	
137	202-3	8:5-6	265
137:7	205		
137:8-9	205-6	***Habakkuk***	
138	188n4	1:13	65
139	202		
140:9-10	202	***Malachi***	
141:6	205	2:1-17	165
147	188n4	3	242
150	214	3:8-10	244-5

Proverbs

10:12	69
11:24	250

Matthew

1:21	371	25	242
3:1	35	25:41	208
3:7	208	25:42	372
3:11	283-4	26:17-30	215
3:13-17	282	26:26-30	166, 273, 310
4:23	35	26:30	191
5:9	353	26:39	222
5:12	192	27:51	214
5:14-16	39-40	28:1	262
5:17-18	237	28:18-20	12, 20, 28, 35, 39, 44, 53, 82, 91, 93, 165, 179-180, 214, 233, 257, 273, 276, 280, 343n18
5:20	250		
5:21-26	352		
5:21-48	46		
5:25	192		
5:29-30	309		
5:43-5	207	**Mark**	
6:1-4	248	1:9-11	282
6:5	221	3:14	334
6:5-6	249	7:6-13	165, 168, 183
6:9-13	254	10:13-16	294
6:10	165	11:25	221
7:23	207	12:31	46
10:7	334	13:10	16
10:15	207	14:22-25	310
10:32-33	51	14:26	191
12:30	98	16:1-2	262
13:24-30	71	16:15	334
13:24-43	17		
13:36-43	71	**Luke**	
15:6	168	1:33	333
15:9	39, 165, 168	1:46-55	198
16:16	21	1:68-79	198
16:18	12, 16, 20, 21, 40, 91	2:29-32	198
		3:21-22	282
16:19	26, 37, 65	4:16	215
17:24-27	248	4:16-21	256
18:15-20	37, 63-5	8:3	54
18:17	12, 71	9:2	334
18:20	13, 66, 276	9:60	334
19:8	152n8	10:7	242, 335
19:19	46	10:40	371
22:39	46	11:2	165
23:23	245	11:2-4	254
23:34	341	11:42	245
24	203	16:1-13	248
24:13-14	45	16:10	181, 220

Scripture Index

16:10-13	250	16:7-8	166, 208
16:19-31	165	16:8-11	52
16:31	152n8	16:12-15	25
18:1-8	204	16:15	194
18:9-14	221	18:36-38	21
18:15-17	294	20:1	262
18:18	246	20:19	263
18:22	246	20:26	263
20:42	195		
21:1-4	240, 247	***Acts (of the Apostles)***	
22:15-20	310	1:8	44
22:41	222	1:15-26	90
24:1	262	1:20	195
24:13-35	171	2	216
24:27	152n8, 171	2:1-4	284
24:35	313	2:14-36	256
24:44	152n8, 189, 195	2:22	197
		2:33	166
John		2:38	291
1:9	69	2:38-41	54, 283, 284, 301,
1:14	137, 155	2:42-47	42, 313
1:17	152n8	2:44-45	247
1:29	308	3	243
1:32-34	282	3:6	239
1:33	343n18	3:22	333
2:1-11	311	3:40-47	246
3:3-5	166	5	246
3:16	251	5:1-11	37, 240
3:27	337n5	5:31-32	23
4:21-24	183, 216	5:42	35
4:23	6	6	242, 372
5:46	152n8	6:1-4	335, 341
6:35	312	6:1-7	47, 55, 90, 166, 371
6:51-57	272, 312	6:3	337, 369
8:58	189	6:4	367
10:22-30	17	6:6	367
10:35	139	6:8	369
12:6	369	6:8-15	367n1
13:1-11	284	7:38	11
14:3	18	8:4	35
14:6	21, 40	8:12	283
14:15	165	8:13	275, 283
14:15-18	25	8:20-23	275
14:26	166	8:26	283, 367n1
15:4	23	8:36-38	283, 291
15:14	165-6	9:18	283, 291
16:5-15	315		

9:36	371	**Romans**	
9:40	222	1:18	203
10:36	91-2	1:21-25	183
10:42	334	2:5	207n11
12:4	267n5	2:5-10	205
13	338	4:3	177
13:2-3	336-7	5:12-20	150
13:33	196	6:4	286
13:47	46	7:22	263
14:15	334	8:1	306
14:23	90, 346, 371	8:4	306
14:28	346	8:9	23
15	81, 87, 137, 155	8:11	194
15:1-31	90	10:5	152n8
15:4	338	10:9-11	51, 140
15:6-29	37	10:13-15	35, 335, 336, 337n5
15:22-29	64		
16:11-15	192, 371	11:4	222
16:15	283, 291, 293	11:9-10	207
16:16-24	192	12:1	41
16:25	192	12:8	87
16:30-34	283, 291	12:15	57
17:1-4	169n4	12:19	205
17:10-12	215	14:5	13, 166
17:11	144	14:11	222
17:30	17	15:9	198
18:8	283	15:25	372
18:24-28	38, 182	16:1-2	371
18:26	371	16:25-27	257
19:1-7	182		
19:32-41	11	**1 Corinthians**	
20:7	263	1	293
20:17	90, 346, 368n2	1:2	11, 32, 238
20:24-27	346	1:11-17	15
20:27-31	17	1:18	34
20:28	22, 37, 90, 346-7, 349, 357, 368n2	1:21	34
		2:12-16	166
20:29-31	359	3:1-4	15
20:33-35	361	3:7	275
20:35	241	4:1	343n18
20:36	169n4, 222, 341	4:7	240-1
20:37-38	347	5:1-8	64
21:5	222	5:7-8	307, 308-9, 310, 311
21:10	332		
28:23	152n8	5:9-13	71
		5:11	256
		6:20	53

Scripture Index

7:14	302-3	13:5	322
7:22-23	27	13:14	257
8:5	251		
9:14	242, 335	***Galatians***	
10:16	312, 315	1:2	11
11	309, 350	1:12	166
11:1-16	227-238	1:13	12
11:23-34	12, 35-6, 51, 54, 166, 215, 273, 275, 294, 310, 312, 314, 319-321, 327, 343n18	4:30	177
		5:12	203
		5:16	38, 306
		5:19-21	145
		5:22-23	322, 332
		5:25	38, 306
12:28	87, 331	6:2	57
13	15	6:6	242, 335
14:19	11	6:10	57, 303
14:26	193, 196`	6:14	315
14:29	332		
14:33-36	11, 229-230, 338, 370	***Ephesians***	
		1:22-23	17, 19-20, 93, 111
15	137, 155, 267	2:20	166
15:9	11	3:3-4	271
15:17-20	262	3:14	222
15:47	150	4:10	91
16	242	4:11	341, 345
16:2	54, 246-7, 263	4:11-13	22, 24, 331
		4:12	336
2 Corinthians		5:1-7	64
3:14-15	216	5:14	199
3:15	152n8	5:18	194
4:1	336	5:19	169, 189, 193-6, 197n21, 215
5:10	92		
5:18	336	5:23	12, 18, 90
5:20	53	5:25	12, 17-18
6:3	336	5:26	18
7:1	309	5:27	12, 18
7:9-11	52	5:32	12
8	215, 242	6:4	302
8:1-7	57, 241	6:10-20	17-18, 332
8:2-3	247	6:13-18	21
8:9	241, 248		
8:19	372	***Philippians***	
9:7	247	1:1	367-8
9:13	336	2:6-11	199
9:15	251	2:10	222
10:4	207	4:6	253
10:7	220	4:9	361
13	258		

4:10-20	243	3:1-13	166
		3:8-13	335, 346, 349, 368-70
Colossians			
1:15-18	93, 189	3:15	40
1:15-20	199	3:16	199
1:18	19, 20, 90	4:11	166
2:16	261	4:14	90, 338
2:18-23	168, 183	5:3-16	371
2:19	23	5:8	249
2:20-23	165	5:9-10	371
3:2-4	18	5:17	87, 335, 346, 357, 362
3:5	309		
3:16	169, 189, 193-6, 215	5:17-28	82
		5:20	72
3:22	218	5:21	166
4:17	336	6:3-5	235-6
		6:15-16	92
1 Thessalonians			
1:1	11	*2 Timothy*	
		1:5	350
2 Thessalonians		1:10	206
1:3-4	58	1:13	70
1:4-10	205	3:1-9	121
1:8	207n11	3:14-17	181, 194, 256
2	123	3:16	40, 133, 139-140, 175
2:1-13	114-6		
2:3-4	113, 119, 120	3:16-17	34, 202
2:5-7	116	4:1-4	34
2:7	117-120	4:1-5	346
2:8-12	113, 118	4:2	169n4, 256
2:9-10	121	4:3	70
3:14	72	4:14	203
3:14-15	70		
		Titus	
1 Timothy		1	350, 357
1:10	70	1:2-3	35
1:12	336	1:5	90, 333, 338, 362, 368n2
2:1-2	169n4, 255		
2:1-3	99	1:5-9	82, 166, 337, 346, 349, 351-4, 356
2:8-15	338, 370		
2:10	371	1:7	90, 332n2, 333, 368n2
2:11-14	232		
3:1	345, 347, 350	1:9	70
3:1-2	332n2	1:13	72
3:1-7	335, 337, 338, 346-7, 349, 351-7, 362, 368,	2:1	70
		2:3-5	350
		2:8	70

Scripture Index

3	285	**1 Peter**	
3:5	281	1:1-2	285
3:9-11	64	1:15-16	57
3:10	71	2:5	253
		2:25	332n2
Hebrews		3:8	54
1:1	175	3:15	146
1:1-3	285	3:18-21	286
2:12	193, 196	4:8	69
4:2	169n4	4:8-10	54-5
4:9	265	5:1	333
4:14-16	24	5:2-3	357, 360-2
5:4	337n5, 343n18	5:4	360
5:6	333		
7	245	**2 Peter**	
8:5	211, 213	1:19-21	40
9:9	213	1:21	175
9:13-14	216	2	121
9:22	285, 308	3:13-14	18
10:1-4	213-4	3:16	153
10:4	285		
10:12	214	**1 John**	
10:22	285-6	1:9	69
10:23-25	12, 43	2:18-19	115-6
10:31	208	2:22	121
11:6	281	4:1-3	115
11:7	165	4:2-3	137, 155
11:16	18	4:3	114, 116, 118, 120-1
12:18-19	222		
12:23	18	5:3	166
12:24	285		
12:29	208	**Jude**	
13:7	58	24-25	257
13:7-17	363-4		
13:15	182, 215	**Revelation**	
13:17	360	1:5	341
		1:10	261-2
James		1:12-13	38
1:22	53	1:13	24
1:27	47	1:17-18	22
2:8	46	1:18	23
2:17-18	52-3	1:20	24
4:7-8	316	2	11, 13, 15, 22, 37, 50, 63, 65, 70, 82, 120, 165
4:8	309		
5:13	198	2:1-5	38
5:14	358, 364	2:9	13

2:26	93	13	115
2:27	207n11	13:6	113
3	11, 13, 15, 22, 37, 50, 63, 65, 82, 120, 165	13:8	308
		14:3	196
		14:6-7	180
3:1-6	49	15:3	196
3:9	13	15:3-4	93, 173
3:20	314	17	115
5:9	196	18	115
6:10	203	19:11-16	99
7:9	221	19:15	93, 207n11
8:2-3	221	21:1	18
11:16	222	21:24-26	93
12:5	207n11	22:18-19	166, 175, 237